Alfred Cave

The Inspiration of the old Testament inductively considered

The seventh Congregational Union Lecture

Alfred Cave

The Inspiration of the old Testament inductively considered
The seventh Congregational Union Lecture

ISBN/EAN: 9783337177065

Printed in Europe, USA, Canada, Australia, Japan

Cover: Foto ©ninafisch / pixelio.de

More available books at **www.hansebooks.com**

*THE INSPIRATION OF THE OLD TESTAMENT
INDUCTIVELY CONSIDERED.*

THE

INSPIRATION OF THE OLD TESTAMENT

INDUCTIVELY CONSIDERED.

*THE SEVENTH
CONGREGATIONAL UNION LECTURE.*

BY

ALFRED CAVE, B.A.,

Principal of Hackney College.

LONDON:

Congregational Union of England and Wales,

MEMORIAL HALL, FARRINGDON STREET,

MDCCCLXXXVIII.

UNWIN BROTHERS, THE GRESHAM PRESS, CHILWORTH AND LONDON.

ADVERTISEMENT

By the Committee of the Congregational Union of England and Wales.

THE CONGREGATIONAL UNION LECTURE has been established with a view to the promotion of Biblical Science, and Theological and Ecclesiastical Literature.

It is intended that each Lecture shall consist of a course of Prelections delivered at the Memorial Hall, but when the convenience of the Lecturer shall so require, the oral delivery will be dispensed with.

The Committee hope that the Lecture will be maintained in an Annual Series; but they promise to continue it only so long as it seems to be efficiently serving the end for which it has been established, or as they may have the necessary funds at their disposal.

For the opinions advanced in any of the Lectures, the Lecturer alone will be responsible.

CONGREGATIONAL MEMORIAL HALL,
FARRINGDON STREET, LONDON.

TABLE OF CONTENTS.

LECTURE I.

INTRODUCTORY.

	PAGE
I. Theme—Supremacy of the Bible as Revelation	3
II. Importance of Theme, shown by Historical Survey ...	4
And by Present Uncertainty of Doctrine of Inspiration...	11
III. Limitation of Theme to Old Testament	13
IV. Method of Treatment—Inductive	16
Three Steps in Inductive Method	19
First Step, Textual Criticism, needs no Enlargement ...	21
Nor does Second Step—Exegetical Criticism	24
Higher Criticism, Third Step, occupies throughout ...	25
V. Headings of Treatment	27
VI. Entire Subject, a Branch of Evolution Controversy ...	31

LECTURE II.

GENESIS AND ETHNIC TRADITION.

First Question—the Divine Origin of the Law	39
A Preliminary Question—the Historicity of Genesis... ...	40
Ethnic Tradition, an important evidence	41
I. Illustration of Ethnic Traditions of a Flood	42
As preserved in Ancient Babylon	44
And in Ancient Egypt	47
And in India	48
In Persia	52
In China, Japan, Siam, Tartary, and Borneo	54
In Phrygia	54

	PAGE
In Greece, Rome, Scandinavia, and Wales	55
And in North and South America	58
Summary as to Deluge Tradition	62
Further Illustration of Ethnic Tradition	63
E.G. of Chaos	66
And of Order of Creation	68
And of Creation of Man *limo terræ*	70
And of Woman from Man's Rib	70
And of Eden	71
And of Serpent as Source of Evil	72
And of Fall	74
And of Tree of Life	77
And of Ten Patriarchs	77
And of Longevity of Patriarchs	78
And of Three Sons of Noah	79
And of Confusion of Tongues	80
Summary as to Illustrative Ethnic Traditions	82

II. Inferences concerning the Traditions of Genesis, viz.—

First, that they are Primitive	82
Second, Original	84
Third, Ancient	86
Fourth, Pure	88
Fifth, Historical	95

LECTURE III.

GENESIS AND SCIENCE.

The Historicity of Genesis still considered	99
Evidence from Parallel Conclusions of Genesis and Science	100
I. The Unity of the Race in Genesis and Science	101
II. The Unity of Language ,, ,, ,,	105
III. The Genealogy of Races ,, ,, ,,	109
IV. God and Divine Things ,, ,, ,,	120
V. Creation in Genesis and Science	127
General Conclusions	145

LECTURE IV.

THE AUTHORSHIP OF GENESIS.

Consequences of the Historicity of Genesis	153
Problem of this Lecture—who wrote Genesis	155
I. History of Criticism of Pentateuch	155
First Phase—Astruc, Eichhorn, &c.	157

		PAGE
Second Phase—De Wette, Bleek, Tuch, &c.		161
Third Phase—Hupfeld, Ewald, Dillmann, &c.		164
Fourth Phase—Reuss, Kuenen, Wellhausen, Renan, &c.		167
Fifth Phase—D'Eichthal, Vernes		171
II. Internal Evidence of Date of Genesis		176
Argument from Anachronisms		177
Argument from Anatropisms		186
Argument from Romancings		189
Summary		190
III. Internal Evidence of Composite Character of Genesis		190
Evidence from Use of Divine Names		191
Evidence from Style		191
Evidence from *Usus Loquendi*		194
Evidence from Contradictory Narratives		196
Summary		205
IV. Theory of Authorship of Genesis		206
Evidence of Revision		207
Evidence from Name Jehovah		208
Evidence from Precision in Use of Divine Names		210
Evidence from Exclusion of Jehovah from Personal Names		213
And from Names of Places		214
Evidence from Characteristics of Jehovist		217
Theory as to Jehovist summarized		220
Theory as to Elohist		221
Summary		222

LECTURE V.

THE AUTHORSHIP OF THE LAW.

Corollary from preceding Lecture	227
Problem of this Lecture—Authorship of Law	229
Two Rival Theories	230
Statement of Journal Theory	230
Statement of Evolutionary Theory	231
I. Evidence for Journal Theory	237
Testimony of the Books themselves	237
Apparent Method of Composition	238
Illustration in the Laws of Passover	243
Reuss's Examination of Journal Theory	247
II. Evidence for Evolutionary Theory	250
Wellhausen's Position	252
Is the Position true	254
The Priestly Code known to Book of Joshua	255

		PAGE
	And to Book of Judges	261
	And to Books of Samuel	266
	And to the Psalms	272
	And to the Prophetical Books proper	277
	As is proved by Amos	278
	And by Hosea	284
	Summary	289
III.	Conclusion in favour of Mosaic Authorship	290
	Collateral Evidence	291

LECTURE VI.

THE DIVINE ORIGIN OF THE LAW.

	Summary of preceding Investigation	297
	Further Question—Is the Law credible as Revelation?	299
	A Priori Objection to Revelation considered	299
	Evidence to the Supernatural Origin of the Law	302
I.	In the Theocratic Nature of Legal Code	302
II.	In its Didactic Significance	305
	Considered generally	307
	And considered specifically, *e.g.*, in its Doctrine of God	309
	And in its Doctrine of Sin	311
	And in its Doctrine of Salvation	313
	And in its Doctrine of the Church	318
III.	In the Evolutionary Process Illustrated	322
	The Law a Supernatural Successor	323
	The Law a Supernatural Forerunner	327
IV.	In the Supernatural Setting of the Legal Code	337
V.	In the Substantiation of Revelation by Miracles	338
VI.	In the Inspiration involved in Revelation	339
VII.	In the Authorship of Moses	341

LECTURE VII.

THE DIVINE ORIGIN OF PROPHECY.

	The Prophets, the Second Section of the Old Testament	345
	Are the Prophetical Books Historical?	347
	Are they of Divine Origin?	347
I.	The Nature of Prophecy	348
	As seen, first, in its History	348
	And, second, in its Claims	350

Contents.

	PAGE
II. The Divine Origin of Prophecy	355
As seen, first, in its Religious interest	355
And, second, in its Predictive element	357
III. The Divine Origin of the Non-Messianic Prophecies	359
Isaiah's Prediction of the Fall of Babylon	361
Predictions concerning Israel, viz.—	
The Exile Generally	365
And the Captivity of Ephraim	366
And the Captivity of Judah	368
And the Return from Exile	372
And the Four Empires	373
Predictions concerning Babylon	374
And Nineveh	377
And Tyre	379
And Edom	381
And Philistia, Moab, Ammon, and Elam	383
And Egypt	383
Tholuck and Kuenen on Jeremiah's Prophecies	385
IV. The Divine Origin of the Messianic Prophecies	393
Two Aspects of all Prophecy	395
Development of Messianic Prophecy	397
Fulfilment in Jesus	403
Revealed Character of Messianic Prophecy	403
V. The Divine Relations of the Prophetical Books	404
The *Prophetæ Posteriores*	405
The *Prophetæ Priores*	406
Summary	414

LECTURE VIII.

THE OLD TESTAMENT DOCTRINE OF INSPIRATION.

The Holy Writings—the Third Section of the Old Testament	417
General Principle applicable to all the Holy Writings	418
The Inspiration of the Old Testament considered generally	420
The Inspiration of the Old Testament specifically considered	423
I. Hagiographic Inspiration	426
II. Prophetic Inspiration	439
III. Transcriptive Inspiration	448
IV. Canonic Inspiration	453
Conclusion	455

APPENDIX I.

Tabular View of Typical Analyses of Genesis 459

APPENDIX II.

Tabular View of the Analysis of Exodus, Leviticus, and Numbers, according to Wellhausen 466

ERRATUM.—*On page* 169, *line* 13, *for* "seventh" *read* "seventeenth."

LECTURE I.

INTRODUCTORY.

LECTURE I.

INTRODUCTORY.

ONE of my predecessors in this Lectureship, upon whose honoured grave I feel it a pleasure to place another wreath, made it a large part of his life-work to remind us of the unique position of the Bible in the literature of the world. If the supremacy of Holy Scripture engaged the earlier manhood of Henry Rogers, as his justly famous *Eclipse of Faith* testifies; the supremacy of Holy Scripture equally engrossed his maturest thinking, as is evident from his latest and finest work, *The Superhuman Origin of the Bible Inferred from Itself.* Very fresh and very cogent at all times was Mr. Rogers's exposition of his favourite theme. As, in his own trenchant and brilliant way, Mr. Rogers concentrated upon his momentous subject his marvellous insight, his exceptional generalization, his easy mastery of detail, his characteristic artistic skill, the old Book once more became new. We saw its catholicity; we understood its popularity; we ceased to wonder at its influence upon human life and thought; we delighted in its prose; we revelled in its poetry. The survival of the Bible was the most natural of things. Once more, as the gifted writer and theologian unfolded his specific thought, it seemed but reasonable that the Book of Books should be the story-book of our childhood, the guide of our youth, the inspirer of our manhood, and the solace of our age.

In his Congregational Union Lecture Mr. Rogers gave us a study *of the Supremacy of Scripture* AS LITERATURE. I desire to approach this important subject of the supremacy of Scripture from another side. I propose to handle, with what faculty I can, the *Supremacy of the Bible* AS REVELATION, all Revelation implying INSPIRATION.

At once in illustration and in defence of my point of view, permit me to take a brief historical survey.

In that gigantic but beneficent struggle, to which the name of the Reformation has been justly given, the supreme arbitrament in matters of religion was re-transferred from the Church to the Bible. The conflict between evangelical and papal—that is to say, between Biblical and ecclesiastical—Christianity having been first fought out in the breast of Luther, a similar conflict, in the Providence of God, was subsequently waged in the Diet of Worms, in the Genevan Republic, in the States-General of France, and in the Parliaments of England and Scotland. For Luther there was something of absurdity in any appeal to a higher standard of faith and practice than the Bible. "To put the Divine word beneath human invention," Luther was wont to say, "was to be deficient in understanding."[1] Again and again, in many forms of speech, Luther

---

[1] *Werke*, edit. Walch, Halle, 1740-1753, vol. xviii. p. 254.

averred that "no Christian can be forced to bind himself by aught but the Holy Scriptures, which alone have Divine right."[1] Being the supreme revelation of God to man, the Bible was to the great initiator of the Reformation the supreme arbiter in matters of religion.

This belief of Luther's as to the supremacy of Scripture as revelation all the Reformers shared. What the miner's son of Erfurt maintained with so much heroism, mother-wit, and persistence, each of the leading Reformers declared in his own place and in his own way. "He is deceived," said scholarly Melancthon, "who seeks the form of Christianity anywhere else than from the canonical Scriptures."[2] Pass from Wittenberg to Zurich, and gentle, large-hearted Zwingli has nothing else to say. "This is my view," writes Zwingli, "that the word of God must be held by us in the highest honour and that to no word such faith should be given as to that."[3] Similarly expresses himself the third member of that triad of theologians, the other members of which are Paul and Augustine, I mean John Calvin, who says, in his immortal *Institutes*, "If true religion is to enlighten us, our principle must be, that it is necessary to begin with heavenly teaching, and that it is impossible for any man to obtain even the minutest portion of right and sound doctrine without being a disciple of Scripture."[4] By common consent the Bible was regarded by the leading Reformers, as well as by

[1] *Werke*, vol. xviii. p. 254.
[2] *Corpus Reformatorum*, Brunswick, 1834 to the present (still publishing), vol. xxi. pp. 453, 685, 732.
[3] *Werke*, Turin, 1828, vol. i. p. 81; compare the extracts given in Hagenbach, *A History of Christian Doctrines*, Edinburgh, 1881, vol. iii. pp. 41-43.
[4] Comp. *Corpus Reformatorum*, vol. xxx. pp. 56-61, or vol. xxxi. pp. 88-98.

Luther, as the supreme revelation of God to man, and consequently as the ultimate rule of human faith.

Naturally enough, therefore, the estimate of the Scriptures, framed by the great formative minds of the Reformation, became the cherished heirloom of the generations immediately succeeding them. Turn where we will in that age of creeds, and the doctrinal standards of Protestantism all avow the same reverence for "the Word of God," as they intelligibly named the sacred volume. "We believe, confess, and teach," runs the Formula of Concord, the confessional standard of the Lutheran Churches, "that the only rule and norm, according to which all dogmas and doctors ought to be esteemed and judged, is no other whatever than the prophetic and apostolic writings both of the Old and New Testaments, as it is written, 'Thy word is a lamp unto my feet and a light unto my path.'"[1] Says the First Helvetic Confession, in which Reformed Switzerland gave voice to its religious convictions in 1536, "The holy, divine, biblical Scripture, which is the word of God, given by the Holy Spirit, and transmitted to the world by the prophets and apostles, is the most ancient, the most complete, and the supreme doctrine," containing "everything which serves for the true knowledge, love, and honour of God, for right and true piety, and for the preparation of a pious, decorous, and blessed life."[2] In almost identical words spake the Huguenot Churches of France. "We believe," reads the *Confessio Gallicana*, "that the word contained in these books has proceeded from God, and receives its authority from Him alone,

---

[1] Schaff, *The Creeds of the Evangelical Protestant Churches*, London, 1877, p. 94.
[2] Schaff, *ib.* p. 210.

and not from men; and inasmuch as it is the rule of all truth, containing all that is necessary for the service of God and for our salvation, it is not lawful for men, or even for angels, to add to it, to take away from it, or to change it; whence it follows," the Confession continues, "that no authority, whether of antiquity, or custom, or numbers, or human wisdom, or judgments, or proclamations, or edicts, or decrees, or councils, or unions, or miracles, should be opposed to these Holy Scriptures; but, on the contrary, all things should be examined, regulated, and reformed according to them."[1] The parallel statements of the Thirty-nine Articles and of the Westminster Confession it is needless to quote. In fact, the citations given are but a few out of very many. It was in harmony with the entire spirit of the historical churches which sprang from the Reformation, that the Bible should be regarded therein as the supreme Divine revelation, and therefore the supreme rule of religious faith and practice.

Three centuries have passed since the birth of Protestantism. They have been centuries of much controversy. Conflict, too, has often gathered thick around the Protestant doctrine of the supremacy of Scripture as revelation. So the extant literature shows clearly. Undoubtedly the religious life of an age is not to be judged wholly by its literature. Human chronicles too frequently describe noisy change rather than silent growth. In every age there are lives spent, victories won, sacrifices made, thoughts moulded, and errors unmasked, the sole memorial of which is in the great book of the recording angel. Who, for example,

---

[1] Schaff, *The Creeds of the Evangelical Protestant Churches*, p. 310.

would undertake, from the extant records—a few letters, and a few brief manuals for catechumens—to tell the true story of that fruitful century which followed the martyrdom of Paul and Peter? The seventeenth and eighteenth centuries shall not therefore be too hastily judged; for they too had their nobleness and self-denial and growth, which no chronicles register or could register, their secret deeds of holiness, their unsung heroism, their great thoughts no less deep and influential for being still and silent. Nevertheless, these centuries were to a great extent iconoclastic and controversial. The followers of Socinus had much to say against the supremacy of Scripture as revelation. So had the Deists. Men like Toland and Tindal desired, by their popular criticism and attack, to unsettle the common faith in the authority of Scripture. Nay, the Deism of England gave birth to the great rationalistic movements of France and Germany, quite naturally, be it observed, for he who plants the seeds of error should expect a crop of heresy. They were Deistic quills, alas, which fledged the arrows of Voltaire. If German Rationalists have brought weapons of precision to bear upon the Bible, let it not be forgotten that it was the English Deists who first taught these skilled assailants to carry arms. There would have been no Semler if there had been no Bolingbroke; there would have been no Strauss if there had been no Woolston. Now far be it from me to deny that these Socinian, Deistic, and Rationalistic attacks upon the Bible have had their use in the great scheme of things. History has shown us again and again that Christian truth never crystallizes so readily and so sharply as under the agitation produced by anti-Christian speculation. To continue the previous mode of expression—had there been no Deists there would have been no Butler, and possibly no Wesley, no Whitefield. Notwithstanding, it is idle to ignore the fact that pronounced Protestant opinions as to the supremacy of Scripture as revelation, are found with less frequency at the close of the eighteenth century than at the close of the sixteenth.

Continuing to descend the stream of time, this nineteenth century itself has also forged peculiar weapons with which to attack the Protestant doctrine of the supremacy of Scripture as revelation. These weapons have been cast in three armouries—the armoury of philosophy, the armoury of the "higher criticism," and the armoury of the physical sciences. The century has produced the agnostic school of philosophy—Agnosticism being a term which has been framed by a dominant school of thought to describe its ignorance concerning any sphere of knowledge outside the human senses; but manifestly if Spencer and Clifford are right, Moses and Jesus cannot but be wrong. Again, splendid as have been the achievements of physical science in recent years—and we cannot forget that this century will be known, *practically*, as the century of the steam-engine, the camera, the telegraph, and the spectroscope, and, *theoretically*, as the century of the regeneration of chemistry, geology, and biology—nevertheless this widespread occupancy with the world of force and matter has fostered a materialistic bias, which, combined with the prevalence of many unwarranted interpretations of Scripture, have engendered much doubt upon the revealed character of Holy Writ. It would be vain to ignore that geology has seemed to many to conflict with the Mosaic narrative of the creation and deluge;

that astronomy has also appeared to many to discredit the biblical account of the origin of the solar and stellar systems; and that biology has apparently elevated the doctrine of atheistic evolution to the position formerly held by the conception of distinct creative acts. Yet again, Biblical Science itself has originated many theories which seem to militate against the Protestant doctrine of the supremacy of Scripture. Much of Biblical Science, it is true, is the child of this century, and has rendered very eminent service; still, in this instance again, it would be blindness to forget that the many recent assaults upon the age and authenticity of the Pentateuch, upon the supernatural character of prophecy, upon the trustworthiness of the biblical miracles, and upon the reliableness of the Gospels and Epistles, have been working largely to the unsettlement of the Protestant doctrine of the supremacy of Scripture as revelation. Whilst cordially allowing that conflicts between rival hypotheses ultimately aid the attainment of truth, one must as frankly concede that a wide and popular grasp of truth cannot co-exist with a wide adherence to rival hypotheses. Good as the end is, one may deplore the means.

Now in these controversies of the last three centuries, and especially in the prominent controversies of our own day, I think I see reason for the inquiry I have ventured to undertake. The Protestant doctrine of the supremacy of Scripture as revelation is manifestly on its trial. The truth concerning it cannot be reached by simply repeating the arguments of the great theologians of the sixteenth and seventeenth centuries. These arguments are in some points as antiquated as the opinions they successfully traversed. Each age must fight its own doubts, and lay its own spectres, and formulate its own creed. In the providence of God, and in the progress of man, the new wine is ever bursting the old bottles. Every religious thinker is in duty bound to be timely. It is his duty to do what in him lies for the religious faith of his contemporaries. He best serves the future who serves the present. The needs of the present afford the best test of what is worth preserving from the past. No contribution to current opinion, however humble, can be useless, which is timely, honest, and painstaking.

If I needed additional warrant to proceed, I think I should find it in the indefiniteness, if not disrepute, into which the doctrine of inspiration has fallen in many quarters. Not so long ago a very precise theory of inspiration was commonly avowed. The entire contents of the Bible, it was thought, were dictated by the Holy Spirit to the several writers, word for word, and syllable by syllable. It was not in parody, but in exposition of this view of inspiration, that Gaussen, one of the latest advocates of this theory, declared in his *Théopneustie*, that "the literary style of Moses, Ezekiel, and Luke was the style of God." Now, whatever be the popular conception of inspiration, it would be difficult to find adherents to this mechanical theory among the theological writers of to-day. The heat, the passion of Coleridge's attack on this theory in his *Confessions of an Inquiring Spirit* seems to the modern reader like flogging a dead horse. Neither in England nor in France, neither in Germany nor in America, so far as I know, has any recent writer of mark declared for the mechanical theory of inspiration, which was nevertheless generally received and maintained by the great theologians of the seventeenth century. A great vagueness, I fear, has fallen of late upon all deliberate statements concerning inspiration. Men know what theory they disbelieve; they do not know how to express their belief in a theory. Even where adherence to the plenary inspiration of Scripture is avowed, what exactly is meant by plenary inspiration is rarely defined with clearness. Many, like Dr. William Lee, rest in the statement that, as humanity and Deity were really, but inexpressibly, united in the incarnate Word of God, so God and man are really but inexpressibly united in the written word of God.[1] Others, again, whilst cleaving tenaciously to the formula of the plenary inspiration of Scripture, so dilute the idea of inspiration, as did Spinoza and many others, that in their view inspiration does not differ from the aroma floating around all works of genius. Schleiermacher and De Wette, Bunsen and Morell, apparently regarded inspiration as the subjective excitement produced by revelation, the exhilaration of the fresh and novel. "The Scriptures *contain* the word of God," was the position of Tholuck, which has been reiterated in England by men like Samuel Taylor Coleridge, Thomas Arnold, and Arthur Stanley. It was in view of this fluidity of opinion concerning the doctrine of inspiration that Dean Milman wrote, and wisely, more than twenty years ago, that "if on such subjects some solid ground be not found in which highly educated, reflective, reading, reasoning men may find firm footing, I can see nothing but a wide, a widening, I fear an irreparable breach, between the thought and religion of England."[2] In similar

---

[1] *Inspiration of Holy Scripture; its Nature and Proof*, 1st edit., Dublin, 1854, 5th edit. 1882.
[2] *History of the Jews*, 4th edit. London, 1886, p. xxxiv. vol. i.

strains Prebendary Row felt himself constrained to say in his Bampton Lecture : "There is no one thing at the present day occasioning a greater amount of difficulty to a number of inquiring and deeply religious minds than some of the theories which have been propounded respecting the nature and extent of the inspiration under the influence of which the different books in the Bible have been composed."[1] And to mention yet another instructive American instance, not to name one nearer home, Dr. Ladd, a Professor in Yale College, recently wrote a book, certainly with much scholarship, thoroughness, ability, and force, which, penned confessedly in the interests of the Christian Faith, and professing to be a monograph upon the entire doctrine of Scripture, announced these notable results—that in his view no scientific contents are to be found in the Bible ; that the genesis and early history of man recorded in the Bible are unhistorical ; that a very different credibility pertains to the miracles of the Old Testament to what pertains to those of the New ; and that prophetical inspiration does not guarantee historical accuracy. I am not criticizing Professor Ladd's contentions, at present ; I am simply citing them as a sign of the times. In such an atmosphere of opinion, no re-examination, in the light of modern research, into the data and doctrine of the inspiration of Scripture, provided that examination be reverent and earnest, can fail to be of some value.

Thus far I have spoken of the general question of the

[1] *Christian Evidences Viewed in Relation to Modern Thought*, 3rd edit. London, 1881, p. 428.
[2] *The Doctrine of Sacred Scripture ; a Critical, Historical, and Dogmatic Inquiry into the Origin and Nature of the Old and New Testaments*, Edinburgh, 2 vols. 1883.

authority of Scripture as the supreme rule of faith. It is now time to state that I have deliberately restricted my inquiry to the Old Testament. I have thus limited my view for several reasons. *First*, the Old Testament is the battlefield just now upon which the advocates of the natural and supernatural origin of things are engaged in a life and death struggle. As Dr. Bissell has well remarked, "it is safe to say, bating from the statement whatever you please for any partiality we might have for favourite studies, that not a few of the problems with which the minds of thoughtful men are grappling to-day, directly concern the Hebrew Scriptures. It is the Book of Genesis that we couple in our thinking with certain puzzling questions of geology and cosmography. It is the same book that serves as point of departure for the still-mooted subject, when human history had its beginning, and how it began. It is to the Old Testament chiefly that the science of archæology, opening up in our day so broad a field and awakening in its devotees so inspiring an ardour, comes to lay down its stores of gathered facts and illustrations. It is significant, too, that an eminent Assyriologist published, not long ago, as the result of special study in this department, a discussion of the question—more practical in its bearing than might appear—*Where was Paradise?* And it is not geography or history or chronology alone that these priceless records are teaching us. They are enriching our lexicons and correcting our grammars as well. As if all this were not enough to quicken our flagging zeal, and teach us that the Hebrew Scriptures can never be divorced from the Greek Scriptures in our reverential study, the heaviest cannonading of Biblical criticism is just now heard among these earliest records of our faith. Around the Gospels and Epistles there is for the moment a comparative lull in the conflict, while Moses and his great work are sharply challenged."[1] *Secondly*, much more attention has been bestowed upon the inspiration of the New Testament than of the Old, a restriction of view which is very natural, seeing that the life, the character, the teaching, and the miracles of Jesus and His apostles, afford such manifest evidence for the revealed character of the Gospels and Epistles. *Thirdly*, the data for the doctrine of Old Testament inspiration whilst less commonly studied, have a fascination all their own. *Fourthly*—a personal reason—Old Testament studies have for some time been peculiarly congenial to me.[2] And *lastly*, the very different contents of the two Testaments, as well as the limitations of time, suggest the desirability of narrowing my theme. To these reasons let me add—that I believe it will be seen, as my subject unfolds, that a similar line of argument is equally applicable to the New Testament, and that I have not selected the easier task.

Two questions, then, are to be discussed in these lectures, namely: *on the one hand*, the DATA, and, *on the other hand*, the DOCTRINE *of the Inspiration of the Old Testament.*

[1] *The Pentateuch; its Origin and Structure. An Examination of Recent Theories*, London, 1885.
[2] Compare my *Scriptural Doctrine of Sacrifice*, 1877; my introduction to the *Pulpit Commentary on Leviticus*, 1882; and various articles on Old Testament subjects, *e.g.*, "The Critical Estimate of Mosaism," in *The Princeton Review* for 1877; "On the Latest Phase of the Pentateuch Question," in *The British and Foreign Evangelical Review* for April, 1880; "Professor Robertson Smith and the Pentateuch" in the same Review for October, 1880, ; "Evolution and the Hebrews," in the same Review for January, 1881 ; "The Old Testament in the Jewish Church," in the same Review for October, 1881 ; also a concise tract published by the Religious Tract Society in several forms *When was the Pentateuch Written?*

From this mode of presenting the subject it will be seen that we are to be engaged upon an *inductive* inquiry.

Two methods have been adopted for proving the inspired character of Scripture—the dogmatic and the inductive methods. According to the dogmatic method, the testimony of the Bible has been cited to its own contents, a series of texts being quoted, in more or less order, and with more or less regard to the historical development of the books quoted. According to the inductive method, the phenomena of the Bible—its history, its law, its miracle, its prophecy, its doctrine, its words—have been critically examined. In these lectures, the latter method will be pursued. Having first classified, criticized, and weighed our data, we shall afterward infer our doctrine. In other words, the doctrine of the inspiration of the Old Testament is to be defined and illustrated in the course of the inquiry; it is not to be initially asserted. All the facts concerning inspiration presented by the Old Testament are to be examined, as far as possible without bias or prepossession, with a view to ultimately ascertaining the conclusions these facts warrant. The familiar conclusions of Protestant theology are not to be assumed at the outset. Seeing that proof-texts can only assure us of the claims made by the Bible on its own behalf, and cannot assure us of the credibility of those claims, start is not to be made with proof-texts. In short, an attempt is to be made to avoid that circle of reasoning by which the book is assessed by the texts, and the texts by the book. The following inquiry is to be inductive.

A parallel case will possibly make the method clearer. Let us suppose ourselves searching, for once, into the truth of Mahometanism. As our search is prosecuted, we speedily discover that the investigation narrows itself down to the question as to the Divine origin of the Koran. Now in the pages of the Koran itself, its contents are ascribed to the dictation of the angel Gabriel. What Gabriel spoke, Mahomet wrote. But do proof-texts from the Koran settle the matter? Assuredly not. We desire information upon the credibility of the Koran. The literary testimony must itself be critically tested; the textual evidence requires evidence extra-textual in support. In brief, an inductive inquiry must be instituted into the veracity of the assertions of the Koran.

Similarly, in examination of the claims of the Bible to Divine origin, an inductive investigation must be undertaken into its contents. Acknowledging the Old Testament to be an ancient religious record, and as such deserving of serious and prolonged study like any other great Sacred Book of the East, investigating the Old Testament by the same critical processes which have been so successfully applied to other literary monuments of the distant past, patient inquiry is to be made into its varied phenomena, with a view to arriving at sound conclusions upon those phenomena, their causes and their implications. Inquiry is to be made indeed whether, so far from being an ordinary book, the Old Testament be not so extraordinary as to belong to a category all its own. We submit the Bible to those critical tests to which all sacred books must submit.

In the opening pages of his *Religion of Israel*, Dr. Kuenen has put this inductive point of view with his usual lucidity. "Surely," Dr. Kuenen says, "it is a fact that the sacred records of the Israelites and the Christians attribute to each of these two religions a supernatural origin. May we simply overlook this fact? By no means. The rise of that belief among Israelites and Christians is one of the most important facts in their religious history, and must be not only acknowledged, but, if possible, explained."[1] The statement is incontestable. "But here," continues the Dutch professor, "it behoves us not to forget that this belief is by no means exclusively characteristic of Israelites and Christians. They hold it in common with the adherents of many, nay, most other forms of religion. Zarathustra, Sakyamouni, and Mahomet pass among their followers for envoys of the Godhead, and in the estimation of the Brahmin the Vedas and the Laws of Manou are holy, Divine books. At the same time, it does not follow from this that the description of these forms of religion must start from this belief. No one expects or requires this for Buddhism or Islam; with what right, then, can it be demanded with respect to Judaism or Christianity?" The case is stated in a strictly scientific spirit, let it be frankly confessed. But then Dr. Kuenen—and here it is necessary to part company with him, if scientific impartiality is to be retained—proceeds to regard all religions as nothing else than so many natural manifestations of the religious faculty of man. In the act of divesting himself of doctrinal assumptions, Dr. Kuenen lays down a postulate of an extreme dogmatic complexion. Instead of presenting us with a rigorous induction from the facts he presents, Dr. Kuenen invites us to accept on the spot, and without proof, a first principle, which is as much an assumption as any advanced by the most illogical advocate of orthodoxy. "If we look," this famous critic continues, "upon those other religions"—of

[1] *The Religion of Israel to the Fall of the Jewish State*, translated from the Dutch by Alfred Heath May. London, 1874, vol. i. pp. 5, 6.

Persia, India, and Arabia—" as so many manifestations of the religious spirit of mankind, are we not bound to examine the Israelitish and Christian religions also from the same point of view?" In other words, having discarded the axiom of the Divine origin of Judaism and Christianity, shall we not straightway lay down the axiom of their purely human origin? Shall we not assume, as self-evident, that all religions are alike in kind? Shall we not commence our inquiry by taking for granted that the religions of Moses and Jesus are, like those of Mahomet, Buddha, and Zoroaster, nothing but "so many manifestations of the religious spirit of mankind"? Certainly not, we reply. Such an assumption is unscientific. It is starting with a proof-text. The scientific inquirer should make at the outset no assumption whatever, either as to the Divine or the human origin of any religion; he should industriously collect all pertinent facts without prejudice; he should rigorously draw those conclusions, and those conclusions only, which the collated facts appear to justify, and he should follow those conclusions faithfully wherever they may lead. If, at the beginning of an inquiry into the place of the Old Testament amongst books, it is unscientific to take for granted that these canonical books are Divine, it is equally unscientific to assert at the outset that they are not Divine. Whether the books of the Old Testament are adequately described by designating them " so many manifestations of the religious spirit of mankind" can only appear at the close, not at the beginning, of a scientific inquiry.

However, the really scientific method of inquiry may be suggested to us by the remarks thus criticized. Let me illustrate the inductive point of view by Zoroastrianism. In the invaluable series of the Sacred Books of the East, now being issued by the Clarendon Press under the editorship of Professor Max Müller, Dr. James Darmesteter has published a translation of the Zend-Avesta, the Bible, so to speak, of the Parsis. A modern inquirer, of some thoroughness of mind, is anxious, let us suppose, to test the Divine claims made by these fire-worshippers for their religion. What course must this inquirer pursue? He must first ascertain, I imagine, whether the translation before him is a fair rendering of the ancient Zend-Avesta. This process would involve two steps. The translation might be poor, or the text might be corrupt. Upon both points he must satisfy himself. By his own investigations, or by conscious reliance upon trustworthy experts, he must convince himself that he is dealing with a tolerably accurate translation. Further, he must have some reasonable ground for supposing that the modern original used by the translator is a fairly accurate transcription of the autographs of the original writers of this sacred book. Should the translation used be bad, some views may be erroneously ascribed to the original, which, after all, are nothing but blunders of the translator. Should the text used by the translator be bad, some opinions may be wrongly attributed to the author which are really mistakes of copyists. It is indispensable, in fact, in any scientific investigation, for the inquirer to satisfy himself both as to the genuineness of his text and the accuracy of his translation; otherwise, if his text be impure, he lays himself open to a charge of misrepresentation, or if his translation be inaccurate, he renders himself liable to a charge of ignorance. These two preliminary problems solved, the inquirer may prosecute with confidence the more immediate object of his search; he may gradually elicit from his translation all the evidence bearing in any way upon the Divine origin of the Zend-Avesta; he may formulate, step by step, a series of conclusions which would substantiate, or invalidate, the conception of the Zend-Avesta as revelation. In brief, from the criticism of the text and the criticism of the translation, which are but means to his end, he may proceed to the end itself—to criticism of contents, to literary and historical criticism.

Substitute the Old Testament for the Zend-Avesta, and the same words might describe the course of the inductive inquirer into the value of the Old Testament. The student of the Divine character of the Old Testament must satisfy himself upon the accuracy of the translation he adopts, upon the genuineness of the text he employs, and upon the correctness of the inferences he draws from the data which the translated text puts in his hands. In effect, the inductive investigation of the Old Testament combines three stages of research, that is to say, *textual criticism*, or the inquiry into the accuracy of the Old Testament text; *exegetical criticism*, or the inquiry into the meaning of the Old Testament text; and the so-called *higher criticism* in its two branches, viz., *historical criticism*, or criticism of the historical contents, and *literary criticism*, or criticism of the literary phenomena. Only by a use of these three varieties of criticism can the Old Testament be examined on its revealed or natural character.

Happily little needs be said in these Lectures either upon the textual or the exegetical criticism of the Old Testament. These two branches of inquiry may, after a few remarks, be dismissed from our view once for all, their results being sufficiently assured to be axiomatic, facts which may be assumed rather than opinions which require to be argued. No scholar would maintain nowadays that impregnable opinions are impossible, either on the score of our comparative ignorance of the genuine words penned by the original scribes of the Law and the Prophets, or on the score of our relative ignorance of the meaning attached to these words by their original readers. The text of the Old Testament is known to be accurate enough for our purpose, and our comprehension of the meaning of that text, if it be not perfect, is practically all that we need. By the industry of many interpreters, and the discoveries of many explorers, throughout generations, throughout centuries, a fairly adequate knowledge of the actual contents of the Sacred Scriptures as known to Moses, to David, to Daniel, and to Jesus, has become the common inheritance of man.

As regards the textual criticism of the Old Testament, let it suffice to say that the results even of the most recent research shall not be forgotten in these Lectures, although, after all, these textual researches are, for the most part, rather of a scholarly than a practical interest. Thus to speak is to minimize in no degree the precious and self-denying labours of textual critics. Seeing that we do not possess the autographs of the writers of the Law and the Prophets, but only numerous and varying transcripts of their writings of much later date, it is indispensable that some men, patient and capable, should compare copies with copies, originals with versions, and manuscripts with printed texts, slowly eliciting sound principles of judgment, and gradually constructing a solid mass of critical opinion. Such examination is rendered necessary by the circumstances of the case. "Certainly," as I have said elsewhere,[1] "had the great Revealer seen fit, He might have preserved to us the identical sheets of papyrus or skins of parchment which passed beneath the styles of the holy men of old who wrote as they were moved by the Holy Spirit, just as by a continuous miracle, He might have scrupulously preserved every scribe from error in copying, and every compositor from error in printing. As a matter of fact, the great Giver of Truth, has not been careful to preserve all past, present, and future copies of the Holy Scriptures from any and every admixture of error, as innumerable minute variations testify. The scribe was no more gifted with infallibility in the past than the printer in the present." Hence the necessity of textual criticism. Nevertheless, the researches of textual criticism, mostly upon *minutiæ*, are not of high value in such an inquiry as ours. It is almost enough, indeed, for us to know that such textual researches, carried on for many years, have had one positive result: they have accentuated the substantial accuracy, the reliableness, of the common Hebrew text for all purposes of doctrinal examination. In many minutenesses of speech, textual criticism may have a large influence in the future, but the general tenour of the Old Testament books will most probably remain unaffected. In short, the practical reliability of the text is now demonstrated beyond gainsaying. There is no book of the Old Testament, for instance, the text of which is not in a more satisfactory state than any literary heirloom of ancient Greece or Rome. However, at points in our inquiry, valuable hints will follow

---

[1] *An Introduction to Theology; its Principles, its Branches, its Results, and its Literature*, Edinburgh, 1886, pp. 258, 259. Compare on the whole subject of Textual Criticism §§ 39–42 of that book.

from textual studies, and nowhere shall textual results be ignored.

Happily also, our knowledge of the meaning of the Old Testament is in even a better position than our knowledge of the text. By many generations of exegetes, the meaning of the Old Testament, in general and in detail, has become increasingly plain. The biblical scholar has to-day a more confident hold than ever upon the laws of Moses or the prophecies of Isaiah. In this field also *minutiæ* doubtless remain to be elucidated; but such minute points of interpretation cannot affect very largely such an inquiry as ours. All that it is necessary to do in this respect is, on the one hand, to lay the best exegetical knowledge of the time under contribution; and, on the other, to occasionally undertake original investigations which may make the meaning of isolated passages clearer.

With regard, therefore, to the two preliminary stages of any inductive inquiry into the value of the Old Testament as revelation, two postulates may be laid down. First, it may be fearlessly asserted that the original words of the Old Testament are sufficiently known to us for the purposes in view, no future suggestions of textual criticism being capable of interfering to any material extent with the general conclusions which will be arrived at. A second postulate is, that the true meaning of the Old Testament is also sufficiently known for our purpose. If our knowledge of the original words of the Old Testament, and our acquaintance with their significance be not perfect—and there is certainly much room for many earnest labourers for a long time to come in both departments of biblical science—it is, notwithstanding, practically all that is needed. No one would have the temerity to maintain nowadays that valid opinions upon the general bearings of the Old Testament are impossible, either on the score of the corruptness of our copies, or on the score of the precariousness of our translation. In fact, we might almost rest satisfied with the Revised English Version everywhere, without going far wrong.

It is with the third branch of Biblical criticism, however, that we are to be especially concerned in these Lectures. It is only occasionally that textual and exegetical criticism are to be pressed into our service, whereas literary and historical criticism, that is, rigorous investigation of the facts of Biblical expression and of the facts expressed, are to provide our entire argument; and necessarily so, seeing that it is only upon the proven veracity of the Old Testament that a doctrine of Old Testament Inspiration can be built. The various classes of contents presented by the Old Testament are to be examined, and cross-examined, and re-examined, with a view to framing just conclusions. Is the Old Testament historically veracious? This is the very question into which we are to inquire; and we must not therefore dogmatize upon the point at the outset. Does the Old Testament afford crucial evidence of the supernatural? A conviction upon the matter is to be the goal, and cannot be the starting-point, of our inquiry. Are the miracles of the Old Testament capable of a purely rational explanation? The question is to be discussed. Can the phenomena of Old Testament prophecy be attributed to a Shemitic genius for religion, and are they explicable therefore by natural causes? The answer is to come after investigation. When the Old Testament professes to guide our beliefs concerning God, sin, retribution, salvation, and a future life, are such momentous doctrines of religion credible? In the sequel only does our method permit us to reply. By criticism we are to strive after results beyond criticism. By comparison the most rigorous, we are to endeavour to arrive at inductions the most rigid. Without fear, without bias, without prejudice, the consistency of related facts is to be minutely tested. Statements made at one moment are to be confronted with statements made at another; the implications of a statement made in one place are to be confronted with the implications of statements made in other places; the subtle harmonies of truth are to be sought out with diligence, the latent contradictions of error are to be unearthed with equal care; the glamour of great names, whether of advocates or opponents of orthodoxy, is to be shut from the eyes as far as possible; all the powers of insight, and of experience, and of research are to be brought to bear, so as to penetrate falsehood and to disclose truth, to unclothe appearance and to reveal reality; inconsistency of every kind, however recondite its hiding-place, is to be laid bare by the engines of logic; coincidences are to be narrowly watched, in order to discover whether they are intentional or casual; and by all forms of the comparison of evidence, whether afforded by the Old Testament itself, or by collateral profane knowledge—first, the data of a doctrine of inspiration are to be elicited, and, subsequently, the doctrine itself is to be formulated. The task is difficult. The result attained may be of the poorest. But one comfort remains. The task is inevitable. The test cannot be refused. Only by literary and historical criticism of such a kind, can the claims of the Old Testament be put aside. Only by literary and historical criticism of such a kind can the claims of the Old Testament be substantiated. If the Old Testament is a purely human composition, this can only be shown by "the higher criticism." If the Old Testament is of composition Divine as well as human, the demonstration can only come from the criticism of contents, as distinct from the criticism of text or of interpretation.

Methods, however, are best appreciated by embodiments. Some sign-posts to mark our way may therefore be of use. A complete inductive study of the Old Testament would occupy many volumes. The salient and more controverted points alone can here come under discussion.

From the nature of the case, the Book of Genesis must always have a large part in deciding the Divine or human origin of the Old Testament. The next three Lectures are occupied with this book, each lecture dealing with a very important feature of its contents. Thus, to start with, there are many extraordinary coincidences between the narratives of Genesis and the traditions of profane antiquity. The series of data relating to these coincidences are at once deeply interesting and profoundly suggestive; for, as a matter of fact, which well repays illustration, wherever there are in the religions of heathendom ancient literary relics, whether in stone or tradition or writing, these antique memorials are found to contain more or less striking parallels to the stories of Genesis. The evidence is full. Attack the theory of a universal Flood, for example, as men may on geological grounds, an important fact, nevertheless, calls for explanation, namely, that traditions of a universal flood have been preserved in the most opposite quarters—in the libraries of stone and clay, of palm-leaf and papyrus, of Babylonia, Egypt, Syria, and India, in the legends of the Scandinavians and the Lithuanians, in the literature of Greece and Rome, and in the folk-lore of the savage tribes of America and Polynesia. Nor is this a solitary instance. Parallels exist between the ancient traditions of heathendom and all the other traditions of Genesis, without exception, prior to the Confusion of Tongues. Here, then, an important series of facts discloses itself. If the early history of our race rests, not upon unsupported testimony, but upon the concurrent testimony of many peoples, the history of Genesis has received a substantial corroboration. Further, if it can be shown, on the one hand, that these Pagan traditions have not been derived from Genesis, and, on the other hand, that the narratives of Genesis have not been derived from these Pagan traditions, another conclusion of manifest moment will follow concerning the origin of these primitive traditions; these traditions, in short, must be the common inheritance of the human race. And yet again, if it can be shown that Genesis preserves most purely these common primeval traditions, the further problem will arise as to whether this purity is not due to a supernatural source, to a Divine inspiration. The SECOND LECTURE will therefore deal with GENESIS AND ETHNIC TRADITION.

Further, it is characteristic of Genesis that it has pronounced views upon several scientific questions. Long anterior to the birth of modern science, this ancient book incorporated in itself definite views upon questions which modern science regards as its peculiar treasure. Genesis presents a cosmogony. It also propounds ethnological opinions concerning the original unity of the race, and the genealogy of peoples. It advances a philological opinion concerning the origin of language. Genesis has distinct pathological theories regarding the early decay of the race and regarding the healthiness of goodness. It has historical views as well concerning the primitive civilizations. And, besides all these varied physical opinions, Genesis advances theological assertions of many kinds, concerning God, concerning man, and concerning the relations of God and man, past, present, and future, assertions which are capable of being tested by later knowledge, and which challenge the most careful attention. In view of all this expression of opinion, the question is inevitable as to its weight. Has Genesis forestalled recent scientific results by many centuries, and if it has, how is this precocity of knowledge to be explained? To teach science before science, would bring us face to face with a profoundly significant fact. The THIRD LECTURE will therefore deal with GENESIS AND SCIENCE.

The progress of the argument will next demand that some conclusion should be arrived at concerning the *authorship* of Genesis. It will be necessary to plunge into the unquiet waves of the "Higher Criticism," as it is called ; and, utilizing the methods by which this sea of literary criticism is navigated by experts, good reasons will appear for retaining the traditional opinion of the Mosaic Authorship, and therefore the high antiquity, of Genesis. The FOURTH LECTURE will treat of THE AUTHORSHIP OF THE GENESIS.

From Genesis it will be needful to pass to the remaining four books of the Pentateuch. Further questions of literary criticism will immediately confront us, those questions which have been at once so congenial and so perplexing to our time. No solid ground can be secured for the Divine origin of the Law until the question of the Authorship of the Pentateuch has been examined. However, after careful inductive inquiry, the Higher Criticism itself of the Pentateuch will give us reason for abiding by the Mosaic origin of the last four books of the Law as well as of the first; a result of the highest importance to our subsequent progress. The FIFTH LECTURE will therefore deal with THE AUTHORSHIP OF THE PENTATEUCH.

The foundations of our inquiry, having thus been well if slowly laid, and the principles of our method having been clearly if tediously illustrated, one great section of the Old Testament may then be finally examined. By a careful inquiry into the contents of the Books of the Law, and into the logical implications of those contents, we shall next arrive at conclusions of the highest importance concerning the revealed character of the Law. Indeed, attention having been called to the various phenomena presented by the Law on its theological, its social, and its ethical sides, no other conclusion, even upon the inductive method, will appear possible, than—that the Law was given by Divine Revelation. The SIXTH LECTURE will therefore be entitled THE DIVINE ORIGIN OF THE LAW.

From the Law we shall pass to the Prophets. As will be seen later on, the remaining data, of specific importance to our inquiry, may be classed under the head of Prophecy. Law and Prophecy, in fact, are the two great supernatural revelations of the Old Testament. In this instance, again, a cautious inductive investigation will supply us with invaluable conclusions as to the non-human, the inspired, origin of prophecy. In the SEVENTH LECTURE, therefore, the DIVINE ORIGIN OF HEBREW PROPHECY will be examined.

Having, thus, industriously marshalled the data which relate to the Inspiration of the Old Testament, and drawn from these data several conclusions as logical as weighty, it will be possible to advance to the doctrine which these data warrant. The subject of the EIGHTH and last Lecture will therefore be—THE DOCTRINE OF THE INSPIRATION OF THE OLD TESTAMENT.

I turn to the last point to which it is necessary to allude in this Introductory Lecture. From the map of the way thus roughly outlined, it will have been manifest that these Lectures are to form a contribution —all too humble when the needs of the case are considered—to the most gigantic problem of modern times, the problem of Evolution. The crucial question, which will arise again and again is just this, Evolution *versus* Revelation, Naturalistic Evolution *versus* Miraculous Revelation. Let me guard myself against misunderstanding. I say deliberately, *Naturalistic* Evolution, *Non-miraculous* Evolution. The idea of development or evolution has shown itself the most energizing and the most fruitful conception of recent years. Evolution is the one generalization which the chemist (the investigator of elements), the geologist (the investigator of the rocky structures of the earth), the astronomer (the student of the stellar motions), the physiographer (the observer of planetary structure), the physiologist (the analyst of the body), and the psychologist (the anatomist of the mind), the moralist (who treats of individuals), and the sociologist (who treats of communities), are all combining to elucidate. Development has shown itself to have illustrations in the tiniest molecule as well as in the most highly organized structure, in the movements of the lowest forms of life as well as in the progress of the most civilized societies, in the nebulæ of the starry heavens as well as in the differentiated planets of the solar system. But this evolution is not necessarily naturalistic evolution. What exactly is meant by evolution is the great conflict of the day. Upon this question the world of thought is divided into two opposite camps. These antagonistic camps range themselves beneath an evolution which is theistic, and an evolution which is atheistic, beneath a development which is Christian and a development which is Spencerian. That there is in the universe a process of development of some sort, no one will disbelieve who believes in a Divine plan, and who therefore doubts not "through the ages one increasing purpose runs"; but, under the exigencies of a philosophic system, men are challenged to surrender all convictions as to the existence of a personal Deity, all persuasions of a Divine interference in human affairs, all hopes of a Divine voice which, breaking the silence and order of nature, speaks of a possible friendship with the Father of all, and promises a blessed immortality,—to surrender, in short, all the indissoluble dictates of the renewed and Christian consciousness. Now, in deciding between a theistic and an atheistic evolution, the religion of the Old Testament presents one of the crucial instances which must be faced. It is a prime necessity, whether for the theistic or atheistic evolutionist, to explain satisfactorily the origin and influence of the Old Testament faith. And, as a matter of fact, the crucial nature of the Old Testament religion has been for some time acknowledged by the adherents of an atheistic evolution of all things. Attempts have been made to explain Mosaism and Prophecy on purely natural grounds. The history of the Old Testament has been reconstructed to demonstrate, if possible, that Sinai and Bethlehem are but stages by which the Goshen of the Pharaohs becomes, by purely natural processes, the Judæa of the Proconsuls. To this end, the Old Testament, in all its parts, has been most minutely studied, and most elaborately remodelled. It was certain that the Old Testament would be remodelled in the interests of a naturalistic evolution sooner or later. Evolutionists, who have not hesitated to say that the life and words of Jesus had a purely naturalistic origin, were not likely to shrink from avowing the religion of Israel to be a purely natural phenomenon as well. The glove has been thrown down, and Christian thinkers are bound to take it up, in Christ's name and for His sake. The question of the natural or supernatural origin of the Old Testament can only be evaded by those who shut their eyes and ears. Graf understated the case, when, in the opening page of his epoch-making work on *The Historical Books of the Old Testament*,[1] he wrote: "The question is worth answering, in what epoch we regard the Mosaic Law as completed, whether conformably to nature and analogy, we are to regard it as a witness and result of a gradual evolution from a fruitful germ, or as something initially perfect and

[1] *Die Geschichtlichen Bücher des Alten Testaments*, Leipsic, 1866, p. 1.

underlying every subsequent development;" the question is not only *worth* answering, the question *must* be answered. Again, it is an inevitable outcome of much of the physical and philosophical speculation of the time,—and it should be frankly recognized to be a consistent outcome of such speculation,—when Kuenen, for example, proceeds, in his investigation of the religion of Israel, from what he is pleased to call "the standpoint of modern science," and declares his desire to show "a natural development both of the Israelitish religion itself and of the belief in its heavenly origin;"[1] and when Kalisch[2] "would fain hope that he has furnished a few available stones for that new edifice which it is the labour of our age to erect, that he has aided, however humbly and modestly, in supporting by arguments derived from his special department of study the philosophical ideas which all genuine science at present seems eager to establish," the ideas, that is to say, "of Buckle," and "the fearless and penetrating investigations of Darwin, Huxley, and Lyell." In short, whether the Old Testament is the outcome of a theistic and supernatural evolution, or of an evolution which is atheistic and purely natural, is one of the pressing questions of the time. To that question much of the Lectures which follow is devoted.

It will be seen, I trust, that the facts presented by the Old Testament are inconsistent with any evolutionary idea which excludes revelation and miracle. The entire discussion will show cause, I hope, for believing, on purely scientific grounds and on the evidence of fact, in a

---

[1] *The Religion of Israel*, vol. i. pp. 4–10.
[2] *A Historical and Critical Commentary on the Old Testament, with a New Translation*, Leviticus, Part I., London, 1867, pp. iii., iv.

Personal Deity, who is unspeakably interested in sinful man and who interferes on his behalf, freely yet lovingly, in human history. Of the nescience of the agnostic, who only knows that the universe of one moment is the consequence of the combined matter, motion, and force of the moment before, we shall see nothing. Of the evolution of the theist, who knows that the universe of one moment is the consequence of all the causes existent the moment before, including the great First Cause and all supernatural causes, we shall see much. Again and again, crucial instances of Divine revelation will present themselves, approving themselves solid rock upon which any atheistic theory of evolution must split. What "integration of matter" can coalesce into a Messianic prophecy? What "dissipation of motion" can crystallize into the Mosaic code? How shall the "indefinite, incoherent homogeneity" of the Patriarchal Age become, of itself and by its own inherent forces, the "definite, coherent homogeneity" of the life at Sinai? Is it possible for the chance metamorphosis of force to evolve an Isaiah or an Ezekiel? In a sentence, of an evolution which explains the universe *by the persistence of force* we shall see, I believe, little evidence: of an evolution which explains the universe by the *persistence of God*, evidence both cogent and consolatory will, I trust, be afforded. Do not the cardinal facts of the Old Testament, frankly faced and fairly considered, compel a belief in a Holy Spirit who spake by the mouths of holy men of old? The sequel will show.

LECTURE II.

GENESIS AND ETHNIC TRADITION.

LECTURE II.

GENESIS AND ETHNIC TRADITION.

THE aim before us, then, in these Lectures, is to inquire inductively into the claims of the Old Testament, which, professedly a record of many events of a supernatural order, asserts again and again that it contains revelations from above. In other words, the distant goal before us is a doctrine of the Inspiration of the Old Testament.

But data must precede doctrine.

Before well-grounded opinions can be framed upon inspiration, careful investigation must be made of those characteristics which lead us to infer inspiration. *The first question* which must be approached is *the Divine origin of the so-called Law of Moses.* In that law, if anywhere, evidence is afforded of revelation ; and the first sure step to be taken in this inquiry *is* to examine the credentials of the Mosaic Law. But here, again, two preliminary questions immediately stop the way. They concern, too, it is true, only a part of the Law, viz., the Book of Genesis. Nevertheless, in dealing with these two questions, although apparently considering but a very small portion of the Old Testament, we are, as will be evident later on, really taking long strides towards the final stage. These questions are two: first, *is the Genesis historical;* and second, *in what age was it written?* These two unavoidable questions will be considered in the next three lectures. After all, Genesis is the battle-ground on which the claims of the Old Testament will be largely decided.

Is Genesis, then, we are compelled by our plan to ask, the product of human art, or of Divine revelation, or of both? Can we find therein conclusive evidence of a Divine interference in human affairs? Are we dealing, in the first book of the Law, with the thinkings or imaginings of the unaided faculties of man, or are we concerned therein with information divinely revealed, and, at the same time, communicated to man under the influence of a supernatural inspiration? Is Genesis, or is it not, explicable on a theory of purely human invention? Reply, as has just been said, will be easier after a prior question has been considered. That prior question is, whether Genesis is historical. Is Genesis history or legend, fact or myth, narrative or allegory, plain prose or imaginative poetry?

The question as to the historical character of Genesis is not unimportant in itself, and is indispensable to our inquiry. Of late years the earlier chapters of Genesis have been studiously represented by some,[1] as little better than a collection of folk-lore, comparable with the legendary tales of classical antiquity, and therefore as little more veracious than the stories of Romulus and Veii, of Cadmus and the μῆνις Πηληιάδεω Ἀχιλῆος. Some, too,[2] have found in the Biblical narratives of the origins of things nothing but myths, the speculative and vain

---

[1] Conspicuously by Ewald.
[2] Like Bauer, Vatke, Schultz, and Goldziher.

attempts of primitive man to explain the problem of his being, whence he came, and whither he was going. Origen, again, the great theologian of Alexandria, agrees with Jacob Behmen, the Lusatian shoemaker and theosophist, in regarding Genesis, not as the narrative of actual occurrence, but as needing to be interpreted in a *spiritual sense*. Others, again,[1] have preferred to see in the earlier chapters of Genesis a great primeval epic, true to life, if unsubstantiated by fact. In the face of such conclusions, it becomes, then, an important question, whether Genesis is historical.

I do not delay to insist that, whether the narratives of Genesis are veracious or not, they have the air of veracity. This *vraisemblance* must come up for consideration later on. At present I simply desire to state fairly and fully certain suggestive facts, which make for the historical character of these early Biblical annals. The evidence about to be adduced argues for the truth—and therefore incidentally, as will be seen later on, for the Divine origin—of those pre-Abrahamic traditions which have appeared to many legendary, if not wholly mythical. Indeed, as this Lecture proceeds, reason will be seen for believing that the primitive history of man as given in Genesis, rests by no means upon unsupported testimony, but upon the concurrent voice of many nations at many times. It will be seen to be matter of fact that numerous pagan traditions so minutely coincide with, as to corroborate strongly, the Old Testament account of the world's infancy.

As a matter of fact, the pre-Abrahamic narratives of Genesis relate to four distinct periods of time, namely,

[1] Like Herder, Eichhorn, and De Wette, to whom some prominent English names might be added.

the Creation, the Deluge, and the centuries which preceded and those which followed the Flood. Now, upon inquiry, it is found that the remembrance of all these four periods has been carefully preserved by many nations of men, more or less distinctly, doubtless, but in a very striking manner notwithstanding. Notable resemblances occur in the primitive traditions of east and west, of north and south. Some of this concurrent testimony has been long known; some is of recent discovery; and additional facts, in all probability, remain to be collected. Nevertheless, whencesoever obtained, the evidence is remarkable, whether it comes from America or Polynesia, Scandinavia or Hindostan.

Let, however, one caution be uttered before proceeding. Should any of the parallels presented appear slight or fanciful, let it be remembered that no single instance affects any other instance. We are not dealing with a chain of examples, so to speak, which wholly breaks if any single link gives way; we are rather forging a cable of many cords, in which any strand may snap without perceptibly affecting the tenacity of the rest.

In this Lecture, therefore, I propose, FIRST, to *illustrate the similarity existing between the traditions of the Genesis, and those extant in the several ethnic religions;* and, SECONDLY, to *draw some important conclusions from that similarity.*

Facts often belie presumptions, and however apparently improbable, perhaps the most widely attested of human traditions is that of a great catastrophe " by which the world that then was being overflowed with water perished." The tradition of a universal flood presents so excellent an example of a corroborative tradition that I swerve from the strictly chronological order, and present this diluvian evidence to begin with. As Lenormant has well said, in his notable work on the *Origins of History*,[1] "the tradition of the Deluge is the universal tradition *par excellence;*" and if he goes on to say that it "would be too much to assert that it is found amongst all peoples," he straightway adds that "it is reproduced in all the great races of humanity save one, the black race." Now, conceding frankly that in some cases apologists have mistaken mere popular recollections of local floods for traditional relics of the great primeval deluge, still the concurrence of testimony is at once so great and so minute, as to throw strong emphasis upon the Biblical narrative. Unmistakable references to the Deluge have been found in the extant remains of the Babylonians and the races of India—the Egyptians, the Phœnicians and the Syrians,—the Greeks, the Etruscans, and the Romans,—the Celts, the Scandinavians, and the Lithuanians,—the native tribes of North America, and the inhabitants of America south of the isthmus of Panama,—the Chinese, the Japanese, and the natives of Borneo,—and even amongst the savages of Polynesia. It was on such evidence that Canon Rawlinson declared in his *Historical Illustrations of the Old Testament*, that it constituted an array of exact coincidences, which cannot possibly be the result of chance, and of which I see no plausible account that can be given except it is the harmony of truth."[2] A similar opinion has been expressed by the eminent philologist, Adolphe Pictet, who writes : "It is

---

[1] *Origines de l'Histoire*, Paris, 1880, vol. i. p. 382.
[2] *The Historical Evidence of the Truth of the Scripture Records stated anew, with special reference to the Doubts and Discoveries of Modern Times.* Bampton Lectures for 1859, London, 1859, p. 65.

known that the remembrance of a formidable flood has been preserved among so many people of the Old World and the New, with the same essential features of a destruction of the human race, and of one family or a single couple saved from the disaster in a boat and re-peopling the earth, that it is impossible to explain such an agreement except by admitting a primitive tradition founded upon an actual fact."[1] The question to be illustrated, be it observed, is not one of geology nor of theology, nor of exegesis, but of transmitted tradition.

I proceed, then, to the illustration of this universal tradition of a Deluge.

I commence with *Ancient Babylon*, Babylon the great, the empire of Nimrod the hunter, Sargon the lawgiver, and Nebuchadnezzar *le grand monarque*. The evidence of a deluge in the extant remains of Babylonia is distinct. There are two versions of the tradition.

One is that of Berossus, the historian of Babylon, who lived some three centuries before the birth of Christ, fragments only of whose writings have been preserved to us in Josephus, Eusebius, and others. Wrote Berossus, as is recorded by Alexander Polyhistor :

"After the death of Ardates, his son Xisuthrus" (said by Berossus to be the tenth king of the Chaldeans) "reigned eighteen sari. In his time happened a great deluge, the history of which is thus described. The deity Cronos appeared to him in a vision, and warned him that upon the fifteenth day of the month Dæsius, there would be a flood, by which mankind would be destroyed. He, therefore, enjoined him to write a history of the beginning, procedure and conclusion of all things, and to bury it in the city of the sun at Sippara ; and to build a vessel, and take with him into

---

[1] *Les Origines Indo-Européennes ou les Aryas Primitifs, Essai de Paléontologie Linguistique*, 2nd edit., Paris, 1886, vol. iii. p. 362.

it his friends, and relatives, and to convey on board everything
necessary to sustain life, together with all the different animals,
both birds and quadrupeds, and trust himself fearlessly to
the deep. Having asked the deity whither he was to sail, he was
answered 'to the Gods,' upon which he offered up a prayer for the
good of mankind. He then obeyed the Divine admonition, and
built a vessel five stadia in length and two in breadth. Into this
he put everything which he had prepared, and last of all conveyed
into it his wife, his children, and his friends. After the flood had
been upon the earth, and was in time abated, Xisuthrus sent out
birds from the vessel, which, not finding any food, nor any place
whereon they might rest their feet, returned to him again. After
an interval of some days, he sent them forth a second time; and
they now returned with their feet tinged with mud. He made a
trial a third time with these birds; but they returned to him no
more; from whence he judged that the surface of the earth had
appeared above the waters. He, therefore, made an opening in
the vessel, and upon looking out, found that it was stranded upon
the side of some mountain, upon which he immediately quitted it
with his wife, his daughter and his pilot. Xisuthrus then paid his
adoration to the earth; and having constructed an altar, offered
sacrifices to the gods, and with those who had come out of the
vessel with him, disappeared."[1]

It is unnecessary to continue the extract, further than
to state that Berossus goes on to describe how the vessel
was stranded in Armenia, and how some part of it
remained to his day in the Corcyrean mountains of
Armenia, the people habitually scraping off the bitumen,
with which it was covered, to make amulets. The
resemblances to the Biblical story are striking—the
command to construct the ship, in order to escape a
general inundation,—the introduction of all sorts of
animals into the vessel,—the despatch of the birds,—the
second despatch,—and the third,—and the reference to
the bitumen with which the surface was smeared. The

[1] Cory, *The Ancient Fragments, containing what Remains of the Writings of Sanchoniatho, Berossus, Abydenus, Megasthenes, and Manetho, &c.* 1828, p. 21. Cory also gives renderings of Berossus from Abydenus and Apollodorus.

divergences from the Biblical story are equally suggestive.

This narrative of Berossus was, however, of so late a date, that, although apparently derived from independent sources, it was possible for some to maintain that it had been in some way borrowed from the Jews. A recent discovery has emphasized the probability of the independent origin of the account. Berossus was, we know, the keeper of the Babylonian archives, and a few years ago, a tablet of burnt clay, inscribed with cuneiform characters, the eleventh of a series of historical tablets, was exhumed at Nineveh, from the buried palace of Assurbanipal, the great Sardanapalus of the Greeks. This tablet also presents, in a form much more ancient than that of Berossus, the account of a general deluge. In the view of the late George Smith, who discovered and translated these interesting tablets, their age may be fairly placed at two thousand years before the Christian era, a date which Professor Sayce also thinks probable.[1] This ancient story of the deluge forms part of a great Assyrian epic. Isdhubar, or Gisdhubar—the name is uncertain—the hero of this epic (identified by George Smith with Nimrod, and rightly in all probability, according to Professor Sayce),[2] afflicted with leprosy, goes to consult the patriarch Hasisadra, who, having been spared in the deluge, has received his apotheosis. Amongst other things, Isdhubar asks the patriarch for an account of the events which won him immortality. Notwithstanding that the response of the patriarch has not been perfectly preserved, and that there are lamen-

---

[1] Sayce, *Lectures on the Origin and Growth of Religion as illustrated by the Religion of the Ancient Babylonians*, Hibbert Lectures for 1887, p. 847.
[2] *Ib.* p. 8.

table gaps in the narrative, to say nothing of the difficulties of interpretation, the following details, amongst others, are indisputable. A command was divinely given to build a ship; the reason for this command is stated to have been the sin of the world; the ship was intended to save the seed of life; beasts of the field entered the ship; the ship was pitched without and within with bitumen; food was taken into the ship; on the bursting forth of the flood, all people were destroyed; after a while a window was opened in the ship; the ship was brought to rest upon a mountain; a dove was sent forth and returned; a swallow was despatched, which also returned; a raven was next allowed to go, " it did eat, it swam, it wandered away, it did not return ; " an altar was built and a sacrifice offered ; "the gods collected at its savour ; " finally, a covenant was made that the deluge should not happen again. So many coincidences between the Biblical and this Ninevite account may well arrest attention.[1]

From the ancient Babylonian Empire let us pass to the *ancient Empire of Egypt*. Doubts have sometimes been expressed as to whether a universal deluge was not wholly unknown in the Nile Valley. But there are good reasons for doubting these doubts. Thus Edouard Naville has published an interesting inscription from the tomb of Seti the First at Thebes,[2] which shows conclusively that, whether the Egyptians had or had not reminiscences of the deluge, they certainly had pre-

---

[1] Compare *The Chaldean Account of Genesis*, by George Smith, London, 1876, pp. 263-289; the *Transactions of the Society of Biblical Archæology*, vol. ii. 1873, pp. 213-234; vol. iii. pp. 530-596; vol. iv. pp. 49-83, 129-131, and 363, 364 ; and *Records of the Past*, vol. vii. pp. 133-149.

[2] Compare *Transactions of the Society of Biblical Archæology*, vol. iv. pp. 1-19, and *Records of the Past*, vol. vi. pp. 103-112.

served in their annals a remembrance of a total destruction of mankind by the gods. "The account," too, as Faber has said, "given by Plutarch, of the Egyptian Osiris, affords some grounds for imagining that he is the same person as the Scriptural Noah. He is said to have been a husbandman, a legislator, and a jealous advocate for the worship of the gods. Typhon conspired against him, and by a stratagem prevailed upon him to enter an ark, the top of which was immediately closed by his perfidious enemy. In this situation he floated down the Nile into the sea. The day in which he entered the ark was the seventeenth of the month Athyr, when the sun passes through the sign Scorpio."[1] Now, as Faber goes on to say, "with regard to this account, it may be observed that Typhon, according to Plutarch, is merely a mythological person, expressive of the ocean; and consequently the tradition signifies nothing more than that the character denominated Osiris was in danger from the sea; and that he escaped by entering an ark." Faber adds, "It is not a little remarkable that the day on which this took place precisely agrees with that of Noah's embarcation, previous to the commencement of the deluge." The evidence, if not quite convincing, is suggestive. Lucian, if he be the author of the *De Dea Syriaca*, also associates a tradition of the deluge with the Egyptian Hierapolis.

From Egypt let us journey to *India*. Four versions of the deluge are found in the ancient literature of India, namely, in the Satapatha Brahmana, part of the White Yajur-Veda, the oldest version of the four—in the great epic of the Mahabharata, the next oldest version—in

[1] *Horæ Mosaicæ*, Bampton Lectures for 1801, vol. i. pp. 134-136; compare Bryant, *A New System, or an Analysis of Antient Mythology*, 1807, vol. iii. pp. 44, 182, 183.

the Bhagavata Purana,[1] a poem of more recent date still, and in the Matsya Purana,[2] a fabulous poem for which the story of the deluge forms the framework. The two last versions may be passed by, because of their late date, and mature extravagance. The version from the Mahabharata I give in the summary of Monier Williams,[3] which runs—

"Manu, the Hindu Noah, ... is represented as conciliating the favour of the Supreme Being by his austerities in an age of universal depravity. A fish, which was an incarnation of Brahmâ appeared to him whilst engaged in penance on the margin of the river, and accosting him, craved protection from the larger fish. Manu complied and placed him in a glass vessel. Having outgrown this, he requested to be taken to a more roomy receptacle. Manu then placed him in a lake. Still the fish grew, till the lake, though three leagues long, could not contain him. He next asked to be taken to the Ganges; but even the Ganges was soon too small, and the fish was finally transferred to the ocean. Here he continued to expand, till at last, addressing Manu, he warned him of the coming deluge. Manu, however, was to be preserved by the help of the fish, who commanded him to build a ship and go on board, not with his own wife and children, but with the Seven Rishis or patriarchs; and not with pairs of animals, but with the seeds of all existing things. The flood came: Manu went on board, and fastened the ship, as directed, to a horn in the fish's head. He was thus drawn along."

The remainder of the narrative Professor Williams

---

[1] Compare Burnouf, *Le Bhagavata, ou Histoire Poétique de Krishna*, Paris, 1867, vol. iii. p. 191; Muir, *Original Sanskrit Texts on the Origin and History of the People of India, their Religion and Institutions*, Collected, translated, and illustrated, 2nd edit., London, 1872, vol. i. pp. 208-209.

[2] Analysed by H. H. Wilson, in his *Vishnu Purana, a System of Hindu Mythology and Tradition*, Translated from the original Sanskrit, and illustrated by Notes, London, 1864, vol. i. pp. lxxx-lxxxiii; compare Muir, *Original Sanskrit Texts*, vol. i. pp. 203-207.

[3] *Indian Wisdom, or Examples of the Religious, Philosophical, and Ethical Doctrines of the Hindus*, 3rd edit., London, 1876, pp. 394-395; comp. Muir, *Sanskrit Texts*, vol. i. pp. 196-203.

presents in a metrical rendering which he claims to be nearly literal :—

"Along the ocean in that stately ship was borne the lord of men, and through
The dancing, tumbling billows, and its roaring waters; and the bark,
Tossed to and fro by violent winds, rested on the surface of the deep,
Staggering and trembling like a drunken woman. Land was seen no more,
Nor far horizon, nor the space between ; for everywhere around
Spread the wild waste of waters, reeking atmosphere, and boundless sky.
And now when all the world was deluged, nought appeared above the waves
But Manu and the seven sages, and the fish that drew the bark.
Unwearied thus for years on years the fish propelled the ship across
The heaped-up waters, till at length it bore the vessel to the peak
Of Himavân ; then, softly smiling, thus the fish addressed the sage,
'Haste now to bind thy ship to this high crag. Know me the Lord of all,
The great creator Brahmâ, mightier than all might—omnipotent.
By me in fish-like shape hast thou been saved in dire emergency.
From Manu all creation, gods, Asuras, men, must be produced ;
By him the world must be created—that which moves and moveth not.'"

However, the oldest and simplest form of the tradition is that found in the Veda,[1] written certainly not later than a thousand years before Christ. The following translation is from Muir :—

"In the morning they brought to Manu water for washing, as men are in the habit of bringing it to wash with the hands. As he was thus washing, a fish came into his hands, (which spake to him,) 'Preserve me ; I shall save thee.' (Manu inquired), 'From what

---

[1] Compare Weber, *Indische Studien*, Berlin, 1850, vol. i. p. 161 ; Muir, *Original Sanskrit Texts*, vol. i. pp. 181-220 ; *Sacred Books of the East*, vol. xii. pp. 216-219.

wilt thou save me?' (The fish replied), 'A flood shall sweep away all these creatures: from it will I rescue thee.' (Manu asked) 'How (shall) thy preservation be effected?' The fish said: 'So long as we are small, we are in great peril, for fish devours fish; thou shalt preserve me first in a jar. When I grow too large for the jar, then thou shalt dig a trench, and preserve me in that. When I grow too large for the trench, then thou shalt carry me away to the ocean. I shall then be beyond the reach of danger.' Straightway he became a large fish; for he waxes to the utmost. (He said), 'Now in such and such a year, then the flood will come; thou shalt, therefore, construct a ship, and resort to me; thou shalt embark in the ship when the flood rises, and I shall deliver thee from it.' Having thus preserved the fish, Manu carried him away to the sea. Then in the same year, which the fish had enjoined, he constructed a ship and resorted to him. When the flood rose, Manu embarked in the ship. The fish swam towards him. He fastened the cables of the ship to the fish's horn. By this means he passed over this northern mountain [Himavat or Himalaya]. The fish said, 'I have delivered thee: fasten the ship to a tree. But lest the waters should cut thee off whilst thou art on this mountain, as much as the water subsides, so much shalt thou descend after it. He accordingly descended after it, as much (as it subsided). Wherefore also this, viz., 'Manu's descent' is (the name) of the northern mountain. Now the flood had swept away all these creatures; so Manu alone was left here. Desirous of offspring, he lived worshipping and toiling in arduous religious rites. Among these he also sacrificed with the pâkâ offering. He cast clarified butter, thickened milk, whey, and curds as an oblation into the waters. Thence in a year a woman was produced. She rose," &c., &c.

Nor is it undesirable to add that, in the version of the Bhagavata Purana, express reference is made to seven days. "In seven days, says Bhagavata, the Supreme God, to Satyavrata, the three worlds shall be submerged by the ocean of destruction."[1] "In yet seven days, said Jehovah to Noah, and I will cause it to rain upon the earth."

Summarizing, therefore, the characteristics of this Indian tradition, they are as follows: *First*, the person

[1] Compare Pictet, *Les Origines Indo-Européennes*, 2nd edit. p. 368.

saved from the waters is the first monarch, the divine chief of the present epoch of the world. *Second*, the salvation of Manu is achieved by divine interposition. *Third*, the deity appears to Manu under the form of a fish. *Fourth*, Manu is rescued by a ship. *Fifth*, Manu saves with him the seven Rishis, and also the seeds of all useful plants. *Sixth*, once saved Manu proceeds to the regeneration of all things.[1] Although in this Indian tradition there are variations peculiarly Aryan, the resemblance to Genesis is significant.

From India let us turn to Ancient *Iran*—modern Persia—another branch of the great Aryan race, which scattered itself abroad from its home in Central Asia. A tradition of the destruction of all men is given in the Zend Avesta, the great legacy of Zoroaster, the sacred book of the Magi, the Bible of the Parsis. According to the Vendidad, most probably written not less than a thousand years before the Christian era,[2] Yima, the

---

[1] Compare Burnouf, *Bhagavata Purana*, vol. iii. preface, xxxiv.-xlvii.

[2] Says Dosabhai Framji Karaka, in his *History of the Parsis, including their Manners, Customs, Religion and Present Position*, London, 1884, vol. ii. pp. 147, 148: "Mr. Karshedji Rastamji Kama, a well-known Oriental scholar among the Parsis, has on the authority of Greek and Jewish writers, and on that of the cuneiform inscriptions, very clearly shown in his Zarthosht Nama (*i.e.*, Life of Zoroaster), that Zoroaster lived at least 1300 years before Christ. Before the light of new scholarship fell upon the point, it was the accepted belief among the learned that Zoroaster flourished in the sixth century before Christ. The mistake arose from the fact that they took the Kayanian king Gushtasp, in whose reign the prophet flourished, to be the same as Darius Hystaspes, the well-known king of the later Achæmenian dynasty, who lived about B.C. 521. Not only did the two kings belong to different dynasties, but the latest researches have shown that a period of more than 800 years intervened between them. This fact affixes as the earliest possible date to the reign of Gushtasp, and in consequence to the birth of Zoroaster also, the year B.C. 1300." That Zoroaster was thus a possible contemporary of Moses, Haug, Windischmann, and Spiegel also agree: see Haug's *Essays on the Sacred Language, Writings, and Religion of the Parsis*, edited and enlarged by E. W. West, 3rd edit., London, 1884, pp. 298, 299; Windischmann, *Zoroastr. Studien*, Berlin, 1863, p. 67; Spiegel, *Eranische*

first man, the first king, and the founder of civilization, is advised by Ahura, the Good Spirit and Creator of all, on the approach of a dire winter which is to destroy every living creature, to build an enclosure in which to preserve the seeds of all animals and plants.

"And Ahura Mazda spake unto Yima saying :
"O fair Yima, son of Vivanghat ! upon the material world the fatal winters are going to fall, that shall bring the fierce, foul frost : upon the material world the fatal winters are going to fall, that shall make snowflakes fall thick, even an *aredvi* deep on the highest tops of mountains.

"And all the three sorts of beasts shall perish, those that live in the wilderness, and those that live on the tops of the mountains, and those that live in the bosom of the dale, under the shelter of stables.

"Before that winter, those fields would bear plenty of grass for cattle ; now with floods that stream, with snows that melt, it will seem a happy land in the world, the land wherein footprints of sheep may still be seen.

" Therefore make thee a Vara (enclosure) long as a riding-ground on every side of the square, and thither bring the seeds of sheep and oxen, of men, of dogs, of birds, and of red blazing fires.

"Therefore make thee a Vara, long as a riding-ground on every side of the square, to be an abode for men ; a Vara, long as a riding-ground on every side of the square, to be a fold for flocks.

. . . . . .

" Thither thou shalt bring the seeds of men, and women, of the greatest, best, and finest kinds, on this earth ; thither thou shalt bring the seeds of every kind of cattle, of the greatest, best, and finest kinds on this earth.

" Thither thou shalt bring the seeds of every kind of tree, of the greatest, best, and finest kinds on this earth; thither thou shalt bring the seeds of every kind of fruit, the fullest of food and the sweetest of odour. All those seeds thou shalt bring, two of every

---

Alterthumskunde, Leipsic, 1871, vol. i. pp. 668–683. Professor Harlez, however, still advocates the later date for Zoroaster ; see his *Avesta, Livre Sacré du Zoroastrianisme*, 2nd edit., Paris, 1881, Introduction, pp. xviii–xxiii, and cxcii–ccvii. As against both views, Darmesteter considers Zoroaster to have been a wholly mythical personage ; see his *Ormazd et Ahriman, leurs Origines, et leur Histoire*, Paris, 1877, and the *Sacred Books of the East*, vol. iv. 1880, Introduction, p. lxxxvi.

kind, to be kept inexhaustible there, so long as those men shall stay in the Vara."

In due course the Vara was sealed, a door having been made and a window "self-shining within." In this instance, as so frequently happens in these ancient traditions, there appears to be some confusion of the tradition of Eden with that of the Flood; nevertheless two additional facts deserve notice. On the one hand, the word translated "frosts" is said by some commentators to signify "rains,"[2] in which case the destruction of all things would have been by water, not cold. On the other hand, the command was given to Yima to build "when six hundred winters" had passed over him.[3] According to Genesis, Noah was six hundred years old when the Flood broke.

In China[4] also, and in Japan, in Siam, amongst the Tartars,[5] and amongst the Dyaks of Borneo,[6] a parallel tradition has been preserved. To these Asiatic traditions may be added the *Phrygian* story of King Naumakos, identified by some with Enoch. This king was fabled to have reached an age of more than three hundred years, to have foretold the Flood, and to have prayed and wept for his people, so clearly did he see the coming destruction. Very curious, too, as showing how deep a root this tradition had taken in the country, is the fact that so late as the time of Septimius Severus, about the

---

[1] *Sacred Books of the East*, vol. iv. pp. 15-21.

[2] *Ib.* p. 17, *note*.

[3] *Ib.* vol. iv. p. 14.

[4] Faber, *Horæ Mosaicæ*, vol. i. pp. 147, 148: Gainet, *La Bible sans la Bible*, 2nd edit., 1871, Bar-le-Duc, vol. i. pp. 189, 190.

[5] Japanese, Siamese, and Tartar legends are given in Gainet, vol. i. pp. 193, 194.

[6] *Trans. of Soc. of Bibl. Archæol.*, vol. ii. p. 265.

second century of our era, a medal was struck at Apamæa commemorating the Flood. The city is known to have been formerly called Kibotos, or the Ark, and it is also well known that the coins of cities frequently exhibited in that age some leading feature of their mythological history. The medal in question represents a kind of square vessel floating in the water. Through an opening in the vessel are seen two persons, a man and a woman. Upon the top of this chest, or ark, a bird is perched, whilst another flies towards it carrying a small branch of a tree between its feet. In front of the vessel the same pair are represented as having quitted their ship for dry land. Singularly enough, too, on some specimens of this medal the letters $N\Omega$ or $N\Omega E$ have been found. Can such a medal celebrate more events than one?[1]

Passing from Asia to Europe, traditions of a universal deluge are found amongst the Greeks and Romans, the Scandinavians, the Celts and the Lithuanians—in fact, among all the great Aryan tribes which have peopled Europe.

The *Greek* diluvian legend, which passed to Rome, exists in two forms. There is the legend of Ogyges, whose very name is derived from a word signifying flood, and there is the well-known legend of Deukalion. In the time of Ogyges, a mythical personage,—"*qui se perd dans la nuit des âges,*" as Lenormant says after Pictet,—the whole country of Bœotia was invaded by a deluge, the waters of which, rising to heaven, destroyed all men but the king and a few companions who escaped

---

[1] Cardinal Wiseman, *Lectures on Science and Religion*, 6th edit., London, 1849, vol. ii. pp. 117-124; comp. Bryant, *Antient Mythology*, vol. iii. pp. 47-49.

in a ship. In this instance, it is true, we see an exemplification of the common law of traditions, that they become localized, as has happened, for example, when the primitive Eden has been identified with Japan and Mexico, with Denmark and Sicily. If, however, some are inclined to think that this Bœotian legend is simply a vague reminiscence of some local flood, the same cannot be said of the legend of Deukalion and Pyrrha, so favourite a story with the ancient writers, with Pindar and Ovid, Apollodorus and Lucian.

"The generation and the present race of men," says Lucian, "were not the first; for all those of that former generation perished. But these are of a second race; which increased from a single person, named Deukalion, to its present multitude. Concerning those men, they relate the following tale. Being of a violent and ferocious temper, they were guilty of every sort of lawlessness. They neither regarded the obligation of oaths, nor the rights of hospitality, nor the prayers of the suppliant; wherefore a great calamity befel them. The earth suddenly poured forth a vast body of water; heavy torrents of rain descended; the rivers overflowed their banks; and the sea arose above its ordinary level; until the whole world was inundated, and all that were in it perished. In the midst of the general destruction, Deukalion alone was left to another generation, on account of his extraordinary wisdom and piety. Now his preservation was thus effected. He caused his sons and their wives to enter a large ark which he had provided. But, while he was embarking, swine and horses and lions and serpents, and all other animals that live upon the face of the earth, came to him in pairs. These he took in with him; and they injured him not; but, on the contrary, the greatest harmony subsisted between them through the influence of the deity. Thus they all sailed together in an ark, so long as the waters prevailed. Such is the narrative of the Greeks."[1]

Lucian goes on to say that the Syrians of Hierapolis believed the flood to have been swallowed up by a large

[1] Quoted from Faber, *The Origin of Pagan Idolatry, ascertained from Historical Testimony and Circumstantial Evidence*, London, 1816, vol. ii. pp. 110, 111; compare Bryant, *Antient Mythology*, vol. iii. pp. 27-29.

chasm in their country, that they had erected a temple over this chasm, and that they held annually a festival in remembrance of the cessation of the deluge. Let another significant detail be added. " It was maintained by mythologists," writes Plutarch, "that Deukalion sent a dove out of the ark; which, when it returned to him, showed that the storm was not yet abated; but when he saw it no more, he concluded that the sky was serene again." [1]

The *Celtic* Druids, also, so unique and yet so conservative in their rites and doctrines, had their diluvian legend.[2] According to their bardic hymns, the profligacy of mankind had provoked the Supreme to send a pestilential wind upon the earth. A pure poison descended; every blast was death. At this time, the patriarch, distinguished for his integrity, was shut up, together with his seven select companions, in the floating island, or sacred enclosure, with the strong door. Here the just ones were safe from injury. Presently a tempest of fire arose. It split the earth asunder to the great deep. The lake Llion burst its bounds; the waves of the sea lifted themselves on high, round the borders of Britain; the rain poured down from heaven; and the water covered the earth. But that water was a lustration, to purify the polluted globe, to render it meet for the renewal of life, and to wash away the contagion of its former inhabitants into the chasms of the abyss. The flood, which swept away from the surface of the earth the expiring remains of the patriarch's contemporaries,

---

[1] Quoted by Faber, *The Origin of Pagan Idolatry*, &c., vol. ii. p. 111.
[2] Compare Davies, *Mythology and Rites of the British Druids*, London, 1809, p. 226; Faber, *ib.* vol. ii. pp. 130-136; Rhys, *Lectures on the Origin and Growth of Religion as illustrated by Celtic Heathendom*, London, 1888, pp. 649-668, 670.

raised his vessel, or inclosure, on high from the ground, bore it safe upon the summit of the waves, and proved to him and his associates the water of life and renovation.

Simply mentioning a diluvian tradition, to some extent parallel to the preceding, in the great Scandinavian epic, the Edda,[1] and another tradition extant amongst the ancient Lithuanians,[2] which, by the way, calls attention to the rainbow, we may further advance from the Eastern to the *Western Hemisphere*, where again reminiscences of a deluge are frequent. Diluvian traditions have been met with, in fact, in North America, in South America, and in the isthmus of Panama. Indeed, as D'Eichthal has said, legends of a universal flood are "spread throughout the New World from one pole, so to speak, to the other;"[3] and, as Dall has said, "a general belief in a deluge is widely spread among American races, and can hardly be attributed to Christian teaching."[4] To give a few instances. The legend in existence among the Cherokees reminds us of the story in the Mahabharata, except that a dog renders the same service to his master that the fish did to Manu.

"This dog," writes Schoolcraft, "was very pertinacious in visiting the banks of a river for several days, where he stood gazing at the water and howling piteously. Being sharply spoken to by his master and ordered home, he revealed the coming evil. He concluded his prediction by saying that the escape of his master and

---

[1] Pictet, *Les Origines Indo-Européennes*, 2nd edit. vol. ii. p. 372.

[2] Hanusch, *Die Wissenschaft des Slawischen Mythus*, Lemberg, 1842, p. 234.

[3] *Etude sur les Origines Bouddhiques de la Civilisation Americaine*, Paris, 1865, part i. p. 65.

[4] Nadaillac, *Prehistoric America*, translated by D'Anvers, and edited by W. H. Dall, London, 1885, p. 525.

family from drowning depended on throwing *him* into the water; that to escape drowning himself, he must take a boat and put in it all he wished to save; that it would then rain hard a long time, and a great overflowing of the land would take place. By obeying this prediction the man and his family were saved, and from them the earth was again peopled." [1]

The diluvian tradition of the Quiches ran as follows:—

"Thus by the will of the Heart of Heaven the waters were swollen and a great flood came upon the manikins of wood. For they did not think nor speak of the Creator who had created them, and who had caused their birth. They were drowned, and a thick resin fell from heaven. . . .

"Because they had not thought of their Mother and Father, the Heart of Heaven, whose name is Hurakan, therefore the face of the earth grew dark and a pouring rain commenced, raining by day, raining by night.

"Then all sorts of beings, little and great, gathered together to abuse the men to their faces; and all spoke, their mill-stones, their plates, their cups, their dogs, their hens.

"Said the dogs and hens, 'Very badly have you treated us, and you have bitten us. Now we bite you in turn.'

"Said the mill-stones, 'Very much were we tormented by you, and daily, daily, night and day, it was *squeak, squeak, screech, screech*, for your sake. Now yourselves shall feel our strength, and we will grind your flesh, and make meal of your bodies,' said the mill-stones.

"And the cups and dishes said, 'Pain and misery you gave us, smoking our tops and sides, cooking us over the fire, burning and hurting us as if we had no feeling. Now it is your turn, and you shall burn,' said the cups, insultingly.

"Then ran the men hither and thither in despair. They climbed to the roofs of the houses, but the houses crumbled under their feet; they tried to mount to the tops of the trees, but the trees hurled them far from them; they sought refuge in the caverns, but the caverns shut before them.

"Thus was accomplished the ruin of this race, destined to be destroyed and overthrown; thus were they given over to destruc-

---

[1] *Notes on the Iroquois, or, Contributions to American History, Antiquities, and General Ethnology*, Albany, 1847, pp. 358, 359.

tion and contempt. And it is said that their posterity are those little monkeys who live in the woods."[1]

Again, concerning the Mexicans, Alexander von Humboldt writes:—

"Of the different nations that inhabit Mexico the following had paintings resembling the deluge, viz., the Aztecs, the Miztecs, the Zapotecs, the Tlascaltecs, and the Mechoacans. The Noah, Xisuthrus, or Manu of these nations is called Coxcox, Teo Cipactli or Tezpi. He saved himself with his wife Xochiquetzatl in a bark, or, according to other traditions, on a raft. The painting represents Coxcox in the midst of the water waiting for the bark. The mountain, the summit of which rises above the waters, is the peak of Colhuacan, the Ararat of the Mexicans. At the foot of the mountain are the heads of Coxcox and his wife."[2]

Of the Mechoacan tradition of a deluge Von Humboldt writes:—

"Coxcox, whom they call Tezpi, embarked in a spacious *acalli* with his wife, his children, several animals and grain. When the Great Spirit ordered the waters to withdraw, Tezpi sent out from his bark a vulture, the zopiloti or *vultur aura*. This bird did not return on account of the carcases, with which the earth was strewed. Tezpi sent out other birds, one of which, the humming-bird, alone returned, holding in its beak a branch clad with leaves. Tezpi, seeing that fresh verdure covered the soil, quitted his bark near the mountain of Colhuacan."

According to Herrera, the Peruvians had a tradition that all men perished in a deluge, "except six who were saved in a float, from whom descended the inhabitants of that country."[3]

---

[1] Brinton, *Myths of the New World, a Treati on the Symbolism and Mythology of the Races of America*, 2nd edit., New York, 1876, pp. 223, 224.

[2] *Researches concerning the Institutions and Monuments of the Ancient Inhabitants of Mexico*, translated by Helen Maria Williams, 2 vols., London, 1814, pp. 226, 227.

[3] *History of America*, translated by Stevens, London, 1725, 1726, vol. iii. p. 250.

For yet further illustration of the diluvian traditions of the Western world, let the quaint chant of the Lenni-Lenape be cited :—

"Long ago," they sang, "came the powerful serpent when men had become evil.
The strong serpent was the foe of the beings, and they became embroiled, hating each other.
Then they fought and despoiled each other, and were not peaceful.
Then the strong serpent resolved all men and women to destroy immediately.
The black serpent monster brought the snake water rushing.
The wide waters rushing wide to the hills, everywhere spreading, everywhere destroying.
At the island of the turtle was Manabozho, of men and beings the Grandfather.
Being born creeping, at turtle land he is ready to move and dwell.
Men and beings all go forth on the flood of waters, moving afloat every way, seeking the back of the turtle.
The monsters of the sea were many, and destroyed some of them.
Then the daughter of a spirit helped them in a boat, and all joined, saying, Come, help,
Manabozho, of all beings, of men and turtles, the Grandfather.
All together, on the turtle then, the men then, all together.
Much frightened, Manabozho prayed to the turtle that he would make all well again.
Then the waters ran off, it was dry on mountain and plain, and the great evil went elsewhere by the path of the cave."[1]

Similar traditions were preserved by the Nicaraguans, the Brazilians, and the Cubans. Indeed, even so antipathetic a critic as Mr. Brinton confesses that "there are no more common heirlooms" than flood traditions—that in these traditions "the person saved is always the first man," and that "the American nations, among whom a distinct and well-authenticated myth of the deluge was found, are as follows—Athapascas, Iroquois,

[1] Paraphrase given in Emerson, *Indian Myths*, Boston, 1884, p. 352.

Cherokees, Chikasaws, Cuddos, Natchez, Dakotas, Apaches, Navajos, Mandans, Pueblo Indians, Aztecs, Miztecs, Zapotecs, Tlascalans, Mechoacans, Toltecs, Natonas, Mayas, Quiches, Haitians, natives of Darien and Popoyan, Muyscas, Quichmas, Tuppinambas, Achaguas, Araucanians, and doubtless others."[1] Nor should we omit the fact that the "Popul Vuh," the sacred book of the people of Guatemala, concerning which Max Müller writes one of his interesting essays in the first volume of his *Chips from a German Workshop*, knows of a first race of men who were destroyed by water.

Even in the many islands of the Pacific references to a deluge have been discovered. Thus the Fijians say that after the islands had been peopled by the first man and woman, a great rain took place by which they were finally submerged, but that, before the highest places were covered by the waters, two large double canoes made their appearance. In one of them was Rokoru, the god of carpenters, in the other, Rokolu, his head workman, who picked up some of the people and kept them on board until the waters had subsided, after which, eight in number, they were again landed on the island. Diluvian traditions have also been preserved in other places in Polynesia.[2]

Here the sketch of deluge traditions, which if recorded fully would fill a large volume, may cease. The sketch is complete enough for the argument. Witnesses have been summoned from all quarters of the globe, there scarcely being a people or a corner of the earth which does not furnish some corroboration of the historical

---

[1] *Myths of the New World*, p. 226; compare pp. 213-228.
[2] Waitz, *Anthropologie der Naturvölker*, vol. vi., Die Völker der Sudsee, Leipsic, 1872, pp. 270-273.

character of this great event. "The deluge was the grand epocha of every ancient kingdom ; ... the renewal of the world ; the new birth of mankind ; and the ultimate of Gentile history."[1] Even the variations of the legends point the more surely to an unvarying, and very ancient, historical nucleus. As M. Pictet has so well said,

> "If the different legends are compared with each other, or with the narrative of the Genesis, they are found to be too divergent to admit the fact of their being borrowed by one people from another, and, on the other hand, too concordant to associate them with the hypothesis of several local deluges. In them all, the place of the event is changed, and the names of the man saved from the waters vary, or they simply signify the ancient mythical renovation of each particular race ; but also, in them all, the destruction is universal, and one single man or a single couple escapes in a ship, with or without animals, so as to recommence life on the earth."[2]

Indeed it would seem that chronology itself has some curious testimony to offer, for there are some grounds for saying that the date assigned in the Genesis to the Flood varies but slightly from the approximate dates of the Indian Deluge and the Chinese.[3]

This diluvian evidence is, to say the least, striking. For the moment I refrain from drawing the inferences which such a series of facts warrant, and content myself with calling attention to the remarkable character of the facts themselves.

I have thus considered the world-wide traditions of a universal deluge at some length. Desiring to illustrate that corroboration of Genesis which may be found in ethnic tradition, I have primarily selected a crucial and

---

[1] Bryant, *Antient Mythology*, vol. i. pp. xxxvii., xxxviii.
[2] *Les Origines Indo-Européennes*, vol. iii. p. 386.
[3] Gainet, *La Bible sans la Bible*, vol. i. pp. 208, 209.

indubitable instance. But it is necessary now to add that the instance given is far from exceptional. Similar corroboration is found in the ethnic religions of other portions of the primitive Biblical history. There is scarcely an incident in the earlier chapters of Genesis which does not exist in some legend or other in some heathen faith. That the world was created in six days, that man was formed of the dust of the ground, that woman was moulded from man, that humanity has sprung from a single pair, that the primitive beliefs of men were monotheistic, all may be found in the records of heathendom as well as of Christianity; there are corroborative traditions concerning a primeval paradise, concerning its location, concerning the fall of our first parents, concerning the serpent as the origin of evil, and concerning a promised deliverer from the effects of sin; there are also corroborative traditions relative to Cain and Abel, to the intermarriage of the sons of God and the daughters of men, to the primitive giants, to the longevity of the patriarchs, and even to the number of the patriarchs from the Creation to the Deluge, whilst the long list of corroborative traditions is brought to a close with the numerous legends extant concerning Babel and the confusion of tongues. It is unnecessary for my purpose to illustrate all these coincidences by lengthy extracts from the extant records; but, seeing that the argument is to some extent cumulative, and that the inductions I am about to draw are generalizations from many particulars, I shall serve the end in view by a rapid enumeration of results. Being about to pass as soon as possible to the conclusions suggested by such community of evidence, I simply outline the testimony available.

Allow me to remark, however, before proceeding, that variations in traditions should cause little surprise. Traditions only become stereotyped by committal to writing; and the literary phase is by no means an early stage in the transmission of religions. On any thoughtful consideration of the circumstances under which legends are handed on from generation to generation, imaginative versions, renderings which are romantic, exaggerated, localized, and personal, will be expected to be the rule; it will be anticipated, that occurrences of remote lands and ancient men will become associated with places nearer home and with names revered and familiar. Indeed, with all the human failings of the custodians of legendary lore, the mode of transmission from mouth to ear, and from father to son, is liable in the extreme to introduce embellishment and error. The story-teller has many a temptation not to restrict himself to the naked truth. *Bon-mots* are apt to be attributed to many authors, doing service from age to age. Great deeds are wont to be ascribed to many heroes of diverse climes. Love of self, or family, or country, leads to the appropriation of exploits which are not our own; and the instinct to regard our own village as the hub of the universe, our own time as the centre of history, our own achievements as the pink of excellence, our own perils as the crater of all catastrophe, is, to use a euphemism, *human*. How *human* it is to slightly colour plain facts, to appropriate to a country what pertains to the race, and to array simple truth in the gaudy garb of allegory! How prone is the tutored as well as the savage man to tell stories, and to varnish them! In face of the mode of transmission of ethnic legends our surprise may well be reserved for the coincidences rather than the dissimilarities which appear. However, it is for the coincidences, for such coincidences as point to a common origin, that we are at present in search.

"*And the earth was waste and void; and darkness was upon the face of the deep, and the Spirit of God was brooding over the face of the waters.*" So runs Genesis. According to the Biblical account the earth was a chaos, a desert; darkness was on the face of ocean; and the creative Spirit hovered like a bird over the aqueous waste. What say the ethnic traditions? Says Ancient Egypt, "There was originally a boundless darkness in the great abyss; but water and an intelligent ethereal Spirit acted by Divine power in chaos."[1] Says Ancient Chaldea, "There was a time in which there existed nothing but darkness and an abyss of waters;"[2] and, in another place, "When the upper region was not yet called heaven, and the lower region was not yet called earth, and the abyss had not opened its arms, then the chaos of waters gave birth to them all, and the waters were gathered to one place;"[3] or, as George Smith translated the same passage, "When above was not raised the heavens, and below on the earth a plant had not grown up, the abyss also had not broken open their boundaries, the chaos Tiamat (the sea), was the producing mother of all of them."[4] Says Ancient Phœnicia, "The beginning of all things was a dark and windy air, or a breeze of dark air, and a chaos turbid and

---

[1] Faber, *Origin of Pagan Idolatry*, vol. i. p. 228.
[2] Cory, *Ancient Fragments*, p. 22.
[3] *Transactions of the Society of Biblical Archæology*, vol. v. p. 426; *Records of the Past*, vol. ix. p. 117.
[4] *Chaldean Genesis*, p. 62; compare Sayce, *Hibbert Lectures*, p. 143.

dark as Erebos."[1] Says Ancient India, "This universe was formerly waters, fluid."[2] Says Ancient Japan, "In the beginning of the opening of all things, a chaos floated, as fishes swim in the waters for pleasure."[3] Says Ancient Scandinavia, "At the beginning of time, when nothing was as yet formed, neither shore nor sea, nor foundations beneath; when the earth was nowhere to be found below, nor the heavens above, all was one vast abyss without plant or verdure."[4] Says Ancient Greece :—

> "First chaos was, next ample-bosomed earth.
> . . . . . .
> From chaos, Erebos, and ebon Night:"[5]

a sentiment more fully expanded by Orpheus, in whose view, "In the beginning was created the ether: Chaos, and gloomy night, the first of all things, enveloped it on every side: nevertheless, there was a being, incomprehensible, supreme, and pre-existing, the creator of the ether itself, as of whatsoever is under the ether."[6] Says Ancient Rome :—

> "Ante, mare et tellus et quod tegit omnia cælum
> Unus erat toto Naturæ vultus in orbe
> Quem dixere chaos, rudis indigestaque moles ;
> Nec quidquam, nisi pondus iners ; congestaque eodem
> Non bene junctarum discordia semina rerum."[7]

---

[1] Sanchoniathon, as preserved by Eusebius, *Præparatio Evangelica*, lib. i. c. x. Sanchoniathon obtained all his knowledge apparently from some very ancient records preserved in an ancient temple.

[2] Muir, *Sanskrit Texts*, vol. i. p. 52.

[3] Faber, *Origin of Pagan Idolatry*, vol. i. p. 249; compare Bousquet, *Le Japon de nos Jours*, Paris, 1877, vol. ii. pp. 66, 67, and Reed, *Japan, its History, Traditions, and Religion*, London, 1880, vol. i. pp. 26, 27.

[4] Edda, fab. i. see, *e.g.*, Mallet's *Northern Antiquities*, London, 1770, reprinted in Bohn's *Antiquarian Library*.

[5] Hesiod, *Theogonia*, v. 116, Elton's Translation, London, 1809 ; compare Aristophanes, *Aves*, line 694.

[6] Suidas, *Lexicon*, under "Orpheus," *vide* Cambridge edition, 1785.

[7] Ovid, *Metamorphoseon*, series i. lines 5–9.

Says the Red-skin of North America, "The great Spirit, the raven, the personification of the black and windy heaven of dark nights, long brooded over an obscure and smoking chaos."[1] Could similarity even of expression go farther?

"*Thus the heavens and the earth were finished.*"—The Biblical order of creation is—light,—the firmament,—seas, dry land and plants,—sun, moon, and stars,—reptiles, fishes, birds,—the higher animals and man. Upon this question of the order of creation ethnic tradition has evidence to offer. Thus the ancient Egyptians used to sing in their hymns to Osiris, "He has made this world by his hands, its waters, its atmosphere, its vegetation, all its beasts, all its flying things, all its fish, all its reptiles, and its quadrupeds;"[2] where, although man is omitted, the order is suggestive. According to the cosmogony of the Bundehish, a collection of fragments in Pehlevi relating to the myths and legends of the Mazdayasnan tradition, the Parsis believe that the order of creation was—the heavens, and the world of light, including the sun, the moon, and the stars,—the waters,—the earth,—the trees,—the animals,—man.[3] Again, George Smith shows cause for saying that, despite the great gaps in the creation tablets discovered at Nineveh, these tablets followed almost identically the order of creation given in Genesis.[4] Yet again, according to the Laws of Manu, one of the sacred books

---

[1] Reville, *Les Religions des Peuples Non-civilisés*, Paris, 1883, vol. i. p. 277.

[2] Chabas, "Hymne à Osiris," *Revue Archéologique*, 1857, vol. xiv. pp. 73, 74.

[3] Du Perron, *Zend-Avesta, Ouvrage de Zoroastre*, Paris, 1771, vol. ii. p. 348.

[4] *Chaldean Genesis*, pp. 72-76; compare Sayce, *Hibbert Lectures*, pp. 394-395.

of India, the order of creation was—the self-existent, the waters, the heavens and the earth.[1] In the cosmogony of the Popul Vuh, of Central America, the order is—dawn,—Huracan, whose signs are lightning and thunder,—the earth with its mountains and plains and water-courses,—stags and birds,—man.[2] And yet again, in the painted records of the Indian tribe of the Lenni-Lenape we may read :—

"At the first there were great waters above all the land,
And above the waters were thick clouds, and there was God the Creator.
He created vast waters, great lands, and much air and heaven ;
He created the sun, the moon and stars ;
He caused them all to move well ;
By His power He made the winds to blow, purifying, and the deep waters to run off ;
All was made bright, and the islands were brought into being.
Then again God the Creator made the great spirits ;
He made also the first beings, angels and souls,
Then made he a man being, the father of men ;
He gave him the first mother, the mother of the early born.
Fishes gave he him, turtles, beasts and birds."[3]

It is further noteworthy, in this connection, that the Parsis expressly attribute the creation to six periods—six very prolonged periods, of time ;[4] that the Etruscans believed that five millenniums preceded the formation of man which itself occupied a sixth millennium ;[5] and that the ancient Mexicans had preserved the remembrance of a creation by the great god Ketzalkohuatl in seven days.[6]

---

[1] *Sacred Books of the East*, vol. xxv. pp. 1–5.
[2] Gainet, *La Bible sans la Bible*, vol. i. pp. 147–149.
[3] Paraphrase from Emerson, *Indian Myths*, pp. 395–397.
[4] Du Perron, *Zend-Avesta*, vol. ii. p. 348.
[5] Suidas, *Lexicon*, article Τυρρηνία.
[6] D'Anselme, *Monde Païen*, vol. ii. p. 441, quoted by Gainet, *La Bible sans la Bible*, vol. i. p. 73.

"*And the Lord God formed man from the dust of the ground.*"—A similar tradition is world-wide, being found in Phœnicia,[1] Libya,[2] Egypt,[3] Greece,[4] Borneo,[5] Peru,[6] the native tribes of America,[7] Madagascar,[8] Tahiti.[9] As said the Mandans of North America, "the great Spirit formed two figures of clay which he dried and animated with the breath of his mouth, the first man and the first woman,"—a turn of phrase which reminds one of Ovid's fresh earth :—

> " Quam satus Japeto, mixtam fluvialibus undis,
> Finxit in effigiem moderantum cuncta deorum."

"*And the Lord God caused a deep sleep to fall upon the man, and he slept ; and he took one of his ribs and closed up the flesh instead thereof, and the rib which the Lord God had taken from the man, made he a woman.*"— The nations of New Zealand say the same, that "the first woman was made out of one of man's ribs ; and their general term for *bone* is *hevee* or, as Professor Lee gives it, *iwi*—a sound bearing a singular resemblance to the Hebrew name of our first mother."[10] The same legend is found amongst the Polynesians of the Union Group, who tell how the first man "made the head, body, arms and legs all of earth, then took a rib from his right side, and thrust it inside of the earth model ;

---

[1] *Sanchoniatho*, edit. Orelli, Leipsic, 1826, p. 18.
[2] *Philosophumena*, lib. v. cap. vii.
[3] Chabas, *Etudes sur l'Antiquité Historique*, p. 87.
[4] Ovid, *Metamorph.* i.
[5] Gainet, *La Bible sans la Bible*, vol. i. p. 131.
[6] Lenormant, *Les Origines de l'Histoire*, vol. i .p. 40.
[7] Emerson, *Indian Myths*, p. 117 ; Brinton, *Myths of New World*, pp. 238, 239.
[8] *Bible Myths and their Parallels in other Religions*, New York, 1883. p. 15.
[9] Lenormant, *Les Origines de l'Histoire* vol. i. p. 40.
[10] Shepheard, *Traditions of Eden*, London, 1871, p. 73.

when suddenly the earth became alive and up started a woman on her feet; he called her Ivi (pronounced Evee) or rib; he took her to be his wife, and from them sprang the race of men."[1] In Ancient Babylonia, too, a similar belief prevailed as to the creation of woman "from the loins of the man."[2]

"*And the Lord God planted a garden eastward in Eden, and there he put the man whom he had formed.*"—Here, again, we touch a tradition which may be not inappropriately termed universal. A primitive state of Edenic felicity is one of the fondest memories of man, preserved by nearly all religions.[3] Thus the Egyptian looked back with tenderness to the days of the God Ra, which inaugurated human history.[4] The Brahman speaks with affection of the bright age of Krita, when "righteousness was perennial," when "the earth was watered by streams of milk and honey," when "men died when they desired, suffered few annoyances, were free from disease, accomplished all their objects and endured no oppression," when "they had an intuitive perception of all duties," and when, alas, "this felicity blinded them."[5] Of a land of Heden, the Magians knew, and of a primeval time of great innocence and happiness.[6] Scandinavia had its Asgard

---

[1] Turner, *Nineteen Years in Polynesia*, London, 1861, p. 526; compare Ellis, *Polynesian Researches*, London, 1829, vol. ii. p. 28, and Max Müller, *Introduction to Science of Religion*, London, 1873, pp. 302-304.

[2] Sayce, *Hibbert Lectures*, p. 395.

[3] Compare Ewald, *Geschichte des Volkes Israel*, 3rd edit. 1874, vol. i. pp. 366-378; Maury, *Histoire des Religions de la Grèce*, Paris, 1857, vol. i. p. 371; Renan, *Histoire des Langues Semitiques*, 4th edit. 1863, Paris, pp. 484-486; Lassen, *Indische Alterthumskunde*, Bonn, 1847, vol. i. pp. 528-529; Burnouf, *Bhagavata Purana*, vol. iii. preface, pp. xlviii-xlix.

[4] Lenormant, *Les Origines de l'Histoire*, vol. i. p. 58.

[5] Muir, *Sanskrit Texts*, vol. i. pp. 145,147; Gainet, *La Bible sans la Bible*, vol. i. p. 85; Lenormant, *Les Origines de l'Histoire*, vol. i. p. 59.

[6] Shepheard, *Traditions of Eden*, p. 49; Faber, *Horæ Mosaicæ*, vol. i. p. 72.

and its Golden Age.[1] Greece, too, had its Golden Age, exempt from care and sorrow, as Hesiod sang, when man led the life of the gods, and old age was unknown.[2] Nor did the Aztec priests ever chant more regretfully than when they sang of Tulan, the cradle of their race, the land of riches and plenty ; of Tulan where the sun rises; of Tulan in the land of shades ; of Tulan where the sun reposes and where God dwells—of Tulan, that is to say, their Paradise Lost, and Tulan their Paradise Regained.[3] Even the location of Eden and its four rivers are known to very diverse ethnic faiths.[4]

"*Now the serpent was more subtil than any beast of the field which the Lord God had made, and he said unto the woman, hath God said,*" &c. ? In the serpent as the origin of evil we again touch a universal tradition. I do not forget that much of ophiolatry is explicable on natural grounds, the serpent being at once so formidable and so uncanny ; nor do I forget, as Max Müller has reminded us, that "there is an Aryan, there is a Semitic, there is a Turanian, there is an African serpent," just as I would bear in mind Max Müller's appended caution when he asks "who but an evolutionist would dare to say that all these conceptions came from one and the same original source, that they are all held together by one traditional chain ?"[5] But I am not now calling

---

[1] Edda, Fab. vii. ; compare, *e.g.*, Mallet, *Northern Antiquities.*

[2] Hesiod, *Opera et Dies*, bk. i. line 108 ; compare Plato, *Opera Omnia*, edit. Stallbaum, vol. ix. p. 194.

[3] Brinton, *Myths of the New World*, pp. 90, 91.

[4] Compare Brinton, *ib.* pp. 87-92 ; Smith, *Sacred Annals, or Researches into the History and Religions of Mankind*, vol. i. Patriarchal Age, London, 1859, 2nd edit. p. 156 ; Warren, *Paradise Found, the Cradle of the Human Race at the North Pole, a Study of the Prehistoric World*, Boston, 1885, much of part iv.

[5] *Academy*, 1874, p. 548 ; compare Deane, *The Worship of the Serpent traced throughout the World*, London, 1833.

attention to serpent worship as such, in which the serpent is approached quite as frequently as a beneficent as a maleficent deity; I am only concerned with traditions of the serpent as the source of moral evil. Traditions of this character are found in many ethnic faiths. If the dragon Tiamat who plays a part in the Babylonian narrative of the Fall of Man be not a serpent,[1] the Babylonians nevertheless certainly did know of a great serpent who was "the enemy of the gods."[2] "We read, too, in the bilingual lists" of Babylonia, "of 'the evil serpent,' 'the serpent of darkness.'"[3] So the Phœnicians told of Ophion, the serpent deity, who was precipitated by Cronos into Tartarus with his companions.[4] The ancient Egyptians again had a serpent Apap, who fought against the sun and whom Horus pierced.[5] In the religion of Zoroaster, also, the evil principle, under the form of a serpent, is thrust down to earth after endeavouring to corrupt heaven, is fought against by Mithra, and will one day be vanquished, chained for three thousand years, and finally burnt up in molten metal.[6] Legends, in which a serpent is the symbol of the evil spirit, are also found in Scandinavia and amongst the American Aztecs. A few details of the Scandinavian legend are worth reciting. According to the Edda, Loki, the evil being, is possessed of great personal beauty, and of a malignant and inconstant nature, surpassing

---

[1] Smith, *Chaldean Genesis*, pp. 87-92; compare Lenormant, *Origines &c.*, vol. i. p. 100, note 2.

[2] *Cuneiform Inscriptions of Western Asia*, vol. ii. plate v. l. 39, c, d, and plate 24, quoted by Lenormant, *ib.* p. 100.

[3] Sayce, *Hibbert Lectures*, p. 283.

[4] Origen, *Adv. Celsum*, vi. 303.

[5] Wilkinson, *Manners and Customs of the Ancient Egyptians*, 2nd edit., London, 1878, vol. iii. p. 155.

[6] Du Perron, *Zend-Avesta*, vol. ii. 351.

all creatures in the depth of his cunning and in the artfulness of his perfidy. Two of his children, born of a demon styled the messenger of ill, are—death and an immense serpent. " The universal Father despatched certain of the gods to bring those children to him. When they were come, he threw the serpent down to the bottom of the ocean. But there the monster waxed so large that he wound himself round the whole of the earth. Death meanwhile was precipitated into Hela. Here she possesses vast apartments, strongly built and fenced with grates of iron. Her hall is grief; her table, famine; hunger, her knife; delay, her servant; faintness, her porch; sickness and pain, her bed; and her tent, cursing and howling." Significantly enough also, in this connection, the deliverances wrought by the great heroes of mythology are often over a serpent. Recall, for instance, the legends of Thor who bruises the head of a serpent with his hammer, of Krishna who tramples a serpent beneath his feet, of Mithra and his combat with a serpent, of Hercules and the Python, Apollo and the snake, Horus and Apap. In this instance, again, our thesis is strongly illustrated.

"*And when the woman saw that the tree was good for food, and that it was a delight to the eyes, and that the tree was to be desired to make one wise, she took of the fruit thereof, and did eat; and she gave also unto her husband with her, and he did eat.*" This story of the Fall is another universal tradition. For example, pictorial representations which can refer to nothing but the first temptation abound. Thus an ancient Babylonian cylinder, which has been reproduced by Layard, George Smith, and others, and which may be seen in the British Museum, shows two people, a man and a woman, seated right and left of a tree, from which hang two large fruits, whilst by the side of the woman a serpent stands, and erect. The representation is rude, but even so competent an authority as the great Assyriologist, Friedrich Delitzsch, avows in his edition of the "Chaldean Genesis," that it can bear no other interpretation.[1] Similarly the central tablet of a large sculpture in the temple of Osiris at Phylæ, " at once tells its own story as, beyond a rational doubt, an Egyptian delineation of the temptation and fall of our first parents; every particular is here depicted to the life; the man, the woman, the serpent, the tree, the forbidden fruit, the fruit, being not on the tree, but in the hands of the man and woman, and the basilisk being here again erect."[2] Once more, a bas-relief in the wall of the Villa Albani, at Rome, of pre-Christian times, depicts a man and a woman, nude, standing at the foot of a tree with fruit, around the trunk of which a serpent is twined. So readily did this bas-relief lend itself to express the episode in Genesis, that, as a matter of fact, the early Christians simply reproduced it in painting and sculpture, for their own purposes of illustration.[3] India has, apparently, a similar representation, for in a cave-temple of Southern India, upon a sculptured column, a human pair appear at the foot of a tree, from the branches of which a serpent

---

[1] Layard, *Worship of Mithra*, 1847, plate xvi. No. 4; Smith, *Chaldean Genesis*, p. 91; Vigouroux, *La Bible et les Découvertes Modernes*, 3rd edit., Paris, 1881, vol. i. p. 201.

[2] Forster, *The One Primeval Language*, part ii. *The Monuments of Egypt, and their Vestiges of Patriarchal Tradition*, London, 1852 : p. 185, compare *Le Cham et l'Adam Egyptiens*, by E. Lefébure, in *Trans. of Soc. of Biblical Archæology*, vol. ix. part i. 1887, pp. 176, 177.

[3] Panofker, *Annales de l'Institut Archéologique*, quoted by Lenormant, *Origines*, vol. i. p. 92.

offers fruit in his mouth.[1] The Mexicans, again, according to Alexander von Humboldt, picture a similar scene upon their monuments. Legendary traditions of the Fall also occur in plenty. The Zend Avesta tells how "Yima, the first man, lost his awful kingly glory by conflict with the snake."[2] The Phœnicians had a parallel tradition.[3] The prose Edda, of the ancient Scandinavians, speaks of the golden age when all was pure, but which ended with the arrival of woman.[4] Who can avoid associating with the Fall of Genesis the Greek traditions of Pandora, and of the Garden of Golden Apples kept by the Hesperides and the dragon?[5] The Thibetan Buddhists tell of the lapse of man from a state of felicity by eating of a plant "white and sweet as sugar," which caused him to become conscious of his nakedness and of a sudden ferment introduced into his body.[6] So too the Malagasy describe the first man as free from bodily appetites, and surrounded by delicious fruit which he was strictly forbidden to eat, but as falling from his state of blessedness, when his great enemy came to him painting in glowing colours the sweetness of the apple, and the lusciousness of the date, and the succulence of the orange.[7] And yet again, traditions are abundant con-

---

[1] Higgins, *Anacalypsis; an Enquiry into the Origin of Languages, Nations, and Religions*, London, 1829, vol. i. p. 404.

[2] *Sacred Books of the East*, vol. xxiii. pp. 294, 295 ; compare Lenormant, *Histoire Ancienne de l'Orient*, 9th edit. vol. v. Paris, 1887, p. 398.

[3] Renan, *Mémoires de l'Academie des Inscriptions*, nouvelle séries, vol. xxiii. 2nd part, p. 259.

[4] Mallet, *Northern Antiquities*, translated by Bishop Percy, London, 1847, p. 409.

[5] Preller, *Griechische Mythologie*, 3rd edit., 1872, Berlin ; vol. i. p. 439 ; compare Gainet, *La Bible sans la Bible*, vol. i. p. 87 ; and Montfaucon, *L'Antiquité Expliquée*, Paris, 1722, vol. i.

[6] Bertrand, *Dictionnaire des Religions*, article "Religion Thibétain Mongol."

[7] Baring-Gould, *Legends of the Patriarchs and Prophets*, London, 1872, p. 31.

cerning the Tree of Life. A Tree of Life was known to many peoples.¹ Such a tree appears on Assyrian and Egyptian monuments and coffins.² The Sabæans had a tree of life which they sagely called "the tree which shades." ³ Sometimes the representations of this tree are conventional and sometimes specific.⁴ When they are specific they are manifestly sketches of the *Asclepias acida*, the plant from which is obtained the sacred Soma of the early Aryans of India, and the sacred Huoma of the ancient Iranians—"*le breuvage d'immortalité* "—the holy juice, a drink of which makes men immortal on the day of resurrection.⁵ "We sacrifice," repeats the Parsi priest, "unto the enlivening Huoma [the sacred juice personified], who makes the world grow; we sacrifice unto Huoma, who keeps death far away."⁶ Nor is it without interest to notice that the ancient name of Babylon, Tin-tir-ki, signifies apparently, "the place of the tree of life." ⁷

Passing on to other pre-Abrahamic traditions, *there are many interesting legends concerning the number of the patriarchs*. According to Genesis there were in all ten patriarchs from the Creation to the Flood. Now this number of ten mythical ancestors occurs in various

---

¹ Compare the very interesting chapter on "The Central Tree," in Warren, *Paradise Found*.

² Schrader, *Semitismus und Babylonismus*, in the *Jahrbücher für Protestant. Theologie*, 1875, vol. i. pp. 124, 125. Compare *Le Cham et l'Adam Egyptiens*, by Lefébure, in *Trans. of Soc. of Biblical Archæology*, vol. ix. pp. 178-180.

³ Norberg, *Codex Nasaræus*, Liber Adami appellatus, Syriace transscriptus, . . . latineque redditus, 3 vols., 1815-6, vol. iii. p. 68.

⁴ See Botta, *Monuments de Ninive*, 1847-1850, vol. ii. p. 150; Layard, *Monuments of Nineveh*, plates 6, 7, 8, 9, 39, 44, &c.

⁵ *Sacred Books of the East*, vol. iv. p. lxix. and p. 72.

⁶ *Ib.*, vol. xxiii. p. 20.

⁷ Lenormant, *Origines*, vol. i. p. 76, note 6.

ancient monuments. Thus, in Ancient Chaldea, nine kings are said to have reigned before Xisuthrus, who, according to the Chaldean legend, was saved from the Flood.[1] So too the Assyrians believed that ten generations of heroes had preceded the foundation of Nineveh.[2] According to the ancient Iranian tradition, Gayomard, the first man, was succeeded by the Paradhata dynasty, that is, the dynasty of the kings of yore, nine in number.[3] In India, Brahma and the nine Brahmaditras are honoured as those "who are the origin of the families who have peopled the world."[4] The Egyptians taught that ten deities reigned before man.[5] The Chinese speak of ten emperors who inaugurated historic times, their names being, as far as their significance is concerned, singularly like the biblical names.[6] Similarly, the Tyrians reckoned ten kings, and the Sibylline Books ten ages, between the Creation and the Deluge; whilst Orientals frequently speak of ten Solimans, or first kings, as having reigned in the world.

Further, it is interesting to note that traditions are numerous, not only as to the number of the early patriarchs, but as to their *longevity*. Thus, in a remarkable passage, especially remarkable, if it is borne in mind that he was citing authors much better known to his readers than to us, Josephus, who had been speaking, on the authority of Genesis, of the great

---

[1] The list is given by four ancient authors, viz., Julius Africanus, Abydenus, Berossus, and Apollodorus; see Gainet, *La Bible sans la Bible*, vol. i. p. 95.   [2] Abydenus, as preserved by Eusebius.

[3] Spiegel, *Eran. Alterthumskunde*, vol. i. pp. 508 and 580; *Sacred Books of the East*, vol. iv. p. 220, note 3.

[4] *Sacred Books of the East*, vol. xxv. p. 14; Burnouf, *Bhagavata Purana*, vol. i. p. 212.

[5] Bonnetty, *Chou-King*, preface, p. 13.

[6] Gainet, *La Bible sans la Bible*, vol. i. p. 96.

age to which primitive man attained, goes on to say, "All those persons, whether Greeks or Barbarians, who have written on the subject of antiquity, agree with me in this point. For Manetho, who wrote an account of the Egyptians, and Berossus, who compiled a narrative of the affairs of Chaldea, and Mochus, and Hestiæus, and Jerome the Egyptian, who were the authors of different histories of Phœnicia—all these bear witness to my veracity. Hesiod likewise, and Hecateus, and Hellanicus, and Acusilaus, and Ephorus, and Nicolaus, relate that the ancients lived a thousand years."[1]

Yet again, just as ethnic tradition has preserved the memory of the ten patriarchs prior to the Flood, it has also preserved some memory of *the triad of patriarchs after the Flood*. That all the generations of men have sprung from three ancestors is a conviction preserved in other religious records besides the Bible. Thus the Egyptians divided men into "the Amou, of yellow colour, inhabiting Asia; and the Tama'hou or Ta'hennou, of white colour, spread through the islands and upon the northern coasts of the Mediterranean, as well as in a portion of Libya—two races corresponding exactly to the families of Shem and Japheth in the Biblical narrative; then the Na'hasiou, that is, the negroes of Africa."[2] The Sabæans traced mankind to Schoum, Yamin, and Japhet.[3] According to the Hindu mythologists (who have apparently generalized from an individual instance), at every renovation of the world, the same three heroes appear—

[1] *Antiq. Jud.*, bk. i. ch. 3; compare Eusebius, *Præparatio Evangelica*, bk. ix. cap. 13; Pliny, *Hist. Natur.*, bk. vii. ch. 48, 49; and Horace, *Carmina*, bk. i. ode 3.
[2] Lenormant, *Origines*, vol. i. pp. 201, 202; compare *Le Cham et l'Adam Egyptiens*, by Lefébure, in *Transactions of Soc. of Biblical Archæology*, vol. ix. pp. 167-181.
[3] Norberg, *Codex Nasaræus*, vol. i. p. 96.

Shama, Cama, and Pra- (or Lord) Japati, words which pronounced native fashion, like the Sabæan names just given, resemble the Hebrew forms of Shem, Ham, and Japheth.[1] Ancient Persia knew Airya, Tura, and Sairima, who became the ancestors of Iran, Turan, and Assyria, and Western Asia.[2] Again, in the fragments of Berossus, we are told that books of the Chaldeans speak of three half-divine brothers, who reigned almost immediately after the Deluge, viz., Cronos, Titan, and Prometheus—"audax Japeti genus"; unfortunately, for these interesting identifications, the Assyrian originals of these familiar Greek names are not known, although Moses of Khorene, who says he borrows from Berossus, gives the names as Zerovan, Titan, and Japedosthe. The Sibylline oracles also give the names as Cronos, Titan, and Japetos.[3]

With one other instance of corroboration, this series of illustrative parallels may close. In Babel and the Confusion of Tongues, we touch another ethnic tradition widely preserved. For example, Josephus cites a declaration from one of the Sibyls to the following effect: "When all men spake one common language, some of them built a most lofty tower, as if with an intention of scaling heaven; but the gods, sending a violent wind, overthrew it, and gave a different mode of speaking to each person; for which reason the city was called Babylon."[4] Eusebius has preserved an analogous story as told by the Armenian Abydenus, who wrote:

---

[1] *Asiatic Researches*, vol. iii. p. 262, and vol. viii. p. 255.
[2] *Sacred Books of the East*, vol. xxiii. p. 62, note 2; compare Harlez, *Avesta*, p. 505, note 2.
[3] Lenormant, *Origines*, vol. ii. pp. 205-212; compare Pietet, *Les Origines Indo-Européennes*, 2nd edit. vol. iii. pp. 379-380.
[4] *Antiq. Judæorum*, lib. i. cap. iv.

"They say that the first inhabitants of the earth, glorying in their own strength and despising the gods, undertook to raise a tower whose top should reach the sky, in the place in which Babylon now stands; but when it approached the heaven, the winds assisted the gods, and overthrew the work upon its contrivers, and its ruins are said to be still at Babylon; and the gods introduced a diversity of tongues among men, who till that time had all spoken the same language; and a war arose between Cronos and Titan; the place in which they built the tower is now called Babylon on account of the confusion of tongues, for confusion is by the Hebrews called Babel."[1] A parallel story was told by Eupolemus, the historian. He wrote that "the city of Babylon owes its foundation to those who were saved from the catastrophe of the Deluge; they were the giants, and they built the tower which is noticed in history; but the tower being overthrown by the interposition of God, the giants were scattered over all the earth."[2] One of the Assyrian tablets, now in the British Museum, unfortunately a mere fragment, seems to have a record of the same event.[3] A tradition of a high tower, whence the workmen were scattered wide, appears to exist in Fiji.[4] A parallel tradition has been found in Mexico.[5] Yet other parallels have been met with amongst the Hindus, the Lithuanians, and the inhabitants of Central Africa.[6]

[1] Cory, *Ancient Fragments*, p. 48.
[2] Bryant, *Antient Mythology*, vol. iv. p. 103.
[3] Smith, *Chaldean Genesis*, pp. 160-166; *Transactions of Society of Biblical Archæology*, vol. v. pp. 305-312; *Records of the Past*, vol. vii. p. 129; Sayce, *Hibbert Lectures*, p. 406.
[4] Shepheard, *Traditions of Eden*, p. 72.
[5] Humboldt, *Researches*, vol. i. p. 96.
[6] *Bible Myths*, p. 36.

Here the illustration of the point before us, namely, of the similarity between the traditions of the primitive ages recorded in Genesis and those which are extant in the ethnic religions, may close. The evidence has been by no means exhausted. I might have called attention to the ethnic preservation of the name of Adam. I might have dwelt upon the legendary location of Eden. I might have presented the various ethnic solutions of the cherubic guardians of the gate of Paradise. I have made no reference to the corroboration, given in ethnic tradition, of the death of Abel. I have passed by the legendary lore concerning the primitive giants. I have also refrained from giving various suggestive reminiscences of the flaming sword which kept the way of the Tree of Life. Is it not evident that the earlier chapters of Genesis record events which are also found petrified, often almost beyond recognition, in the mythologies of the world? "The cosmogony and mythology .. of all nations are evidently primitive history altered by oral tradition, transformed by the imagination and symbolized."[1] From illustration I now turn to application. Having sufficiently shown the similarity existing to a greater or less extent between the Biblical and ethnic records of primitive times, I now proceed to draw some important conclusions from that similarity.

The first inference which the above facts seem to warrant is this—that *the earlier chapters of Genesis contain primeval traditions*, meaning by primeval those early traditions of the race which date from a time prior to the dispersion from the central home.

In supporting such an inference, happily, there is no

[1] Biart, *Les Aztèques, Histoire, Mœurs, Coutumes,* Paris, 1885, p. 72.

need to decide between the rival theories, now so warmly advocated, concerning the origin of myths. It is only with one small section of these stories of the beginnings of things—of men, of sun and moon and stars, of animals, of death, of the "great globe itself,"—that we are in any way concerned. Whether many of these mythical stories have originated in a disease of language, as Max Müller affirms; or whether they are really the metaphysics of savages, as Mr. Lang thinks, it is unnecessary to discuss. All that is required by the argument of these Lectures is, to remind mythologists that some traditions as to the earlier history of our race are universal to man. There are, so to speak, primitive rocks in human traditions as well as strata of later origin. M. Darmesteter has clearly shown that in the religion of the Magi, for example, some beliefs are due to the ancestral Aryan race, and some are peculiar to the Iranian offshoot.[1] What is true of Mazdeism is true of all religions whatever; they possess generic as well as specific traditions. As M. Pictet says, "There are traditions of historical times preserved by means of the recital of epics; there are indigenous mythical traditions, the spontaneous products of the imagination when interpreting in its own fashion nature and its phenomena; and besides both these, there are traditions of a more remote past, mounting to the very origin of the human race, but obscured and altered in more than

---

[1] *Ormazd et Ahriman*, p. 4, and *Sacred Books of the East*, vol. iv. p. lvii.: "The Mazdean belief, therefore, is composed of two different strata; the one contains all the gods, myths, and ideas which were already in existence during the Indo-Iranian period, whatever changes they may have undergone during the actual Iranian periods; the other comprises the gods, myths, and ideas which were only developed after the separation of the two religions."

one sense."[1] Nor is the importance of these early traditions to be judged by their number. Being primitive traditions, fragments of antediluvian theology, pages of antediluvian history, they have an incalculable interest and importance. It is true, alas, that priests and poets have all too frequently added colour—*rebus gestis addiderunt quemdam colorem ;* still, notwithstanding this imaginative process, the bare facts are visible beneath, upon careful comparison. In short, in view of the multitudinous fragments dispersed in many lands, the conclusion is inevitable that some of the religious traditions extant are lovingly cherished remains of a primitive system of belief, heirlooms, more or less decayed, from the days when the race occupied a common home and held a common faith. The evidence in the preceding pages, outlined as it has been rather than fully presented, points to the existence of a primitive tradition. Of that tradition, the opening chapters of the Genesis—at least present one form.

But the evidence warrants a further conclusion—*The primitive traditions preserved in Genesis are original.*

For whence is derived the similarity of tradition in Genesis and in the ethnic faiths, some scanty illustration of which has been given in the preceding pages? Four hypotheses are conceivable. First, the traditions in Genesis would of course resemble the ethnic traditions if they had been actually drawn therefrom. Or, secondly, the similarity would be explicable, if, as was maintained in Gale's well-known *Court of the Gentiles,*[2] the several

---

[1] *Les Origines Indo-Européennes,* 2nd edit. vol. iii. p. 360.
[2] *Court of the Gentiles, or a Discourse Touching the Original of Human Literature, both Philology and Philosophy, from the Scriptures and Jewish Church,* 1st edit., Oxford, 1669.

ethnic faiths obtained their traditions from Genesis. Or, thirdly, the manifest likeness might be attributed to like ways of thinking, similar traditions having spontaneously arisen in different quarters because of "the natural tendencies of the human mind in its evolution from a savage state."[1] Or a fourth possible theory remains, that the resemblance is due to the fact of a common inheritance, the Genesis handing on from age to age traditions which the ethnic religions have also preserved with more or less admixture.

Now let any one carefully examine the facts previously collated, and ask which of these four hypotheses is most congruous with those facts. It will be straightway found impossible to show the dependence of Genesis upon any of the ethnic faiths, even upon those of Egypt or Babylon, for the narratives of Genesis are so much more full, so much more ordered, and so much less extravagant; no comparison of the ethnic religions could render superfluous the guidance of Genesis in the arrangement of the primitive traditions themselves; no possible eclecticism could have constructed the Genesis from the records, whether literary or monumental, of any ethnic faith known to us. Genesis does give some clues to the unravelling of the ethnic mythologies; the heathen mythologies in no way explain Genesis. In a word, the first hypothesis of the origination of the traditions of Genesis from extraneous ancient religions is out of court, as is generally conceded.

Nor do the facts of the case afford reason to believe that the ethnic faiths have borrowed their early tradi-

---

[1] Nadaillac, *Prehistoric America*, p. 531.

tions from Genesis. One fact alone negatives the probability of any such dependence of heathen upon Jewish Scriptures. Let the fact be weighed. The traditions common to Genesis and heathenism *end at the Dispersion*.[1] Now how is it that the religions of India and China, America and Ancient Europe, know of Adam and Noah, and know nothing of Abraham and Jacob? If the Arabian religions are exceptions, they are exceptions which point the moral; since none would deny either the intimacy which existed between the sons of Ishmael and the sons of Isaac, or the partial dependence of Mahomet on Christian sources. That the entire Genesis as such was known to the founders of the extra-Christian religions of Europe, Asia, Africa, America, and the islands of the Pacific, who would venture to affirm? The second hypothesis, which would derive the ethnic traditions from Genesis is also out of court.

The third hypothesis scarcely merits reference. That remote peoples might hit upon similar explanations of common natural phenomena, inventing parallel sun-myths and serpent-myths and birth-myths, is within the range of possibility; but consider the subject matter of these universal and primitive traditions! Is it within the range of credibility that different peoples, without contact, by the exercise of the common human faculties, should invent such detailed myths as those of the deluge, and the tree of life, and the creation of woman, and the number of the patriarchs, and the triad of founders of the post-Noachian race? Without contact, even the

---

[1] Compare Ebrard, *Apologetics, or the Scientific Vindication of Christianity*, translated by Rev. John Macpherson, vol. iii. pp. 321, 322. Edinburgh, 1887.

wonderful mind of man, with its similarity of functions in Malay and Negro, Mongol and Caucasian, is surely incapable of inventing, in form so largely identical, the world-wide traditions of a flood and of the salvation of one family. The mind of man might just as well be credited with spontaneously imagining, in many quarters, the historical circumstances of the landing of the Puritans on Plymouth rock. More or less distorted versions of some original story known to all the early races of man these diluvian legends may be; but, remembering their resemblances as well as their differences, spontaneous and distinct births of the mind of man they cannot be.

The only remaining hypothesis is the fourth, and to this the opinion of experts steadily inclines. All religions, it is seen, may be traced back to a comparatively small number of stocks; and if there are still religions, the genesis of which is as yet not understood, the belief grows in their ultimate derivation from some older and perverted faith. Now when these several primary religions are carefully compared, they are each seen to consist of two very different classes of facts, those which are individual and those which are common. Of those features which are common, some are undoubtedly due to the common nature of man; but as clearly some can alone be explained by a common inheritance. All religions of any antiquity bear witness to a few common traditions handed down, with more or less divergence, from a very remote past. Examine where we will, and the leading religions of the world testify to the existence of some primary and common traditions. In plain speech, the early·races of man, wherever they wandered from their original Asiatic home, took with them the primeval traditions of their ancestors, modifying these traditions more or less in the lapse of time and by the method of oral transmission. Thus, wherever man went, he carried with him the stories of a Paradise, and a Fall, and the early consequences of the Fall. It was not that one ancient religion borrowed these universal traditions from another, but that to each early religion these traditions were original. Ham did not learn of Japheth, or Japheth of Shem, but the descendants of each branch of the Noachian family took the traditions of their common family into their diverse and distant homes. In a word, the traditions of Genesis, which are common to the ethnic faiths, are original.

Yet a further inference respects age — *The traditions preserved in Genesis are of the highest antiquity.* So much follows from the preceding conclusion; for, if original, they are necessarily ancient. At least these traditions are long prior to Moses, seeing that they have been preserved, with more or less distortion, in religions with which, as far as our knowledge goes, Moses and the earlier Jews never came into contact. And even supposing that Moses utilized materials in his writings which he had obtained either from earlier writings or from oral tradition, Moses, or his successors, could not have been the channel by which these traditions became known in India and Iran, Scandinavia and Mexico.

And yet another inference is — *The primitive traditions preserved in Genesis are pure.*

Not without great cogency this unadulterated character of the early traditions of Genesis might be inferred from their simplicity and rationality. There is a truthfulness and a credibility about these early Biblical narratives, which not even rare literary genius seems able to impart. Nor does their veraciousness lessen upon comparison. There is an air of truth about the Biblical story of the Flood which there is not about the North American or the Indian story. Often the legends of heathenism appear to be a grotesque masquerade of the beliefs ascribed in Genesis to the Patriarchal Age.

Further, the veracity of these early Biblical traditions follows upon careful scientific and theological inquiry, a branch of proof which will be presented later on.

But, further still, a third method remains for demonstrating the purity of these early traditions, a method which, although a little recondite, is very suggestive. Do not the *manifest misconceptions of Heathenism* emphasize strongly the purity of the Biblical traditions from Adam to Shem?

This point of the comparative purity of the early narratives of Genesis repays illustration. A few instances shall be given, which doubtless might be very largely multiplied.

One good illustrative instance is found in the narrative of Creation. According to the Hebrew form of the tradition, the earth was without form and void (*thohu wabhohu*), where *thohu* and *bhohu* are archaic forms even to Biblical Hebrew. Now in Babylonian and Assyrian the original meaning of *bhohu* has manifestly become lost, and instead of "chaos" we find a "goddess of chaos," Bahu the wife of Hea. In fact, the Mesopotamian religions, in ignorance, made a divine personage of what was originally apparently a mere name expressive of disorganization and disorder.¹ Who will contend that *Bahu* the goddess is of earlier date than *bhohu*, chaos?

Parallel instances abound. The Assyrian goddess Tihavti, also pronounced Tihamti, the goddess of the sea, would appear to have arisen from a misconception of the antique word *th'hom* preserved in Hebrew and translated the "deep"; "and darkness was upon the face of the deep." Similarly the Babylonian "Tiamat or Tiavat, is the *t'hom* or 'deep' of the Old Testament."² Again, according to one of the fragments of the Phœnician cosmogony, which have reached us under the name of Sanchoniathon, we read that of the god Colpias and of his spouse Baau was born the first human pair, Protogonos and Æon, this Æon having discovered the eating of the fruit of the tree.³ Now here the names Protogonos and Æon, which are Greek, are very probably renderings of Adam Qadmun (a common name for the first man), and of Chavah (Eve, the first woman). Yet more curiously, as Bochart pointed out long ago, in the god Colpias we seem to have a transliteration of Qolpiach (the voice of the breath), with some confusion of "the voice of the Lord God," and of the "breath of God" which moved on the face of the waters, just as in the goddess Baau we certainly have a transliteration of the ancient name for chaos. Have we not possibly in this legend a misconception of the primary narrative which has been pre-

---

¹ Compare Vigouroux, *La Bible et les Découvertes Modernes*, vol. i. p. 175; and Sayce, *Hibbert Lectures*, p. 151. "She," the goddess Bahu, "seems to have been the Bohu of Genesis," *ib.* pp. 262, 263. "Bau, or Bahu, is the *bohu* of the Old Testament, the Baau of Phœnician mythology," *ib.* p. 375.

² Sayce, *Hibbert Lectures*, p. 374. ³ Edit. Orelli, p. 14.

served purely in the second verse of the first chapter of Genesis?

Similarly, are not the various ethnic traditions, so common, which make man autochthonous and androgynous, misconceptions of the simpler version given in Genesis? Thus, as we have seen, the religions are numerous which regard man as sprung in some fantastic way from the soil; but have we not possibly in these often ludicrous statements the product of human imagination working upon the phrase, possibly perplexing enough if taken apart from its context, "And the Lord God formed man of the dust of the ground"? And is it not allowable to see in those ethnic extravagances, which represent the first pair as first created in physical union and as subsequently disparted, the working also of perplexed imagination upon the primary tradition as to the creation of woman, preserved purely in Genesis, a tradition naturally incredible to the heathen mind, and therefore calling for some sort of speculative explanation?

Here is another suggestive example of this variety of misconception. Receiving from tradition the name of Ararat, the Babylonians tried to find an etymology for it, and built thereupon a mythology. Of course they framed a wrong etymology. As M. Lenormant has pointed out, "the lexicographic documents of the library palatine of Nineveh show us that the Assyro-Babylonians sometimes called the Ayrarad of Armenia *Urtu*, whence we must conclude that by a mistaken etymology they decomposed *Urartu* or Arartu into ar-Urtu, the mountain of Ourtou."[1] Surely the name of Ararat must be prior to its mistaken interpretation.

[1] *Les Origines de l'Histoire*, vol. ii. p. 38.

Again, is it not probable that the Indian Meru, the Mazdean Airyana-Vaedja, and the numerous ethnic conceptions of a golden age now lost, are mythological distortions of the Biblical Eden? And, amidst all the extravagances and mythical accretions of the Vishnu Purana,[1] is there not ground for seeing in the river divided into four streams and in the tree which gives life and immortality to all who drink thereof, reminiscences sure, if faint, of a primitive tradition preserved in purer form in Genesis? The very name of Paradise was retained by Persian monarchs for their enclosed parks or gardens, as Xenophon has told us.[2]

Or again, who can resist the impression of a distortion of a tradition preserved more purely in Genesis when he reads the Brahman myth concerning King Nahusha,[3] who moved through the sky in a celestial car, acquired the sovereignty of three worlds, was hurled from heaven because of his overweening pride, and was changed into a serpent? The very name Nahusha is apparently a simple transference of the word translated "serpent" (*nachash*) in the first verse of the third chapter of Genesis. There is even some ground for tracing back the name of the god Dionysos to the same primary tradition.

Further, does not a common confusion in ethnic religions afford an additional series of instances of misconceptions, and accentuate the purity of the traditions preserved in Genesis? As a matter of fact the stories of Adam and Noah, or, to speak more accurately, of the first man of pre-diluvian and the first man of post-

---

[1] *Vishnu Purana*, translated by Wilson, pp. 166-171.
[2] *Hellenica*, iv. 1, 15; *Cyropædia*, i. 3, 14.
[3] Muir, *Sanskrit Texts*, i. pp. 307-316.

diluvian times, and the stories of the Creation and of the Deluge, the first beginning of historic times and the second beginning, are so frequently confounded in the religion of heathendom, as to point strongly to the impure character of ethnic tradition. The fact of their confusion is so commonly acknowledged that instances need not be cited. Faber called attention to the fact again and again in his famous work on *Idolatry*, and Lenormant has done the same in his *Origines*. Possibly a couple of modern testimonies from writers who certainly do not write in the Christian interest, may have large weight. Says Mr. Brinton, concerning what he is pleased to call the deluge-*myths* of Asia and America, "It has been a peculiarity of the latter (and he shows afterwards of the former as well) that in them the person saved is always the first man: this, though not without exception, is certainly the general rule: but these first men were usually the highest deities known to their nations, the only creators of the world, and the guardians of the race,"[1] and, a little later on in his book, he speaks of "the intimate connection that once existed between the myths of the deluge and those of the creation."[2] M. Reville makes a similar remark in his recent *History of Religions*.[3]

And yet again, is not the common heathen representation of the world as originating in a world-egg probably another misconception of the primitive tradition, a misconception, however, not seen in Genesis? "Black-winged night produced an aerial egg," sang the Orphic poet; and this mundane egg, at once the source and the fitting

[1] *Myths of the New World*, p. 217.
[2] *Ib.*, p. 220.
[3] *Histoire des Religions*, Paris, 1883, vol. i. p. 353.

symbol of the universe, has been celebrated by other priests and poets in many climes. But the thought arises as to whether the idea of this generative egg has not sprung from a misunderstanding of the primitive tradition of creation. At any rate, in the version of this ancient tradition given in Genesis, it is said, that when "the earth was waste and void," and when "darkness was upon the face of the deep," the "spirit of God *moved* upon the face of the waters," where the word *moved*, more accurately rendered, would be "was brooding upon," as a hen does over an egg. Has this figurative description of the creative activity of God, handed scrupulously down from a very high antiquity, become so misapprehended in the course of time as to give rise to these numerous legends of a world-egg? The question is at least suggestive.

And yet again, do not the various exaggerations in heathen lands of the longevity of the early races of men point to an original fact, the remembrance of which, again, has been preserved purely in Genesis? The Babylonian tradition made its antediluvian kings to have lived from ten thousand to sixty-eight thousand years apiece;[1] and the Egyptians and the Greeks and other nations spoke of long-lived giants as their earliest ancestry. In such legends have we not another instance of the mythical tendency working upon early traditions, which have become, in the course of time and in the absence of written records, partly forgotten, and, therefore, largely misconceived?

Have we not, too, in the several instances of the heathen association in worship of women and serpents,

[1] Vigouroux, *La Bible*, &c., vol. i. pp. 211-217.

as in the case of the Epirote woman who was made priestess over the sacred wood of serpents, and in the case of the grove at Lavinium with its cave and great serpent ministered to by young girls, and in the African dedication of their most beautiful maidens to the worship of serpents,—have we not in such instances an outgrowth of the narrative told in pure form in Genesis?

And, not to continue further these suggestive instances of misconception, which might be almost indefinitely increased, have we not in the notion, which has prevailed widely both in the Eastern Hemisphere and the West, of four successive ages in the history of man, symbolized by the metals, gold, silver, brass, and iron, ages during which mankind steadily degenerated from a state of peace and holiness to one of violence and wickedness, another example of the distortion of an original tradition given purely in Genesis? Genesis also knows of a golden age of Eden, and a silver antediluvian age, and a brass antediluvian age, and an iron post-diluvian age, in each of which an augmenting degeneration is manifested. The legend of the four ages may have sprung from the primitive history of the race, as purely recorded in Genesis; the narrative of Genesis can scarcely have originated in the ethnic tradition of successive ages of degeneration. Surely altogether these manifest distortions of the primary traditions accentuate the purity of the form they have in Genesis.

A final inference remains. If the contents of the first twelve chapters of Genesis are traditions concerning the human race, at once primitive, original, ancient, and pure, they *must be historical.* The conclusion is inevitable. These chapters contain history, not legend,—narrative, not allegory,—prose, not poetry. Such a conclusion is no unimportant contribution to our subsequent discussion, as will be seen presently. Such a conclusion turns the edge of much modern criticism, and provides solid ground for a reasoned belief in Divine inspiration.

LECTURE III.

GENESIS AND SCIENCE.

LECTURE III.

GENESIS AND SCIENCE.

IN our inductive study of the Divine origin of the Law, one branch of preliminary evidence has been sufficiently investigated in the preceding Lecture Ethnic traditions of many kinds, as we have seen, corroborate the view that Genesis records facts and not fictions. Another branch of preliminary evidence now calls for examination.

In this Lecture we are still concerned with the historical character of Genesis. On the side of the argument for historicity many traditions of religious antiquity have presented themselves as cogent and yet independent witnesses. Another series of independent witnesses is to be now arraigned. The crucial question is to be tested, whether coincidences also exist between the narratives of Genesis and the conclusions of Science.

We are to ask whether or not the independent researches of scientists and exegetes mutually support each other. We are to inquire whether the historical character of Genesis is substantiated in any degree by the discoveries of science. In a word, do Genesis and Science agree or differ?

That Genesis is not a science handbook may be conceded at once. As a recent writer has said: "The first chapter of Genesis is not a geological treatise; it is absolutely valueless in a geological discussion."[1] A manual of Science must be ordered, reasoned, technical, complete, and, being science and not literature, is addressed to students of science as such, not to man as man. Genesis, beyond a question, is no systematized nor scholastic, specialistic nor balanced, text-book upon any branch of knowledge, physical, mental, social, or religious. Neither in form nor contents, neither in method nor audience, is Genesis a scientific manual. Genesis is literature, not science. It addresses itself to the world, and not to a class. Genesis has all the naturalness, the freedom, the picturesqueness, the apparent disorder, the ready intelligibility of popular annals. Genesis, whilst not itself systematized, is like a piece of nature, from which the scientific mind may extract a system if it will. It would be a gross misnomer to call Genesis in any sense a manual of science.

But, by conceding on the spot that Genesis does not contain scientific knowledge of any kind expressed in scientific language, the whole problem of the relations of Genesis and Science is not solved. For example, it is only the shallowest dogmatism when the writer previously quoted goes on to say, not only that the first chapter of Genesis is valueless in geological discussion, but that it "has no authority whatever, save as representing what the Jews borrowed from the Babylonians, and as preserving for us an early cosmology to be compared with those prevailing among other early peoples suffi-

---

[1] Howorth, *The Mammoth and the Flood, an Attempt to Confront the Theory of Uniformity with the facts of Recent Geology*, London, 1887, preface, p. ix.

ciently cultivated to have been inquisitive about such things."[1] Quite another question besides the scientific value of Genesis arises. Is it possible that Genesis, literary and popular as it is in its form, affirms, upon men and things, certain definite conclusions, which have themselves only been reached in quite recent years by the methods of science? Is there any reasonable ground for saying that, centuries before the birth of Science, Genesis asserted precise views upon the origins of things, views which to-day are the most treasured, because the hardest won, conclusions of scientific research? In short, are Genesis and Science at one upon many points? For if they are, such startling anticipation of modern results, is a noteworthy feature in deciding the position of the Jewish Law in the literatures of the world.

In this Lecture, FIRST, *it will be made clear that Genesis and Science do show remarkable coincidences; and* SECOND, *the conclusions (inferrible from such coincidences) as to the historicity of Genesis will be summarized.*

One concurrence of opinion between Genesis and Science is seen in their identical views upon the original unity of the human race.

Genesis very distinctly asserts that the entire human race, all the numerous progeny of Shem and Ham and Japheth, has sprung from a single parental pair. "And the man called his wife's name Eve; because she was the mother of all living." Notwithstanding apparently irreconcilable differences of form and colour, all the

---

[1] Howorth, *Mammoth and the Flood*, preface, p., ix.

varieties of mankind, according to the teaching of Genesis, are descendants of the first man and the first woman. Now what says anthropology? Does it declare for monogeny or for polygeny?

The answer is tolerably definite. A little after this nineteenth century had broken, Baron Cuvier, the greatest naturalist of his day, expressed himself with decision upon the problem of race. "We are fully warranted," he wrote, "in concluding, both from the comparison of man with inferior animals, so far as the inferiority will allow of such comparison, and beyond that, by comparing him with himself, that the great family of mankind loudly proclaim a descent, at some period or other, from one common origin." Nor has later inquiry weakened the force of this deliberate scientific opinion that God "hath made of one blood all nations of men, for to dwell on all the face of the earth." A few decades later Dr. Prichard, the father of modern ethnology, published his splendid work entitled *Researches into the Physical History of Mankind*,[1] showing by a very careful and exhaustive examination of the physical characteristics of the races of man, their common descent. True, it has become fashionable to shelve biological and anthropological works written prior to the publication of Darwin's epoch-making book upon the *Origin of Species*, as if all scientific knowledge of man and men dated from the year 1859; but, notwithstanding this common prejudice, Dr. Prichard's researches are confessedly to-day a rich mine of useful observation. M. Quatrefages, too, one of the most prominent comparative anatomists of the time, has also, in wide and justly

---

[1] *Researches into the Physical History of Mankind*, 5 vols., vol. i. 4th edit., London, 1861.

esteemed investigations, shown good ground for believing in the primitive unity of the race.[1] Besides, Darwinian speculations have rather accentuated than otherwise the theory of primitive unity, and, as Dr. E. B. Tylor has pointed out, Darwin himself presents, in his *Descent of Man,* "as distinctly a monogenist argument as those of Blumenbach, Prichard, or Quatrefages."[2]

Nor is it easy to see how Science could arrive at any other conclusion. The facts which have been collated are irresistible. There are all the facts, as convincing as varied, afforded by minute inspection of the known races of men—their skin, their hair, their skulls, their forms. There are all the facts associated with the known history of the races of men, rendering a common ancestral home highly probable. Then, too, there is a mental unity in man. Differ as races, as well as individuals, may in mental power, there is the same psychological classification for all; there is, in all races, the same senses, the same intellect, the same affections, the same instincts, the same volitional and ethical faculties, the same religious sense. All races apparently are susceptible of amelioration by Christianity.[3] Circassian and Negro and Mongol, the philosophic Hindu and the barbarian Fuegian, the degraded Hottentot and the civilized Englishman, all possess, it would seem, the same list of mental faculties, including capacity for religion. Nay, dig skulls from the most ancient repositories available, and there is no average diminution of nerve power, it would seem, upon

---

[1] *Unité de l'Espèce Humaine,* Paris, 1861 ; compare *Histoire Générale des Races Humaines, Introduction, Questions Générales,* Paris, 1887, especially chapter ii.

[2] *Encyclopædia Britannica,* 9th edit. vol. ii. p. 114.

[3] Compare a suggestive little book by S. R. Pattison, *Gospel Ethnology,* London, 1887.

measurement. Yet again, the members of the human race do not become sterile by intermarriage, as animals of what we are compelled to call different species do; nay, the several races of men illustrate forcibly the well-known law, that when individuals marry of different varieties, the offspring tends in a very few generations to become at once more prolific and better endowed, mentally and physically, than their parents. In this question of intermarriage the American continent has shown a magnificent, a prolonged, and a conclusive experiment, an experiment extending over four centuries; all races of the Eastern Hemisphere have mingled with all races of the Western Hemisphere, without any interference with the fecundity or endowments of the offspring. Yet again, closer investigation has diminished the mysteriousness of the black colour of the Negro, that one physical fact which seemed to argue for a plurality of origin for the human family. Livingstone met Negroes of a coffee-colour. The Bicharis, of Shemitic and not a Hamitic birth, are as sable as Negroes. Some East Indians combine with features of a purely Aryan type the pronounced tint of Africa. Indeed, such acknowleged facts are now seen to be readily explicable. Colour is due to a pigment secreted in the skin by nature. But animal secretions of all kinds are known to be peculiarly influenced by circumstances. The very name of Melanism has had to be framed for a by no means uncommon disorder in which the skin becomes black. Brown Norway rats have been seen in zoological collections in the process of turning black. The Jews, again, as has often been remarked, are a proof of the impermanence of facial colour. Indubitably descended from a common stock, restricted by all their laws from intermarriage with Gentiles, yet

scattered over the face of the globe, they are white in England, brown in Italy, olive in Syria, coffee-coloured in Arabia, and almost black in Abyssinia.

In short, anthropology finds in all the races of men the same anatomical structure, the same mean duration of life, the same disposition to disease, the same disposition to diseases which only attack man, the same mean temperature of the body, the same mean movement of the pulse, the same period of pregnancy. Such is the evidence, in fact, that even Dr. Tylor, whose whole bias and deliverances are against the Biblical standpoint, is constrained to say, that "on the whole, it may be asserted that the doctrine of the unity of mankind now stands on a firmer basis than in previous ages," and, though he goes on to say, "it would be premature to judge how far the problem of the origin of races may be capable of exact solution," he immediately adds, "but the experience of the last few years countenances Mr. Darwin's prophecy, that before long the dispute between the monogenists and polygenists will die a silent and unobserved death."[1]

What, then, Genesis narrates as history, concerning the derivation of the human race from a single pair, Science declares, many decades of centuries afterwards, as inference.

A second noteworthy concurrence of Biblical and scientific opinion is seen in identical views upon the original unity of human speech.

From anthropology let us turn to philology.

By a scene as unmistakable as vivid the writer of Genesis stakes his veracity on the unity of human

---

[1] *Encyclopædia Britannica*, 9th edit. vol. ii. art. "Anthropology."

language as well as of human descent. According to his pictorial view, the families of men originally spoke one common speech, which, however, ultimately became confused and diverse after a precise turning-point in the primitive history. At Babel arose confusion; from Babel radiated emigration.

Now what has modern philology, reasoning according to its own methods and from its own data, to say concerning the primary unity of language? When the tribunal of Science has, according to its inductive method, stripped the author of Genesis of his claim as an inspired writer, "may he," to use the phrase of Max Müller, take, before that rigorous tribunal, "the modest title of a quiet observer"?

A few decades ago it would have been difficult for Science to reply either way; and even at the present moment, in face of the vast subject-matter of philology and also in face of the languages still wholly or largely unstudied, some modesty of expression best harmonizes with scientific calm and absence of bias. Nevertheless, it is not too much to say that every step of late has been towards the demonstration of the primary oneness of speech. Any summary, however brief and untechnical, of the line of recent linguistic discovery emphasizes the high probability of this primary oneness.

Comparative philologists are now no more perplexed before the numerous varieties of speech than comparative biologists are before the many varieties of life. For the same reason in both cases. Comparison has disclosed the type under the instance, the genus under the species; the individual examples under examination have ceased to be individual; they have become individuals which have been gathered into a great classification. System has grown under the ardent prosecution of observation, and law out of the inchoate. Stage by stage the generalizing process has been pushed to higher issues. In single languages Science has seen varieties of speech, in varieties genera, in genera branches, and in branches families. A small number of families are now understood to embrace the entire realm of spoken utterance. Every advance, therefore, in classification has been an advance to unity.

Further, the advance to unity has not stopped at the few ultimate families. It was much for the earnest band of comparative philologists to bring within the bonds of an indubitable relationship languages as remote in appearance, in age, and in position, as Sanskrit and English, Italian and Celtic, Greek and Scythian. It was also much to add to the demonstration of the existence of the great Aryan family, represented by such opposite languages as the dialects of the peoples ruled over by the Queen of England and the Empress of India, that of the great Shemitic and Turanian families. But more still has been done towards the proof of the primeval unity of all languages. The great Aryan family is seen to consist of all sorts of compounds made of roots and inflections (themselves transformed roots): the great Shemitic family is also seen to consist of all sorts of compounds of roots and inflections (themselves transformed roots); whereas the great Turanian family is seen to consist of roots agglutinated together. Thus all three families point back to a time when language consisted of nothing but what are called "roots," that is to say, intelligible sounds used to express thoughts. It is on such evidence that Max Müller, having put the question, "Can we reconcile with the three distinct forms of speech—the radical, the terminational, and the inflectional — the admission of one common origin of human language," says, "I answer decidedly, Yes." The decomposition of all speech into these elements, which men call roots, emphasizes strongly the primary unity of language. An identical law of composition seems to point to community of origin.

Further, philological research suggests yet another step towards the primeval unity of language. All languages are referrible, it has just been said, to a few great families; these families, it has also been said, point, by their common structure from roots, to their being descendants, more or less remote, from one and the same parent; further, the roots themselves apparently belong to one and the same original language. Here come in voluminous recent researches as fascinating as recondite. The Englishman, the Frenchman, the Greek, and the Hindu make themselves understood by their fellows by their use of verbal roots which they have inherited from the language which became the sacred Sanskrit; the Arab dragoman of to-day, not above baksheesh, speaks with roots employed by Ishmael; John Chinaman converses by the aid of roots which were not new in the days of Confucius. All this is sufficiently interesting. But there is matter of profounder interest yet. Indian and Englishman, Frenchman and Arab, Greek and Chinee, all draw apparently upon the same original stock of verbal roots which have passed from father to son, and from dynasty to dynasty, and from people to people, and from age to age, and from hemisphere to hemisphere. The coin, so to speak, which bears to-day the impress of every nation under the sun, has simply been again and again new minted; its metal has been handed down from a far-distant past when humanity had but one home. The very controversies of philology point the same moral. Theories antagonistic to the primary unity of language, and theories which preferred a sort of animal origin for human speech, are now remembered simply as the vanquished in past battles. To-day the opinion is almost universal among philologists that primitive man, settled in his original Asiatic home, possessed one parent language, rude it may be as well as rudimentary, but none the less the origin of all the dialects of the world, simple or elaborate, savage or civilized. Indeed, one of the most brilliant chapters in Max Müller's latest work, the *Science of Thought*, traces the entire speech of man to about a hundred and twenty roots, or mother ideas. "All that we admire, all on which we pride ourselves, our thoughts, whether poetical, philosophical, or religious, our whole literature, our whole intellectual life, is built up with about one hundred and twenty-one bricks." "The Science of Language startled the world some years ago with the announcement that it could reduce the 250,000 words, now filling an English dictionary, to about 1,000 roots; the Science of Thought goes beyond this, and assures us that every thought that ever crossed the mind of man can be traced back to about one hundred and twenty-one simple concepts."[1]

Again, then, what Genesis states as history, science maintains as inference.

From philology let us turn to *ethnography*. A third noteworthy concurrence in Biblical and scientific opinion concerns the Genealogy of Races.

[1] *Science of Thought*, 1887, pp. 418, 419; compare the entire chapter, pp. 330-419.

In fact, the tenth chapter of Genesis, which claims to give a careful and minute description of the original dispersion of mankind, narrating at once the birth, the growth, and the spread of the primitive nations, their ancestry, their habitat, and their migrations, is an indiscreet audacity if it be not naked truth. For the whole chapter provides a series of tests of historicity as unexceptionable as crucial. The historian who wrote for immediate recognition might so far presume upon ignorance and credulity as to give a speculative view of the journeying of the Noachidæ from their central home; but time and inquiry could not fail, in the long run, to render his statements suspect if they were not true

Now what says the modern science of man to the contents of this ethnographic Register of Genesis? It declares this Book of the Generations of Noah at once a document of a very high antiquity and an authentic record of the affiliation of peoples. To use the phrase of Canon Rawlinson, these " *Toldoth Beni Noah* . . . . have extorted the admiration of modern ethnologists who continually find in it anticipations of their greatest discoveries." [1]

Not that this tenth chapter of Genesis is without its difficulties. There are difficulties in what it says, difficulties of interpretation; and there are difficulties in what it does not say, difficulties in omission. With respect to the former there are points not clear even now, after the persistent efforts of recent inquirers. With respect to the latter, the table does not itself pretend to be complete. Thus Japheth is said to have

[1] *The Historical Evidence of the Truths of the Scripture Records Stated Anew*, London, 1859, lecture ii., compare note 75.

had seven sons; whereas the line of two alone, Gomer and Javan, is pursued; and whereas, as history teaches us, great and important nations were derived from Magog and Madai and Tubal and Meshech and Tiras. To Ham, again, five sons are ascribed, but the descendants of four only are given, Phut being passed over. Shem, yet again, is said to have had five sons, but the children of Arphaxad and Aram are alone given. Further, it is manifest that the whole migrations of men are not named, for we hear nothing of the peopling of Eastern Asia, Central and Southern Africa, America and Australasia. Let these difficulties be frankly admitted. But the point of real emphasis is, not whether there are facts in this ethnological chapter which are beyond comprehension, but whether there are facts which are manifestly historical. That there are, an inductive investigation demonstrates. Possibly, too, the difficulties themselves which appear insoluble are really consequences of the great age of the document itself which has been manifestly laid under contribution by the author of Genesis.

For this chapter bears evidence to its own high antiquity. There would seem to be no reference therein, in the original portion of the chapter, to a time posterior to the days of Abraham. For example, this register has very little to say about the tribes of Japheth who, towards the close of the pre-Christian era, attained to the first eminence; whereas this register has very much to say about those Hamitic nations, the Egyptians and the Canaanites, the first founders of great empires, who so early achieved historic eminence. The Canaanites too, at the time of writing, were in undisputed possession of Canaan, and were not spread abroad;[1] thus the chapter would appear to antedate the great Hittite conquest, of which we have recently heard much. Nor had the Philistines[2] (who are mentioned in what looks very like a later addition to the text, made not improbably by Ezra, the writer of the Chronicles) concluded their migration from the Casluhim. Does not the mention, again, of Resen, otherwise unknown, as "a great city" indicate a time anterior to the great kings who ruled at Asshur and Calah?[3] Nor is it without weight that Tyre, a fortified city in the days of Joshua, and a city of considerable importance in the days of David and Solomon,[4] is not so much as noticed. On the other hand, Sodom and Gomorrah[5] are spoken of as familiar and existent landmarks. The Kittim,[6] again, apparently the inhabitants of Cyprus, who were assuredly Phœnician in the days of Solomon, and therefore Shemite, are assigned to Japheth, as is Tarshish also, the well-known Phœnician Tartessus. The conspicuous omission, too, of the ancestry of the Edomites and Moabites and

---

[1] Gen. x. 18.
[2] Gen. x. 14; compare 1 Chron. i. 12. "I think it manifest, that the Casluhim and the Caphtorim, mingled together, occupied the district, which lies between the delta of the Nile and the southern extremity of Palestine. This appears from the circumstance of the Philistine being said in one place to have come out from the Casluhim, and in another to be the remnant of the land of Caphtor (Gen. x. 14: Jerem. xlvii. 4). Now the Philistim, in the days of Abraham, were just beginning to penetrate into the country, which from them was afterwards called Palestine, or Pallisthan; and they clearly entered it from the south-west; because at that period even Beer-Sheba was not in the land of the Philistine, though at length, as they gradually spread themselves northward up the coast, it became a town in their most southerly province (Gen. xxi. 31–34)."
—Faber, *Pagan Idolatry*, vol. iii. p. 456.
[3] Gen. x. 12.
[4] Josh. xix. 29; 2 Sam. v. 11; and 1 and 2 Kings frequently.
[5] Gen. x. 19. [6] *Ib.*, x. 4.

Ammonites and Ishmaelites would appear to imply that the table was written before the days of Ishmael and Esau, and even Lot. Further—and the fact has peculiar weight—from his elaborate study of Javan and his sons, M. Lenormant, in his great work, infers that this ethnographical table belongs to a time, when the Dorians had not entered upon the scene of history, when only Æolians were to be found on the Greek continent, when the Carians (who lost their domination of the Ægean before the Trojan war) were unknown, a date at least as remote as the Exodus.[1] Lenormant, it is true, expressly guards himself from seeming by such an admission to imply anything concerning the date of Genesis as a whole, this table being, in his view, simply a very early document used by a late writer; "the writer, who desired to make an ethnogeny would by preference follow the most ancient documents to which it was possible to remount." But we are not, in our inductive examination, at present concerned with the date of the whole of Genesis, but simply with the date of this tenth chapter; and it is, from our present standpoint, a highly significant fact that the latest and best investigator of the difficult details of this chapter, himself an advocate of the post-Mosaic authorship of Genesis, should find in this register of races a document possibly older than Moses. For many strong reasons, in fine, it may be said with confidence, that this ethnographical table is an heirloom from a remote antiquity, very probably coming to us from within a century or so of the days of Abraham. It is difficult to see how the high antiquity of this table can be disputed.

[1] *Les Origines de l'Histoire*, vol. iii. pp. 179, 180. Lenormant's whole examination of this chapter, occupying more than 500 pages of his great work deserve, and will repay, careful study.

Has, then, this ancient genealogical monument the venerableness of truth as well as of age? This tabular tree of races—so full of singular theories and of singular explicitness, so full, be it added, of singular daring if it be not true,—is it historical or imaginative? Does this table heighten the repute of its author for veracity, or environ him with suspicion? The considerations of a few facts in these "Generations of the Sons of Noah," the commonplaces of modern research, may aid decision.

Thus, this summary history of the sons of Noah places the first home of the human race, after the Flood, eastwards of the plain of Shinar, that is to say, eastwards of the great alluvial tract through which pass the renowned rivers, the Euphrates and Tigris. What says comparative philology concerning the primeval home of man? As far as it is able to decide, philology places the original centre from which the race radiated just in such a spot. According to large consent, the steppes of Central Asia were the birth-place of human speech. To such a spot the primary Indo-European languages may be traced. To such a spot equally may the earliest Shemitic speech be referred. And, most probably, to such a spot may the Turanian languages also be attributed. The conclusion is so largely recognized, after the able advocacy of such scholars as Lassen, Burnouf, Ewald, Renan, Obry, D'Eckstein, Senart, Maspéro, and Lenormant, that it is needless to delay upon it.[1] As Sir Henry Rawlinson has said, "Ethnography pronounces that we should be led to fix the

---

[1] Compare Renan, *De l'Origine du Langage*, cap. xi.; 5th edit., Paris, 1875, pp. 219-236; and especially, Obry, *Le Berceau de l'Espèce Humaine selon les Indiens, les Perses et les Hébreux*, Amiens, 1858.

plains of Shinar as a common centre from which the various lines of migration radiated."[1]

Again, the Biblical narrative divides all the races of mankind into three primary races. Of this triple division modern ethnology also knows something. Cuvier spoke of Caucasian, Mongolian, Ethiopian; Prichard, according to skull formation, of Oval, Pyramidal, and Prognathous; Latham of Atlantidæ, Japetidæ, and Mongolidæ; Max Müller of Aryan, Semitic, and Turanian; whilst Hamilton Smith speaks of Bearded, Beardless, and Woolly Type. Nearly a hundred years ago Sir William Jones wrote his conclusions as follows: "First, that the various languages of the world are traceable to three primitive ones: that these are essentially different in their construction from each other; but that all the languages of Asia and of the world finally resolve themselves into these. Second, that the several nations of mankind are, in a similar manner, found to have descended from three distinct races, or families. And, thirdly, that there is ample reason for believing that those several tribes of mankind, and those several primitive languages, are clearly traced to, and are found to have emanated from, Ancient Iran—an important district, and which is geographically the same as that described in the Scriptures as the plains of Shinar."[2] Despite the eccentric opinion of Professor Sayce,[3] it is possible to say that a century of further investigation has simply

[1] *Journal of Royal Asiatic Society*, vol. xi. part ii. p. 232.
[2] *Origin of Families and Nations*, vol. iii. pp. 34, 53, 178, 186.
[3] *Introduction to the Science of Language*, vol. ii. p. 323, London, 1880: "The attempt made in the infancy of linguistic science to reduce these groups to a mystical triad has long since been abandoned by the scientific student."

emphasized the conclusions of Sir William Jones. From the days of this pioneer of comparative philology the triple division has ruled.

Yet another point deserves notice. The Genesis table places a Shemitic population in Assyria and Elam, and a Cushite, a Hamitic, population in Babylon. Can these unexpected statements be true? Here again modern inquiry is on the side of Genesis. That the Assyrians were Shemites, allied in language, physical constitution, manners, and customs, with the Tyrians and Phœnicians and Israelites has been long held; and recent monumental discovery has entirely confirmed the conclusion. "We now possess," says Canon Rawlinson, in his great work on the Oriental Monarchies, "in the engraved slabs, the clay tablets, the cylinders, and the bricks, exhumed from the ruins of the great Assyrian cities, copious documentary evidence of the character of the Assyrian language, and (so far as language is a proof) of the ethnic character of the race. It appears to be doubted by none who have examined the evidence that the language of these records is Shemitic. However imperfect the acquaintance our best Oriental archæologists have as yet obtained with this ancient and difficult form of speech, its connection with the Syriac, the later Babylonian, the Hebrew, and the Arabic does not seem to admit of a doubt."[1] To-day, also, this consanguinity of the languages of Assyria and Palestine seems likely to throw large light upon the Hebrew of the Old Testament, ancient Assyrian in the hands of Delitzsch the Younger being a more fertile field of study than modern Arabic in the hands of Ewald.[2]

[1] *Five Great Monarchies*, 2nd edit., 1870, Second Monarchy, chap. iii.
[2] Compare *The Hebrew Language Viewed in the Light of Assyrian Research*, by Frederic Delitzsch, London, 1883.

In this instance scientific archæology has but emphasized the popular conviction that the Assyrians were Shemites, allied in language and origin to the Hebrews. But what shall be said about the Babylonians? Are they not allied to the Assyrians? Are they not Shemites, too? Certainly many great men have so thought. Baron Bunsen, in his *Philosophy of Universal History*,[1] regards the fact of the Aramæan origin of the Babylonians as completely established, thus making the Babylonians closely akin to the Assyrians. A similar impression has been fostered in the popular mind by the *vulgarization*, as the French say, of Cyclopædias and Historical Compends. But the Biblical statement is precise : " And Cush begat Nimrod . . . and the beginning of his kingdom was Babel, and Erech, and Accad, and Calneh, in the land of Shinar." According to this genealogy the early Babylonians would be Hamites, not Shemites—Ethiopians, not Aramæans—cousins-german of the Egyptians and Abyssinians, not of the Syrians and Phœnicians. Here, then, there is a decided conflict of opinion. As a matter of fact, however, the recent discoveries of records in stone and clay have given the solution of the difference of view. Both parties are right. The Babylonian language in the time of Nebuchadnezzar was indubitably Shemitic; the language of Lower Mesopotamia at the date of the first establishment of a Chaldean kingdom was as indubitably Hamitic. Such is the testimony of the Inscriptions. It is also the testimony of tradition, when carefully weighed. Let the words of Canon Rawlinson be again cited. "The conclusions," he says, "recommended to us by the consentient primitive traditions of so many

[1] Vol. i. p. 193.

races, have lately received most important and unexpected confirmation from the results of linguistic research. After the most remarkable of the Mesopotamian mounds had yielded their treasures and supplied the historical student with numerous and copious documents bearing upon the history of the great Assyrian and Babylonian Empires, it was determined to explore Chaldæa Proper, where mounds of less pretension, but still of considerable height, marked the sites of a number of ancient cities. The excavations were eminently successful. *Among their other unexpected results was the discovery, in the most ancient remains,* of a new form of speech, differing greatly from the later Babylonian language. . . . In grammatical structure this ancient tongue resembles dialects of the Turanian family, but its vocabulary has been pronounced to be *decidedly Cushite* or Ethiopian." [1] Thus the Cushite or Hamite origin of the ancient Babylonians seems demonstrated; and Egypt and Babylon, the great pioneers in civilization, the founders, apparently, of alphabetic writing, astronomy, history, chronology, architecture, plastic art, sculpture, and navigation, were, as Genesis says, twin sisters of Hamite birth.

Yet again, the several members attributed by this chapter to the Japhetic race, forestall by fifty centuries a great philological discovery, that concerning the affinity of such languages as Greek and Celtic, Gothic and Scythian. If philology declares such opposite languages to be of one great family, Genesis does the same, and

---

[1] *Five Great Monarchies*, First Monarchy, chap. iii., the whole chapter should be read; compare, Sayce, *Lectures on the Origin and Growth of Religion, as illustrated by the Religion of the Ancient Babylonians*, Hibbert Lectures for 1887, p. 5.

Genesis did not get its view from philology. Let the descendants of Japheth, the members of the great Japhetic family, be attentively considered.[1] Amongst those descendants are the sons of Gomer, the Gimirrai of the cuneiform tablets, the Cimmerians of the Odyssey —the sons of Magog, generally understood to be the Scythians—the sons of Madai, or the Medes—the sons of Javan, identical with the Greek 'Ιάfoves, or Ionians —and the sons of Tiras, or the ancestors of those maritime Tyrrheni, who have left their marks so perceptibly on the coasts of the Mediterranean, to say nothing of the sons of Tubal and Meshech, peoples already extinct in the days of Ezekiel.[2] Now to class, as Genesis does, all these peoples as members of one Japhetic family is as astonishing as the philological classification of Celtic, Gothic, Scythian, Median, Greek, and Tuscan under one great Aryan family.

Then, passing from the Japhetic to the Hamite list,[3] it is not without its strong interest to see that such widely-separated peoples as the Ethiopians, the sons of Cush, and the Egyptians, the son of Mizraim, and the Copts, the sons of Phut, and the several Canaanite peoples, the sons of Canaan, are attributed to a common ancestor. In this instance, again, modern linguistic and ethnographical inquiry generally have no objections to take. The cuneiform monuments and other lines of proof have established the fact that the primary Babylonians, and the inhabitants of Upper and Lower Egypt, and the Hittite, the Jebusite, the Amorite, the Girgashite, the Hivite, the Arkite, the Sinite, the Arvadite, the Zemarite, and the Hamathite, in short, all the several tribes of Canaan, some of whom, like the Hittites, sub-

---

[1] Gen. x. 2.   [2] Ezek. xxxii. 26, 27.   [3] Gen. x. 6.

sequently became great peoples, are descended from Ham.

And, finally, passing on to the Shemitic list,[1] however surprising at first sight it may be to find in close association of descent the children of Asshur and Elam and Eber, the Assyrians, that is to say, and the Hebrews, and the inhabitants of Elymais, this affiliation of peoples has also been borne out by recent inquiry; the connection, for example, of Hebrew with Assyrian having been but recently verified by Orientalists.

What, then, Genesis narrates as history, concerning the genealogy of races, Science, many centuries afterwards, declares quite independently as inference.

A fourth noteworthy concurrence of Biblical and scientific opinion concerns the theological views advocated by both.

To some, doubtless, it will seem strange to put Genesis into such an antithesis, and for two opposite reasons. Some will say Theology is not Science; let this class of objectors remain content with the assurance that, in strict regard for the limits of an inductive argument such as these lectures contain, nothing in theology shall be deemed to be science which is not fact, or legitimate inference from fact. Others will express surprise that Genesis, which is part of the data of Theology as generally understood, should be put in contrast with Theology, the whole which contains the part; for how can the part be opposed to the whole? Let such objectors be good enough to bear in mind that, at the present juncture, revealed religion as such is not in question. For the moment we are not concerned with

[1] Gen. x. 21, &c.

the revealed character of any part of Genesis, although valid grounds for belief in that revealed character will appear later on. For the moment the position to be emphasized and illustrated is simply this—that the theological statements of Genesis are substantiated by the common facts of the religious life of man. Genesis and the religious life of mankind are at one, it is believed, in their several statements concerning God and man and their relations.

Let the point to be considered be otherwise stated.

On the one hand, Genesis confronts its readers with certain pronounced deliverances of a religious kind. That these deliverances are presented in a historical, and not in a philosophical, setting, does not make them less religious. Quite characteristically Genesis contains teaching about God and His relations with man, but enforces this teaching, not by the demonstrations of argument, not by elaborate logical processes, not in any abstract way indeed, but by a concrete method all its own, by a historical narrative of facts concerning the Divine dealings. We are taught therein that God is, and that He is supremely interested in man, by being informed what God does. Therein the doctrine of God is not deduced from admitted principles, but forms the background of lives exceptionally influenced by Deity. Genesis narrates, it does not speculate; it is history, not philosophy; it presents life in God by a record of God in life. This being so, the question straightway arises, whether its historical statements concerning the supernatural side of human life are credible? Are its theological utterances an additional proof of its historicity?

On the other hand, man is not wholly dependent upon

the Bible, and certainly is not dependent upon Genesis, for his religious convictions. Common exercise of the faculties of observation and reason suggest the existence of a world beyond sense and of a personality beyond self. Face to face with the facts of life men have arrived at beliefs which transcend those facts. Prayer and worship, the sense of dependence, and the devout mind, indeed, the entire religious attitude, so peculiarly human, have found their *rationale* in convictions concerning God and the soul, concerning present duty and a future life. In short, religion is natural to man, and religion is the outcome of convictions concerning the supernatural natural to man. *Even an agnostic would confess that it requires a philosophical training to make an agnostic.* It is as human to pray as to sing. Awe in the presence of the infinite is as universal as laughter. "The invisible things of Him from the creation of the world are clearly seen, being understood by the things that are made, even His eternal power and Godhead; so that they are without excuse, because that when they knew God, they glorified Him not as God, neither were thankful." Do these natural religious convictions of men countenance or contradict the religious atmosphere and history of Genesis?

On the one hand, as has just been said, Genesis assumes the truth of certain religious facts, which constitute its theological postulates everywhere; and, on the other hand, as we have also seen, the natural reason declares for certain religious conclusions at which it has independently arrived, putting them forth as its axioms everywhere. Now do Genesis and Natural Religion hold any religious convictions in common? Does the reason accept after argument religious beliefs which Genesis assumes as facts? The question is worth asking. As has been already remarked, the testimony of Genesis upon various anthropological, ethnographic, and philological matters, closely harmonizes with the results attained by modern science upon those matters; does the testimony of Genesis upon theological matters also coincide with the deliverances of modern theological science, expressly restricting the term for the moment to theological science which does not assume the revealed character of Scripture?

To ask the question is a long way towards a reply. Many have found the sole aim and interest of Genesis in its religious atmosphere, which has seemed to them peculiarly native to man as man. They have possibly not regarded the first chapter of Genesis as historical, and yet have eulogized its religious background. These advocates of the religious, but not the scientific importance of Genesis, may be cited as unimpeachable witnesses. They are as numerous as unbiassed. There is a very wide agreement amongst them in saying that the common reason of man rather substantiates than otherwise the theological assumptions of Genesis.

Let a few instructive examples of parallel religious teaching in Genesis and in religious philosophy be cited.

Note, then, that Genesis teaches, or, to speak more accurately, assumes the unity of Deity. The elaborate Theistic Argument, in which the existence of one God is inferred from the contemplation of man and of the visible universe—an argument which many have attacked, but which settles more surely into its place as a great beacon in the seas of thought the more the waves of passing winds rock it—also gives rational grounds for a belief in Monotheism. Here, then, there is a striking consensus of belief. Both Genesis and Reason declare for a First Cause of all things, a Person, a Spirit, eternal, self-existent, infinite in intelligence, feeling, and will, free, of whose freedom all other freedom is but an image, the supreme Truth, the supreme Beauty, the supreme Good, the supreme Holiness. Man asks, and must ask, what the Psalmist so pertinently expresses, "He who planted the ear, shall He not hear, He who hath formed the eye, shall He not see?" As said Jacobi, in one of his flashes of insight, giving utterance to the common sentiment of the profounder thinker, "My watchword and that of my reason, is not I, but one who is more than I, better than I, one who is entirely different from what I am, I mean God—I neither am, nor care to be, if He is not."

Genesis declares for the creation of the visible universe. Nor has the reason of man ever been able to rest for long either in the idea of a universe without beginning, an endless cycle, or in a universe self-evolving, an endless progress, chaos becoming order without cause.

Genesis describes the constant Divine occupation with the concerns of man, testifying, by incident after incident, to a ceaseless moral government of us by God, and to an unrelaxing providence which cares for us in all relations, physical, individual, social, and religious. The providential and rectoral sides of life and history are equally insisted on by Natural Religion. "No sooner does one epoch in the history of the world come to an end than a new creative day dawns, the words 'let light be' are spoken anew by the Divine creative word."[1] The preservation of the world does not argue

---

[1] Martensen, *Christian Dogmatics*, Eng. trans., Edinburgh, 1871, p. 122.

the cessation of the Divine working. The only difference between creation and preservation is this:—Creation implies a new Divine resolve as well as a Divine working. Conservation means a continuance of the Divine working, upon the same resolve.

Genesis has, too, an historical explanation to offer of the existence of evil in our midst. It traces evil to an express act of disobedience, necessitating Divine disapproval, and causing, therefore, in the providential, and, as we must believe, wise arrangement of things, a great moral disturbance, subtle and far-reaching. The theory, so to speak, of Genesis, concerning the introduction of evil into human history, deserves explicit mention. Man had been created in fellowship with God. In his primitive state, and so long as that state lasted, man was, by the gift of God, and by the influx of Divine life, immortal. Spiritual intercourse between man and his Maker being unbroken, deathlessness resulted, and, in addition to incapability of death, the flow of Divine life into man maintained a harmonious interaction of both sides of human nature, of body and spirit. Further, besides immortality and moral balance, the continuity of Divine intercourse imparted that superhuman life by means of which the natural man becomes the spiritual man. All this is taught under the form of history in Genesis. Further, according to Genesis, the Divine regenerating life ceased to flow immediately upon an act, not less shameful because so trivial, of human disobedience. Immediately, consequently, mortality ensued, disturbance of moral balance ensued, and the loss of sonship ensued. Not only so, not only were the originally disobedient thus involved, but Genesis also insists, in pictorial form, that the posterity as well as the parents suffered; and that the Divine regenerating life in consequence of the disobedience, no longer flowing as at first, the race degenerated, death reigning in man's body, passion ruling in man's mind, and man becoming his own selfish and self-centred master. Now, what have the facts of life rationally interpreted to say to this clear, if terrible, history? Is not a widespread disturbance of things more and more evident? Has not man evidence of faculties, once possessed, but now largely lost? Does not restored contact with God counteract the frightful effects which have become embodied in human nature? Is it not evident that heredity affects the moral as well as the physical structure? In short, does not the reason of man, when frankly confronting the facts of life, compel belief in a moral ideal, which is, alas! no longer realized, and, in a moral defection, which propagates itself from generation to generation, and from age to age, and which is only effectively counteracted by those who consciously live in restored contact with Deity! Natural Religion has its collections of the multiform facts of the moral life, and its facts and inferences correspond suggestively with the moral postulates of Genesis concerning the original state, the sin, and the sinful degeneration of man.

Genesis also points, in a historical manner, to a possible restoration of humanity, and a possible neutralization of the disastrous effects of the first act of disobedience. Detailed remark upon this primary evangel would be out of place here—it will follow, however, later on—but the question is timely, whether the facts of the common religious life of man do not point to a similar method of restoration. What hope can there be of an eradication of death, of a rectification of the moral disturbance, or a restoration of the Divine Spirit, except by a renewed flow of that Divine life into man, the cessation of which gave preponderance to the animal side of man's nature? Must not man's salvation depend on the restored solidarity of man and God? So much the religious mind can see outside of revelation proper; though silence is the only possible attitude when the *anima naturaliter Christiana*, as Tertullian put it, is asked whether such a restored flow of Divine energy can be looked for. As to whether God is able upon any grounds to reimpart to man the spiritual life He felt it necessary to withhold, the religious nature as such can say nothing definite.

The illustration is slight, but sufficient. The more carefully the matter is considered, however, in the light of this bare illustration, the more evident it will become that, apart from express revelation, man has some knowledge of God. The point insisted on is this: formulate that knowledge with what accuracy and fulness we can, and it will be found to harmonize closely with the historical presentments of Genesis.

Again, therefore, what Genesis narrates as fact, the reason of man, acting legitimately upon the common religious data of life, teaches, after laborious processes, by inference.

A fifth noteworthy concurrence between the teaching of Genesis and Science appears in their common views upon the generations of the heavens and the earth.

Should it seem strange to many to cite the narrative of the Creation in such a connection, it certainly were not surprising. Has it not been this very story, which, in the advance of physical researches, has seemed to be irrecoverably discredited? Upon reading this ancient cosmogony, has it not often seemed to the man of science that he must either surrender his science or his faith? How often, too, the religious man has had to front the discomposing dilemma that the Bible and Geology could not both be correct. All this is true, and is not forgotten. But a mediating word may be said. Perhaps there has been truth on both sides, which will become evident as the scientist gains a little more theology, and the theologian gains a little more science. Is there not something to be said from the side of Science, when rightly guarded and understood, for the Scriptural view of the origin of this mundane system of things?

Certainly very different views have been held upon this Biblical cosmogony. Some have regarded the first chapter of Genesis as a *legend*, that is to say as the description of what was originally an actual fact, but which, as necessarily as naturally, has become altered, possibly beyond recognition, in its transmission from generation to generation. Others have thought the story a *myth*, a popular and purely imaginative explanation of effects at once manifest and unintelligible. A third, and much more numerous class have thought this cosmogony historical, though they have differed much in their estimate of what this history actually conveyed. Thus, there have been the so-called *Traditionalists*, the favourite position with those who know little but theology: they claim that this creation narrative is historical in the most literal sense, the universe and the solar system having been created in six ordinary literal days. Then there are the so-called *Restitutionalists*, who confine the Scriptural account of the six days to this present late phase of the earth's history, and who find in the two opening verses of the chapter sufficient margin for all the preceding formations, deposited through myriads of years, and catalogued surely to-day by geological science. According to this theory, supported by many names deserving of the profoundest respect, the Mosaic six days record the restitution of a preceding creation which had been many times previously disorganized and overwhelmed; in a sentence, the genesis is a palingenesis. Both these schools of interpreters, be it observed, are really literalists, being advocates from different standpoints of the actual literality of the six days. A third class, the *Visionists*, also maintain the literal character of the days mentioned, but offer an entirely different explanation from either of the other two classes. In their view the days do not refer to the express days of creation, but to the actual days of the *revelation* of the creation; in six successive days, it is thought, a Divine knowledge was imparted, by vision, of things necessarily beyond human cognizance. Yet a fourth class, the *Epochists*, reject altogether the literal interpretation of the days assigned; they regard the days as epochs; they so regard them, sometimes on Scriptural grounds, and sometimes on grounds that are scientific, and sometimes for reasons both of Scripture and Science. These are the several views of this cosmogony of Genesis, very generally stated. The diversities under each class are naturally numerous. If an attempt is made to steer clear amongst these many hypotheses, it shall be because of the intrinsic importance to our inquiry of the question at stake.

There are two points to be considered, namely, first,

What does the Genesis itself say concerning the Creation? and secondly, How does what Genesis says harmonize with what Science says? Let us regard each point in order.

In examining the relations between Genesis and Science, especially as regards the creation of all things, nothing is more necessary, and at the same time nothing is so rare, as to inquire with exactness what the testimony of Genesis is. Here the frequent oversight must not be permitted. Let the precise words of Genesis be carefully ascertained. In ascertaining these words the method to be pursued is purely grammatical. Neither scientists nor theologians can proceed to comparison until they have valid ground for thinking they know exactly what Genesis says. As a matter of fact, the Biblical story reaches us in Hebrew, and its interpretation is a matter of language; and, beyond a doubt, there is great gain in knowing just what the laws of language permit this story in its details to mean. When the linguistic interpretation is secure, much else will be suggested in the way of interpretation. Further, Hebrew is better known than Babylonian, and the Genesis creation tablet, so to speak, should be at least as interesting as the Assyrian, which was the talk of the civilized world a short while ago. Besides, a little Hebrew would have saved many a sorry sight of recent controversy!

One postulate has been laid down, namely, that in asking just what the Biblical narrative of Creation says, we are to be guided simply by the laws of Hebrew. Let a second postulate follow. It is, that in seeking the meaning of the ancient words, we should choose those which are the most elementary and concrete, those which accord best both with very ancient narrative and with very undeveloped civilization. If the Hebrew says nothing else than that "great long things" were created in the seas, we are not to import into the translation later and more developed ideas such as sea-monsters, or even whales, to say nothing of ichthyosauri. If the Hebrew says nothing about a firmament, a solid sky, the idea is not to be imported into the text. Everything in the structure of the narrative points to the very high antiquity of the account we have. It contains words which are not used in Biblical Hebrew, except as express quotation, and it manifestly belongs to a very early date in the history of man. This being so, let the natural implication be frankly acknowledged. Secondary and tertiary strata of meaning only become attached to words in the process of time. It is an error to read into ancient monuments ideas not current in the days when they were written. What we have in this chapter is simple conceptions, elementary knowledge, concrete and not abstract words, a phase of language which a few hours in the nursery will interpret better than years in the study of the philosopher. The postulate is important, as will appear presently on several occasions; and the postulate is warranted, as the previous lecture has shown us, for this tradition in its original form is older than Moses, nay, is older than the dispersion, seeing that its contents, often its very expressions, have spread across the world with the races of men.

Read in the light of these two postulates, What is the Creation story of Genesis? Instinct with life, athrob with energy, with its own simple power and thrilling beauty of expression, one wishes it could be read somehow by us as if it were a newly-discovered page from some stone or papyrus just unearthed. What, exegetically regarded, and judging purely by the laws of language, is the story of the creation in Genesis?

The Biblical narrative of Creation begins with a general statement concerning the activity of God and the rudimentary condition of the earth, a statement as notable for its reticence as for its actual contents. It runs as follows: *In the beginning*—or, more literally, *at the head* (of His deeds)—*God created the heaven and the earth.* Here two points especially deserve close attention. On the one hand, the word translated "create" does not mean, as is so often said, "made out of nothing"; such a conception is wholly foreign to the Biblical circle of ideas; but the word does imply express Divine interposition; the word is never used of human activity; and further, such Divine activity as the word connotes is of the rarest occurrence; in this Creation narrative, for example, the word is only used three times—here, and at the introduction of animal life, and at the introduction of man. This usage of the word translated "create" is one noteworthy feature. A second is that "heaven and earth" is an inclusive phrase, apparently, for the entire universe. "Heaven" in Hebrew is used, it is true, for the sky primarily, the place of the clouds, and the stars, but it is also frequently employed, with the latitude so familiar in most languages, for the dwelling-place of Deity, that mysterious and supersensuous world which mortal eye cannot see. In short, this opening verse calls attention to two facts, viz., that all being originated in God, and that this mundane sphere was not the first creation of God.

This generalized statement having been made concerning the Divine activity, a further preliminary remark is made upon the initial state of the planet we inhabit. *And*—the common copulative "and," there is no close connection between the previous statement and this, for though the Hebrew has a method of representing close consecution, that method is not employed for a sentence or two—*The earth was waste and void*, the words translated "waste and void" being archaic words even in Biblical Hebrew, and being relics very possibly of some language prior to Hebrew. Nor was the earth, in the rudimentary state, simply devoid of structure and inhabitant, it was also devoid of light, *darkness was upon the face of the ocean*, where the word translated "ocean," is another antique word, signifying a wild rush and roar of things.

The sentences, exegetically regarded, thus far considered, are purely introductory. They describe, as has been said, the Divine Originator of all things, and the raw state of the terrestrial globe. Only now begins the narrative of Creation proper. We are no longer dealing —the Hebrew copulative conjunction shows this clearly —with somewhat disjointed remarks. From this statement on, the entire story is welded—by that Semitic peculiarity and beauty, the consecutive *waw*—into one magnificent narration, which moves as rapidly as grandly from its first incident to its last.

And the spirit of God hovered upon the face of the waters.—By the waters more is meant than seas, it would seem; for, a little later on, seas and clouds, which both form parts of the waters, are separated. *And God said, Let there be light. And light was. And God saw the light that it was good; and God divided between the light and the darkness; and God called to the light, (Thou art) Day, and to the darkness He called, (Thou art) Night.*

And there was dusk (gloaming would be the exact rendering) *and there was dawn, one day.* At present, be it remembered, we are simply dealing with philological interpretation. Linguistically regarded, these words imply, first, that Deity acted upon the waste and empty earth; secondly, that God evolved light; thirdly, that this light was periodic, and formed a contrast with the darkness; and fourthly, that this union of the time of light and the time of darkness—of the duration of the light and darkness nothing whatever is said—formed one day, one cosmogonic day; what was meant by a day was a period of darkness succeeded by a period of light.

And God said, Let there be an expanse—all the erroneous associations of the word "firmament," suggested by a Greek and a Latin word and not by the word of the Hebrew text, should be carefully avoided—*in the midst of the waters* (the circumambient waters); *and let it divide between the waters and the waters. And God made the expanse, and divided between the waters which were under the expanse and the waters which were above the expanse, and it was so. And God called to the expanse, (Thou art) Heaven. And there was dusk and there was dawn, a second day.* Thus, during the second alternation of darkness and light, the great air space was formed around the earth, and the clouds and the sea were formed. If the heavens only are named, that is because the earth and the sea are only definitively distinguished next day.

And God said, Let the waters under the heaven be gathered together into one place, and let the dry land appear; and it was so. And God called to the dry land, (Thou art) Earth, and to the gathering together of the waters He called, (Thou art) Sea. And God saw that it was good. And God said, Let the earth grow green with greenness—herbage seeding seed, fruit tree making fruit after its kind, the seed of which is in the fruit, upon the earth. And it was so. And the earth produced vegetation (literally *greenness*), *herbage seeding seed after its kind and tree making fruit which has its seed in it after its kind; and God saw that it was good. And there was dusk and there was dawn, a third day.* On this third day, that is to say, the separation became determinate between dry land and sea, whereupon the dry land sprouted vegetation of two kinds, plants with seed and plants with fruit, Gymnosperms and Angiosperms as would be said to-day.

And God said, Let there be lights in the expanse of heaven to divide between the day and the night; and let them be for signs and seasons and days and years. And let them be for lights in the expanse of heaven to give light upon the earth: and it was so. And God made the two great lights, the great light into the ruler of the day and the little light into the ruler of the night, and the stars. And God appointed them to give light upon the earth. And there was dusk and there was dawn, a fourth day. Let the exact words be carefully observed, as remarkable for their silence as their speech.

And God said, Let the waters swarm with swarms, with living breathing things, and let flying things fly upon the earth upon the face of the expanse of heaven. And God created the great long things—the word used, applied, *e.g.*, to crocodiles and serpents, means no more—*and every living breathing thing which roams, with which the waters swarmed after their kind, and every winged flying thing after its kind; and God saw that it was good. And God blessed them, saying, Fructify, and multiply, and fill the waters in the seas, and let the flying thing multiply in the earth; and there was dusk and there was dawn, a fifth day.* Thus, upon this fifth day, animal life first appears, and that in the seas and the atmosphere.

And God said, Let the earth produce living breathing things after their kind, the brute and the roaming thing, and the living thing of the earth after its kind; and it was so; and God made the living thing of the earth after its kind, and the brute thing after its kind, and everything which roams upon the ground after its kind; and God saw that it was good. Elementary zoological classification doubtless, but not inefficient! *And God said, Let us make Adam after our image, according to our likeness. . . . And God created the man in His image; in the Divine likeness He created him; male and female He created them. . . . And there was dusk and there was dawn, a sixth day.*

Such is the narrative, simple, naïve, effective, touching. Is it fact or fiction, history or poetry, truth or imagination? Ethnic religions would lead us to reply, as we have seen—fact, history, truth. What says physical science?

Perhaps, however, before the question is examined in the light of Science, it may be well to emphasize one other philological fact. Again and again, this narration has mentioned "days"—one day, a second day, and so on. What is the exact significance of this word *day*, the significance, that is to say, upon purely linguistic data. The query is worth considering; for here again, many prepossessions may vanish. What then does the word translated "day" mean in Hebrew? Exegetical considerations compel a sure, if somewhat complicated, reply. As a matter of fact, " day " is used in a variety of senses, the word manifestly possessing considerable latitude of meaning. Even in this Creation narrative itself the word has more meanings than one. The word, indeed, is used in this Creation story in five different senses. First, the pre-solar periodic light is called day : " And God called to the light, (Thou art) Day." Second, the alternation of the cosmic darkness and the cosmic light is called Day ; " and there was dusk and there was dawn, one day." Third, day means a day of twenty-four hours, as when we read of the heavenly lights that they are to be for seasons and *days* and years. Fourthly, the word is used for the light part of the twenty-four hours' day, as when we are told that "the great light is to rule the day." Fifthly, the whole time of creation is called a day in the fourth verse of the next chapter, where it is said, "these are the generations of the heaven and the earth when they were created, in the *day* that the Lord made earth and heaven." All this points to a fluid use of the word day, a use which requires the exact significance to be decided by the context. And this fluid use is manifest throughout the Old Testament, which speaks of "the day" of wrath, and " the day " of salvation, and " the day " of judgment, and " the day " of redemption. Do sticklers for literalism regard these days as of twenty-four hours? The fact is that what is called a day is one alternation of darkness and light, whatever its length. " As in the growth of the plant we distinguish the germinating, the leafing, the flowering, and the seeding processes, as so many organic phases which might be called the days of the plant's history, without reference to the length of time allotted to each, so we have here the day of the cosmic light, the day of the heavens, the day of the earth, the day of the solar light, the day of the lower animals, the day of the mammals and man ; which are really the great phases of God's creation."[1]

In comparing the teaching of Genesis and Science upon the origin of the earth and man, it will facilitate inquiry to remember that this Biblical Creation story stands or falls by nine points. Firstly, Genesis avers that our present earth once existed without structure or inhabitants. Secondly, the first stage of the elaboration of our present planet was the appearance of light (but not the light of the sun), which produced alternate night and day. Thirdly, in further elaboration of our earth, the atmosphere was formed. Fourthly arose the differentiation into earth and sea, the earth straightway producing vegetation, and this growth of vegetation preceding the appearance either of animal life or of sun and moon. Fifthly, sun and moon are made to superintend day and night, summer and winter, month and year. Sixthly, animal life began to swarm in the waters and in the air. Seventhly, cattle and wild beasts at length roam upon the earth. Eighthly, and almost contemporaneously, man is made. Ninthly, creation, the express and exceptional interposition of Deity, is restricted, as the language employed shows, to the original creation of the earth, to the creation of the primary types of animal life —insect and fish and bird, small and great—and to the creation of man. Here, then, are so many crucial instances for examination. What has Science to say to these several points?

Taking the last point first, and working backwards, is it not a fact that a large agreement is arising upon the mysteriousness, the unintelligibility, to scientific methods,

[1] Guyot, *Creation, or, The Biblical Cosmogony in the Light of Modern Science*, Edinburgh, 1883, p. 53.

of these three events, viz., the birth of things, the origin of life, and the genesis of man? Does not the theory of a thoroughgoing evolution begin to lose its charm under the stress of the study of facts? Of course there is a spell about a conception of the universe at once so homogeneous, simple, and comprehensive, which arranges beneath one law the minutest molecular change and the progress of constellations, the slow accretion of a flint and the complicated conditions under which a civilized society advances. But fascination is one thing and proof is another. That there is a process of development of some kind or other in the history of the universe, on many grounds one is fain to believe; but that the hypothetical primary atoms simply by growing long enough became a planet and life and man, calls for evidence. And that any evolution of force can coalesce into life, evidence is not forthcoming. Life comes from life, without life no life, says Science in its almost universally accepted law of Biogenesis. Further, man comes from man, says Science mostly, regarding the Darwinian theory of human descent as hypothesis, and nothing but hypothesis. Similarly, Science finds itself unable to explain in any way the origin of the primary atoms it postulates. Now is it not remarkable that the three cardinal facts, the existence of which Science finds it impossible to explain, viz., the primary existence of matter and life and man, are just the three facts in mundane history in which Genesis sees an express Divine interference? God works ever in creation, Genesis says, but He expressly intervened on the birth of the earth and the birth of animal life and the birth of man.

Again, despite the diversity of view as to the antiquity of man, is not Science also agreed that man belongs to the latest comers upon this earth? Primary rocks, geologists tell us, know nothing of man; nor do Secondary; nor do Tertiary. Traces of man first appear in Post-tertiary formations. In other words, man belongs to the modern period of the geological record, and to that period alone. As Sir J. W. Dawson well says: " The day when the first man stood erect upon the earth and gazed upon a world which had been shaped for him by the preceding periods of the creative work, was the definite beginning of the Modern Period in Geology: if that day could be fixed in the world's calendar, on reaching it the geologist might lay down his hammer, and yield the field to the antiquarian and the historian."[1] That man makes a period all his own, that man gives his name to a period, that the Recent is the Human Period, these are the commonplaces of every geological handbook. That man "is the end towards which all the animal creation has tended, from the first appearance of the Palæozoic fishes," to use the words of Agassiz, in his *Principles of Zoology*, is universally accepted. An attempt is even being made to show that the difficulty of the co-existence of the remains of man and of extinct animals like the Mammoth has a ready solution; for pre-historic is simply pre-diluvian man.[2]

Yet again, Science finds no fault with the succession of life, as rapidly and broadly sketched in Genesis. On the fifth day of creation we read of swarms of living things in seas and of flying things in the air, as well as of marine animals; and on the sixth day we read

---

[1] *Fossil Men and their Modern Representatives, An Attempt to Illustrate the Character and Condition of Pre-historic Men, &c.*, 2nd edit., 1883, p. 1.

[2] Howorth, *The Mammoth and the Flood*; compare Warren, *Paradise Found, the Cradle of the Human Race at the North Pole.*

of the brute creation and wild beasts as created
just prior to man. The geological order of appearance is the same, the swarms of invertebrate animals,
the swarms of fish, then huge reptiles, then mammals, then man. As says Dr. Arnold Guyot, "The
fifth and sixth days offer no difficulties, for they
unfold the successive creation of the various tribes of
animals which people the water, the air, and the land,
in the precise order indicated by geology."[1] In fact,
the coincidences between the Biblical and Geological
records are most marked, and have been admirably summarized by Principal Dawson as follows: "*First*, according to both records, the causes which at present regulate
the distribution of light, heat, and moisture, and of land
and water, were during the whole of this period much
the same as at present. . . . The Bible affirms that all
the earth's physical features were perfected on the fourth
day, and immediately before the creation of animals.
Second, both records show the existence of vegetation
during this period. . . . *Third*, both records inform us
that reptiles and birds were the higher and leading forms
of animals and that all the lower forms of animals
co-existed with them. In both we have especial
notice of the gigantic Saurian reptiles of the latter
part of the period. . . . *Fourth*, it accords with both
records that the work of creation in this period was
gradually progressive; species after species was locally
introduced, extended itself, and after having served its
purpose, gradually became extinct. . . . *Fifth*, in both
records the time between the creation of the first animals

---

[1] Guyot, *Creation, or, The Biblical Cosmology in the Light of Modern Science*, pp. 95–121.

and the introduction of the mammalia as a dominant class forms a well-marked period."[1]

Yet again, in passing behind the phenomena of the fifth day, to the great cosmic changes attributed to the first four days, if the geological record fails us, and if the method of the origination of the earth is rather inferential than evidential, nevertheless, on the comparison of the hypotheses of science with the narrative of Genesis concerning the first four days, striking coincidences appear. For example, Genesis speaks of some ordering of the solar system upon the fourth day which was of great and permanent influence. What says Science? As a matter of fact, Science distinctly declares, as we have already seen, that from the time of the introduction of animals, " land, sea, atmosphere, summer and winter, day and night—all the great inorganic conditions affecting animal life—have existed as at present. . . . The fourth day, then, in geological language, marks the complete introduction of existing causes in inorganic nature, and we henceforth find no more creative interference, except in the domain of organization ; this accords admirably with the deductions of modern geology."[2] Thus Genesis and Science are agreed that just prior to the appearance of animal life, sun and moon and stars, and all the phenomena dependent thereupon, have been in full force. If Science cannot say whether the final adjustment of the solar system immediately preceded the introduction of animals, it can say clearly that since that introduction the solar system has remained in the same condition. Is not this one of those undesigned coin-

---

[1] *The Origin of the World according to Revelation and Science*, London, 3rd edit., 1884, pp, 219, 220.
[2] *Ib.*, p. 202.

cidences which suggest the truth of the narrative in Genesis?

And yet again, according to the dominant nebular hypothesis of the origin of our planet, a very remarkable series of coincidences appears. Genesis knew nothing of Laplace, and Laplace had little esteem for Genesis; yet, notwithstanding, the famous theory of Laplace renders singularly intelligible to modern readers the otherwise almost unintelligible words of Genesis. Genesis speaks of a world without structure and inhabitant; Genesis gives the first stage in the evolution of this void world as the appearance of light; Genesis perceives the second stage in the evolution of our present earth in the formation of an atmosphere; and Genesis announces as the third stage in the advancing evolution the appearance of dry land and seas. To append clear conceptions to these several stages in mundane history is difficult in the extreme, and if it is no longer so difficult, this is largely because of the solar theory of Laplace, his "magnificent nebular hypothesis, which explains the formation of the whole solar system by the condensation of a revolving mass of gaseous matter." If Genesis begins with an earth waste and void, Laplace begins with his nascent nebulous planet thrown off, upon contraction, from the gigantic nebulous solar mass. If Genesis advances to the birth of light, Laplace advances to his incandescent period, when the earth was a sort of sun, a fiery, fused, mineral mass, surrounded by a luminous atmosphere. If Genesis proceeds to the formation of an aerial space, the nebular hypothesis proceeds to argue for the disappearance of the luminous envelope upon the cooling of the heated globe, and therefore for the formation of our modern atmosphere. Further, if

Genesis speaks of the calling forth of dry land and seas, the nebular theory also goes on to assume disturbances of the solidifying crust of the earth, resulting in the settling of the seas and the elevation of the land. In short, Genesis puts the order of development—chaos, light, atmosphere, land and sea; and Laplace and his followers put the order—nebula, photosphere, atmosphere, land and sea. Speculation as all this is on the part of the student of the cosmical relations of our planet, it is also profoundly interesting.

With a few words upon one other point, this series of parallels between Genesis and Science may end. That point is the primary advent of plant-life, a great difficulty in the way of this interpretation in the view of some. According to Genesis, the advent of vegetation preceded the final settlement of the solar system, and thus belongs to so remote a time as to be beyond the observation of the geologist, at least so it would seem. In reference to this first appearance of vegetation, it will suffice for the purpose of these lectures to give a quotation from the discoverer of the earliest forms of life in the rocky structure of the globe. Says Sir J. W. Dawson: "The oldest geological formations are of marine origin, and contain remains of marine animals, with those of plants, supposed to be allied to the existing algæ or seaweeds. Geology cannot, however, assure us either that no land plants existed contemporaneously with these earliest animals, or that no land flora preceded them. These oldest fossiliferous rocks may mark the commencement of animal life, but they testify nothing as to the existence or non-existence of a previous period of vegetation alone. Further, the rocks which contain the oldest remains of life exist, as far as yet known, in a condition so highly metamorphic as almost to preclude the possibility of their containing any distinguishable vegetable fossils; yet they contain vast deposits of carbon in the form of graphite, and if this, like more modern coaly matter, was accumulated by vegetable growth, it must indicate an exuberance of plants in these earliest geological periods, but of plants as yet altogether unknown to us. It is possible, therefore, that in these Eozoic rocks we may have remnants of the formations of the third Mosaic day."[1] Surely the absence of our knowledge of the earliest gymnosperms and angiosperms is sufficiently explained.

What, then, it may once more be said, Genesis narrates as history concerning the order of creation, Science, the geological science almost born in this nineteenth century, declares as inference.[2]

Again, then, is not the conclusion inevitable, upon the inductive method, that these opening chapters of Genesis contain history, not legend; narrative, not allegory; prose, not poetry; fact, and not fiction? A series of tests has been applied to this book of the origins of the

[1] *The Origin of the World*, pp. 192, 193.
[2] Those who may desire to read further on this rapidly spreading harmony of Genesis and Geology may read with profit: Dawson, *The Origin of the World according to Revelation and Science*, 3rd edit., 1884; Guyot, *Creation, or, The Biblical Cosmogony in the Light of Modern Science*, 1883; and especially Camille Flammarion, *Le Monde avant la Création de l'Homme, Origines de la Terre, Origines de la Vie, Origines de l'Humanité*, 1886 (with remarkable illustrations). Other noteworthy books are: P. W. Grant, *The Bible Record of Creation True for Every Age*, 1877; Tayler Lewis, *The Six Days of Creation, or, The Scriptural Cosmology, with the Ancient Idea of Time—Worlds, &c.*, 1879; Reusch, *Nature and the Bible*, 1886; Reynolds, *The Supernatural in Nature, a Verification by the Free Use of Science*, 1878; and Ritchie, *The Creation, The Earth's Formation on Dynamical Principles in accordance with the Mosaic Record and the Latest Scientific Discoveries*, 5th edit., 1874.

earth and man, and the book has stood the tests marvellously. On the evidence of several sciences, are we not in a position to say that, whatever be the source of the information it contains, the information itself is true? In short, wherever it is possible to compare the testimony of Genesis with the testimony of Science, the result shows that Genesis is historical.

But a further question arises, Whence has Genesis obtained this true information concerning the unity of the race, and the unity of language, and the descent of man, and the origin of the heavens and the earth, and the Divine relations of mundane things? Whence came the secular and religious knowledge of Genesis?

An adequate cause is suggested by Genesis itself. The contents of Genesis take the form of a history, and, as far as we are able to test, are actually historical; historical knowledge is preserved by testimony, which, as handed on from age to age, is called tradition; a line of persons, peculiarly interested in religion and the religious aspect of things, is constantly kept before the reader's eye as he moves on from the days of Adam to those of Joseph. It thus appears highly probable that the historical contents of Genesis were traditions handed on from father to son, and from age to age, in the line of Seth. The unity of the race, the fact of a primeval language, the genealogy of men, the record of Divine revelations, and the story of Creation, would appear to be ancestral traditions carefully and reverentially treasured.

Be it added, too, that the purity of this historical testimony would be very intelligibly preserved, if the tradition of Genesis as to the great age of the early patriarchs be true; nor can such tradition be simply laughed out of court, at least, not by the inductive inquirer.[1] Parallel traditions of longevity, as we have seen in the last lecture, have been preserved in many quarters, and must have apparently some element of truth at their base. Further, the physical inheritance of these long-lived patriarchs was bequeathed from a good stock, upon which the effects of a sinful career was of the slightest. Disease, decay, a poor vital record, speedily followed, doubtless, upon the disarrangement produced by sin; the shortening of life told speedily, as the bodily constitution became vitiated from generation to generation; but this righteous line was just that in which the vitiating effect was least. If simplicity and purity of life raise the average of years to-day, especially when that simplicity and purity are characteristic of several generations, is it altogether foolish to believe that the same causes produced the same effects at the beginning of human history? At any rate, the truth of the record given by Genesis would be fully accounted for by a transmission from father to son in the godly line.

Nor is it altogether improbable that some of these cherished traditions of the Sethite and Shemite families may have been committed to writing. As has been seen, the Genealogical Table of the descendants of Noah is, it would appear, as early in date as the days of Abraham. Very probably this table was preserved in writing. There would be no insuperable difficulty in believing that the author of Genesis, whoever he was, employed for his work earlier records extant in his day.

Genesis, then, is historical. It is historical because it

---

[1] Compare Bunsen, *Egypt's Place in Universal History*, vol. iii. p. 340. Bunsen calls a belief in the longevity of the "antidiluvian patriarchs as well as Noah and Shem"—"an infatuation"—a "purely childish delusion"—a great cause of "doubt and unbelief."

is based on a series of reliable traditions of primitive history; and it is also historical apparently because it embodies some of those traditions as they were committed by early historians to writing. So much seems probable. But the whole problem of the case has not yet been faced. Genesis, in the course of its narrative—shown already to be largely historical—tells of sundry Divine interpositions in human affairs. Are these interpositions facts, too? This inquiry is not yet prepared to enter upon the vital question as a whole. But one weighty fact may be emphasized at this point. That fact concerns the Creation narrative. Whence came that narrative? From tradition, it may be said. Well and good. Adam handed it on, perhaps, or Enoch, or Noah. So much seems highly probable. But a further question straightway arises. How came the original teller of the narrative by his story? The narrative has too many points in common with the conclusions of modern science to be the offspring of imagination, whether poetical or myth-making; whence, then, came the story? To ask the question, is it not to answer it? Does not the ironical verse in Job immediately come into mind—"Doubtless thou knowest, for thou wast then born!" Whence came this narrative of Creation?

The fact is that, if this narrative has any truth whatever, preceding as its events all do the creation of man, the narrative must be an instance of Divine revelation. Only Divine revelation could inform concerning such pre-historic, because pre-human, events. As we shall see later on, the Old Testament has much to say about Divine revelations concerning *future* events which were made to prophets in vision. Have we not in this Creation story, which harmonizes so strikingly with many conclusions of physical and theological science, a Divine revelation concerning a *past* event made to some patriarch in vision? If Adam, or Enoch, or another, was the human source of the narrative, was there not also a Divine source, a vision of God disclosing the past, as visions subsequently disclosed the future by Divine condescension? Let the question be weighed by the inductive inquirer. It deserves thought. If one instance of Divine Revelation be proved, other instances are not impossible.

LECTURE IV.

THE AUTHORSHIP OF GENESIS.

LECTURE IV.

THE AUTHORSHIP OF GENESIS.

IN the two preceding lectures the historical character of Genesis, so important a feature in any doctrine of the inspiration of the Old Testament, has been illustrated. The next question that arises, in any inductive examination of the Books of the Law, is—*By whom and at what time was Genesis written?* Is Genesis part of the oldest literature of the world, as many say, or does it belong, as some contend, to a date much more modern?

It is true that, from the vantage ground already attained, this question as to the authorship of Genesis might be not unfairly shunted. For if Genesis is historical, one of two conclusions follows. It is historical, because it is compounded of narratives, written or oral, contemporary in origin with the events narrated; this might be one conclusion—but such a conclusion would straightway deal a death-blow to many modern critical theories. Or else, if the theory be maintained that Genesis was written late in the evolution of Judaism, then, seeing that Genesis is historical, and so remarkably historical, nothing but the supernatural assistance of the writer can explain its accuracy to fact. In other words, seeing that Genesis is historical, a true record of actual events, the book must be due to contemporary knowledge handed down from father to son without flaw, or else it must be due to express revelation. No effort of the historical imagination, apart from supernatural assistance, could so resuscitate the past without materials bequeathed by the past. Indeed, this question of the historical character of Genesis, a character which is strengthened from year to year by every fresh inquiry, should be frankly faced by the advocates of the late date of the Law. This historical character has, in fact, implications which annihilate the evolutionary theory of the origin of the Pentateuch. The following inquiries cannot be long shelved. If Genesis is a veracious record of the origin of our race, whence comes this truthfulness? Does it come from traditions carefully preserved and transmitted? Does it come from traditions stereotyped in memory or in writing? Does it come from specific revelation? In short, if the historical character of Genesis be denied—as it consistently is by Colenso and Kuenen and others — the facts adduced in the two previous lectures must be reckoned with : if the historical character of Genesis be asserted, then the later the date assigned to its composition, the greater is the evidence for supernatural revelation.

Nevertheless, although the dilemma is certainly formidable, that the original sources of Genesis are either *contemporary* or *divine*, it would be scarcely prudent to ignore the trend of much of the literary criticism of the Pentateuch for the last hundred years. The wise inquirer answers his opponent's case as well as states his own. It is advisable, therefore, to ask, in the light of modern research, when and how Genesis was written?

To propose the question is to plunge headlong into one of the fiercest eddies of modern controversy.

Until recently, doubts upon either the date or the authorship of Genesis were rare. Genesis, it was commonly said, was the first book of Moses, and Moses died in the fifteenth century before Christ. So the traditional view, as it is called, was wont to express itself. To-day, however, side by side with this traditional view, which has been handed down from Jew to Christian, and from Romanist to Protestant, another view is largely advocated, which denies the Mosaic authorship of Genesis. This later view must be carefully, and of course inductively, examined.

The *problem*, then, which is to be investigated in this Lecture is this—*What conclusions concerning the date and authorship of Genesis are warranted by the facts which Genesis itself presents?*

The solution of the problem proposed is not as simple as at first sight appears. Let the inquirer take up a good book upon any branch of Biblical Criticism, and he will find much that is apparently irrelevant and possibly unintelligible. A prior knowledge is lacking. The inquirer is like a man who opens a book in an unknown tongue. Indeed many prominent Biblical critics themselves, acutely sensible, even proud, of their succession to an inheritance of critical tradition, hold themselves absolved from stating, for beginners, the entire evidence for their conclusions. It is with the tyro in the "Higher Criticism" very much as it is with the tyro in modern Biology. The student of recent biological theory finds it indispensable to take a survey of the effects produced by the publication thirty years ago of Darwin's *Origin of Species*, if he would understand his science intelligently; for he finds again and again that Darwin's conclusions, as reasoned as revolutionary, are rather assumed than argued in modern works upon the evolution of life. Similarly the student of modern Biblical Criticism soon learns that he cannot proceed securely, before he too has taken a survey of the recent history of his science. To understand the last step in any movement you must understand the last step but one. The study of causes is as necessary to the pathologist of mind as of body. Such a book, for instance, as Dr. Kuenen's *Religion of Israel*, or such an article as Dr. Wellhausen's article on "Israel" in the current edition of the *Encyclopædia Britannica* cannot but appear to the English reader a tissue of baseless assumptions, unless he has previously acquainted himself with the course of recent criticism upon the Pentateuch. In short, *an intelligent appreciation of the positions of modern Biblical critics can only follow an intelligent appreciation of the recent history of Biblical Criticism.*

Let a summary view be therefore presented of the "Higher Criticism" of Genesis, nay, of the entire Pentateuch, for in a paragraph or so it will become apparent how impossible it is to dissever the course of critical inquiry into the authorship of Genesis from the course of critical inquiry into the Pentateuch as a whole. The comfort is that, although the circuit travelled seems wide, every step taken will be a step to the solution of wider problems than those of Genesis. Let the reader prepare himself therefore, if he would vindicate his position as an inductive inquirer, for a little difficult reading for a few pages, remembering, for his encouragement, that these pages will facilitate, indeed are indispensable to, subsequent progress.

Happily, in order to place oneself upon that altitude from which a survey of the criticism of the Pentateuch is possible, it is unnecessary to regard the views of men like Aben-Ezra,[1] the learned Jew of Toledo ; Carlstadt,[2] the famous opponent of Luther; Maes,[3] the Belgian commentator; Hobbes,[4] our English philosopher ; Peyrerius,[5] the author of the theory of the Pre-Adamites ; or Spinoza,[6] or Le Clerc,[7] who, with a few others, prior to the middle of the last century, promulgated doubts, rather sentimental than exegetical, as to the Mosaic authorship of the whole or parts of the Genesis. The so-called "*Higher Criticism*," "a name new to no Humanist," as Eichhorn [8] so well says—"a sense and measure of the harmonious and the contradictory," as Hupfeld [9] defines it—that criticism which deals on internal evidence with the date and authorship of the Books of Scripture, *is a little more than a hundred years old.*

The critical movement, which has led of late to an entire reconstruction by some scholars of the Old Testament, *dates from the year* 1753, when a book [10] was published anonymously at Brussels and at Paris,

[1] Aben-Ezra, *Commentary on the Pentateuch*, Lucca, 1152.
[2] *De Scripturis Canonicis*, Wittenberg, 1521.
[3] *Josuæ Imperatoris Historia, illustrata atque explicata*, Antwerp, 1574.
[4] *Leviathan*, London, 1651, chap. xxxiii.
[5] *Systema Theol. ex Præadamitarum Hypothesi*, 1655, lib. iv. c. 1, 2.
[6] *Tractatus Theologico-politicus*, Hamburg, 1670, cap. vii.
[7] *Sentimens de quelques théologiens de Hollande sur l'histoire critique du V. T.*, Amsterdam, 1685.
[8] *Einleitung in das A. T.*, Göttingen, 1823, vol. i. p. vii.
[9] *Die Quellen der Genesis*, Berlin, 1853, p. 1.
[10] *Conjectures sur les mémoires originaux, dont il paroit que Moïse s'est servi pour composer le livre de la Genèse.* A German translation was published at Frankfort in 1783.

but really written by one Jean Astruc, a French physican and a Roman Catholic. Astruc was impressed, as Augustine[1] had been before him, with the ordered and apparently discriminating use of the Divine Names in Genesis. How deliberate this usage is even the English reader may see, who takes the trouble to observe how the word "God" will occur in passage after passage of the English version, whilst in contiguous passages the word "Lord" is exclusively used. Concentrating attention upon this ostensibly deliberate usage of the Divine names, Astruc made an analysis of Genesis. Astruc thought he had valid grounds for the conjecture (he only put his views forward as conjectures) that Moses had compiled Genesis from two principal documents, characterized respectively by the employment of the Hebrew words Elohim and Jehovah for God, and at the same time for the further conjecture that Moses obtained additional materials for his book from nine smaller memoirs still extant in his day, various pedigrees and poems inserted in Genesis giving him this idea. It is only fair to add that, by these conjectures of his, Astruc assuredly did not dream of becoming the founder of a school of marked revolutionary tendency, just as he assuredly had no thought of extending his analysis to the other books of the Pentateuch. This FIRST PHASE in the history of modern Pentateuch criticism dealt, and meant to deal, solely with Genesis.

In Belgium and in France Astruc's book attracted little notice. In Germany this suggested method of analysis fell into prepared soil. There the age of criticism was already born. There Rationalism—which, with

---

[1] *De Genesi ad Litteram*, lib. viii. c. 11.

all its faults, is, on its good side, a legitimate request for evidence—was in the air. There, too, the appetite for literary criticism had been whetted by the birth of the new historical method, which regarded history as a sphere for accuracy and the minutest truthfulness, rather than for rhetorical display. This new historical school, which preferred fact to style, was doing a marvellous thing. It was replacing, in classical story, legend by history, and was reconstructing—not without shock—important sections of the past of the world. And in this historical reconstruction literary (or the "higher") criticism was playing a large part. By the careful comparison of passage with passage, and of narrative with narrative, by alert watchfulness for any forms of inconsistency however slight, by rigorous search for anachronisms, by cultivated sense of tone and expression, by searching study, in short, of all varieties of what is not inappropriately termed internal evidence, of all evidence, that is, that bears upon the date and credibility of extant records, supposed to be contemporaneous, or nearly so, with the events they record, by such methods profane history was being largely remodelled. Was it not probable that, by similar critical devices, sacred history might be re-shaped as well as profane? At least, so men in Germany were beginning, under the influence of Lessing, to inquire. Into such an atmosphere Astruc's book fell ; and, as any piece of wood or stone will initiate crystallization in a solution just about to crystallize, so Astruc's *Conjectures* became the nucleus around which the criticism of the Biblical records took palpable shape.

In the new criticism Eichhorn led the way.[1] Eichhorn

[1] *Einleitung in das Alte Testament*, 4th edit., 1823, vol. iii. pp. 106–135.

saw, however, clearly that, valuable as was the critical principle of the Divine names, such a principle alone could not furnish all the critical aids he desired. "It is an acknowledged impossibility, in fact, to found a rational theory of separable documents on the use of the Divine names *as they now appear* in the Genesis."[1] Eichhorn therefore combined Astruc's suggestion with the critical methods already used in classical history, and, collaterally with the analytical test of the Divine names, employed careful examination of diction, style, and general contents. According to Eichhorn's view, after the application of this composite method of analysis, Genesis and the opening chapters of Exodus were a compilation of two documents, the one of which was characterized by the use of the word Elohim for the name of Deity (and by other critical marks), and the other of which was characterized by the use of the word Jehovah for the Divine name (as well as by other critical marks). Eichhorn also saw reason to believe that some portions of Genesis, such as the fourteenth chapter (which treats of the Battle of the Kings, and introduces another name for Deity—God Most High) were interpolations in the two leading documents.[2] Such was Eichhorn's theory, which at present I am only stating.

Several critics of note speedily declared for this theory, and it was fully elaborately by men like Möller,[3] Bauer,[4] Gramberg,[5] and Stähelin,[6] who, whilst exhibiting many

[1] Bissell, *The Pentateuch, its Origin and Structure*, p. 57.
[2] See the analysis in Appendix I.
[3] *Ueber die Verschiedenheit des Styls der beyden Haupturkunden der Genesis*, Göttingen, 1792.
[4] *Entwurf einer histor-kritischen Einleitung in die Schriften des A. T.*, Nürnberg, 1806.
[5] *Libri Geneseos secundum fontes rite dignoscendos adumbratio nova*, Leipsic, 1828.
[6] *Kritische Untersuchungen über die Genesis*, Basel, 1830.

minor differences, showed also a substantial agreement —as it was probable they would, seeing that they started from the same premises. In this first phase, then, of the criticism of the Pentateuch—the Earlier Documentary phase, as it is often called, the phase of the *Urkunden-Hypothese*, as the Germans say—the Genesis was regarded as a compilation from two original sources, together with a few interpolations; although one writer of this school, Ilgen,[1] declared for three original sources, a view which was revived later on as we shall see. Of course side by side with this earlier form of the Compilation Theory of authorship, there were those who contended, and contended ably, for the Mosaic authorship of the whole of the book in question. Further, an extreme radical section of critics followed out the minor analysis of Astruc, and declared Genesis to be a compilation, long after the time of Moses, not from two original sources, but from many fragments of various dates.[2] This Fragmentary Hypothesis was, however, speedily abandoned in face of the striking unity visible in Genesis.

But this first phase of the Higher Criticism of the Pentateuch soon merged into a SECOND PHASE. The Compilation Theory of the authorship of Genesis became a New-Edition Theory. With the temerity of discoverers, critics speedily desired to apply their new analytical method, not to Genesis only and the opening chapters of Exodus (where the distinctive employment

[1] *Die Urkunden des Jerusalem-Tempelarchivs in ihrer Urgestalt*, Leipsic, 1798.
[2] Compare Hasse, *Aussichten zu künftigen Aufklärungen über das Alte Testament in Briefen*, Jena, 1785; J. S. Vater, *Commentar ü. die Pentat.*, vol. iii., Halle, 1802-1805; and A. T. Hartmann, *Hist.-krit. Forschungen ü. Bildung, Zeitalter und Plan der 5 Bücher Moses*, Rostock, 1831.

of the Divine names is patent to every careful reader), but to the remainder of the Pentateuch as well (where this distinctive use of the Divine names no longer obtains). This enlargement of application was greatly due to De Wette,[1] who called attention to the individuality [2] of Deuteronomy, and to what he was pleased to regard as the unhistorical character of the other four books of the Pentateuch, a character which pointed, as he thought, to a later author than Moses. It was also due to Ewald, who maintained that the two documents, the Elohim record and the Jehovah record, were traceable, if not by the peculiar usage of the Divine names, at least by phrase and style and plan, throughout the whole five books of the Pentateuch. This extension of view to the entire Pentateuch—nay, to the Hexateuch, to use the word which has been coined to represent the five books of Moses and the Book of Joshua—was one prominent characteristic of this second phase. Another characteristic was the separation of Deuteronomy from the other books. Yet a third feature was, that, almost as a matter of course after the change of general view, the theory of compilation passed into a theory of editorship. The author of the Pentateuch was no longer supposed to have combined, almost mechanically, two original documents known to him, but he was now credited with having before him an original writing, that of the Elohist (who preferred the name Elohim for the Deity), and with supplementing that primary text, wherever he felt so disposed, by materials of his own, whether derived

[1] *Dissertatio Critica, qua Deuteronomium a prioribus Pentateuchi libris diversum*, Jena, 1805; and *Beiträge zur Einleitung in's A. T.*, Halle, 1806; and *Kritik der Mosaischen Geschichte*, 1807.

[2] *Composition der Genesis kritisch untersucht*, Brunswick, 1823; and *Theologische Studien und Kritiken*, 1831.

from tradition or from other records with which he was familiar. Thus the *Earlier Documentary Theory* of the composition of Genesis became a *Supplementary Theory*, a more organic and fascinating theory of the origination of the Pentateuch by editorial additions to earlier writings. Stated generally, in short, this Theory of Supplementing *(Ergänzung-Hypothese*, as the Germans say), took the following form: according to it the original sources of the whole Pentateuch as well as Genesis were two, an Elohistic record (in which a few yet more ancient fragments were embedded), and the Book of Deuteronomy, these two original sources having been largely added to by a subsequent writer, the Jehovist, who at once edited and supplemented the whole from Genesis to Numbers. Perhaps I should add that, to some advocates of the theory, the Jehovist and the writer of Deuteronomy were one and the same person.[1] Such was the theory of authorship advocated, with many minor differences, especially as to the dates of the component parts, by De Wette,[2] Bleek,[3] and Tuch,[4] to mention the more important writers only. As regards the age of the component parts, the age of the Elohist, the writer who preferred the name Elohim for God, was placed at the earliest in the time of the Judges, opinions varying; whereas the age of the Jehovist, the writer who preferred the name Jehovah for God, was necessarily placed somewhat later, Bleek says in David's days, and Tuch says some time between the reigns of Solomon and Uzziah. In this second phase, then, of the

[1] *E.g.*, Stähelin.
[2] *Beiträge zur Einleitung in's A. T.*, Halle, 1806.
[3] *Einleitung in die Heilige Schrift*, 1st part, *Einleitung in das Alte Testament*, Berlin, 1860.
[4] Tuch, *Kommentar über die Genesis*, Halle, 1838.

Higher Criticism of the Pentateuch,—Textual Criticism being the Lower Criticism, and Historical and Literary Criticism the Higher—the Pentateuch was regarded as consisting of one main story, which had been re-written and completed by a later writer, himself either the author or the adapter of the Book of Deuteronomy; moreover, this main narrative—the Original Story, as Colenso named it, the *Grundschrift*, as the Germans say—a connected account of the entire epoch from the origin of the world to the conquest of Canaan, was traceable, it was thought, not by the comparatively coarse test of the Divine names, but by those more subtle critical methods which distinguish between variations of style, diversities of plan, differences of aim, divergent modes of presentation, recondite inconsistencies of statement, minute peculiarities of diction, latent psychological assumptions, axiomatic theological predilections, in short, by all those critical methods which a cultured and sensitive criticism can detect, or—imagine.[1]

However, this second phase of Pentateuch analysis was destined to give way to a THIRD PHASE. As the Compilation Theory of authorship had been displaced by the Revised-Edition Theory, so this New-Edition Theory, in the turn of the wheel of criticism, was itself to disappear before a *More Elaborate Compilation Theory*. This new form of the composite theory followed upon the publication by Hupfeld in 1853 of his *Sources of Genesis and Method of their Composition*.[2] In this book, instead of speaking of two authors of the Genesis, an original Elohistic writer and an accomplished Jeho-

---

[1] See Appendix I.
[2] *Die Quellen der Genesis und die Art ihrer Zusammensetzung*, Berlin, 1853.

vistic editor, as had been maintained by his immediate predecessors in criticism, Hupfeld declared for three writers and an editor besides, being compelled, as he believed, to distinguish in the Genesis three independent sources—an Elohist, who preferred the name Elohim for God ; a Jehovist, who preferred the name Jehovah for God ; and a *second* Elohist, who also had a preference for Elohim in describing the Deity. At the same time, Hupfeld maintained that no one of these three writers had anything to do with the others, but that a fourth, a much later writer, who also knew and utilized for his purpose the Book of Deuteronomy, combined these various records into one consecutive whole, using, however, a large editorial liberty of alteration. Many later critics have accepted these views of Hupfeld's with one important amendment. According to the rejoinder of Nöldeke,[1] which has largely commended itself to those who start from the same principles, the second Elohist does not form an independent section of the whole, but only exists in extracts embodied by the Jehovist in his own writing. Thus, in this third phase, the Pentateuch was still regarded as compiled from two original sources, the one being characterized by a preference for the name of Elohim for God, and the other being characterized by a preference for the name Jehovah ; this latter writer, however, incorporating into his narrative various extracts from another writer known to him, who showed a preference for the name Elohim ; and, at the same time, it was thought, that these two original sources, together with the Book of Deuteronomy which had come from an independent pen, had undergone careful combination and revision at the hands of

[1] *Untersuchungen zur Kritik des Alten Testaments*, Kiel, 1869.

a later writer. Such is the Later Documentary Theory, as it has been called, which has been substantially, though with minor variations, advocated by such leading exegetes as Ewald,[1] Knobel,[2] Dillmann,[3] Vaihinger,[4] Schrader,[5] and Samuel Davidson.[6] According to this third phase, in its latest and most mature form, the Pentateuch (or rather the Hexateuch) was the work of a late editor—himself the author of Deuteronomy say some—who, speaking generally, used for his own purposes the previous work of an Elohist, a priest writing about the time of David—who also employed the work of the Jehovist, an Ephraimite, a man of prophetical leanings, writing two centuries later, that is to say, about the year 800 B.C.—who adopted as well the Book of Deuteronomy, written a little before the reign of Josiah, this editor himself (supposing him not to have been the Deuteronomist) of course writing at a later date than the seventh century before Christ. The theory is elaborate and not without precision. What facts it has for its basis we shall see presently.[7]

Attention is sometimes called to the great unity of conviction that distinguishes the advocates of the composite theory of the authorship of the Law, as if it were something wonderful that men who start from the same premises should reach similar conclusions. Surely the

[1] *Geschichte des Volkes Israel*, 3rd edit., Göttingen, 1864, vol. i., translated under the title, *The History of Israel to the Death of Moses*, London, 1867.
[2] *Die Bücher Numeri, Deuteronomium und Josua*, Kritik des Pentateuch und Josua, Leipsic, 1861.
[3] *Die Genesis*, 4th edit., Leipsic, 1882.
[4] Article "Pentateuch" in Herzog, *Real-Encyklopädie*, 1st edit. vol. xi. pp. 292-368, Gotha, 1852.
[5] De Wette, *Lehrbuch der hist.-krit. Einleitung, bearbeitet von H Schrader*, Berlin, 1869, pp. 232-325.
[6] *Introduction to Old Testament*, vol. i., London, 1862.
[7] Compare Appendix I.

wonder is—to an inductive inquirer at least—that after a century of criticism a larger unanimity should not be apparent. Three phases in the decomposition of the Pentateuch have already passed under brief review. A FOURTH PHASE follows. It shows a great change of view. As has been well, if sharply, said, "Experiments without number have been made of running the dissecting knife through the Pentateuch; and each fresh operator has pronounced, with the utmost positiveness, upon the various age of its several portions, &c.; and now everything has been thrown into a fresh jumble again; everything must be reconstructed on a new basis." [1]

This fourth phase, singularly enough, accepts the main lines of the analysis just sketched—remaining still a *More Elaborate Compilation Theory*—but marks a gigantic revolution of opinion, nevertheless. The revolution of view concerns the date at which the writer wrote who prefers the name Elohim for the Deity. From being thought the earliest writer of all, who lived not later than the times of Solomon, the Elohist becomes in this new theory the latest writer of all, and contemporary with Ezekiel. Nor is this view without prominent advocates. Dr. Robertson Smith has described this theory as "the growing conviction of an overwhelming weight of the most earnest and sober scholarship." [2] Similarly Dr. Kuenen has dubbed this theory "the received view of European critical Scholarship." [3] If the words are hasty, as a reaction in opinion is beginning to show, nevertheless it should be said that this theory

[1] *Presbyterian Review*, 1882, p. 109.
[2] *Old Testament in the Jewish Church*, Edinburgh, 1881, p. 216.
[3] *An Historico-Critical Inquiry into the Origin and Composition of the Hexateuch*, translated by Philip H. Wicksteed, London, 1886, p. xl.

commends itself to such leaders in Biblical Science as
Reuss,[1] Graf,[2] Kuenen,[3] Duhm,[4] Schultz,[5] and Wellhausen,[6] and as Kalisch,[7] and Colenso,[8] and Renan [9] (in
their later writings). Of the quiet inculcation of this
theory in general terms by Reuss, of its more accurate
formulation by Popper [10] and Graf, of its independent
discovery and skilful advocacy by Kayser [11] and by
Kuenen, and of its masterly and novel presentation by
Julius Wellhausen, I need not speak.[12] In its essential
features, and in the form which is most prominent
to-day, this critical theory—"the growing conviction of
an overwhelming weight of the most earnest and sober

---

[1] *L'Histoire Sainte et la Loi*, Paris, 1879. "The venerable Strasburg professor showed himself, in his admirable introduction to this work," says Kuenen, "to be not so much a distinguished convert to the Grafian hypothesis as its real author. . . . In the lecture-room of Strasburg, then, we might look, in no small measure, for the ultimate source of Graf's and Kayser's inspiration, and Reuss had the satisfaction of seeing the views he had enunciated in his youth taken up and elaborated by his distinguished pupils, and commanding ever-increasing assent as he incorporated them, matured and consolidated, into the works of his old age" (*Hexateuch*, pp. xxxiv., xxxv).

[2] *Die Geschichtlichen Bücher des A. T.*, Leipsic, 1866.

[3] *Religion of Israel: Hexateuch.*

[4] *Die Theologie der Propheten als Grundlage für die innere Entwickelungsgeschichte der Israelitischen Religion*, Bonn, 1875.

[5] *Alttestamentliche Theologie, Die Offenbarungsreligion auf ihrer vorchristlichen Entwickelungsstufe*, 3rd edit., 1885.

[6] *Die Composition des Hexateuchs*, published in 1877, and reprinted in *Skizzen und Vorarbeiten*, 2nd part, Berlin, 1885; *Geschichte Israels*, vol. i., Berlin, 1878, 2nd edit., 1883, translated under the title of *The History of Israel*, Edinburgh, 1885.

[7] *A Historical and Critical Commentary on the Old Testament, Leviticus*, London, 1867.

[8] *The Pentateuch*, part vi., London, 1872.

[9] *Histoire du Peuple d'Israel*, vol. i., Paris, 1887.

[10] *Die biblische Bericht über die Stiftshütte, Ein Beitrag zur Geschichte der Composition und Diaskeue des Pentateuch*, Leipsic, 1862.

[11] *Das Vorexilische Buch der Urgeschichte und seine Erweiterungen*, Strasburg, 1874.

[12] A good outline of the history of this theory may be found in Kuenen, *The Hexateuch*, Introduction.

scholarship"—is, that the oldest part of the Pentateuch (which, we are told, has certainly an ancient air) is the chapters of Exodus containing the Ten Commandments and the Judgments which follow (that is to say, the twentieth chapter to the twenty-third, and also the thirty-fourth); that the Jehovist comes next, seeing that he wrote in the period subsequent to the division of the kingdom of Solomon, thus committing to fixed writing what had previously circulated orally and had manifestly been subject to frequent change; that the Deuteronomic laws and revision subsequently followed, towards the end of the seventh century B.C.; that then certain chapters of Leviticus, from the seventh to the twenty-third, were written, most probably by Ezekiel; that later still lived the priestly Elohist, who composed the "Priests' Code," as it has been technically called, consisting of the laws of the Pentateuch not included by the Jehovist in his work, together with their historical setting, and a preface giving the history of the creative days; and that, lastly, the entire work was completed by an editor, and put into circulation, about the year 444 B.C. According to this fourth phase of the decomposition of the Pentateuch, speaking briefly, the final result was produced at the close of the Babylonian Exile by a compilation from three sources, these sources being a Jehovist document of a prophetic tendency written before Deuteronomy, of Deuteronomy written about the time of Josiah, and of the Priestly Code, the Elohistic document, written soon after the Exile.

Such is the theory, both detailed and guarded, which all Biblical students are being called upon to accept or reject—"the growing conviction of an overwhelming weight of the most earnest and sober scholarship" as we are bidden believe. Nor do its advocates shrink from the consequences of their theory. Rather has its revolutionary and evolutional character itself a charm, "supporting" as Kalisch says, "the philosophical ideas" dominant at present in many quarters. Darwinism has its fascination to some theological as well as some biological minds. It was to be expected, in fact, that attempts would be made to trace a purely naturalistic evolution of religious ideas and institutions amongst the ancient Israelites; just as it was to be expected that an ingenuity of accommodation should be brought to bear in making such attempts. In fact, such attempts should be as welcome as inevitable. A theory cannot be disproved until its most able presentation be disproved. It remains to be seen whether the prepossession in favour of a naturalistic evolution has not placed a false accent upon the Biblical facts. For the consequences of this evolutionary theory are clear. On this theory, as is avowed, Sinai and its events are myths, or, at best, legends told a thousand years after the occurrence of the events they encrust; the Tabernacle, with its Court and Holy Place and Holiest, is pure fiction, an imaginative sanctuary made on the rough-and-ready method of halving the dimensions of the Temple of Solomon, itself a study from the Phœnician; and the entire narrative of the Books of the Law, is, so to speak, a religious novel, written for ecclesiastical purposes, and based upon the slenderest modicum of fact. All this is clearly acknowledged. "At one stroke," as has been said by one of its advocates, "the Mosaic period is wiped out."[1] Even Colenso, cautious as he usually was in expression,

[1] Duhm, *Die Theologie der Propheten*, p. 18.

ventured to say that "perhaps the most important result of the criticism of the Pentateuch is this, that it strikes a death-blow at the whole system of priestcraft, which has mainly been based upon the notion that the Levitical laws . . . were really of Mosaic, or rather of Divine origin."[1] Quite consciously the alternative is placed before the world by this fourth phase, of the critical decomposition of the Law, that either the theory it advocates *must be disproven*, or—the Old Testament *must be reconstructed.* As Reuss says, "The entire history of the Israelites, civil, political, literary, and religious, depends on the answer which will be given to the question whether these books (of the Pentateuch) belong to the first beginnings of the nation as the primary base of its life and of its social and spiritual development, or whether they are the fruit of a labour of centuries, to which twenty generations have ministered, and which have only been completed at the hour in which this development has been stopped and the productive sap has been exhausted."[2] Truly the question at issue is capital; for when "the name of Moses" is used either as speaker or hearer, it is simply employed, we are told, "by the anonymous writer, as Merlin, Solomon, and Ossian"[3] are employed in "other literatures."[4]

Assured as the results of this fourth phase are represented as being, it is of some interest to notice that there are clear signs of entrance upon a FIFTH PHASE. In a work published posthumously, a M. D'Eichthal, remark-

---

[1] *The Pentateuch and the Book of Joshua*, part vi. pp. 631, 635, 637.
[2] *L'Histoire Sainte et la Loi*, p. 13.
[3] Russell Martineau, article on the "Legislation of the Pentateuch" in *The Theological Review* for 1872.
[4] Compare Appendices I. and II.

ing that a rigorous criticism of Deuteronomy has not been made as yet, but that it has been too commonly assumed that Deuteronomy is an original work, homogeneous and well knit in all its parts, lays claim to the honour of showing, by the critical methods which have issued in the four preceding phases, that Deuteronomy has been composed as the remaining books of the Law are declared to have been composed. Deuteronomy also is said to be a compilation from various sources by an accomplished editor. As D'Eichthal says, "The fifth book of the Pentateuch is a complex of documents, all or almost all of previous date, 'reconciled, cut up, parcelled out, mixed' with more or less art and care, in order to serve the purpose the editor had in view."[1] Further, M. D'Eichthal contends that the date of Deuteronomy has been placed much too early, and that it too belongs to the epoch after the Babylonian Exile,—to the fifth century before Christ, or the fourth, and not to the seventh. All this might seem of little importance, were it not that M. Maurice Vernes, who has popularized the views of Graf, Kuenen, and Wellhausen in France, as efficiently as Robertson Smith has popularized them in the English-speaking countries, has given in his adhesion to this view of Deuteronomy, in a remarkable tractate.[2] M. Vernes accepts the two views, first, of the composite character of Deuteronomy, and second, of its Post-Exilic date; and, at the same time, M. Vernes reconstructs the Grafian hypothesis accordingly. Adhering strictly to the Grafian view of the succession of documents, M. Vernes still maintains the order of composition

---

[1] *Mélanges de Critique Biblique*, Paris, 1886.
[2] *Une Nouvelle Hypothèse sur la Composition et l'Origine du Deutéronome, Examen des Vues de M. G. D'Eichthal,* par Maurice Vernes, Directeur Adjoint a l'Ecole des Hautes Etudes (Sorbonne), Paris, 1887.

to be—the Jehovistic source, Deuteronomy, the Priests' Code ; but believing now as he does, that Deuteronomy is a product of the age of Ezra, and not of the age of Josiah, he asserts that the whole Pentateuch could not have existed at an earlier date than the fourth century. In his view Deuteronomy is Post-Exilic, say of the fifth century, and the Priests' Code (and of course the entire Pentateuch) is Post-Exilic, and later in date than Deuteronomy. Further, M. Vernes does not stop here. He proceeds to inquire whether even the Jehovistic document, regarded by the Grafian theory as prior in date to the time of Josiah, can be regarded as of an earlier date than the Exile, and replies in the negative. His words are as follows : " And if I were asked, Have you decisive reasons for affirming that at least the nucleus of the Jehovistic and prophetic document had been composed before the Exile, I should venture to reply humbly and quite in a whisper : I have not. That is, indeed, what I am coming to, viz., at no longer recognizing in the Jehovistic-prophetic document, although I hold it as of more ancient date than Deuteronomy, and than the Elohistic-priestly document, a work bearing the specific characters of the times anterior to the destruction of Jerusalem by the Chaldeans." Let the words be weighed. They are an *indirect testimony to the homogeneousness of the Pentateuch.* One may disagree entirely with M. Vernes as to the dates he assigns to the constituent portions of the Law, and thank him nevertheless for his expressed conviction that the Jehovist and Elohist and Deuteronomist do not belong to diverse centuries, nor present different standpoints. It is not an advocate, be it remembered, of the traditional standpoint, but an advocate of the most anti-traditional theory yet proposed, who writes: "When there is seen (in the Pentateuch) documents of three distinct epochs, the monuments of three different and incompatible spirits, each of which has made a civilization in its likeness, of the epoch of Isaiah and Hezekiah, of the epoch of Josiah, and of the epoch of Ezra, I contest it formally."[1] The position is suggestive. Nor does the suggestiveness lessen when M. Vernes continues:

"In drawing up its lines, as criticism has done, in multiplying its divisions, in establishing its fundamental contradictions, in wishing to remake the history of a religious evolution as complex as long by means of documents extracted conjecturally from a final combination into which they have entered, criticism—and our remark does not specially apply here to the school of Graf—appears to us to have fallen into the contrary fault to that into which traditional opinion has fallen. The latter has ignored too readily the divergences of the text and the incompatibility of the diverse assertions they contain; convinced of the unity of inspiration of such a work as the Hexateuch, it has thought it expedient to seek that unity even in details. The critical schools, in their turn, present us with a conception of the Hexateuch, which compels disquietude, because we see therein, not an effort directed to a precise end, but a series of attempts of opposite tendency, and because the definitive reunion of these divergent and contradictory works into a single code rather affords us a lumber-room than a legislation."

And M. Vernes continues in golden words:

"It is necessary at this point to carefully represent the thought which has guided the last editors of the first six books of the Bible. Are they virtuosos, doing the work of dilettantism, more sensitive to the unsuitability of permitting the loss of an original feature of an ancient chronicle, of an unusual text of common law, than to that of leading the reader astray by the multiplicity of versions of the same fact and especially by their disagreement? Assuredly not. They are historians and lawyers, desirous of giving their contemporaries a book in which they may find at once 'the holy history' of their early past, and the 'Law,' the authority of which

---

[1] *Une Nouvelle Hypothèse*, pp. 50, 51.

they recognize? However great may be the differences between the Oriental and Occidental genius, I should never admit that the last editors of the *Mosaic Law* had introduced into their works considerable fragments of the *Jehovistic* document or of Deuteronomy if they had recognized therein a spirit sensibly different from that of the *Elohistic*-priestly Document, which saw the light last. These documents were, in their eyes, different versions of the great facts of the past, concurrent editions of the legislation of the present, which, by reason of their gravity, their eloquence, the varied information they contained, deserved to be preserved side by side. . . . All this would be readily intelligible if the last redaction of the Pentateuch and Joshua belongs to the third century, and if the principal documents which entered into its composition date from the times immediately preceding. All this would be intelligible with difficulty if the three great constituent documents represent three phases, eminently distinct, of the religious and social evolution of the ancient Jews."

The extract is long, but it is worthy of careful consideration. The eloquent protest is notable. It has a weight far beyond what M. Vernes himself realizes. It destroys his own references to date. This appeal from pedantry to common-sense should ring the death-knell of the theory, which is "the growing conviction of an overwhelming weight of the most earnest and sober scholarship." Extremes seem about to meet. The course of the literary criticism of the last hundred years seems about to complete its cycle, and to return with a surer conviction than ever to the traditional belief concerning the Pentateuch. Let the arguments concerning the composition of the Five Books of the Law once confine themselves to the evidence as to their date, *on the prior assurance of their practical contemporaneousness*, and the Pentateuch will come forth from the fires of recent criticism, as the Gospel of John has done, a little dross of human thought possibly consumed, but purer gold. The fifth phase of the history of the criticism of the Pentateuch would speedily enter upon a sixth in which the contemporaneous character of the contents of the Law, and *therefore its Mosaic origin*, will be maintained.

But it is time to pass from the survey of the history of recent criticism upon the Genesis and the Law, instructive as that history is, to the criticism of criticism. Proceeding then, in the next place, to the criticism of the results of criticism, and, more especially, to the criticism of critical views upon the Genesis—seeing that it is desirable for many reasons which will appear as we proceed, to confine attention at present to Genesis—two cardinal questions call for investigation. As the previous history of criticism has shown us, it is now necessary to ask, on the one hand, *what evidence Genesis itself affords of the* DATE *of its composition;* it is also needful to ask, on the other hand, *what evidence does Genesis itself offer as to its* SIMPLE OR COMPOSITE CONSTRUCTION. These two questions answered, a third will present itself, viz., *what* THEORY *of the date and authorship of Genesis seems to be most in harmony with the facts of the case.* To these three crucial questions I advance.

FIRST, then, *must we*, upon an examination of the evidence forthcoming in Genesis, *necessarily declare for the post-Mosaic authorship of Genesis?* To the Law and to the Testimony.

In entering upon this question, it is encouraging to read in the pages of the most scholarly advocate of the post-Mosaic date of Genesis that "the date . . . is a task beset with no small difficulties." "The facts," continues Dr. Kuenen, "we have to go upon are comparatively few and are often ambiguous; and sometimes, too, it is doubtful whether the evidence refers to the original narratives themselves or to the more or less modified form in which they have come down to us." "We must therefore," this eminent Dutchman goes on to say, "be content, when the circumstances require it, with a more or less vague result."[1] All this means that Dr. Kuenen finds it exceedingly difficult to support from Genesis his particular evolutionary theory of the origin of the Law.

The fact is, that the evidence advanced for the late date of Genesis, from Genesis itself, is of the scantiest. Professedly the evidence for the post-Mosaic date is of three kinds, viz., *anachronisms* (or evidence as to the possession of knowledge impossible in the days of Moses); *anatropisms*, to coin a parallel word (or evidence as to the possession of knowledge impossible in the location of Moses); and *romancings* (or evidence of unhistorical, and, therefore, non-contemporary, contents). Let each class of evidence be reviewed.

On the principle that a book must have been written later than any circumstances that it records—that Genesis, for example, was written posterior to the death of Joseph—the evidence of anachronisms, if such there be, is crucial. The more important of these anachronisms is as follows; they have been repeated again and again, as the stock instances, since Le Clerc wrote his *Prolegomena to the Old Testament;* and Le Clerc borrowed from Aben Ezra.

One supposed *anachronism* is this. In the twelfth chapter of Genesis and the sixth verse, it is said that "Abram passed through the land into the place of Shechem, unto the oak of Moreh ; *and the Canaanite was then in the land.*" Now these last words imply, it is said, that at the date of writing, the Canaanite was *not*

[1] *Hexateuch*, p. 227.

then in the land, and this being so, the date of the composition of Genesis would be subsequent to the conquest of Canaan. But will the instance bear the strain put upon it? Is there not another explanation of the phrase at least as natural? Is not the statement a mere statement of fact without ulterior or prior reference of any kind? The Lord appears to Abram, and notwithstanding the fact that "the Canaanite was then in the land," promises this very Canaanitish land to his posterity: "unto thy seed will I give this land." As Dillmann well says, "The observation is made with reference to the promise in the next verse; the land, the possession of which God promises to the descendants of Abram, was not a land which nobody owned, the Canaanites dwelt there, but these Canaanites, according to the Divine plan, were afterwards to bow the neck to the seed of Abram."[1] Nay, is not the cited phrase a peculiarly Mosaic phrase? Moses knew all too well that the Canaanite dwelt in the land—was it not the Canaanite who kept Israel from Canaan—and supposing Moses to have written this book, there would have been a peculiar appropriateness, a characteristic touch of realism, if in recording the narrative of the promise to Abram, Moses had inscribed such a sentence, to remind his followers that what did not stagger the faith of Abram should not stagger theirs. The Canaanite was in the land when the promise was made; if the Canaanite was still in the land, it did not make the promise vain. At least this instance is too slight to build the theory of a post-Mosaic date upon.

A *second* apparent *anachronism* is like to the preceding. In the thirteenth chapter of Genesis and the seventh

[1] *Die Genesis*, 4th edit., Leipsic, 1882, pp. 210, 211.

verse we read: "And there was a strife between the herdsmen of Abram's cattle and the herdsmen of Lot's cattle. *And the Canaanite and the Perizzite* dwelled then in the land. And Abram said unto Lot, Let there be no strife, I pray thee, between me and thee, and between my herdsmen and thy herdsmen." Here, again, the allusion to the Canaanite and the Perizzite has been supposed to point to a later time than Moses, seeing that it was only subsequent to the days of the great leader of the Exodus that the Canaanite and the Perizzite ceased to be in the land. But is not the inference far-fetched? Is there not a much more natural explanation of the allusion? Friendly nomads in a land of enemies cannot live at strife. Does not the introduction of the Canaanite and the Perizzite give peculiar force to Abraham's pacific appeal to his nephew? With the Canaanite and Perizzite in the land, how suicidal would be the policy which made antagonists of allies! Neither is this passage conclusive.

A *third* instance of *anachronism* often quoted is this. "And these are the kings," we read in the thirty-sixth chapter of Genesis and the thirty-first verse, "that reigned in the land of Edom, *before there reigned any king over the children of Israel.*" The natural inference is, it is said, that Genesis was written *after* "there reigned a king over the children of Israel," that is to say, not prior to the days of Saul. Have we not, in this allusion to a king, it has been asked, "a note of time which betrays a date subsequent to the introduction of monarchy in Israel"?[1] The point is strong, but I am by no means sure it is as strong as at first sight it looks.

[1] Marcus Dodds, *Genesis*, Edinburgh, 1882, p. 152.

It cannot be shown, for example, that any of the Edomite kings mentioned belong to a later time than Moses—a conclusive argument if it could be shown. But there is another reason which may make one pause before ascribing this verse to a post-Mosaic date. Is it possible that we are reading a later technicality into earlier times? Modern historians are wont to speak of Saul as the first king of Israel. Is this Biblical language? Is this not to read into a flexible Hebrew term our later notions of kingship? Certainly Moses does not hesitate to call himself, or, if the turn of expression be challenged, certainly the author of Deuteronomy did not hesitate to put into the mouth of Moses the name of—a king in Israel. "Moses commanded us a law, an inheritance for the assembly of Jacob, *and he was king in Jeshurun*."[1] Balaam, too, says of Israel, not improbably with reference to the leadership of Moses, "The Lord his God is with him, and *the shout of a king* is among them."[2] According to the Old Testament conception, therefore, it would appear that Moses was the first king of Israel, king meaning no more than leader or ruler. According to the earlier Old Testament conception, it would appear that the king was a judge,[3] the judge was a king,[4] and a ruler might be called either judge or king. At least, if we assume that a judge was often called a king, several parallel passages in Judges, which have given the commentators much trouble, become clear at once. I refer to the frequent phrase "in those days there was no king in Israel," every man doing that which was right in his own eyes,[5] phrases which are not necessarily anachro-

---

[1] Deut. xxxiii. 5.   [2] Numb. xxiii. 21.
[3] 1 Sam. viii. 5, 20.   [4] *Ib.* ii. 10; Judges ix. 6, 15, 16.
[5] *Ib.*. xvii. 6; xviii. 1; xix. 1; xxi. 25.

nisms, but which contrast the political state of Israel, not with its future, but with its past, not with the days of kings to come, but with the days of judges who had done their work and died. If, too, this more flexible use of the word "king" (as equivalent to political head) be Scriptural, another perplexing passage immediately becomes clear, namely, the passage where Moses commands every king to write and read diligently a copy of the Law,[1] a passage which seems an anachronism if four hundred years were to pass before a king was appointed, but at once pertinent and impressive if Moses understood by king any subsequent leader like himself. In which connection, it is significant that, on the appointment of Joshua to leadership, instructions are given him concerning the keeping of the Law, this book of the Law, which Joshua must copy if he is to meditate therein day and night.[2] Further, whether the above explanation appear probable or not, some have thought that there are good grounds for regarding the entire passage as an interpolation.[3] That a subsequent reviser of the early Law did make a few explanatory and supplementary additions has been long recognized, and the phrase before us may certainly be such an interpolation. It is evident that the passage is perfectly intelligible if the phrase in question be read as a later insertion.

Other anachronisms supposed to militate against the Mosaic authorship of Genesis are found in those passages which mention the city of Hebron. Thus we read " How Abraham removed his tent, and came to dwell in the plain of Mamre, which is Hebron, and built there

---

[1] Deut xvii. 14-20. [2] Josh. i. 58.
[3] Kennicott, *Remarks on Select Passages of the Old Testament*, p. 35.

an altar unto the Lord."[1] Now in the Book of Joshua it is distinctly said that "the name of Hebron before-time was Kirjath-Arba (that is, the city of Arba), which Arba was the greatest among the Anakim."[2] Here then, it is contended, there is definite evidence of a post-Mosaic author, seeing that neither in the time of Abraham, nor in that of Moses, was the name of Hebron known. But is not the leverage in this name Hebron small for so long a leap? If there is revision anywhere, surely this word points to the modernizing of a reviser. Let the facts of the case be carefully weighed. This name Hebron occurs in three passages in Genesis, and in each instance the name is a superfluity, the meaning being perfectly clear and complete, if the clause containing the name be altogether omitted. If Hebrew had known the modern use of brackets, when additions were made to the primary text, would not brackets have been used in these three passages? Let us see how the three passages look so written. The above-cited text would run thus: "Abraham removed his tent, and came and dwelt in the plain of Mamre [which is Hebron], and built there an altar to the Lord." The second passage would run: "And Sarah died in Kirjath-Arba [the same is Hebron] in the land of Canaan."[3] And the third would run, in the similar fashion, "And Jacob came unto Isaac his father to Mamre, to Kirjath-Arba [the same is Hebron], where Abraham and Isaac sojourned."[4] Are not these allusions to Hebron manifest interpolations of a later hand? In this instance, then, the evidence is rather of a post-Mosaic revision than of a post-Mosaic

---

[1] Gen. xiii. 18.   [2] Josh. xiv. 15; xv. 13.
[3] Gen. xxiii. 2.   [4] *Ib.* xxxv. 27.

authorship of Genesis. The distinction will rise again presently.

Yet another anachronism is found where we read that "Abraham pursued" Chedorlaomer and the confederate kings "as far as Dan";[1] inasmuch as in Judges we also read, "and they (the Danites), called the name of the city Dan, after the name of Dan their father, who was born unto Israel; howbeit, the name of the city was Laish at the first."[2] Now, if the Dan of Abraham be the same as the Dan of the Danites, there seems here also to be the handiwork of a writer who wrote subsequently to the time of the Judges. But the evidence is not conclusive, seeing that there seems to be some doubt as to the original reading. Further, copyists, to say nothing of revisers, have been known to modernize names: and the probability of a later revision has just been pointed out. May not a reviser have substituted the familiar Dan for the obsolete Lais?

Attention has also been called, as an instance of *another anachronism*, to the use of the word "prophet" in the verse, "Now, therefore, restore the man his wife, for he is a prophet,"[3] whereas, in Samuel, the name prophet is apparently described as a newly introduced term.[4] The explanation of the matter is not quite clear. But whatever be the meaning of the statement in Samuel—and very various meanings have been attributed thereto—it is evident that the word prophet occurs constantly in the Pentateuch in the sense assigned to it.[5] Indeed, so conclusive is the evidence, that some

---

[1] Gen. xiv. 14.
[2] Judg. xviii. 29.
[3] Gen. xx. 7.
[4] 1 Sam. ix. 9.
[5] Exod. vii. 1; Numb. xi. 27, 29; Deut. xiii. 1, 3, 5; xviii. 18.

have doubted the authenticity of the passage (manifestly a parenthesis) in Samuel.

Yet *another anachronism* has been found, in the view of some, where Joseph tells Pharaoh's chief butler that he was stolen "out of the land of the Hebrews;"[1] whereas the land of Canaan was not yet "the land of the Hebrews." The contention is against the evidence. Was it, or was it not, a matter of fact that Abraham, and Isaac, and Jacob, were known to their contemporaries as Hebrews? There can be no doubt about the reply. Abraham was known as "Abram *the Hebrew*,"[2] and Potiphar's wife complains to her servants that her husband had "brought in *a Hebrew*"[3] to mock the Egyptian, and the chief butler calls Joseph a Hebrew to the face of his master.[4] It is unnecessary to trouble ourselves with the difficult question of the etymology of the term "Hebrew;" the Biblical usage is sufficient reply.

An *additional anachronism*, sometimes cited, has been found in the verse which tells how Abraham was bidden get with Isaac into "the land of Moriah," the mountain of Moriah only receiving its name at the building of the Temple of Solomon. The identity of the Moriah of Abraham's faith with the Moriah of the Temple is exceedingly doubtful, and quite as doubtful is the reading "land of *Moriah*." However, this point will require discussion later on, when it is necessary to inquire whether the reading Mount of Jehovah (or Moriah) is defensible in pre-Mosaic times.

Reviewing all this *evidence* as to *anachronism*, is it not manifestly too weak to bear the strain it is called upon

---

[1] Gen. xl. 15; compare xxxix. 14, 17, and xli. 12.   [2] *Ib*. xiv. 13.
[3] *Ib*. xxxix. 14.   [4] *Ib*. xli. 12.

to bear? Of the several instances put forth as demonstrating the post-Mosaic date of Genesis, crucial instances as they are supposed to be, some are wholly inconclusive, whilst the remainder appear to point rather to the work of a reviser than of an author later than Moses.

And here let the probability of a later revision be emphasized. For the high probability of a later revision of the Law has been long acknowledged, not on the demands of any critical theory, but because of ancient evidence. Ezra, for example, has been credited again and again with rendering the ancient Book of the Law more intelligible to his contemporaries. "It is generally received," says Bishop Cosin,[1] "that after the return of the Jews from their captivity in Babylon, all the Books of Scripture having been revised by Ezra (then their priest and leader), . . . were by him, and the prophets of God that lived with him, consigned and delivered over to all posterity." The learned bishop so wrote on the authority of Jerome and Theodoret; he might have added extracts from Tertullian, Irenæus, Clement of Alexandria, and Chrysostom.[2] Indeed, the evidence is conclusive, that in the early belief of the Christian Church, as well as in the tradition of the Jews,[3] Ezra restored, corrected, and edited the entire sacred records of his day, including the Law. Even the words of the Old Testament themselves receive almost a more suit-

[1] *A Scholastical History of the Canon of Holy Scripture*, London, 1672, p. 13.
[2] Hieronymus, *Contra Helveticum*, cap. i. 7; Theodoret, *Præfatio*, in Cant.; Tertullian, *De Habitu Muliebri*, cap. iii.; Irenæus, *Adversus Hæreses*, iii. 23; Clemens Alex., *Stromata*, i.; Chrysostom, *Hom. viii. in Epistolam ad Hebræos*.
[3] Prideaux, *The Old and New Testaments Connected, &c.*, 5th edit. 1718, vol. i. pp. 270-272.

able, as well as a fuller meaning, if this tradition of a revision be thought probable. Such a tradition, in fact, gives added weight to such words as these, which call Ezra "a ready scribe in the Law of Moses," which represent him as having "prepared his heart to seek the law of the Lord, and to do it, and to teach in Israel statutes and judgments," which describe the mission of Ezra to be the teaching "the law of his God to such as knew it not." [1] Ezra, for some peculiar and personal act, was worthy of the title, given him by the heathen Artaxerxes, "the scribe of the law of the God of heaven." [2] How this conception of Ezra had laid hold of pre-Christian Judaism is seen in the Book of Esdras, where we read of Ezra praying, "If I have found grace before thee, send the Holy Spirit into me, and I will write all that hath taken place in the world since the beginning, which were written in thy law, that men may find a path, and that they who would live in the later days may live;" [3] and where we find Ezra named "the scribe of the knowledge of the Most High for ever." [4] Such a tradition points to the current belief that Ezra was an inspired interpreter and not a mechanical copyist of the Law.

On the whole, therefore, one is entitled to say that the evidence for anachronisms is altogether too frail for so elaborate a structure of theory as has been built thereon. On the other hand, when the counter-evidence—as to knowledge manifestly contemporaneous—is considered, this foundation of apparent anachronisms will show itself as friable as frail.

A *further class of evidence*, supposed to negative the

[1] Ezra vii. 6, 10, 11, 12, 21, 25. [2] *Ib.* vii. 12, 21; compare v. 6.
[3] *Ib.* xiv. 22. [4] *Ib.* xiv. 50.

possibility of the Mosaic authorship of Genesis, is thought to be found in phrases which imply that Genesis was written after the Israelites had entered Canaan, *anatropisms*, as I have ventured to call them. The entire geographical standpoint of the writer, some contend, is that of a resident in Canaan. The proof lies, as far as Genesis is concerned, in two words, only the Hebrew words for West and South. When the Israelite wished to say "west," he said "seawards" (*yam*); and when he wished to say "south," he said "towards the desert" (*negeb*).[1] Now, in Egypt, "seawards" was "north," and not "west;" and at Sinai "seawards" was not "west," but "south." The turn of phrase, it is contended, cannot therefore have originated either in Egypt or during the Wanderings in the Wilderness; in short, as Reuss puts the matter, the turn of phrase "betrays a Palestinian pen." Or such phrase "betrays a Palestinian origin," it might suffice to reply; and only the exigences of a theory stand in the way of acknowledging that the origin of the phrase lay with Abraham, or one of his immediate descendants. To Abraham, after his migration, seawards *was* west, and desert-wards *was* south. Even if these same designations lingered in use long after this original meaning ceased to hold, this is only what happens in all languages when we employ a useful or common word. We do not always adhere to, or even think, of its etymology. When one says "lunatic" he does not necessarily mean "influenced by the moon;" nor when one says "candidate" is he straightway to be understood to mean "dressed in white;" nor when one says "jovial" does he naturally intend "born

---

[1] Reuss, *L'Histoire Sainte et la Loi*, pp. 134, 135; Robertson Smith, *Old Testament in Jewish Church*, p. 323; Dillmann, *Numeri*, p. 594.

beneath the planet Jupiter." Neither when an Anglo-Indian talks at Calcutta about the Orientals, is it self-evident that he cannot possibly mean the Turks, say, seeing that they are to the west and not to the east of him. Etymologically, I believe, east-wind is ice-wind, and west-wind is wind of the home of the sun, and south-wind is sun-wind; but when I use these words, to-day, whether here or at the antipodes, I certainly do not think of "ice" when I say "east," nor of "sun" when I say "south," nor of the "home of the sun" when I say "west." Similarly, supposing the Patriarchs, when resident in Canaan, to have coined these words, using them with precision for a while, a time would, nevertheless, undoubtedly arrive, when the terms precisely coined at first would come to be used for their practical rather than their etymological value. Often, from this tendency of language, etymologists are pedantic rather than practical guides to the use of speech, and shallow rather than sound guides, let me add, to the criticism of speech. The above reply, however, does not commend itself to Dr. Robertson Smith, who says, "The answer attempted to this (that Negeb is South), is that the Hebrews might have adopted their phrases in patriarchal times, and never have given them up in the ensuing four hundred and thirty years, but that is nonsense." I am not quite sure which of the two statements is said to be "nonsense," whether, that is to say, it is nonsense to affirm that the patriarchs coined the term *Negeb*, or whether it is said to be "nonsense" that the descendants of the patriarchs did not surrender this term during their four hundred and thirty years in Egypt; if the former is meant, the opinion so forcibly described is only "nonsense" on a foregone conclusion; and, if the latter is meant, the opinion controverted is only "nonsense" on a gratuitous assumption. So far as Genesis, at least, is concerned, with which book alone I am dealing at present, the entire argument as to geographical standpoint, *anatropisms*, is worthless.

Upon the *remaining branch of evidence* relied upon for proving that Genesis could not have been written by Moses, viz., *romancings*, or the fictitious character of its contents, little more need be said, after the conclusions arrived at in the two preceding Lectures. Seeing that Genesis is palpably unhistorical, this argument runs, Genesis cannot have originated in contemporary knowledge or in early and therefore reliable tradition. This unhistorical vein is a favourite one with Colenso, who "thinks he has proved abundantly that the statements in the first eleven chapters of Genesis—whatever value they may have, whatever lessons may be drawn from them—cannot be regarded as historically true, being contradicted in their literal sense again and again by the certain facts of modern science;"[1] in fact, as Colenso has said in another place, " the two main conclusions for which he has contended are the facts of the *non-Mosaic authorship* of Genesis and the *unhistorical character* of a great portion of its contents." Kuenen, too, regards Genesis as utterly unhistorical, and therefore as necessarily committed to writing centuries after Moses and Joshua.[2] Similar quotations could readily be multiplied. As a matter of fact, however, little examination of a destructive kind has been bestowed upon the narratives of Abraham, Isaac, Jacob, and Joseph, and as for the

---

[1] *The Pentateuch and the Book of Joshua*, part iv. p. vii. ; and part v. p. 305.

[2] *Hexateuch*, p. 42.

pre-Abrahamic chapters of Genesis, science, as we have already seen, has had to learn caution in pronouncing them unhistorical, easy as it has seemed to some to signalize the contradictions of Science and Scripture upon the Creation, the Deluge, the Confusion of Tongues, *et hoc genus omne historiarum.* The unhistorical character of Genesis is one of those common assertions more easily made than proved.

A *definite reply* therefore can now be given *to the first of the critical questions* proposed concerning Genesis, viz., as to the evidence Genesis itself affords as to the date of its composition. This question, as we have seen, really resolves itself into another—as to what evidence Genesis itself affords antagonistic to the traditional belief (of its having been written by Moses). Three branches of evidence to a post-Mosaic date have been proposed. But on close inductive examination the *first* branch has shown itself *inconclusive*, the *second, irrelevant*, and the *third, superficial.* Thus no solid ground has been discovered as yet for a belief in the post-Mosaic date. This negative evidence will be supplemented a little later on in this Lecture by positive evidence associating Genesis with Moses.

Having thus dealt with one great critical question concerning Genesis, I now pass to a SECOND. *What evidence does Genesis itself proffer upon its simple or composite authorship?* Was it apparently written by one hand? And if written by one hand, to judge by internal evidence, was it wholly original, or did its author employ for his purpose oral or written records known to him?

The data relied upon as showing more hands than one

in the composition of Genesis may be arranged in several classes?

First comes the well-known fact of *the singular usage of the Divine names* already alluded to more than once. The fact is unquestionable. The inference also appears unquestionable. A law manifestly underlies the employment of the terms Elohim and Jehovah, which seems to point to more than one author. The evidence will be resumed presently.

Side by side with this distinctive usage of the Divine names comes, *secondly*, a *manifest difference of style*, so marked indeed as to argue variety of mind. On the one hand, we have a writer, the Elohist, whose style is simplicity itself, clear but often diffuse, neither laboured nor embellished, free from the art of the writer or the orator, rich in repetition, given to technicalities, circumstantial, frigid, yet with great fulness of expression at command, wont to emphasize a minute and consistent chronology, utilizing apparently various ancient genealogies,[1] and statistical summaries,[2] and written traditions, whose religious standpoint is everywhere pronounced, but non-Levitical. On the other hand, we have a writer, the Jehovist, who is pointed and terse, smooth yet spirited, ornate and rhetorical, even brilliant, revelling in colour, who is fond of the derivation of names,[3] who likes to intensify the milder language of the Elohist, who shows great skill in narrative (as in the stories of Paradise, the Fall, Cain and Abel, and the Confusion of Tongues), who delights in indicating the religious and moral implications of events, who possesses much more pronounced convictions than the Elohist upon the nature and history of

---

[1] *E.g.*, xi. 10, &c.; xxxv. 22, &c.
[2] *E.g.*, x.; xxv. 12, &c.; xxxvi.
[3] *E.g.*, ii. 7, 23; iii. 20; iv. 1, 16, 25; v. 29; ix. 27; x. 25; xi. 9.

man, and upon the nature and history of revelation, nay, who does not shrink from many anthropomorphic expressions[1] never found in the Elohist, and who occupies everywhere a more fearless and developed religious position, scrupulously pointing out, wherever possible, the links of connection between the pre-Levitical worship and the more elaborate cultus of later days. Note, in illustration of the diversity of manner of the two writers, a few marked instances. It is the Elohist who likes the frequent phrase, "after his kind," and who indulges in such formulas as "Noah, and his sons, and his wife, and his sons' wives with him." It is the Elohist who tabulates the command, "And of every living thing of all flesh, two of every sort shalt thou bring into the ark; of fowls after their kind, and of cattle after their kind, and of every creeping thing of the earth after his kind, two of every sort shall come unto thee:" and it is the Elohist who afterwards informs us, "in the self-same day entered Noah, and Shem, and Ham, and Japheth, the sons of Noah, and Noah's wife, and the three wives of his sons with them, into the ark, they, and every beast after his kind, and all the cattle after their kind, and every thing that creepeth upon the earth after his kind, and every fowl after his kind, every bird of every sort; and they went in unto Noah into the ark, two and two of every kind:" and it is the Elohist who tells us yet again how the command to leave the ark ran, "Go forth of the ark, thou, and thy wife, and thy sons, and thy sons' wives with thee; bring forth with thee every living thing that is with thee, of all flesh, of fowl, and of cattle, and of every creeping thing that creepeth

---

[1] *E.g.*, the whole narrative of the Fall; v. 29; viii. 20–22; ix. 18–27; xii. 2, 3; xviii. 17–19.

upon the earth:" and who goes on to say, "And Noah went forth, and his sons, and his wife, and his sons' wives with him, every beast, every creeping thing, and every fowl, and whatsoever creepeth upon the earth after their kinds, went forth out of the ark." Thus the Elohist. Now contrast with all this lawyer-like circumlocution the terse phrase of the Jehovist, who is content to say, "Come thou and all thy house into the ark." Here is another remarkable diversity of manner: the Elohistic sections of Genesis never refer in any way to the blessing of Abraham, which forms so frequent a subject of the Jehovistic sections. Further, as instancing the rudimentary religious position of the Elohist, observe that he certainly has a sense of sin and of its evil consequences, as when he speaks of the antediluvian earth as "corrupt before God and filled with violence,"[1] and when he also speaks of the determination of God to destroy this corrupt earth; but how much stronger are the statements of the Jehovist, who writes the narrative of the Fall, with its curses upon the serpent, the woman and the man, who pens the story of Cain with its curse, and who recites the drunkenness of Noah, also with its curse. Yet again, it is the Jehovist only who has anything to say about sacrifices;[2] and it is the Jehovist who lays stress on the numbers seven[3] and forty,[4] a stress which reappears in the subsequent books of the Pentateuch. It is scarcely dubitable that Genesis does show traces of at least two hands, differing both in style and standpoint.

Further, in the *third* place, this difference of style and

[1] Gen. xii. 3; xviii. 18; xxii. 18; xxiv. 7; xxviii. 14.
[2] *E.g.*, *Ib.* iv. 3, 4; viii. 20, 21.   [3] *E.g.*, *Ib.* vii. 2, 3, 4, 10; viii. 10, 12.
[4] *E.g.*, *Ib.* vii. 4, 12, 17; viii. 6.

of standpoint extends to the *usus loquendi* : Elohist and Jehovist each has his peculiarities of phrase and vocabulary—his favourite words, and his characteristic turns. It is difficult, it is true, to convey the force of this linguistic evidence to those who know no Hebrew ; nevertheless, a few instances in point may give a little faint insight into the conclusive nature of the evidence. In comparing, for example, the Elohistic and Jehovistic narratives of the Creation, the following peculiarities are found. The Elohist speaks of " the living thing of the earth,"[1] and the Jehovist of " the living thing of the field."[2] The Elohist speaks of "grass" and "herb" and "tree,"[3] and the Jehovist speaks of "plant."[4] The Elohist speaks of " the herb (or green thing) of the earth," and the Jehovist of " the herb of the field." The Elohist affects the term " earth," and the Jehovist prefers the term " soil." Again, so simple and frequent a copulative as "also" is found *ninety-two* times in Jehovistic passages, and only *once* in Elohistic ; and so common an adverb as "now" is found thirty-five times in Jehovistic passages, and only once in passages that are Elohistic. Further, the lengthened form of the Hebrew personal pronoun for the first person singular occurs *fifty-four* times in Jehovistic sections, and but *once* in the Elohistic ; indeed, it is a characteristic of the Jehovist to have a predilection for this pronoun. A parallel instance occurs with the Hebrew personal pronoun for the third person singular, which is found one hundred and twenty-eight times in the Jehovist, and but three times in the Elohist. Elohistic sections always call Mesopotamia Padan-Aram, and Jehovistic sections always call the same country Aram-Naharaim. Where-

---

[1] Gen. i. 24. [2] *Ib.* ii. 19 ; iii. 1, 14. [3] *Ib.* i. 11, 12. [4] *Ib.* ii. 6 ; iii. 18.

as the Elohistic sections always write of "giving" or "establishing", Jehovistic sections always write of "cutting" a covenant. The distinctive Hebrew idiom which associates the indicative and infinitive (for example, dying thou shalt die, or thou shalt surely die) is employed by the Jehovist thirty-eight times and by the Elohist but once. The Jehovist is fond of the phrase "I pray," which the Elohist never uses. The Jehovist has also a preference for the name of Israel as a personal name for Jacob, whereas the name Israel is never found in Elohistic sections. The Jehovist, too, has a love for telling us the exact time of day when an event happened whether in the "morning," at "noon," in the "afternoon," in the "evening," or at "night," whether at "daybreak" or at "sunset," whether in the "cool" or the "heat" of the day, a peculiarity of style which nowhere occurs in the Elohistic sections. The Jehovist, again, finds great attraction in lively and picturesque phrases. "Thus it is only in the non-Elohistic portions of Genesis that we meet with such expressions as 'lift up the eyes and see,' 'lift up the feet and go,' 'lift up the voice and weep,' 'fall upon the neck and weep,' 'do mercy to,' 'mercy and truth,' 'be kindled to,' 'find favour in the eyes of,' 'see the face of,' 'go to meet,' 'rise to meet,' 'run to meet,'—'sin,' 'swear,' 'steal,' 'smite,' 'slay,' 'fear,' 'hate,' 'comfort,' 'embrace,' 'kiss,' and even 'love.' . . . If Abraham 'loves' Isaac, so, too, does Isaac 'love' Rebekah, 'love' Esau, 'love' savoury meat, and Rebekah 'loves' Jacob, Jacob 'loves' Rachel, Israel 'loves' Joseph, Shechem 'loves' Dinah."[1] It

---

[1] Colenso, *The Pentateuch and Book of Joshua Critically Examined*, part v. p. 34: compare part v. pp. 18-57, from which the above numerical statements have been drawn.

is upon such evidence that Kuenen has said (and most justly as regards Genesis, with which alone we are at present concerned): "The narratives differ so widely in respect (of linguistic evidence) that without reference to their contents, and where, from the nature of the case, these contents can give us no help, we are still able to place the diversity of authorship above the reach of doubt by merely noting the divergences of form."[1]

Yet another class of evidence, a *fourth*, has been frequently cited in favour of the composite character of Genesis. Two *accounts* of the same event are often found side by side, it has been said, and *mutually contradictory*. But *only a superficial criticism can thus speak*. Indeed, the very existence of apparent contradictions should suggest a pause before deciding hastily; for is not every instance of contradiction a reflection upon the judgment and the artistic skill of the editor, whoever he was, who, nevertheless produced, from a variety of materials, this very remarkable unity, the Book of Genesis? Surely to condemn so remarkable a compiler of permitting self-evident contradictions to appear in his work, should be the last and not the first resource of the critic. By the nature of the case the critic is bound to search for a possible reconciliation. What, to the superficial observer, may appear contradiction, may cease to be contradiction to the observer who is more patient and profound. *Insolentior lectio potior est ea quæ nil insoliti continetur.* Of these irreconcilable accounts in Genesis a great deal too much has been made; at least, so any inductive inquirer will say.

For example, confident assertions have been made as to the *contradictions* to be found in the Elohistic and

[1] *Hexateuch,* p. 41.

Jehovistic *accounts of the Creation*.[1] There is not one which does not vanish on a closer inspection. Critics should consider how improbable it is that any editor of divergent accounts would insert them side by side. No legend is so dear to a writer as his own reputation for consistency. As a matter of fact, there is not a statement in the second chapter of Genesis[2] which is not perfectly harmonious with the statements of the first chapter, and which may not have been written with perfect intelligence by a writer who had the contents of the first chapter before him. If a hasty reader infers from the first chapter that man and woman were created together, the fault lies, not with the second chapter which states that the woman was created from the man, but with the hasty reader, who forms an opinion as to time without data. If a commentator interprets the statement, "And out of the ground the Lord God formed every beast of the field, and every fowl of the air; and brought them unto Adam to see what he would call them," to mean, that man was created before birds and beasts, the interpretation certainly does contradict the statements of the first chapter, but the originator of the contradiction is not the compiler of Genesis.

However, the point is crucial, and must be carefully considered. Kuenen and Reuss, for instance, summarizing the contentions of their predecessors, have both given carefully prepared lists of these contradictory accounts.[3] These lists it is desirable to examine.

We are said to have in Genesis, *two contradictory accounts of the origin of the name Beersheba*. According

---

[1] Gen. i.–ii. 3.   [2] *Ib*. ii. 4, &c.
[3] Kuenen, *Hexateuch*, pp. 38–40; Reuss, *L'Histoire Sainte et la Loi*, pp. 39–43.

to the one account,[1] the well to which the name Beersheba, or "well of swearing," was given, was dug by Abraham, and received its name because there Abraham and Abimelech made a covenant with an oath. In the second account,[2] the origin of the name Beersheba is attributed to an occurrence precisely similar, in which Isaac and Abimelech are concerned. But let the two accounts be carefully read. It will be seen that they are not contradictory; indeed *the second account expressly refers to the first*. Beersheba was not a modern city, so to speak, but a place of wells, and the wells made by Abraham had been destroyed by Abimelech, and thus the name had lapsed. Isaac re-digs the wells, renews the covenant with Abimelech, and re-names the place. The testimony is express: "And Isaac digged again the wells of water which they had digged in the days of Abraham his father; for the Philistines," Abimelech was their king, "had stopped them after the death of Abraham; and he called their names after the names by which his father had called them."[3]

Again, we are said to have *two different accounts of the origin of the name Bethel*. According to one the name was given by Jacob to the spot where God appeared to him, in the vision of the ghostly ladder, as he fled to Padan-Aram;[4] according to the other the name was given by Jacob to the same spot, when he returned from Padan-Aram.[5] But here also the narrative expressly negatives any contradiction, as the context shows clearly. *The story of the second visit names the first.* "And God said unto Jacob," while he was in Padan-Aram, "Arise and go up to Bethel and dwell

[1] Gen. xxi. 31.   [2] *Ib.* xxvi. 31-33.   [3] *Ib.* xxvi. 18.
[4] *Ib.* xxviii. 19.   [5] *Ib.* xxxv. 14, 15.

there" — then Bethel was already known as such to Jacob. "So Jacob came to . . . Bethel, and he built there an altar, and called the place El-Bethel; because there God appeared unto him, when he fled from the face of his brother." The passage might even read, "So Jacob came . . . to Bethel, and he *had* built there an altar, and *had* called the place El-Bethel; because there God *had* appeared unto him, when he fled from the face of his brother." The act of obedience is followed by a further Divine revelation. "And God appeared unto Jacob again, as he came out of Padan-Aram and blessed him. . . . And Jacob set up a pillar"—additional apparently to the altar—"in the place where he talked with him, a pillar of stone; and he poured a drink offering thereon, and he poured oil thereon. And Jacob called the name of the place where God spoke to him, Bethel." Surely the contradiction lies not in finding in these two accounts two Divine revelations at the same spot, but two divergent accounts of the same event. The circumstances in each instance are as diverse as the time.

Again, we are said to have *two divergent accounts of the origin of the name Israel*.[1] But in this case also it is a superficial criticism which erects a solemn confirmation of the name given on an earlier occasion into a manifest contradiction of that earlier name.

Yet again, we are said to have *two contradictory accounts of the names of Esau's wives*, a statement which one wonders how Dr. Kuenen can repeat, after the fully satisfactory explanation of the apparent diversity which has been long known. Undoubtedly, in this instance, there is a difficulty which is not easy of solution, but it

[1] Gen. xxxii. 24–32 and xxxv. 10.

is not the difficulty to which Dr. Kuenen refers. The difficulty is this. On the first mention of these wives,[1] Esau, we are told, married a daughter of Beeri, the Hittite, named Judith, and a daughter of Elon the Hittite, named Basemath, to whom he subsequently added Mahalath, the daughter of Ishmael and the sister of Nebajoth.[2] Afterwards, however, when these wives are mentioned, the daughter of Elon is called Adah, and the daughter of Ishmael and the sister of Nebajoth is called Basemath, whilst the third wife is described as Oholibamah, the daughter of Anah, the daughter (the Samaritan and Septuagint Versions read "son"[3]) of Zibeon the Hivite.[4] Thus the real difficulty is that Basemath appears as the daughter of Elon in the one case and of Ishmael in the other, which seems to point to some copyist's transposition. The other differences of statement vanish on examination. Anah would seem to have obtained the name of Beeri, or "man of the well," because he found the hot springs in the wilderness, as he fed the asses of Zibeon his father.[5] Further, if Anah, or Beeri, is called a Hittite in one place,[6] and a Hivite in another,[7] this is explained by the fact that "Hittite" is often used in a wide sense for Canaanite, and thus includes "Hivite," Hittite being the generic name for the specific Hivite.[8] That the names of the wives should vary should cause little surprise, seeing how common it is in the East to change names on important occasions, marriage included.[9]

[1] Gen. xxvi. 34.   [2] *Ib.* xxviii. 9.
[3] "Son" is manifestly correct : see *Ib.* xxxvi. 24, 25.
[4] *Ib.* xxxvi. 2, 3.   [5] *Ib.* xxxvi. 24 (Revised Version).
[6] *Ib.* xxvi. 34.   [7] *Ib.* xxxvi. 2.
[8] 1 Kings x. 29 ; 2 Kings vii. 6 ; Josh. i. 4 ; Gen. xxvii. 46, and xlviii. 1.
[9] Ranke, *Untersuchungen über den Pentateuch, aus dem Gebiete der höhern Kritik*, Erlangen, 1834, vol. i. p. 2

Yet again, there are said to be *two divergent accounts of Esau's settlement in Seir*, which, according to one passage it is said, took place during Jacob's sojourn in Mesopotamia,[1] and according to another passage took place after his return therefrom.[2] But is not this to read into the second passage a meaning it does not necessarily contain, seeing that not a word is said there as to this being Esau's first settlement in Seir? May not nomads return to an old camping-ground?

And yet again there are said to be *two incompatible accounts of the sale of Joseph into slavery*, one account describing Joseph as sold to the Ishmaelites,[3] and another account asserting that he was sold to Midianites. But Ishmaelite is a synonym for Arab, and Midianites are a tribe of Arabs. One would have thought that a single reading of the verse concerned would have silenced the objection; for what does the verse say: "Then there passed by *Midianite* merchantmen; and they drew and lifted up Joseph out of the pit, and sold Joseph to the *Ishmaelites* for twenty pieces of silver."[4] If the original writer of the passage saw no difficulty in calling Midianites Ishmaelites, of what weight is modern punctiliousness?

The supposed contradictions cited are all Dr. Kuenen's "absolutely irrefragable proofs . . . of diverse renderings of a single tradition." It is on the strength of these contradictions that he thinks it "very probable that certain other narratives, which strongly resemble each other, must also be regarded as doublets, that is, as diverse renderings of a single tradition, or as variations of a single theme." With these probabilities we need

---

[1] Gen. xxxii. 3.
[2] *Ib.* xxxvi. 8.
[3] *Ib.* xxxvii. 25, 27.
[4] *Ib.* xxxvii. 28.

not concern ourselves here. If the "absolutely irrefragable proofs" show themselves so questionable, there is no need to busy ourselves with the readily adaptable instances. By the very form of Dr. Kuenen's expression it is manifest that these probable doublets are capable of a different classification. So much for Dr. Kuenen's list.

Nor needs much be said about the *additional* instances of *incompatible traditions* given by Dr. Reuss. Observe the cardinal law of all just criticism, and never regard an eminent author as inconsistent until after the most patient inquiry, and Dr. Reuss's instances melt away. The solid pillars of his argument fade like an unsubstantial vision. Let his most carefully elaborated example of various renderings of one fundamental legend serve as an instance. To do Dr. Reuss no injustice I translate his words:—

"In Gen. xii. we read," Reuss says, "that the patriarch," Abraham, "compelled by dearth to emigrate to Egypt, advised his wife to call herself his sister, because he feared being killed on her account, the Egyptians desiring to carry her off because of her beauty. Indeed, hardly arrived in Egypt, Sarah, considered as unmarried, was led into the harem of Pharaoh. But he, punished by heaven for having carried off a married woman, restores her to her husband, and begs him to depart from the country. This same story," Reuss continues, "is told again in two other places."

Chap. xx.	Chap. xxvi.
Abraham sojourns at Gerar.	Isaac sojourns at Gerar.
Fearing death, because of his wife, he makes her pass as his sister.	Fearing death, because of his wife, he makes her pass as his sister.
The king Abimelech carries her of, but warned by God of the true condition of Sarah, he restores her to her husband.	The king Abimelech discovers the truth, and reproves Isaac.

Afterwards, Abraham makes an alliance with Abimelech and his general Pikol (xxi. 22.)	Afterwards, Isaac makes an alliance with Abimelech and his general Pikol (xxvi. 26.)

"This alliance," Reuss goes on to say, "is made near a well, the possession of which had been a subject of dispute (chap. xxi. 28, &c.). Abraham gives to the Philistines seven lambs and keeps the well. Hence the name Beersheba (well of the seven or of the oath). There is the same history in chap. xxvi. 31; only this time it is Isaac who makes an alliance with Abimelech, and the place receives its name on this occasion as if it had not done so previously."[1]

So writes Reuss. His statement is eminently artistic. It accentuates the points of agreement in the several accounts, and conceals those of divergence. But it is a perfectly gratuitous assumption that Abraham's half-truth to Pharaoh should not have been subsequently repeated to Abimelech. At least, whoever wrote Genesis in its final form, allowed both instances of deceit to stand. Upon the assumption that the incident in Philistia is but a legendary variation of what happened in Egypt, it is unnecessary to say anything; does Dr. Reuss think that the several writers he argues for, regarded the incident as praiseworthy that they vary it so as to repeat it? But the parallel between Abraham and Isaac requires more consideration. Here again the plain fact that the editor of the Genesis allowed the two narratives to appear in all their manifest resemblance rather argues for their truth than their manufacture (or at least the literary construction of one). Then, the differences in the two narratives call for recognition as well as their resemblances; and possibly the best reply to Reuss's insinuation would be a careful reading of the two chapters concerned, side by side, the twentieth and the twenty-sixth, close attention being given to the

[1] *L'Histoire Saint et la Loi*, pp. 40, 41.

different setting in the two accounts, to the variant colouring, and to the numerous contrasts. These divergences more make for the truth of the two accounts than the resemblances make for the fictitiousness of one. For mark the following details which, after the manner of Reuss, are presented in tabular form :—

CHAP. XX.	CHAP. XXVI.
For a reason not stated, Abraham goes to Gerar.	Because of famine, Isaac goes to Gerar.
Fearing death, because of the beauty of his wife, Abraham, by express arrangement with Sarah, passes her off as his sister.	Fearing death, because of the beauty of his wife, Isaac, without any arrangement with Rebekah, and without her knowledge apparently, passes her off as his sister.
Abimelech places Sarah in his harem.	Isaac and Rebekah live together.
Straightway a sickness falls upon Abimelech and his house.	No parallel.
Straightway, too, a vision from God is sent to Abimelech, disclosing the relationship of Abraham and Sarah.	After some time Abimelech (another man apparently—the title being the Philistine equivalent of the Egyptian Pharaoh) sees Isaac and Rebekah so behaving that their relationship is inferred by him.
Abimelech expostulates on the ground that he himself might have been led into sin.	Abimelech expostulates on the ground that some of his people might have been led into sin.
Abraham excuses himself on the ground that he had told an half-truth.	Isaac has no reason to offer.
Abraham also excuses himself	Isaac nowhere, implies that

on the ground of a compact with Sarah.	Rebekah had given assent to, or even knew his subterfuge.
Abimelech propitiates Abraham with gifts.	No parallel.
And propitiates Sarah.	No parallel.
Abraham prays for the removal of Abimelech's sickness.	No parallel.
Some time after Abimelech and Phichol (titles equivalent to King and General) make a covenant with Abraham.	Some time after Abimelech and Phichol *and Ahuzzath* (titles equivalent to King and General *and Counsellor*) make a covenant with Isaac.
The covenant is ratified by gifts of sheep and oxen and seven ewe lambs.	The covenant is ratified by eating and drinking.

Does not such a tabulation show that Dr. Reuss has been as artistic in the omission of some of the circumstances of the two cases in question, as in the antithetic use of other circumstances?

Summarizing, therefore, the evidence adduced for the composite authorship of Genesis, it may be said, *first*, that the use of the Divine names assuredly does point to a duality of authorship; *second*, that the manifest differences of style also unmistakably point to at least two hands; *third*, that the very phraseology employed as manifestly indicates more writers than one; whereas, *fourth*, no valid ground has been seen for speaking of twofold and mutually contradictory versions of the same event.

To the solution of the problem of the authorship of Genesis, implied by such inferences as well as by other data, let us now proceed.

THIRDLY, then, *What theory as to the date and author-*

ship of Genesis seems best to harmonize with all the facts of the case? In asking such a question, we approach the goal of this consideration of the authorship of Genesis.

Let the three conclusions already reached be borne in mind. One conclusion was that, in Genesis itself, no sure ground has been discovered for declaring the Mosaic authorship impossible. In fact, as the contents declare, Genesis could not have been written much earlier than Moses, and no valid reasons have been found in Genesis itself for believing that it must have been written much later. A second conclusion arrived at concerned the mode of the composition of this Book of Origins. From the data afforded by the Book itself, the work of at least two hands has become evident, an Elohist and a Jehovist. For, besides the methodical employment of the names of Elohim and Jehovah for the Deity, other data declare for at least a duality of authorship, viz., the great differences of style characteristic of the sections where the name Elohim alone occurs as contrasted with those sections in which the name Jehovah is prominent, a difference of style so radical as to argue diversity of historical and theological standpoint as well as variation in vocabulary and diction. A third conclusion attained was that, notwithstanding the fact that evidence has accumulated for a duality of authorship, no irrefragable instances have been forthcoming of contradictions in the annals of these two historians of primitive times. Proceeding upon these three conclusions, the great question now is, how the relation existing between these two authors is to be expressed. Is it possible, by the use of critical methods, to look in, so to speak, upon the author who virtually gave final form to Genesis, as he is writing his book, and to ascertain, with some approach to certainty, the mode in which he composed?

As a matter of fact a fourth conclusion has been reached in the previous inquiry, and it will clear the way to recall, at this point, this fourth conclusion also. Good grounds have been seen for believing, that here and there Genesis has been *touched up* so to speak, modernized, by a later reviser or revisers, occasional elucidations having been introduced into the text, where expressions were liable to be either ill-conceived or misunderstood. There are frequent instances of these illustrative interpolations in Genesis. Amongst them are, it would seem, the following:—"And Abram moved his tent and came and dwelt by the oaks of Mamre [*which are in Hebron*], and built there an altar unto the Lord;"[1] "The king of Bela [*the same is Zoar*];"[2] "All these joined together in the vale of Siddim [*the same is the Salt Sea*];"[3] "And they returned, and came to En-Mishpat [*the same is Kadesh*];"[4] "the vale of Shaveh [*the same is the King's Dale*];"[5] "Wherefore the well was called Beer-lahai-roi [*behold, it is between Kadesh and Bered*];"[6] "And Abraham called the name of that place Jehovah-Jireh [*as it is said to this day, in the Mount of the Lord it shall be seen*];"[7] "And Sarah died in Kirjath-Arba [*the same is Hebron*];"[8] "And after this Abraham buried Sarah his wife, in the cave in the field of Machpelah before Mamre [*the same is Hebron*], in the land of Canaan;"[9] "And Rachel died and was buried in the way of Ephrath [*the same is Bethlehem*];"[10] "And when the inhabitants

---

[1] Gen. xiii. 18.   [2] *Ib.* xiv. 2.   [3] *Ib.* xiv. 3.
[4] *Ib.* xiv. 7.   [5] *Ib.* xiv. 17.   [6] *Ib.* xvi. 14.
[7] *Ib.* xxii. 14. Here probably the whole verse is an interpolation, as will appear a few pages on.
[8] *Ib.* xxiii. 2.   [9] *Ib.* xxiii. 19.   [10] *Ib.* xxxv. 19.

of the land, the Canaanites, saw the mourning in the floor of Atad, they said, This is a grievous mourning to the Egyptians, wherefore the name of it was called Abel-Mizraim [*which is beyond Jordan*]." [1] If it is somewhat uncertain whether the additions in chapter xiv. are, or are not, by the author of Genesis himself, do not the rest suggest, upon their face, that they are the elucidations of a reviser? Nevertheless, if this be so, the work of this reviser—whether Samuel or Ezra, whether some prophet or priest, whether some school of prophets or assembly of priests—was apparently of a very circumscribed kind. All the data available point to a revision as conservative as respectful. Such a revision need not complicate our present inquiry. The problem before us is—whilst acknowledging that some conservative revision of the text of Genesis may have been instituted subsequently—to gain what light we can upon the manner of the composition of Genesis.

Is not the clue at once to the method of composition and to the composer himself, *to be found in the use of the Divine Names?* That is to say, is there not a perfectly clear statement as to the origin and date of the first use of the name Jehovah? Is not this statement fully supported by all the collateral evidence accessible? Was not Jehovah, as a Divine Name, first given to Moses? In short, *is not Moses the Jehovist*, and did he not utilize for his own specific end, the pre-existing writing of the Elohist? At any rate, let us ask, what light Genesis throws upon so interesting an hypothesis.

First, then, travelling for a moment into the book which follows Genesis, *the origin of the name Jehovah is indubitably associated with Moses.* The statement of

[1] Gen. l. 11.

Exodus is categorical. Jehovah was the name given to Moses at the Luminous Bush, as his credential to the Israelites: "And Moses said unto God, Behold, when I come unto the children of Israel, and shall say unto them, The God of your fathers hath sent me unto you; and they shall say unto me, What is his name? what shall I say unto them? And God said unto Moses, I AM THAT I AM, and he said, Thus shalt thou say unto the children of Israel, I AM hath sent me unto you. And God said moreover unto Moses, Thus shalt thou say unto the children of Israel, Jehovah, the God of your fathers, the God of Abraham, the God of Isaac, and the God of Jacob hath sent me unto you; this is my name for ever, and this is my memorial unto all generations." [1] And this name Jehovah is also explicitly declared to be a new name: "And God spake unto Moses and said unto him, I am Jehovah, and I appeared unto Abraham and Isaac and unto Jacob as El Shaddai (God Almighty), but by my name Jehovah was I not known to them." [2] The assertion is unmistakable. Further, the assertion is borne out by inquiry. Though there are many doubts as to the exact pronunciation of the Sacred Tetragrammaton *JHVH*, evidence against the Mosaic origin of the sacred name is of the slightest. As so careful an investigator as Canon Driver has said, "No ground appears at present to exist for questioning either the purely Israelitish origin of the Tetragrammaton, or the explanation of its meaning which is given in Exod. iii. 14." [3] Seeing then that the name of Jehovah was associated at the first with Moses, is it not probable that

---

[1] Exod. iii. 15-18.   [2] *Ib.* vi. 2, 3.
[3] *Studia Biblica*, Oxford, 1885, "Essay on the Origin and Nature of the Tetragrammaton," p. 19.

Moses is the author of the Jehovistic sections of Genesis? Is it not highly probable, that whilst freely using pre-existing materials (as Luke confesses to have done in writing his Gospel), Moses has employed this Divine Name which was first revealed to himself, and employed this new name, as deliberately as artistically, in order to expressly connect the various Jehovistic sections, which he had penned, with himself as author? Is not the use of the word Jehovah in Genesis a sort of Mosaic signature?

In this connection, therefore *observe, secondly, that there is a very remarkable precision in the use of the name Elohim and some other Divine names in the earlier Jehovistic sections of Genesis.* The fact has not been observed as fully as it merits. A careful consideration, it is true, of context and style and phraseology led Hupfeld, years ago, to see that, whilst the name Elohim always stands alone in the Elohistic sections, in the Jehovistic sections the name Jehovah is the predominant but not the exclusive name employed, Elohim being occasionally used as well. This fact of usage led Hupfeld to speak of a second Elohistic writer. A less superficial examination of the use of Elohim, however, in Jehovistic sections might have suggested another conclusion. The name Elohim, it would appear, only occurs in Jehovistic sections under special circumstances, these circumstances falling under two laws. Thus Elohim is used either to avoid the anachronism of implying that the name Jehovah was known in pre-Mosaic days (an avoidance peculiarly evident in the earlier chapters of Genesis), or else to suggest, without possibility of mistake, that the Elohim of patriarchal days was the Jehovah known to the Israelites of the

Exodus—that, as said in so many words, Jehovah was the God of Abraham, the God of Isaac, and the God of Jacob. As instances of the former usage (to avoid anachronism) let the following passages be weighed. All critics who believe in the composite authorship of Genesis,[1] agree that the third chapter was written by the Jehovist. But observe the usage. The name of Jehovah certainly occurs there again and again, but always in narrative, *never in dialogue*. The serpent uses the name Elohim for Deity, and never Jehovah: "Yea, hath Elohim said," the serpent asks, "Ye shall not eat of every tree of the garden?" Eve, too, is made by the author equally discriminative, for she says in reply "Elohim," not Jehovah, "hath said." And the serpent continues, "Ye shall not surely die, for Elohim doth know." Similarly, in another Jehovistic section, it is Elohim, concerning whom Eve says, "Elohim hath appointed me another son instead of Abel."[2] Again, in another Jehovistic section, we are told that "the sons of Elohim" associated with the daughters of men.[3] In yet another Jehovistic section, it is Elohim who is regarded as "enlarging Japheth."[4] Another instructive instance occurs later on, in a passage, which from its use of the word Jehovah, has given many critics trouble, where we read, "And when Abram was ninety years old and nine, Jehovah appeared to Abram and said unto him," *not* I am Jehovah, "but I am God Almighty" [El Shaddai].[5] Similarly, it is El Roi, God of Light, which, in another Jehovistic passage, Hagar calls Jehovah who appeared to her at the fountain in the wilderness.[6] Contrast, too, Eve's mode of speech, in another

---

[1] Compare Appendix I.   [2] Gen. iv. 25.   [3] *Ib.* vi. 2, 4.
[4] *Ib.* ix. 27.   [5] *Ib.* xvii. 1.   [6] *Ib.* xvi. 13.

Jehovistic section, concerning Seth, "Elohim hath appointed me another seed instead of Abel," with the writer's subsequent comment, "Then began men to call upon the name of Jehovah."[1] To the Jehovist, then, apparently, both the names for Deity, Jehovah and Elohim, are known; he freely uses both in his own comments, with a strong preference for the name Jehovah; but he takes special pains, it would seem, for many chapters in his narrative, to avoid putting the name Jehovah into the mouths of the Patriarchal subjects of his narrative.

Elohim, then, is sometimes used by the Jehovist to avoid seeming to imply that the name Jehovah was known in Patriarchal times, although in the same sections he employs his favourite name Jehovah in describing events of Patriarchal times. But the Jehovist on occasion also used the name Elohim and other Divine names, it would seem, to expressly declare the identity of Jehovah and Elohim, to expressly associate the Elohim of pre-Mosaic times with the Jehovah of Mosaic times. Observe, for instance, the frequent use of the phrase Jehovah Elohim in the second and third chapters. As a transition from the Elohistic narrative of Creation to the Jehovistic narrative, lest it should seem that Elohim is one God and Jehovah another, the Jehovist blends the two names. The transition is striking. The last Elohistic verse reads, "And *Elohim* blessed the seventh day and sanctified it, because that in it he had rested from all his work which *Elohim* created to make." The first Jehovistic verse runs, "These are the generations of the heaven and the earth when they were created, in the day that *Jehovah Elohim* made the

[1] Gen. iv. 25, 26.

earth and the heaven;" the Jehovist adding the name Elohim to Jehovah lest confusion should arise. In the blessing of Noah another instructive instance arises, in a Jehovistic passage, where we read, "Blessed be Jehovah, the God of Shem."[1] Observe, too, how at Salem,[2] El-Elyon is called Jehovah, God Most High; how at Hagar's well,[3] El-Roi, the visible God, is called Jehovah; and how at Beersheba,[4] El-Olam, the Everlasting God, is called Jehovah. Further, Jehovah is named the Elohim of Abraham,[5] and the Elohim of Lot,[6] and the Elohim of Isaac,[7] and the Elohim of Jacob.[8] The Jehovist seems to put himself to some trouble to show that the same God, who afterwards revealed His new name of Jehovah, had nevertheless been the Divine Guide and Inspirer of the earlier Patriarchs.

Would not such a prevision of usage be eminently characteristic of the man to whom the new name was first revealed?

Thirdly, in further evidence at once of the revelation of the name Jehovah to Moses, and of the probable Mosaic origin of the use of this name, *mark the exclusion of the name Jehovah from the list of personal names in Genesis*. Names compounded with Elohim are frequent, names compounded with Jehovah are wholly absent. As Colenso says—to whom are due many parallel numerical calculations, and who is, as an advocate of the non-Mosaic authorship, an unexceptionable witness —Genesis gives us 112 names in all; among them eight are compounded with El (Mahalaleel, Ishmael, Adbeel, Israel, Jemuel, Jahleel, Malchiel, Jahzeel); but not one

---

[1] Gen. ix. 26.   [2] *Ib.* xv. 23.   [3] *Ib.* xvi. 12.
[4] *Ib.* xxi. 33.   [5] *Ib.* xv. 27, &c.   [6] Gen. xix. 13.
[7] *Ib.* xxvi. 2, &c.   [8] *Ib.* xxxi. 3, &c.

of these 112 names is compounded with Jehovah.[1] In fact, during the time described by the Pentateuch, the use of Jehovah for naming is of the rarest, whereas, in the days of David, the case was very different, for three of the sons of David, and his nephew, wear names compounded with Jehovah (Adonijah, Shephatiah, Jedidiah, and Jonadab), and, at the same time, we read of two Jonathans, and two Benaiahs, of Jehoiada and Jehoshaphat, and Uriah,[2] all names compounded with Jehovah. In such a fact, then, as the omission in Genesis of the the name Jehovah from the names of persons, another strong evidence is found for the Mosaic authorship of Jehovistic passages. Such exclusion was not found for any long time after the death of Moses.[3]

And, *fourthly*, there is good ground for saying that *the name Jehovah is excluded from the names of places in Genesis*. The state of the evidence is this. The names of places are derived from Elohim in Genesis; it is doubtful whether they are ever derived from Jehovah. Thus we read of Bethel,[4] and of El-Elohe Israel,[5] but not of any House of Jehovah or Place of Jehovah. The two apparent exceptions are found in the narrative of the Trial of Abraham's Faith, which took place in "the land of Moriah,"[6] a spot subsequently named by

---

[1] Colenso, *Pentateuch*, part vii., appendix, p. 137; cf. part ii. pp. 236-239.

[2] 2 Sam. iii. 4; xii. 25; xiii. 3; xv. 27; xx. 23, 24; xxiii. 30, 32, 39.

[3] If difficulty seems to arise because of the name of Moses' mother, let it be borne in mind that change of name was not unfrequent, especially with women. As the name of Hoshea was altered by Moses into Joshua (Numb. xiii. 16), so it is not improbable that, by a similar process, the name of the mother of the Hebrew leader became Jochebed. At least it would be perilous in the extreme to argue from this one name alone that the name of Jehovah was known at the birth of the mother of Moses.

[4] Gen. xxviii. 19.   [5] *Ib.* xxxiii. 20.   [6] *Ib.* xxii. 2 and 14.

Abraham, in memory of the wondrous Divine interference, "Jehovah-Jireh." Both these names, Moriah and Jehovah-Jireh are, many think, equally compounded with Jehovah. Concerning the etymology of Moriah, and even the accuracy of the reading, grave doubts have been expressed,[1] and with good reason. It certainly does seem extremely unlikely that this should be the only instance in Genesis where any name of place or person is compounded with Jehovah, especially remembering that the name Jehovah is distinctly stated in Exodus to have been first revealed to Moses. Further, if the name be a compound of Jehovah, the mountain cannot have received its name until after the event pourtrayed. As for the name Jehovah-Jireh, and indeed the verse where it occurs, is not this verse, too, an interpolation of some later reviser? At least so the facts of the case seem to imply. For read the narrative carefully, and what do we find? Here also, as elsewhere in Genesis, there seems a strong desire not to introduce the name Jehovah, lest it appear an anachronism. "And it came to pass," we read, that "*Elohim* did try Abraham." "And (Abraham) went unto the place *Elohim* had told him," the narrative continues. "My son, *Elohim* will provide himself a lamb," Abraham explains to Isaac, using the very word which subsequently occurs in Jehovah-Jireh, the Hebrew reading *Elohim* JIREH. "And they came to the place which *Elohim* had told him of." Thus far all through the story the name Jehovah is carefully kept out. Then appears the name Jehovah for the first time in the phrase, which is so characteristic of the Old Testament, the "angel of Jehovah," manifestly inserted for the purpose of deliberately associating this Divine ap-

[1] Compare Colenso, *Pentateuch*, part ii. pp. 240-247.

pearance with all the other appearances of that exalted, that Divine messenger, the mysterious angel of Jehovah. But even this angel of Jehovah is not represented as using the name Jehovah to Abraham, for he says, "I know that thou fearest *Elohim.*" All through the narrative, therefore, there seems to be a scrupulous care bestowed not to attribute to Abraham any knowledge of the name Jehovah. Then follows the verse we are especially occupied with, "And Abraham called the name of that place Jehovah-Jireh" (Abraham's words to Isaac were, be it remembered, *Elohim Jireh*); "and it is said to this day, In the Mount of Jehovah it shall be seen," or "he shall appear," whichever rendering be preferred. Is there not here a reference to some proverb concerning Moriah, the Temple mountain? Is there not here therefore an interpolation of some date posterior to the building of Solomon's Temple, an interpolation expressly made to associate the altar of the Moriah of Solomon with the altar of the Moriah of Abraham? If the answer be affirmative, the explanation of the form Jehovah-Jireh is simple. After the days of Moses Jehovah and Elohim are used as synonyms for the Deity. Abraham said, "Elohim Jireh," meaning "God will provide." The reviser said Jehovah-Jireh, meaning just "God will provide," and no more. In short, Moses used the names for Deity with great precision: in after times the Jews used the names Jehovah and Elohim as interchangeable names for Deity, without thinking about etymological differences, any more than the Englishman means by God simply the Good Being, limiting his attention to but one Divine attribute. Does not, then, this remarkable precision in the use of the name Jehovah point to Moses as the author of the Jehovistic section? As is confessed by all parties, the distinctive use of Elohim and Jehovah ends with the revelation of the name Jehovah quite early in Exodus. There is great care before the sixth chapter of Exodus to avoid implying that Jehovah as such was known before the incident of the Burning Bush; after that incident the names Elohim and Jehovah are used without any such scrupulous care; is there not therefore reason to doubt whether any other Hebrew besides Moses had so tense a grasp upon the exact moment when the name was made known? Surely the evidence is not without force. The name Jehovah was first revealed to Moses. Therefore the Jehovistic sections of Genesis could not have been written before Moses. But further, is it not also certain, that these Jehovistic sections could not have been written much after, seeing that Jehovah and Elohim speedily became as interchangeable names in Hebrew for Deity as God and Lord are with us, of very different etymology though the words be?

Fifthly, amongst other evidence of the Mosaic authorship of the Jehovistic sections, let it be borne in mind, that *all the characteristics of the Jehovist*, as previously catalogued, *would, as far as we know Moses, admirably suit him.* For what, by common consent, are the idiosyncrasies of this writer who strongly prefers the name Jehovah for God? Are they not these—that he has a large skill in the use of words; that he shows everywhere a depth of tone due as ever to a depth of sympathy and experience; that he displays a genius in utilizing all events for moral and religious ends; that he has very pronounced convictions upon the nature and history and Divine relationship of man; that he almost punctiliously emphasizes wherever possible the links of connection between the pre-Levitical and the Levitical worship, that he even has somewhat of self-assertion, and is fond of the pronoun " I "? Supposing, for the moment, that the Five Books of Moses were Mosaic, would they not be a vivid commentary upon the above character-sketch of the critics? Does not Deuteronomy disclose a singular gift of addressing popular audiences? Does not the whole career of the great Hebrew leader testify to largeness of view, to strength of conviction, to grip upon moral and religious principle, to profound knowledge of men, to wide and keen personal experience, even to occasional self-obtrusion?

Three points of similarity between Moses and the Jehovist are worth dwelling upon for a sentence or two.

One point is the fearless exposure by both of human weakness. Moses even tells the truth to and of his people; no attribute is more characteristic: follow the narrative of the Exodus and the Wanderings, and the great leader is seen to as ruthlessly expose as to punish fault; with a strong sense of redemption, he has also a strong sense of sin. Now note this same feature in the Jehovist of Genesis. It is he who "gives us all the *darkest* parts of the histories of individual life," as Colenso observes; it is he who writes of the drunkenness of Noah, the cowardice of Abraham, the greed of Lot, the incest of Lot and his daughters, the partiality of Isaac, the selfishness, the duplicity, the fear of Jacob, the dishonour of Dinah, the hatred of the brethren of Joseph, &c., &c.[1]

Another point of similarity is the great knowledge of Egypt. The acquaintance of the Jehovist with Egyptian

[1] *Pentateuch,* part v. pp. 39, 40.

life and manners and customs and polity has often been remarked, as well by Egyptologists as Biblical critics. Says Brugsch,[1] in his admirable *History of Egypt under the Pharaohs*, "the account in Holy Scripture of the elevation of Joseph—of his life at court, of the reception of his father and brothers in Egypt with all their belongings, is in complete accordance with the manners and customs, as also with the place and time." In short, the study of the ancient Egyptian monuments shows that the narratives of the sojourn of Abraham and Joseph in Egypt disclose a very intimate acquaintance with manners and customs, which only an eye-witness could pen, so local are the descriptions, so subtle the touches, so characteristic the incidents. Were Moses the Jehovist, this rather striking point of similarity would be readily explained.

A third point, also readily explicable on the theory that Moses was the Jehovist, is this: the acquaintance the Jehovist shows with certain technicalities of the Levitical law. This Levitical knowledge of the Jehovist is absolutely ignored by Wellhausen and his school, according to whose theory it is the Elohist in Genesis who should show familiarity with the Levitical system,—which he nowhere does, only mentioning religious ritual of any kind in one passage, and that a ritual wholly foreign to Leviticus.[2] As a matter of fact, it is the

[1] London, 1879, vol. i. pp. 264-271. The details given by Brugsch are worth reading. Compare, also, Kellogg, *Abraham, Joseph, and Moses in Egypt*, New York, 1887. Perhaps, however, the most convincing proof of familiarity, on the part of the writer of Genesis, with Egyptian manners and customs is afforded by reading such careful comparisons of the History of Joseph with the facts exhumed by Egyptologists, as is found in Hengstenberg, *Egypt and the Books of Moses*, translated from the German, Edinburgh, 1845, pp. 21-73 (a book not yet obsolete), and in Ebers, *Ægypten und die Bücher Moses*, Leipsic, 1868, pp. 261-353.

[2] Gen. xxxiv. 14.

Non-Elohistic and not the Elohistic sections of Genesis which show intimacy with the Levitical Law. The Priests' Code in Genesis (to use the phrase of Wellhausen) does not know, the Jehovistic document does know, the Levitical Law. If the cases in point are not numerous, they are decisive. For example, it is in the Jehovist, and not the Élohist, that we find the Levitical technicality for a "burnt-offering."[1] Again, it is in the Jehovist alone that the Levitical technicality "clean," as applied to animals, occurs.[2] Yet again, it is in the Jehovist alone that we find the term "plague," used in Leviticus for leprosy, applied to the judgment of God upon Pharaoh.[3] Again, it is the Jehovist who uses frequently the well-known and characteristic Levitical words translated "righteous" and "righteousness"[4]; and it is the Jehovist who uses the striking word used in connection with righteousness, "counted," a word also largely used in Leviticus.[5] Note, too, the quite Levitical use of the word sacrifice (*zevach*) in reference to Jacob.[6] On the theory, then, that Leviticus is due to the time of the Exile, it is necessary to explain how the above technicalities became known to the Non-Elohistic writer, whilst the Elohistic or Priestly writer is silent concerning them. On the theory, on the other hand, that Moses wrote the Law as such, Moses and the Jehovist would be closely identified.

On the whole, therefore, seeing that the evidence as to the late date of the composition of Genesis has failed, it

---

[1] Gen. viii. 20; xxii. 2, 3, 6, 7, 8, 13.   [2] *Ib.* vii. 2, 20.
[3] *Ib.* xii. 17; compare Lev. xiii., xiv.
[4] Gen. vii. 1; xviii. 23, 24, 25, 26, 28; xx. 4; xv. 6; xviii. 19; xxx. 33.
[5] *Ib.* xv. 6; xxxi. 15; xxxviii. 15; l. 20; compare Lev. vii. 18; xvii. 4; xxv. 27, 31, 50, 52; xxvii. 18, 23.
[6] Gen. xxxi. 54; compare *Scriptural Doctrine of Sacrifice*, pp. 479, 480.

may be said that Moses himself wrote the Jehovistic sections of Genesis.

But if Moses was the Jehovist, who was the Elohist? One fact concerning the Elohistic Narrative seems clear, on an inductive study of the available data—the Elohistic sections were written earlier than the Jehovistic. The evidence is as follows:—First, *it is the Jehovist who supplements the Elohist*, and not conversely. For compare the genealogies of the two documents. The Elohist " gives only the *lineal* ancestors of Abraham (v. 1, &c., xi. 10, &c.), and his descendants by Ishmael (xxv. 12, &c.), and Isaac, viz., Edom (xxxvi. 9, &c.), and Israel (xlvi. 8, &c.) ; whereas the Jehovist gives—in addition to the line from Adam through Kain (iv. 16, &c.), and the seventy nations sprung from Noah (x.)— the *collateral* races claiming kindred with Edom and Israel, viz., Moab and Ammon, descended from Lot (xix. 30-38), twelve tribes from Nahor (xxii. 20-24), sixteen from Keturah (xxv. 1-6)." So far Colenso,[1] who adds, " since these last were manifestly intended to *supplement* the former notices, this fact implies that E (the Elohist) wrote before J (the Jehovist)." Or consider the Jehovistic interpolation in the " book of the generations of the seed of Adam, and other interpolations. "The fact that Gen. v. 29 (J) occurs in the midst of E (v. 1-28, 30-32) and vii. 16[b] (J) after 13-16[a] (E), and vii. 20-22 (J) after v. 14-19 (E) and xi. 28 (J or D) after v. 27 (E) *in all which instances J is unintelligible without the data of E*, whereas there are no similar instances of the contrary relation existing between E and J—tends to show that J wrote merely to supplement E."[2] Or

---

[1] *The Pentateuch and Book of Joshua*, part vii., appendix, p. 129.
[2] *Ib.* p. 129.

weigh the latent references of the Jehovistic document to the Elohistic. "In Gen. l. 12 J refers distinctly to xlix. 29-31 (E), in which passage only does Jacob charge his sons about his burial, which they carry out in l. 13 (E), without which verse the whole story limps, since there is no other account of the actual burial of Jacob."[1] Again, in Gen. xlvii. 30 "(J) 'their burial place' refers loosely to the notices in E about the cave of Machpelah having been acquired as a burial-place by Abraham (xxiii. &c.)." Here, again, although the final conclusions of Colenso are not accepted, some of the facts which he so industriously marshalled may be utilized. This variety of evidence, of which only a few examples have been given, seems to prove conclusively the priority of the Elohistic sections.

Secondly, as has just been shown, and as a fuller examination would strongly emphasize, *the religious position of the Elohistic writer in Genesis is much less differentiated than that of the Jehovist.* All the words, and their implications, of the Elohist point to the pre-Sinaitic period; many of the words, and their implications, of the Jehovist point to the post-Sinaitic period.

Summarizing, then, what has been said in this Lecture, our inductive examination of the authorship of Genesis has led us to the following conclusions :—

Firstly: Genesis shows manifest traces of a post-Mosaic revision of its contents, a revision, however, of a very respectful and conservative nature.

Secondly: Genesis received its substantial form from a writer who distinctly prefers the name of Jehovah for the Supreme Being.

[1] *The Pentateuch and Book of Joshua*, part vii., appendix, p. 130.

Thirdly: This Jehovistic writer, in composing his work, utilized the pre-existing materials which had been got together by a previous writer who preferred the name Elohim for Deity.

Fourthly: This Elohistic writer very probably laid earlier sources, both oral and written, under contribution.

Fifthly: There is strong reason for believing that Moses himself was the Jehovistic writer.

And, sixthly: If any one should feel inclined to say that the Elohistic writing was also the work of Moses, I should see no insuperable objections to the statement in the facts manifested in Genesis itself, with one proviso. If Moses were the Elohist as well, he must have penned his Elohistic document at a sufficient time before the events at Sinai to account for the change of literary style, as well as of religious standpoint.

LECTURE V.

THE AUTHORSHIP OF THE LAW.

LECTURE V.

THE AUTHORSHIP OF THE LAW.

GENESIS, then, is not myth, nor legend, nor romance, but history; and history committed as a whole to writing not later than the days of Moses. So the preceding inquiry entitles us to affirm. Straightway a further question arises. If Genesis is historical, if, that is to say, Genesis presents a true narrative of the subjects with which it deals, and may therefore be regarded as an unimpeachable authority upon those subjects,—if Genesis affords fully reliable information upon the Fall and the Deluge, the migrations of Abraham and the life-stories of Isaac and Jacob,—a further question immediately arises, whether Genesis is also a first-class authority when it treats, as it certainly professes to treat, of Divine revelations to man. This further question is vital. Genesis claims to be a veracious record of the early founders of Israel, and its claims have been sustained upon inquiry; but interwoven with this biographical element there is a distinctive supernatural element; is this woof of revelation as strong as the warp of history? In other words, seeing that Genesis may be regarded as a veracious chronicle of the common life of its day, may it also be regarded as a veracious record of words and events transcending the sphere of human intellect and ability? Can a human chronicle of Divine interference be credited? Is it possible to accept the statements of Genesis as facts, not only when they present the non-miraculous data of men and peoples, which are the usual materials of the historian, but also, and as surely, when they concern professed Divine deeds and declared Divine revelations? The question is of supreme importance in any inductive inquiry into the place and purport of the Old Testament.

But this important question is not quite ripe for discussion. As has been seen in the preceding Lecture, it is impossible, in the face of the problems raised by the "Higher Criticism," to make any solid investigation into the *Law as* REVELATION until we have first investigated the *Law as* FACT. The question as to the Divine origin of the Law is complicated by extant theories as to its human origin. Some progress, however, has been made in the needful preliminary study of the Law as Fact, especially as regards the Book of Genesis. Indeed, it was desirable, for several reasons, to confine attention to Genesis for a while. Genesis shows a unity of plan not visible in the four later books of the Law. Genesis is more manifestly the product of one casting, the later books showing a very different mode of composition. Genesis presents, too, a usage of the Divine names of high analytic value, which wholly fails us early in Exodus; consequently the analysis of Genesis has a certainty all its own. Genesis, again, crucial test though it be of all critical processes, has been much neglected by critics of late, a hasty analysis of Genesis having been accepted, on the exigencies of a theory which has left Genesis out of sight, whereas, as a matter of fact, the data offered by Genesis should have rendered this theory itself suspect. For such reasons, Genesis has been selected for the first critical essay. And progress has been facilitated by this prior inquiry. The main conclusions arrived at—that *Genesis is historical*, and that *Genesis was probably written by Moses*—are of great value in our inquiry. Of so high a value are they that it would be possible to proceed at once to the consideration of the Divine element in Genesis. Nevertheless a preferable order of discussion is, to complete the survey of the Higher Criticism of Genesis by a survey of the Higher Criticism of the remaining books of the Law. For, that survey taken, it will be possible to make a great stride, and to treat, not of the Divine element in Genesis only, but of the Divine element in the entire Law. The time spent will be time saved.

Are, then, the four subsequent books of the Law, as well as Genesis, first, historical, and, second, of Mosaic origin?

The questions are not two, but one, it will soon appear. If Exodus and the succeeding books are historical, they must from the nature of their contents have been written contemporaneously with the events they record, that is to say, during the lifetime of Moses; and, on the other hand, if these books were written by Moses, there would be little reason, from an inductive standpoint, for regarding them as other than historical.

The question before us therefore in this Lecture is,— HOW THE FOUR LATER BOOKS OF THE PENTATEUCH WERE WRITTEN.

The starting-point of this new branch of our inductive

inquiry is this. There is a remarkable unity of plan and purpose in the several Books of the Law. Upon this striking unity all are agreed. Critics of all schools sound the praises of the order and march of these books, speaking enthusiastically of their exquisite literary finish, of the studied progress of their narrative, of their strict observance of the unities of place and time and person. But critics are not agreed as to the explanation of this unity. They have reached no unanimous opinion as to how this singleness of purpose, this oneness of plan, this harmony of style, have been attained. Critics are divided as to whether this acknowledged unity is a product of art or of fact. Is the written result, the beauty and force of which all confess, due to genius which simulates history, or to history which baffles genius? This is the question at issue.

Two theories of the origin of the four later books of the Pentateuch are in the field at the moment. These theories may be not inappropriately called the JOURNAL THEORY and the EVOLUTION THEORY.

According to the Journal Theory, Exodus, Leviticus, Numbers, and Deuteronomy—confessedly but divisions made for convenience *of one continuous book*—were written down in the days of Moses, as the events successively occurred,—Moses kept a journal, in fact; and Genesis was deliberately penned as a suitable introduction to this journal. According to the Evolution Theory the entire five books—nay, the entire six books, for Joshua is included, and we hear again and again of the Hexateuch instead of the Pentateuch—were written at intervals during centuries, the final symmetry being imparted by an editor, who, with great skill, made a homogeneous blend of materials not a little heterogeneous. Thus, on the Journal Theory, the unity of the Law is due to the actual consecution of the facts narrated; whereas on the Evolution Theory that unity is due to the literary skill of the editor who gave to the Law its final form.

On the one hand, then, the homogeneity of the Books of the Law is ascribed, by the Journal Theory, to their contemporaneousness with the events recorded. Moses, or some scribe of his, kept a journal. In this view, in addition to serving his own day by his splendid initiatives, Moses (for it is immaterial whether Moses himself wrote the Law or whether a scribe wrote it at his command) served all after-times by preserving an accurate record of his age. What happened in Egypt was written in Egypt; what happened at Sinai was written at Sinai; what happened in the steppes of Moab was written in Moab. Further, this journal had, so to speak, a preface and an epilogue. The preface, our present Genesis, was a history of the Divine dealings with men from the Creation to the death of Joseph, compiled, like the Gospel of Luke, from the records, whether oral or written, of "eye-witnesses and ministers of the word." The epilogue, our present Deuteronomy (with the exception of a few verses at the close narrating the death of Moses), was a report of the final addresses made by Moses to Israel immediately prior to his ascent of Pisgah. This Journal Theory is so simple that it requires but few words in exposition, however many it may need in defence.

On the other hand, however, the homogeneity of the Books of the Law is ascribed, by the Evolution Theory, in a directly opposite manner, not to literal fact, but to literary faculty. The very lateness of their date rendered their several authors the more free to employ what literary faculty they had, with such success, as one of the greatest advocates of the theory avows, that art has "actually been successful, with its movable tabernacle, its wandering camp, and other archaic details," in "concealing the true date of composition."[1] In fact, according to this Evolutionary Theory, as was stated in the preceding Lecture, the present Pentateuch consists of three main portions, viz., the separate work of a Jehovistic writer, say of the time of Uzziah (who utilized earlier materials, written and oral), the work of the Deuteronomist, say of the time of Josiah (who also utilized some earlier materials), and the work of an Elohist, who wrote after the Exile (and who also utilized various writings of others), these three main portions being harmonized and blended by an accomplished editor, who of course completed his work after the return from Exile. On this theory the Law is really a fiction, founded on fact, small in amount, be it added, and legendary in character—a sort of religious novel.

It is desirable to state this theory at a little more length.

The general outline of this Evolutionary Theory runs as follows. The children of Israel once resided in Egypt, and were polytheists. They had previously been fetichists, and worshipped trees and stones. The first step to a purer faith was taken when Moses, who was possibly a monotheist, during a period of wandering in the Sinaitic desert, called the tribal god by the name of Jahveh, or Jehovah, and imparted the Ten Words or the Ten Commandments (in some rudimentary form of words which became the nucleus of the present Deca-

---

[1] Wellhausen, *History of Israel*, pp. 9, 10.

logue), thus "connecting the religious idea with the moral life of the nation." It was in the days of the Judges—largely mythical as the extant accounts evidently are, when the tribes had ceased to be nomads and had become agriculturists—that the second step in religious advance was taken. This ensued upon the rise of that astonishing type of character, the prophetic, which exercised such gigantic influence upon the entire subsequent history of Israel. To tribes disjointed and antagonistic, fighting to the death with the Canaanitish aborigines, the prophets gave the cohesion of monarchy. They also established monotheism; for, by gradual steps, and reiterated teaching during centuries, they succeeded in erecting Jehovah—who had been since the days of Moses simply what Chemosh was to the Moabites, the patron god of the tribe—into the one supreme and only God. The further development of the religion of Israel was the result of the contest of the prophetical with the ecclesiastical order, prophets and priests, in the fell struggle for existence, furthering the survival of the fittest. Indeed, the Pentateuch, or rather the Hexateuch, was the product of both the prophetic and the priestly party in the struggle for power; for neither in the days of David nor of Solomon was there, it is said, any trace either of the elaborate ritual known as Mosaism, or of sacred books embodying that system. It was in the reign of Hezekiah that the prophetic party, the party of pure religion, set themselves to formulate their desires, to ascribe them to Moses, to commit them to writing, and to place them in the Temple, where they were soon after *found* by the high priest, Hilkiah, as we *find* a letter which has been dropped into our letter-box. This prophetic programme—for the most part a rhetorical expansion of two principles, namely, no God but Jehovah, and no worship apart from the Temple—constitutes the larger portion of the Book of Deuteronomy which, read to the king, gave the initiative to Josiah's reformation. Thus commenced, the Evolution theorists maintain, the momentous epoch of subjection to the written law. Not that the snake of idolatry was more than scotched, for the worship of Baal and Ashera continued until the days of the Exile; the formulation of Deuteronomy (in its earliest form) was simply the first draft of that method of attack which finally proved victorious. This first draft was still further elaborated by Ezekiel during the dreary days by the river Chebar, when, fully assured in his own mind of the certainty of speedy return, he drew up "a complete plan for the organization of the new Israel," giving, in the first place, a minute description of a new temple; appending, in the second place, a series of detailed precepts concerning religious worship, the staff of ministrants and the rights and obligations of the prince; and regulating, thirdly, the division of the land. In thus giving utterance to his scheme for the future, Ezekiel, himself a priest as well as a prophet, commenced the committal to writing of the priestly tradition, which had been accumulating for many years. The priests in Babylonia, the kernel and flower of the Jewish nation, followed in his footsteps. A first essay in legislation (remains of which have been preserved to us in Leviticus xxiii.–xxvi.) was speedily followed by others, until a complete system at length arose, set in a historical frame and presented as a restoration of the remote and glorious past. The two leading details of this system were, that the tabernacle, a convenient fiction, occupied the central position of a fictitious camp, and was the only legitimate place of sacrifice; and that a sharp line of demarcation was everywhere drawn between priests and Levites, and consequently between their status and immunities. What wonder, then, it is asked by the Evolutionary theorists, if on the return of the exiles, the ecclesiastical party having an overwhelming advantage in social position and organization, the first duty assumed was to rebuild the temple? What wonder that the hierarchy thenceforth monopolized the first place in the annals of Judaism? And when Ezra took his stand with fourteen priests upon his lofty platform, on that memorable first day of the seventh month, and read the priestly ordinances of this deftly manufactured Book of the Law absolutely for the first time to the assembled and enthusiastic multitude, what wonder if the legalism which had been sown like a grain of mustard-seed in the days of Hezekiah, sprouted into a tree that could shelter a nation? But not even yet was the work of the priesthood complete. The book from which Ezra read cannot have fully met, say the Evolutionary theorists, the state of affairs which he found around him, nor could it have been introduced with effect without the co-operation of the priesthood. An understanding must be arrived at with this ecclesiastical interest, its wishes and advantage must be taken into account, modifications must be made as circumstances required, and, in a word, such measures must be framed and placed on record as were indispensable to the success of the undertaking. This Ezra did at his leisure, and somewhere between the years 458 and 444 B.C., it is said, completed his final redaction of the law. Emendations were made by later hands, but no alterations of moment. With the recension of Ezra the fabric of so-called Mosaism may be regarded as practically completed; thenceforward it was current, substantially under the form of the present Pentateuch, as the Jewish rule of faith and life. Thenceforth Judaism stood before the eyes of the world like its own temple: Moses had first imparted its idea; Samuel and David and Solomon had endowed that idea with a local habitation and a name; Hezekiah and Josiah restored its buried glories; by the rivers of Babylon it had formed the subject of Ezekiel's dreams, and fired the priesthood with enthusiasm; it was rebuilt with more than pristine magnificence in the days of Nehemiah and Ezra, becoming the centre of a people's hopes and the spring of a people's joys; every change throughout its chequered course had been an enlargement, and every period of oblivion a night of growth; and the splendid structure at length complete, if embellishment and restoration may be undertaken at intervals, of vital alteration there will be no trace, for letter has usurped the place of spirit, the written of the oral word, the scribe of the prophet, the Aaronic priest of the priesthood open to every son of the nation.[1]

In short, according to the Evolution Theory of the Origin of the Pentateuch, that remarkable book, however apparently one, is really the natural, if slow, outgrowth of the religious instincts of the Jewish nation, a survival of the fittest, a final victor in a bitter and prolonged struggle for existence. The rubric of Judaism would, on this theory, resemble that of the Vatican, being really the product of the religious conflicts of

---

[1] This outline has been abridged from Kuenen's *Religion of Israel*; upon all the minuter details here presented possibly all Evolutionary theorists might not be agreed.

centuries. According to this theory, Sinai and its Divine Voice are inventions; the Tabernacle, and its propitiatory, and cherubim, are inventions; the association with Moses of any portion of the so-called Mosaic legislation, with the single exceptions of a wavering predilection for monotheism and the germinal moral code which subsequently grew into the Decalogue, is the pious fraud of prophets, the pious fraud of priests.

Such is the Evolution Theory, broadly stated.

It is between these two theories, the one of which makes the Book of the Law largely a Journal, and the other of which makes the Law largely a Fiction written in the interests of a tendency, and between these two theories alone, that the great critical conflict of the present day lies. Less prominent divergences of opinion may be prudently, therefore, omitted from view, whilst attention is concentrated upon the two leading issues.

What is the evidence for the JOURNAL THEORY?

Evidence in favour of the Journal Theory appears in *certain direct statements of the Books under examination.* At very different times in the course of the narrative Moses is described, directly or indirectly, as committing part of his life-story to writing. These express references to a committal to writing have a cumulative character. Thus, almost at the outset of his career as leader, after the discomfiture of Amalek, we read of Moses writing, by Divine command, his experience of the notable event "in a book:" "And the Lord said unto Moses, Write this for a memorial in a book" (the Hebrew reads "in *the* book").[1] Again, on arrival at Sinai Moses perpetuates the covenant by inserting its

[1] Exod. xvii. 14.

details in a book: "And Moses wrote all the words of the Lord,"[1] these words including, at least, the Ten Commandments of the twentieth chapter, and the additional statutes contained in the three following chapters. Yet again, after the long years of wandering, the fact is signalized that Moses made a written record of the various halting-places of the sojourn in the wilderness: "And Moses wrote their goings out according to their journeys by the commandment of the Lord."[2] And yet again, just before his death, Moses is said to have given permanent form to his parting words of reminiscence and prospect by writing them in a book, which is expressly called "the book of the Law," and which he explicitly commanded should be carefully preserved: "And it came to pass, when Moses had made an end of writing the words of this law in a book, until they were finished, that Moses commanded the Levites, which bear the ark of the covenant of the Lord, saying, Take this book of the law, and put it by (or in) the side of the ark of the covenant of the Lord your God," &c.[3] In view of such a series of statements, is it wholly unreasonable to regard Moses, as the Journal theorists do, as having written again and again in one book, rather than in many, especially remembering that a book exists which contains, amongst other things, all the details cited?

Further, *the apparent method of the composition* from Exodus to Deuteronomy largely favours the Journal Theory. This method of composition can be best shown by contrast. In Genesis, be it repeated, we have a book apart, moulded, so to speak, "at one flow" (as the Germans say), showing an elaborate plan formed from the beginning and steadfastly adhered to; whereas in

---

[1] Exod. xxiv. 3-7.   [2] Numb. xxxiii. 2-49.   [3] Deut. xxxi. 24-26.

the remaining four books quite another mode of writing is visible.

Let this contrast between the plan of Genesis and the absence of plan in the subsequent books be emphasized. After an introduction, giving the exquisite account of the seven creative days,[1] Genesis is clearly—I was going to say *frigidly*—divided into ten sections. Indeed, the author goes out of his way, and repeats the history of Creation from another standpoint, in order to complete the tale of ten sections, this number irresistibly reminding us of the Ten Commandments and the Law of Tithe. These ten sections run as follows. The "generations," or *origines*, of the Heaven and the Earth are given;[2] then succeed the generations of Adam,[3] the generations of Noah,[4] the generations of the sons of Noah,[5] the generations of Shem,[6] the generations of Terah,[7] the generations of Ishmael,[8] the generations of Isaac,[9] the generations of Esau,[10] and the generations of Jacob.[11] These ten sections it is next to impossible to miss, for they all commence with the identical formula, "These are the generations of." The arrangement is evident, *and suggests a plan formed prior to writing.*

Now compare with this set and inflexible framework of composition the easy and unstudied flow of Exodus and the books that follow. In them there is no adherence to a mechanical arrangement. The bones cannot be seen. Growth takes place according to an invertebrate pattern. The completed skeleton, so to speak, is not subsequently clothed with the flesh of fact and figure, but member is added to member by a process of

---

[1] Gen. i.–ii. 3. [2] *Ib.* ii. 4–iv. 26. [3] *Ib.* v. 1–vi. 8.
[4] *Ib.* vi. 9–ix. 29. [5] *Ib.* x. 1–xi. 9. [6] *Ib.* xi. 10–26.
[7] *Ib.* xi. 27–xxv. 11. [8] *Ib.* xxv. 12–18. [9] *Ib.* xxv. 19–xxxv. 29.
[10] *Ib.* xxxvi. 1–xxxvii. 1. [11] *Ib.* xxxvii. 2–l. 26.

continuous accretion. The style of writing is that, not of the balanced history, but of the flexible journal. In evidence of this diary-method of construction, let the observant reader note the entire arrangement of material from the beginning, or nearly the beginning, of Exodus to the close of Deuteronomy. Certainly, supposing these books to have been written in journal fashion, they could not have been more vivid or less prescient. Event follows event with no order but that of time. Commands given at one moment are completed soon afterwards. If the narrative is often inexplicable without knowledge of what has gone before, it is never inexplicable for the want of information which is given subsequently; although occasionally, it is true, what one day brings another day explains. Everywhere the objective order of events appears; nowhere the subjective order of author. If a Divine injunction is given in one spot and at one juncture, its record appears in the story of that place and hour. These books, in fact, are no more divisible than a journal. Exodus is not all history: Leviticus is not all law; Numbers has as much legislation as census; Deuteronomy repeats quite as much of the events of the Wilderness as of its laws. The characteristics of a diary appear everywhere. Everywhere law and life, revelation and history, are fused. As we read we are made eye-witnesses of the events in Egypt, law being already interwoven with narrative in the first institution of the Passover.[1] From Egypt we pass to Sinai, the covenant at Sinai being described in full detail, as well as the injunctions given at Sinai concerning the future priesthood and the future place of worship.[2] On the breach of the covenant, by the rebellion and

[1] Exod. xii.–xiii. 16.   [2] *Ib.* xix. 1–xxxi. 18.

idolatry of the people, the covenant is mercifully renewed;[1] and then, in strict accord with the injunctions previously given, the Tabernacle and its furniture, the Priesthood and its attire, are prepared for actual service.[2] Here there occurs a strong point for the Journal Theory. What author writing, after the event, would have inserted the minute and tautologous repetition of the injunctions previously given concerning the Tabernacle and its ministrants, which is found in these last chapters of Exodus? Then immediately follow—although our modern division of books somewhat conceals the immediateness—the laws of the several sacrifices spoken by Jehovah from the newly-erected Mercy-seat.[3] After an interval, in which the ceremonial of the consecration of the priesthood is both ordained and executed (the record of the consecration of the Tabernacle had been given at the close of Exodus), a variety of supplementary laws, also announced by Jehovah from the recently constructed Mercy-seat, is catalogued from chapter to chapter to the close of Leviticus. Then, after all these laws, ceremonial, constitutional, civil, and criminal, have been announced by Jehovah at Sinai, whether in the Mount of Vision or from the Propitiatory of the Tabernacle, preparations are next made, we read, for the departure from the scene of so much express revelation; the tribes are grouped;[4] a few additional laws are given;[5] the offerings of the princes at the Dedication of the Tabernacle are described (as an after-thought, so to speak);[6] yet again additional laws are appended concerning the holy lamps;[7] the Levites are solemnly set apart for their duties;[8] and the

---

[1] Exod. xxxii. 1–xxxiv. 35. [2] *Ib.* xxxv. 1–xl. 38. [3] Lev. i–vii. 38.
[4] Numb. i–iv. 29. [5] *Ib.* v. 1–vi. 27. [6] *Ib.* vii. 1–89.
[7] *Ib.* viii. 1–viii. 4. [8] *Ib.* iiiv. 5–26.

feast of the Passover is renewed.[1] If all this is not the order of fact, it is the order of very clumsy writing. At length the departure from Sinai to Moab takes place, and the several events which happened in the steppes of Moab are chronologically recorded.[2] Various supplementary laws are still given from time to time to meet new emergencies, the rebellion of Korah, for example, giving rise to new laws concerning the priesthood,[3] the injunctions concerning the partition of the Land of Promise generating the laws as to the cities of refuge,[4] the incident as to the daughters of Zelophehad originating a new law of female inheritance.[5] Again passing on, still in the strict order of events, to the last month of the fortieth year of the Exodus, three successive farewell addresses of Moses are recorded,[6] and the last is heard of the great leader—his resignation of headship,[7] his swan-song,[8] the announcement of his death,[9] his dying blessing,[10] whilst as a brief epilogue to the entire preceding narrative, a subsequent hand, perhaps Joshua's, perhaps Samuel's, perhaps Ezra's, has completed the autobiography by the shortest and most colourless statement of the death of Moses.[11] From beginning to end of these four books, numerous circumstantial details, the subtlest transitions, the most improbable if not the most natural characterizations of time, the frankest freedom and the most transparent ease, all give point to the Journal Theory. As has been said, possibly the best argument for the Journal Theory would be a consecutive and attentive reading (at one sitting say, or two),

---

[1] Numb. ix. 1–14. [2] *Ib.* x. 11–xxxvi. 13. [3] *Ib.* xviii. 1–xix. 22.
[4] *Ib.* xxxv. 9–34. [5] *Ib.* xxxvi. 1–15.
[6] Deut. i. 3–iv. 43; iv. 44–xxvi. 19; xxvii. 1–xxx. 20.
[7] *Ib.* xxxi. 1–15. [8] *Ib.* xxxi. 16–xxxii. 47. [9] *Ib.* xxxii. 48–52.
[10] *Ib.* xxxiii. 1–29. [11] *Ib.* xxxiv. 1–12.

from the beginning of Exodus to the close of Deuteronomy. By such a reading the most lively impression of unity and contemporaneousness is produced, which no pedantry can destroy. Facts may so read; romance never. The evidence which can destroy this impression of veracity must be sure indeed. The art that can conceal such art is itself miraculous. Not Defoe, Cervantes, or Swift, has produced anything parallel. The Passage of the Red Sea is told in as straightforward and naked a manner as the journeying from Elim to Rephidim. The Ten Plagues are recorded without a note of exclamation. Divine commands or appearances seem no more to the author than the most commonplace occurrences of the march. On the supposition that a contemporary was writing what his eyes had seen and his ears had heard, this matter-of-fact, this photographic, narration is intelligible. If these Books be imaginative, the product of the genius of long subsequent days, they stand alone in the literature of the world for fictitious naturalness and ideal reality. To tell such marvels in so non-marvelling a manner seems impossible unless the marvels be true.[1] In this instance also the Bible itself is the best reply to attacks upon the Bible.

Further, this Journal Theory does not appear less reasonable upon *minute examination*. Examine, for instance, *the laws concerning the Passover*. Had these laws been written centuries after the Flight from Egypt, in the priestly interest, as the Evolutionary Theory maintains, we should have expected that the Paschal injunctions, attributed to a long-distant past in order that they might awaken the reverence so readily aroused by antiquity, would have been compact, clear,

---

[1] Compare Rogers, *Superhuman Origin of the Bible*, &c., Lecture VI.

readily intelligible, of the easiest possible application, as simple in statement as evident in design. But what are the facts of the case? These laws, as they actually appear, have no air whatever of being afterthoughts— late customs, set in a frame of antique history, for a partisan purpose. These laws assuredly have an air of being pages from a journal. When these Passover laws first appear, they are manifestly adapted to the peculiar condition of an enslaved people, on the eve of liberation.[1] "And the Lord spake unto Moses and Aaron in the land of Egypt saying"—so the passage runs; and all its details befit the land of Egypt, and only the land of Egypt. The lamb is slain by the householder, and not by a priest (as was the case later); the blood was sprinkled on the lintels of the houses, and not on an altar (as was also subsequently the case); the flesh was eaten with loins girt for the march, and staff in hand; the very bread baked cannot be leavened, because the kneading-troughs are bound up with the clothes, ready for hasty departure. Such is the first mention of the Passover. A few months pass, according to the narrative, and we meet with the Passover injunctions again. At Sinai instructions are given concerning the set feasts which are to be observed in the Wilderness, and amongst these Festal Seasons the Passover appears.[2] In this later reference the earlier commands are evidently assumed to be known,—indeed, it is enough to name the Passover without further reference; nevertheless, the entire environment being altered, some changes of detail are made; thus the Passover is the beginning of a seven days' festival, the first day of this Paschal Feast being ordered to be a holy con-

[1] Exod. xii.   [2] Lev. xxiii. 4–8.

vocation, in which no servile work should be done, and the seven days being days in which offerings should be presented by fire. Yet a few months later, whilst the Israelites are still sojourning at Sinai, we again come across the Passover, which was kept "according to all that the Lord commanded Moses." Here again a further commandment is given to meet the needs of a special case which had arisen; for, at this first Passover after leaving Egypt, a disability, a legal disability (which, by the way, implied the previous announcement of uncleanness caused by contact with the dead) [1] stood in the way of the celebration of the Passover by a few men, to whom permission was given to celebrate the feast at a later date.[2] Still reading on in the narrative, and reaching the events which took place whilst the camp was pitched in the plains of Moab, the injunctions concerning the Passover are a third time renewed, whilst minuter instructions for the offerings by fire, mentioned in general terms before, are now delivered.[3] Still reading on, it appears that when the Israelites are about to cross the Jordan, and Moses is reiterating the various Divine laws in the popular hearing, once more, in this fortieth year of the Wanderings, injunctions are given concerning the Passover, largely similar to what had preceded, it is true, and yet differing in one notable particular.[4] Thenceforth the Passover was to be slain and eaten, not in any house or tent, as at first; or by all the people in the immediate proximity of the Tabernacle, as during the years of Wanderings; but only "in the place which the Lord thy God shall choose to put his name in," a well-understood euphemism

---

[1] Numb. v. 2; compare Lev. xxii. 5.   [2] *Ib.* ix. 1-14.
[3] *Ib.* xxviii. 16-25.   [4] Deut. xvi. 1-8.

for the Altar of Burnt-offering in the Tabernacle, the location of which beyond Jordan was not as yet known; in other words, the Passover was not to be observed by all the people, but only by those who could conveniently attend the Tabernacle. Does not such a series of commands, so carefully adjusted to their environment, bear their truth upon their face? Are they not manifestly beyond the invention of any later writers whatever? *Do they not support strongly the Journal Theory?* For, mark *the alternative.* If the Evolution Theory be true, then, according to the predominant form of that theory, the first statement in Exodus as to the origin of the Passover was written amongst the last of all the accounts[1]; further, the brief statement in Leviticus, which assumes the statement in Exodus, was written, a little earlier, by Ezekiel; the statements in Numbers, with their supplementary laws, were written at the same time as the Exodus passage; and, finally, the Deuteronomic version was written before the Exodus version, before the Leviticus version, and before the Numbers versions. No theory can stand before such a series of contradictions. Let any reader carefully compare these several versions of the Paschal Laws, and he will speedily come to the conclusion, without requiring much further evidence, that there is little to be said, after all, for the Evolutionary Theory, and much for the Journal Theory. On the Journal Theory every variation in command is clear; on the Evolution Theory these several variations produce confusion worse confounded.

So much for positive evidence in favour of the Journal Theory.

[1] See Appendix II.

Now let us turn to the rebutting evidence. How hard bestead the Evolution Theory is, when confronted with the Journal Theory, let an extract from one of the most prominent of the Evolution theorists show. Says Dr. Reuss, in his great work on the Bible, evidently impressed by the strength of the Journal Theory: "If the history of the Exodus has been written by Moses himself, and if the legal code, which is framed in this history, has been drawn up by him, we must necessarily admit that we have in all this the Journal of the Prophet, as that theory alone will explain the incoherence of the matters treated therein, and the absence of all systematic order in the innumerable articles of laws, throughout connected with certain localities, or with certain epochs of sojourn in the wilderness." And Dr. Reuss goes on to say—*his words are noteworthy*—" The idea of a journal is especially supported by two facts, without strain. If the narrative is detached from what belongs to the legislation strictly so-called, an almost continuous story is obtained of the life of Moses from his birth to his death, in an order which may be called chronological, and often determined by precise dates. On the other hand, the numerous repetitions and contradictions in the legislative part lose whatever they have in their actual form which embarrasses us; for it would be possible to admit that in a space of time of some length, many an injunction may have been repeatedly inculcated, or even changed according to the necessities of the moment, or because of a more exact appreciation of the means of execution."[1] The points are well put. The wonder is that their cogency did not lead Dr. Reuss to reconsider his position.

[1] *L'Histoire Sainte et la Loi*, pp. 126-128.

However, it is but fair to Dr. Reuss to say that he has simply mentioned the Journal Theory, as he says, lest "he should appear to recognize therein any probative force." And it is also but fair to Dr. Reuss to state upon what evidence he has the temerity to assert that "the hypothesis of a Journal explains nothing at all and itself has no value." All the details, which in Dr. Reuss's view make against the Journal Theory shall be given. These details are of the scantiest.

How, for example, on the Journal Theory, asks Dr. Reuss, can the immense lacuna of thirty-eight years be explained in the narrative, all the facts detailed being concerned with the first two years and the last few months of the Exodus? But how is this lacuna to be explained on the Evolutionary Theory? By a lack of invention? By the comparative unimportance, in the view of the writer, of these intermediate years? If the latter explanation is given, it equally applies to the Journal Theory. Moses suppressed the events of those thirty-eight years because of their comparative unimportance, from his point of view. Be it remembered also that the date of Miriam's death is uncertain.[1]

Then Dr. Reuss objects to the Journal Theory, that, in the beginning of the Journal, reference is made to what happened years afterwards. The point is crucial. But the instances cited in proof are not conclusive. First, the remark is cited, from the first description of the fall of manna, that "the children of Israel did eat the manna forty years, until they came to a land inhabited; they did eat the manna, until they came unto the borders of the land of Canaan."[2] But who, who has

[1] Numb. xx. 1. [2] Exod. xvi. 35.

not a theory to support, will fail, on a close perusal of the context, to see in this remark—what we have seen in Genesis more than once—a later interpolation, whether made by Moses himself or by another? A second instance of anachronism cited concerns the census, which is only made at the first chapter of Numbers, whereas its result is known at the close of Exodus.[1] But what then? The number of the people is inferred in the Exodus from the quantity of silver subscribed and actually employed for the construction of the Tabernacle. Further, should surprise be expressed that the numbers given at that time and at the more deliberate census, taken later, are the same, let it be remembered, first, that *but a few months intervened*, according to the narrative, between the two numberings for tax and for war; and, second, that the earlier census for tax was probably utilized for the later military census. Another instance of anachronism is seen by Dr. Reuss, in the command to the priests to sanctify themselves at Sinai, before a priesthood had been appointed;[2] but is it not a gratuitous assumption that the Israelites had no priests either in Egypt or on leaving Egypt? A parallel instance is cited by Dr. Reuss where a tent is spoken of as the place of the manifestation of the Divine Glory before the Tabernacle was built;[3] but, according to the statement of Exodus, as a matter of fact, prior to the more elaborate Tabernacle, there was a temporary tent, a tabernacle, erected, not within the encampment as the official place of worship was, but afar from the camp, without the camp, this temporary tabernacle being the

---

[1] Exod. xxxviii. 26.   [2] *Ib.* xix. 22.
[3] *Ib.* xxxiii. 7; compare with xxxv., xxxvii. 21, and xl. 2, 17.

scene of Divine revelation:[1] is it not sheer caprice, or worse, to ignore this deliberate statement? Yet again, Dr. Reuss objects that the law of the Sabbath is supposed to be known, prior to its actual promulgation;[2] but is the evidence for a Patriarchal observance of a Sabbath to be so quietly ignored? Dr. Reuss also urges us to compare Exod. xl. 4 with Lev. xxiv. 4, and Numb. xiv. 36 with Numb. xiv. 29 and Deut. ii. 14, and we shall find further anachronisms. In these passages which Dr. Reuss simply mentions, I can see nothing relevant to the issue.

Dr. Reuss's proofs, which, in his view, negative the Journal Theory, have been fully and carefully stated. If this is all the destructive evidence so acute a critic is able to adduce, such evidence cannot even outweigh his own statement of the case for the Journal Theory. Where Reuss has failed, who shall succeed?

Whether, therefore, the Biblical evidence *for* the Journal Theory, or the Biblical evidence thought to be against this theory, be examined, the theory itself has certainly much to commend it.

But it is probable that the advocates of the Evolution Theory of the origin of the Books of the Law rely more upon their constructive than their destructive criticism. They consider their case so strong in itself, that they do not trouble themselves with the case of other people. If the attitude of mind is unwise, it is human. *What, then, is the evidence advanced in favour of the* EVOLUTIONARY THEORY?

The evidence mainly relied upon to-day by the advocates of the Evolution Theory, "The received view of

---

[1] Exod. xxxiii. 7–11.   [2] *Ib.* xvi. 26.

European critical scholarship," as Kuenen says, is of a historical and not a literary kind. Comparatively little is heard of divergencies in phraseology, seeming anachronisms, dual or triple or multiple repetitions of narrative, apparent contradictions, and all the paraphernalia of literary criticism, acquaintance with the method of which has been made in the last Lecture. The conflict concerning authorship has been transferred from the arena of literary to that of historical criticism. In this there is cause for thankfulness. The decisive battle-ground has been at length recognized. By the minutiæ of literary criticism, the most uncertain of weapons, no sure issue was likely to be reached. Wellhausen was quite right when he said, pungently enough it is true and in a different figure, that, in all this by-play of literary criticism, "the firemen never came near the spot where the conflagration raged." And Wellhausen was also right when he added, that "it is only within the region of religious antiquities and dominant religious ideas that the controversy can be brought to a definite issue."[1] A revolution in method has taken place. From the minor and inconclusive questions as to literary expression and style and method, critics have turned of late to the more serious and decisive questions as to the Revealed or Evolutionary character of the Law itself. From form they have turned to matter; from style to contents; from mode to fact. In this there is, as has been said, cause for congratulation. As there is ground for rejoicing when opponents move from outworks of miracle and prophecy and chronology and history, and plant their storming ladders against the character and claims of Jesus, the impregnable fortress

[1] *Prolegomena to the History of Israel*, p. 12.

of the Christian faith; so there is reason for thankfulness when the engines of criticism are removed from subordinate lines of defence, and are turned upon the Moral and Ceremonial Law, the supreme pre-Christian testimony to a Divine interest in human affairs. No critic of Christian convictions will do other than rejoice that the true point of attack and defence has become more evident of recent years. The facts of the Jewish history are more than their literary dress.

This revolution in method was effected by the publication of Wellhausen's *Prolegomena to the History of Israel,* "the first complete and sustained argument," says Robertson Smith, "which took up the question in its historical bearings;"[1] "the crowning fight in the long campaign,"[2] says Kuenen. The several positions of Wellhausen, the acknowledged apostle of the Evolution Theory of the authorship of the Pentateuch, it is desirable to examine. Wellhausen does not, it is true, and it is to be lamented, handle in any direct way the evidence for the revealed character of the Law (he does not concern himself in any way with the arguments which will appear in the next Lecture), nevertheless he does attack, from the historical side, and with much skill, the problem of the evolutionary character of the Law. At any rate, no Old Testament study can have at the present moment any pretension to completeness which leaves Wellhausen out of view.

Wellhausen's positions are as follows: "I start," he says, "from the comparison of the three constituents of the Pentateuch—the Priestly Code, Deuteronomy, and the work of the Jehovist;" for "it is admitted," he continues (he is referring, of course, only to the admissions

---

[1] Wellhausen, *Prolegomena,* p. viii. [2] *Hexateuch,* p. xxxix.

of those who deny the Mosaic authorship of the Law) " that the three constituent elements are separated from each other by wide intervals." It will be remembered that the existence of these three strata in the Pentateuch, in the belief of many scholars, was made evident in the historical survey of Old Testament Criticism, given in the last Lecture. Assuming, then, the existence of these three constituents, or strata—the Priestly Code (Elohist), Deuteronomy, and the work of the Jehovist, Wellhausen proceeds to inquire in what order they were written. This is the problem he desires to solve, the relative order of the component parts of what to-day we call the Five Books of the Law.

The solution of this problem is attempted by Wellhausen by means of a twofold method of comparison. On the one hand, the three constituents themselves are compared, with a view to showing that the order disclosed is always and invariably Jehovist, Deuteronomist, and Priests' Code (Elohist). On the other hand, the three constituents are individually compared with the writings of contemporary prophets and historians, with a view to showing that the legal contents of Deuteronomy are known at the time of Josiah, and not earlier, whereas the legal contents of the Priestly Code are known after the Exile, but not earlier. By means of this twofold method—namely, a comparison of the three constituents with each other, and a comparison of each with an independent standard, Wellhausen claims to have demonstrated the unhistorical character of the Law. The Law, so long called "of Moses," in his contention, really consists, not of a contemporaneous and consistent whole, but of three constituents of very different dates, the latest having been written a thousand years after the death of Moses; these constituents being, first, the work of the Jehovist (a simple history, embodying earlier records scarcely separable to-day, and written " in the period of the kings and prophets which preceded the dissolution of the two Israelite kingdoms by the Assyrians "); secondly, Deuteronomy (an independent law-book, composed about the time of Josiah); and, thirdly, the work of the Elohist (called the Priestly Code, because written in the interests of the priesthood, itself a complete product like the work of the Jehovist, showing at least the hand of the Elohist and of a later editor, the whole of this Priests' Code having been written not earlier than the *closing years of the Babylonian Exile*).

If these contentions are correct, it is manifest that they will demand an entire reconstruction of the Old Testament, and will have a considerable influence upon the formulation of any doctrine of the Inspiration of the Old Testament.

But are these contentions, so radical and so revolutionary, really warranted by the facts? This is an inductive inquiry, and as such is to be conducted without fear or favour, without fear of great names or favour of popular theories; the sole concern being with those conclusions which the facts of the case appear to warrant. Now is it true that nothing is known of the Priestly Code and its characteristic contents, until after the Exile? Is it true that, prior to the Exile, there is no evidence either of a Levitical Tabernacle or of a Temple constructed upon the model of the Levitical Tabernacle? Is it true that the Levitical sacrifices as such, at once so rounded in ritual and so complete in function, are not to be met with before the Exile, their technique being as unknown as their atoning idea? The critical contest has been transferred from the language to the theology of the Old Testament ; and upon that theological ground the battle must be fought. Is it, therefore, contrary to the facts available that the Law was revealed to Moses ? This is the real point at issue. If this main contention be shown to be inconsistent with the facts of the Old Testament, minor curiosities of exegesis and minor theological theories may be left out of sight. Whether, for example, the several Feasts of Judaism were evolved from Harvest Festivals, or whether the sacrificial cultus of later days was a purely natural evolution from patriarchal and universal usage, being largely affected by the political centralization of worship at Jerusalem, both of which theories Wellhausen holds, are points comparatively unimportant in our inquiry. *The important point is, whether the Law said to be divinely given to Moses was so given, or whether the Law was only given at intervals during a thousand years.*

Did then the Law, the Levitical Law, the Law proper, the Law concerning the sacred Tabernacle and its ministrants, services, and festivals—what Wellhausen calls the Priestly Code—*come by Moses or by Ezra ?* Reply is not uncertain. One branch of evidence settles the question. *From the days of Moses onwards, the Books of the Old Testament bear witness to the prior existence of the Ceremonial Laws*, the so-called Priestly Code (supposed by the Evolutionary theorists to have first taken form in the days of the Exile). The evidence is fairly full, and entirely conclusive. Let the evidence be outlined.

In the Book of Joshua we are certainly confronted by the entire Levitical system. At the outset of the book, Moses being said to be dead, Joshua is appointed by

Jehovah as leader, in words as weighty as memorable. "Only be strong and very courageous, to observe to do according to all *the law which Moses* my servant commanded thee; turn not from it to the right hand or to the left, that thou mayest have good success whithersoever thou goest." And the injunction continues: "This book of the law shall not depart out of thy mouth, but thou shalt meditate therein day and night, that thou mayest observe to do according to all that is written therein."[1] How much more is meant by this Book of the Law than the Ten Commandments (which the Evolutionary theorists concede to be the Law of Moses), the subsequent narrative shows. Joshua is said to "have read all the words of the Law, the blessing and the curse, according to all that is written in the Book of the Law; there was not a word of all that Moses commanded which Joshua read not."[2] Can all this be nothing but a laboured reference to the Ten Commandments? Further, this Book of Joshua, as a matter of fact, manifests an unmistakeable familiarity with significant details of the Levitical legislation, supposed by the Evolutionary theorists to belong to the age of the Babylonian Exile. Wherein, for example, lay the stress and point of the ceremonial at the passage of the Jordan? Was it not in the presence of the ark—"the ark of the covenant," "the ark of the testimony," "the ark of Jehovah," phrases so familiar in the so-called Priestly Code, and in the presence of the priestly attendants of the ark, who performed their religious functions in true Levitical fashion?[3] In such a scene, in fact, are we not "en pleine Leviticisme"? to use the phrase of Reuss. And

---

[1] Josh. i. 7, 8; compare vers. 1-11.
[2] *Ib.* viii. 34, 35.   [3] *Ib.* iii. and iv.

are we not also "in full Leviticism" at the environment of Jericho, with its priests and ark and rams' horns?[1] And a little later on, a noteworthy technicality, occurring in connection with the destruction of Jericho, recalls a characteristic formula of the so-called Priestly Code: "The city shall be devoted," we read, or should read, "the city shall be *cherem*." What is the signification of this *cherem*? A thing was *cherem* which was sacrificed, given to God, made the Lord's portion, "devoted" to Divine uses, whether of destruction or consecration. "Every *devoted* thing is most holy unto the Lord," says the Priests' Code.[2] "No *devoted* thing that a man shall devote unto the Lord of all that he hath, whether of man or beast or of the field of his possession, shall be sold or redeemed: . . . none *devoted* which shall be devoted of men, shall be ransomed, he shall surely be put to death," the same passage continues. And the same technicality is known to Deuteronomy: "Of the cities of these peoples, which the Lord thy God giveth thee for an inheritance, thou shalt save alive nothing that breatheth, but thou shalt *devote* them, the Hittite and the Amorite, the Canaanite and the Perizzite, the Hivite and the Jebusite."[3] Similarly Jericho was to be "devoted," sacrificed, presented as a whole burnt-offering before Jehovah, and the technicality plunges us into full Leviticism.[4] Further, it was in the personal appropriation of what had been "devoted," in other words it was in the utilization for his own selfish ends of what had been wholly given to God, that Achan's sin consisted.[5] If it was a small matter to appropriate spoil, it was a glaring offence to appropriate spoil consecrated to Divine pur-

[1] Josh. vi. [2] Lev. xxvii. 28, 29. [3] Deut. xx. 16, 17.
[4] Compare Appendix II. [5] Josh. vii.

poses. By express statement the trespass committed by Achan was in the *devoted* thing : " Achan ... took of the *devoted* thing " (unfortunately translated *accursed* in the Authorized Version). What follows? Does not this— that the Book of Joshua knows a characteristic technicality of the so-called Priestly Code? Nay, will not the Evolutionary theorists see that, in this Jehovistic section written, as they say, not later than the eighth century B.C., a characteristic technicality of the Priestly Code appears, written, they suppose, in the fifth century? Another suggestive instance of deliberate reference in Joshua to the prior existence of the so-called Priestly Code, an instance none the less conclusive that it is somewhat subtle, occurs in connection with the division of the land by the great warrior-leader when he was "old and stricken in years." "Only unto the tribe of Levi," we read, "he gave none inheritance."[1] Why? "The offerings of the Lord, the God of Israel, made by fire, are his inheritance, *as he spake unto him ;* " a fact also expressed thus: "The Lord God of Israel was their inheritance, *as he said unto them ;* "[2] and also thus : " the priesthood of the Lord is their inheritance."[3] Now when did Jehovah say that the offerings by fire, and He himself, and His priesthood, were the inheritance of Levi? Is not the reference manifestly—the agreement in sentiment even extends to the words used—to the words in Deuteronomy: "The priests, the Levites, and all the tribe of Levi, shall have no portion nor inheritance with Israel, they shall eat the offerings of the Lord made by fire, and his inheritance, and they shall have no inheritance among their brethren, the Lord is their inheritance, *as he hath spoken unto them.*"[4] Joshua thus refers to

[1] Josh. xiii. 14. [2] *Ib.* xiii. 33. [3] *Ib.* xviii. 7. [4] Deut. xviii. 1, 2.

Deuteronomy. But, as the closing words of the passage show, Deuteronomy in turn refers to a prior Divine utterance. Where, then, is this prior utterance made? Does not Deuteronomy clearly refer back to Numbers: "And the Lord spake unto Aaron, and I, behold, have given thee the charge of mine heave-offerings, even all the hallowed things of the children of Israel, unto thee have I given them, by reason of the anointing, and to thy sons, as a due for ever; this shall be thine of the most holy things, reserved from the fire; every oblation of theirs, even every meal-offering of theirs, and every sin-offering of theirs, and every trespass-offering of theirs, which they shall render unto me, shall be most holy for thee and thy sons.... I have given them unto thee, and to thy sons and thy daughters with thee, as a due for ever;" and the passage goes on to include amongst these dues all firstfruits, "the fat of the oil, and the fat of the vintage, and of the corn," and all things "devoted," and all the first-born, or their commutation money, and all the tithe.[1] Joshua then refers back to Deuteronomy, and Deuteronomy to Numbers. But, further, who will regard this passage in Numbers as self-explanatory? Is not this passage manifestly a rapid summary of many details, injunctions concerning which are only to be gathered from a large part of Leviticus, its laws of offerings and its hints as to manipulation? Have we not, then, in such a series of related passages, one of those test cases which substantiate so marvellously the traditional theory of the authorship of the Hexateuch? On the traditional theory all is clear; Joshua refers to the earlier Deuteronomy, Deuteronomy quotes an earlier passage in Numbers, Numbers implies the yet earlier laws em-

[1] Numb. xviii. 8–32.

bodied in Leviticus. But, on the Evolutionary theory, what shall be said? A passage in Joshua, written, as the theory contends,[1] not later than the eighth century before Christ, is only explicable by a passage in Deuteronomy written in the seventh century, as the theory also contends, and this seventh-century passage in turn is only explicable by a passage written by the Elohist in the fifth century, summarizing many other passages written in the fifth century. After such an instance, surely it is scarcely needful to add further examples from the Book of Joshua, although they abound. The Book of Joshua shows us the splendid dawn of the Mosaic Era still unclouded. And the close connection between the Book of Joshua and the five preceding books of the Old Testament, the Evolutionary theorists themselves allow. So Law-like indeed is the Book of Joshua that the Evolutionary theorists of the origin of the Old Testament, contrary to the entire traditional evidence, and on theoretical grounds, have asserted that this book is but a sixth book of the Law, the last book of the Hexateuch as they like to express themselves, receiving its main composition and its final form from a writer who flourished after the Babylonian Exile. Thus, in his attempts to show "discrepancy between the traditional view of the Pentateuch and the plain statements of the historical books and the prophets," Professor Robertson Smith says explicitly: "I exclude the Book of Joshua." For why? "Because it in all its parts hangs closely together with the Pentateuch,"[2] an exclusion which looks singularly like shelving, from the exigency of theory, an awkward series of facts, which renders the

[1] Compare Appendix II.
[2] *Old Testament in Jewish Church*, p. 218.

theory suspect. Further, let any careful critic investigate scientifically and inductively, that is to say fully, dispassionately, and without bias, the literary and historical character of the Book of Joshua, and he will soon be constrained to acknowledge that such a book could never have been written, without miracle, at the late date the Evolutionary theorists assign to it. A true literary instinct will see that such episodes, for example, as that of the Gibeonite ambassadors with their old sacks and old wine bottles,[1] and such minutiæ as the names of the kings of Canaan [2] (both supposed to be part of the Jehovistic writings), or such details as the cities of Judah,[3] and the cities of the other tribes,[4] supposed to be part of the Priestly Code, could not have been invented or even compiled in any other age than that of Joshua himself; that, in short, they bear on their face the clearest evidence of synchronism with the times of which they speak. The Book of Joshua, as the Evolutionary theorists confess—and the admission will one day bear unexpected fruit—cannot be cited in illustration of the "discrepancy between the traditional view of the Pentateuch and the plain statements of the Historical Books."

But while the Levitical tone of much of the Book of Joshua is not denied—only the attractiveness of the Evolutionary Theory, however, concealing the importance of the admission—the Book of Judges and the later historical and prophetical books are said to be absolutely silent as to the existence of the Levitical Law. "The leaders of the nation," it has been categorically said of the days of the Judges, "divinely appointed deliverers like Gideon and Jephthah, who were zealous in Jehovah's cause, were as far from the Pentateuchal

[1] Josh. ix. 3-15.   [2] *Ib.* xii. 9-24.   [3] *Ib.* xv. 20-62.   [4] *Ib.* xviii.-xxi.

standard of righteousness as the mass of the people, . . . the whole religion of the times of the Judges was Levitically false."[1] So it has been alleged. But this being an inductive inquiry, we ask, where, and what, is the evidence for such a statement? The evidence proffered is of three kinds.[2] First, it is said, "breaches of the Law were not confined to times of rebellion against Jehovah." Secondly, it is asserted, the "divinely chosen leaders knew not the Law," seeing that they sacrificed at other places than the central sanctuary. Thirdly, it is also said, that at "Shiloh itself, the central sanctuary, the ritual observed was not according to the Levitical Law." The relevance of this evidence is not apparent. That the days of the Judges, when compared with the Levitical legislation, were days of irregular religious performance, the Book of Judges itself declares beyond dispute; but that the Levitical legislation was *known*, though poorly practised, this same book also places beyond dispute. It is possible that over some advocates of the traditional theory of authorship, who have over-hastily regarded the Levitical ceremonial as constantly practised in all its details when once the Law was given, the Evolutionary Theorists find victory easy; but we are no more concerned with the Traditional than the Evolutionary theory as such. What we are asking is, What theory the facts of the case appear to warrant? And what the facts appear to warrant is, that in the days of the Judges the Levitical legislation was well known, but largely ignored.

That the Levitical legislation was largely ignored, let the summary the book itself gives of its times be witness: "And the children of Israel did that which was evil in

[1] *Old Testament in Jewish Church*, pp. 220, 225. [2] *Ib.* pp. 255-258.

the sight of the Lord, and served the Baalim ; and they forsook the Lord, the God of their fathers, which brought them out of the land of Egypt. . . . And the anger of the Lord was kindled against Israel. . . . Whithersoever they went out, the hand of the Lord was against them for evil, as the Lord had spoken and as the Lord had sworn unto them,"—it would solve much to ask—*where?* —" And the Lord raised up judges. . . . And yet they hearkened not unto their judges; they turned aside quickly out of the way wherein their fathers walked, obeying the commandments of the Lord." [1]

On the other hand—scanty as is the evidence on the one side as on the other—that the Levitical legislation, in other words, that the so-called Priestly Code was known, the following facts conclusively show. Note the Nazirite vow of Samson. For how is this vow of Samson, who was to be *nezir elohim*—consecrated, separated, to God—from his birth, intelligible apart from the Levitical legislation belonging to the supposed Priestly Code of Ezra's day, be it observed. It was the Priestly Code which had ordained as a Divine command: "Speak unto the children of Israel, and say unto them, when either man or woman shall make a special vow, the vow of a Nazirite (of a *nazir*, or consecrated man), to consecrate himself to the Lord, he shall separate himself from wine and strong drink; he shall drink no fermented wine, or fermented strong drink, neither shall he drink any liquor of grapes, nor eat fresh grapes or dried ; all the days of his Naziriteship (or consecration), there shall no razor come upon his head ; until the days be fulfilled in the which he separateth himself unto the

[1] Judg. ii. 10-23. The whole passage should be carefully read and weighed.

Lord, he shall be holy," &c., &c.[1] Manoah's wife, again, after her husband has offered a sacrifice under conditions which are not strictly Levitical, uses nevertheless a technicality for the sacrifice, not found as such in pre-Mosaic times, but occurring frequently in the Levitical legislation; for, with perfect Levitical exactness Manoah's wife speaks of "a burnt-offering and a meal-offering."[2] In this connection, too, attention may be fittingly called to another sacrificial technicality, where we read that "All the children of Israel, and all the people went up, and came unto Beth-el, and wept, and sat there before the Lord, and fasted that day until even; and they offered *burnt-offerings and peace-offerings* before the Lord";[3] "peace-offering" is a technicality peculiarly Levitical. Again, let the injunction to Manoah's wife to "eat not any unclean thing"[4] be observed, for the idea of uncleanness of food is another notion peculiarly Levitical. And yet again, does not the expression of Micah, "Now know I that the Lord will do me good, seeing I have a Levite to my priest," imply a knowledge of an express Levitical priesthood, a limited priesthood, a feature so eminently characteristic of the Levitical legislation?[5] On the whole, therefore, as far as the Book of Judges is concerned—whilst it should be frankly admitted by both sides in

---

[1] Numb. vi. 1–21.

[2] *Olah uminchah*, Judg. xiii. 23; compare, *e.g.*, Exod. xxx. 9; Lev. xxiii. 37; Josh. xxii. 23. *Minchah*, it is true, does occur in Genesis, in the narrative of Abel's sacrifice, but there the usage is distinctly different to the usage here, and there, too, as the Evolution theorists allege, we have the product of a writer of the fifth century before Christ.

[3] Judg. xx. 26 and xxi. 4; compare Lev. iii. 1, &c.

[4] Judg. xiii. 4; compare Lev. xi., &c. The injunctions of Deut. xiv. are manifestly reiterations of Lev. xi.

[5] Judg. xvii. 13.

this controversy that decisive evidence either way is of the slightest—what evidence there is, is not in favour of the Evolutionary Theory.

Fatiguing as is the examination of these numerous quotations, their importance should neutralize their tedium. These quotations really afford the best possible means of testing any theory of the authorship of the Books of the Law. Indeed, if these quotations have weight, they preclude the necessity of minute examination of any hypothesis which contradicts them, however fascinating, brilliant, or recommended. Two main theories, be it remembered, are before us for adjudication. The one regards the several Books of the Law as substantially contemporaneous and uniform; the other regards these books as heterogeneous in composition, and widely divergent as to date of constituents. It is this latter theory which we are at present investigating, the theory which has been named for convenience, the Evolutionary Theory of the Origin of the Pentateuch. And this Evolutionary Theory we are examining rather indirectly than directly. We are submitting the theory to the crucial test of Old Testament quotation. Large parts of the Pentateuch, according to this Evolutionary Theory, especially the legal portions of the Book, were not written until the days of Ezra, or a little before, so it is said. Manifestly therefore the important question is, whether there is any evidence of quotation from the legal portions of the Pentateuch, thus attributed to the days of Ezra, in books written before Ezra's days. If characteristic features of supposed post-Exilic laws are quoted in pre-Exilic books, the date assigned by the Evolutionary Theorists to the Priest's Code must be incorrect. As for the theory itself, it will be time enough to examine its several points, when it has come unscathed through this furnace of trial. If the Evolutionary Theory cannot stand this test, it would be time wasted to trouble oneself with the theory further. From the Book of Judges, therefore—the evidence of which, if it be of any weight, makes against the Evolutionary Theory—we now advance to the remaining pre-Exilic books.

Passing, then, to the history of the times of Samuel, Saul, and David, here and there very distinct evidence is afforded of the prior knowledge of characteristic portions of the Law, attributed by the Evolutionary Theorists to the days of the Babylonian Exile or later. There do exist, it is true, in the Books of Samuel and of Kings, many abuses of the Law as judged by a strict Levitical standard, but the question is whether forgetfulness of the Law necessarily argues non-existence. The facts of the case can alone decide. Irregular, for example, when judged by the Levitical standard, as is the cultus at Shiloh,[1] it is, notwithstanding, difficult to see how such a worship originated, unless as a perversion of a ritual once Levitical. Three hundred years of degeneration from the days of Moses might well, in such times as those of the Judges, have wrought many a change of procedure? The wonder is that the cultus at Shiloh remained at all, not that it survived in an altered form. A religion which has ceased to be enthusiastic has entered upon decadence. It should cause little surprise, therefore, that illegal irregularities occur in the affecting story of Hannah and her infant son, whereas any touches whatever of a purely legal kind, characteristic of the so-called Priestly Code, should straightway

[1] 1 Sam. i. 24.

fix our attention. Now the salient features of the ceremonial at Shiloh are decidedly Levitical. There is an acknowledged centre of religious life; there is an acknowledged chief priest, of the family of Aaron; Hannah's thank-offering observes the legal form, and consisting as it did of a bullock of three years' old (for so the true reading appears to be) shows how the grateful recipient of blessings could find an outlet for special thankfulness in a large, but still legal, gift, in a valuable bullock rather than in almost valueless doves. If the fatty portions of this thank-offering should have been presented, according to the Levitical form, by fire, by omitting this legality the sons of Eli are expressly stated to "sin"[1]: "They knew not the Lord, nor the due of the priests from the people,"[2] where the word "knew" is manifestly equivalent to "did not heed." The whole context implies that there were legal dues which they might demand, whereas by preference they made claims which were illegal. Indeed, wherein lay the "sin" of these young priests? Was it not in causing the people to "abhor" the offering of the Lord? And how came the people to abhor the divine offering? Was it not because in demanding part of the festal offering *after it was cooked*, these venal priests were contravening a familiar command of the Levitical law, which only permitted a share in the offering, the wave breast and the heave-shoulder, *before* it was returned to the sacrificer that he might make merry with his friends? The anxiety, too, shown by the sacrificer that the fat should be burnt, pointed to the great characteristic in the ritual procedure with peace-offerings, ordained in Leviticus, according to which, not the entire animal was burnt, but

[1] 1 Sam. ii. 17.   [2] *Ib.* ii. 12.

only the separable portions of fat.¹ Was not little Samuel's ephod, again, an express imitation of the Levitical ephod for the priesthood? And does not the reference to the women "who did service at the door of the tent of meeting"² recall the cursory reference in the so-called Elohistic, and therefore by supposition the last written, portion of Exodus,³ to "the women which assembled to minister at the door of the tent of meeting," and who gave their brass mirrors to make the Brazen Laver for the Court of the Tabernacle? When, too, the official duties of Eli are said to be "to offer upon mine altar, to burn incense, to wear an ephod before me,"⁴ all this strictly harmonizes with the provisions of the Levitical legislation, according to which only the priest could wear an ephod,⁵ or offer sacrifice,⁶ in both functions acting as the deputy of the high priest,⁷ and according to which only the high priest could burn incense.⁸ The phrase, again, "the offerings of the children of Israel made by fire"⁹ is peculiarly Levitical. Lastly, this long list of Leviticisms in the Hannah episode may be brought to a close by noting that there also occurs there the express Levitical technicality for the Tabernacle—the Tabernacle of Assembly—the Tent of Meeting—the *ohel mo'ed*¹⁰—the *Fixed* Tent. So strong an evidence of the prior existence of the legal portions of Exodus and Leviticus is this Fixed Tent, that Wellhausen¹¹ feels it necessary to discredit the verse

---

[1] 1 Sam. ii. 22.
[2] Compare Lev. iii. and vii. 11-36, and *Scriptural Doctrine of Sacrifice*, p. 78.
[3] Exod. xxxix. 8.   [4] 1 Sam. ii. 18.   [5] Lev. vii. 1-8.
[6] *Scriptural Doctrine of Sacrifice*, p. 70.
[7] *Ib.* pp. 93-95.   [8] Exod. xxx. 7, 8, 34-38.   [9] 1 Sam. ii. 28.
[10] 1 Sam. ii. 23: compare Exod. xxix. 18, 25, 41, and frequently in Leviticus.   [11] Wellhausen, *History of Israel*, transl., p. 41.

by saying that "from its contents it is suspicious." But are all the previous Leviticisms we have discovered to be adjudged "suspicious" too? Will they not rather render the theory of Wellhausen suspicious? The whole ritual of Shiloh, despite aberration from Levitical orthodoxy, is so manifestly dependent upon the Levitical legislation, that it is difficult to believe that the former preceded the latter by centuries. So cogent is the evidence, that, to rebut it, the Evolutionary theorists will have to treat this part of the First Book of Samuel as they treat the Book of Joshua; they will have to maintain that the First Book of Samuel too was written in the days of Ezra.

Further, throughout the Books of Samuel, evidences are frequent of a knowledge of the provisions of the Law. Thus, in the revelation to young Samuel, it is said that the iniquity of Eli's house shall not be "atoned with blood-sacrifice nor bloodless sacrifice for ever,"[1] where in the words "atone" and "blood and bloodless sacrifice" eminently Levitical technicalities are employed, the former being the express Levitical term for the forgiveness of sin,[2] and the latter being compounded of two express Levitical terms for the two legal classes of sacrifices, bloodless and bloody.[3] Again, in the phrase "the ark of the covenant of the Lord of Hosts which dwelleth between the cherubim,"[4] who can refuse to see a reference to the ark of Exodus, with its mercy-seat and overshadowing cloud and attendant angels;[5] and such a reference would argue a prior existence of

---

[1] 1 Sam. iii. 14.
[2] *Scriptural Doctrine of Sacrifice*, pp. 482, 486.
[3] *Ib.* pp. 479, 480.
[4] 1 Sam. iv. 4.   [5] Exod. xxxvii. 1–9.

the so-called Priests' Code? And who will hesitate, upon mature consideration, to associate the trespass-offering (*asham*), which the Philistines returned of with the ark,[1] with the peculiarly Levitical sacrifice restitution, though, be it remembered, this technicality only occurs in what is called the Priestly Code? Let, too, the strictly Levitical usage of the words "burnt-offerings and festal offerings,"[2] in the same Philistine episode, be remarked; the kine of the cart, which carried the ark back, were offered as a burnt-offering, and subsequently, in their adoration and joy, festal offerings were offered by the men of Beth-Shemesh. Indeed this exact adherence to Levitical terminology is characteristic of the First Book of Samuel, witness such phrases as these: "sacrificed sacrifices of peace-offerings" (more literally—"slaughtered peace-offerings"[3]), "burnt-offerings and festal offerings,"[4]—"the fat of rams,"[5] in all which we see a ritualistic language evidently moulded on the terminology of the so-called Priestly Code. When, too, after the Battle of Bethaven, it is said that the people sinned against Jehovah "in that they eat with the blood," it is an important query to ask where the statute lies which determined this sin. It does not lie in the first draft of statutes which alone are regarded by the Evolutionary theorists as Mosaic in origin if not in writing; but the statute is found in both Deuteronomy and Leviticus; the former written, say these theorists, in the days of Josiah, and the latter in those of Ezra, neither of which dates helps us much in account-

---

[1] Sam. vi. 3, 4; compare Lev. v. 6, &c. [2] 1 Sam. vi. 3, 14.
[3] *Ib.* xi. 15; compare Lev. xvii. 5.
[4] 1 Sam. xv. 22; compare *Scriptural Doctrine of Sacrifice*, p. 480.
[5] 1 Sam. xv. 22.

ing for what is attributed to the days of Saul.[1] Again, when we read of "the shew-bread that was taken from before the Lord, to put hot bread in the day when it was taken away," is there no reference to the "shew-bread" of Exodus, and to the "bread" of Leviticus, "set in two rows, six in a row, upon the pure table before the Lord . . . every Sabbath set in order continually," "holy bread" as Abimelech calls this bread, "most holy" as Leviticus describes it?[2] Surely the evidence is conclusive: the First Book of Samuel displays a somewhat minute acquaintance with the characteristic terminology of the Priests' Code.

The Second Book of Samuel shows a similar minute acquaintance with the Levitical system. This its sixth, seventh, and last chapters are sufficient to prove. Let the last chapter be considered. Much difficulty, for example, of a moral and religious kind has been made by many because of the severity of the punishment visited upon David for his census. But wherein lay the sin of the census? Was it not that the census was taken for the glory of man and not for the praise of God? Nay, does not the sin of David really resolve itself into a dereliction of Levitical duty? An express command had been given concerning every act of numbering, which David sinned in ignoring. "And the Lord spake unto Moses," runs the Priests' Code, "saying, When thou takest the sum of the children of Israel, according to those that are numbered of them, then shall they give every man a ransom for his soul unto the Lord, when thou numbered them, that there be *no plague among them*

---

[1] 1 Sam. xiv. 32-34; compare Lev. iii. 17, vii. 26, xvii. 10, xix. 26; Deut. xii. 16, 23, 24.
[2] 1 Sam. xxi. 1-7; compare Exod. xxv. 30; Lev. xxiv. 5-9.

when thou numberest them."[1] If such a command was known to David, a command which constituted the people the servants of a heavenly, not the soldiers of an earthly king, then David sinned against light. How speedy his own sense of wrong-doing was is manifest. Unless such a command was given prior to David's time, this incident of the census must remain a serious problem for all who know of it. If such a command was known at that time, part of the Priestly Code was also known.

In the face of such evidence as has been produced, is it not the merest superficiality to declare that the Books of Samuel know nothing of the Levitical laws?[2]

Further, that the Levitical system played a large part in moulding the life of the Jewish nation long prior to the days of Ezra, one would have thought that the Psalms of David afforded sufficient evidence. Taking, for instance, those Psalms expressly ascribed to David, there is abundant proof of the existence of just such an ecclesiastical system as is depicted in the so-called Priestly Code of the Evolutionary theorists. Whole pages might be filled with the minute features of the Law which are incessantly appearing, whilst undesigned coincidences innumerable suggest that the Levitical Law was at once the source and the stimulus of all the genuine religious life of the people. The Tabernacle of Jehovah, with its ministrants, sacrifices, and feasts, forms the unvarying background for all the play of spiritual emotion, with this result, that what is the express testimony of the Nineteenth Psalm may be taken as the latent testimony of the entire Davidic

---

[1] Exod. xxx. 11–16.
[2] Robertson Smith, *Old Testament in Jewish Church*, pp. 258–262.

cycle: "The law of Jehovah is perfect, restoring the soul; the testimony of Jehovah is sure, making wise the simple; the statutes of Jehovah are right, rejoicing the heart; the commandment of Jehovah is pure, enlightening the eyes; the judgments of Jehovah are true, righteous altogether: more to be desired are they than gold, yea, than much fine gold, sweeter also than honey and the droppings of the honey-comb; moreover, thy servant is enlightened by them, and in keeping of them there is great reward." The Fortieth Psalm alludes to *burnt-offerings* and *sin-offerings*, and indeed employs the common sacrificial classification which was framed, at an early date apparently, to summarize *the whole round* of Levitical offerings (bloody and bloodless offerings). In the Fiftieth Psalm, with dramatic force, Jehovah is represented as commanding His angels "to gather His beloved—those that have *made a covenant by blood-sacrifice*." A similar technicality occurs in the Twenty-seventh Psalm, where David tells how, when he has come to the one legal place of sacrifice and worship, he will offer "in His TABERNACLE *jubilant thank-offerings*"; whilst in the picturesque liturgy contained in the Twentieth Psalm, David puts into the mouth of the congregation led by the Levites the expressive prayer: "Jehovah hear thee in the day of distress, the name of the God of Jacob defend thee, send thee help from the *holy place*, and uphold thee out of Zion, remember all thy *bloodless offerings*, and regard thy BURNT-OFFERINGS AS FAT," a phrase with a history which plunges us at once into the regulations of the Priestly Code. Or analyse the Fifty-first Psalm, and the same result follows. As surely as it paints a vivid remorse, it also calls up a picture of the Levitical salvation, and, it may be added, of that soteriology alone. There is a sense of outlawry throughout such as only the Law could create. The sin bemoaned is no error *bishgagah*, or *without deliberate intent*, which a sin-offering might expiate, but wilful, egregious, violent, presumptuous, and *beyond the atonement of the constituted Levitical sacrifices*. For so awful a sin no sacrificial atonement was provided; from so great a sinner no sacrifice whatever was acceptable. A clean heart is a Divine gift to be implored, not a ritual exculpation to be purchased. The Psalmist knows himself an alien from the commonwealth of Israel, and therefore, "Create in me a clean heart, O God," is his significant prayer. "Thou delightest not in blood sacrifice" in such cases as mine; "restore unto me the joy of Thy salvation." Yet is there no hopelessness. The writer looks through rites to doctrines. He believes in a possible Divine detergent; and as faith in almighty compassion grows stronger, he is able to rejoice in that renewal of favour which can once more transform *burnt-offerings* and *holocausts* into *righteous sacrifices*. To a close student of the Levitical plan of salvation, in short, this gem of the Penitential Psalms is as luminous from what is latent as from what appears. And let this further fact be attentively considered. In the so-called Priests' Code there is a somewhat minute terminology for the Tabernacle and its several divisions. In the Psalms *expressly ascribed to David*, and discredited by no internal evidence, that terminology is repeated again and again. If the Priests' Code speaks of *bayith* or House of God, *ohel* or Tabernacle, *mishkan* or Habitation, *miqdash* or Sanctuary, and that in various combinations, the Davidic Psalms employ the same technicalities at sundry times and in divers manners. The divisions of the Tabernacle, so characteristic of the Priests' Code, are also reproduced, and David recognizes his place in the "*great congregation*," the restriction of his sacrifice to the "*altar of burnt-offering*," and the nearer revelation of Deity confined to the *Holy Place*, or, as he says, with more accuracy still, to the "*Holy Places*." In short, the references in the Psalms to those parts of the Pentateuch regarded by the Evolutionary theorists as of the latest date are numberless.

What, then, do the Evolutionary theorists make of this testimony of the Davidic Psalms to the prior existence of their so-called Priests' Code? It is instructive to observe what their procedure is. Two courses are open. They may surrender *either* their theory *or* the Davidic authorship of the Psalms expressly ascribed to David. They prefer to relinquish the Davidic authorship, and to say that no single Psalm in the Psalter is of David's time, nay, that the probability is that these profoundly Davidic Psalms are all later in date than the Babylonian Exile. Is not this an astounding conclusion to arrive at on theoretical grounds? For, be it remembered that the superscriptions of the Psalms, many of which attribute certain Psalms to David,—unlike the analytical headings of our Authorized Version, which are intentionally so printed as to show that they form no part of the original text,—are part and parcel of the primary Hebrew text. Is not the temerity great which thus desires to emendate an original text? Is not the temerity remarkable, for example, which would put aside altogether the superscription of the Fifty-first Psalm, because, forsooth, its sense of sin is "contrary to the *naïveté* of antiquity." Surely, to the end of time, sanctified and cultured common-sense, which is truest criticism, as it reads that penitential outcry, will picture the suppliant king, alone in that most terrible, if most blessed, of all solitudes, alone with God, and will also picture him, as thought grows calmer, and conscience more potent, as the touching parable of the ewe-lamb and his own passionate condemnation of wrong-doing are more and more self-appropriated, telling his hard-won experience of sin and shame and contrition and forgiveness to his harp, and through his harp to the world. A theory is hard bestead which requires so to accommodate facts.

Let the foregoing examination of the testimony of the historical books of the Old Testament suffice for our purpose. Two conclusions have appeared in process. One conclusion is that the Evolutionary Theory is contradicted by a manifest fact. According to this theory the larger part of the legal portions of the Pentateuch was not written until the time of the Babylonian Exile, whereas, as a matter of fact the characteristic terminology of these legal portions is found in Joshua, Judges, the Books of Samuel, and the Books of Kings, centuries prior to the date of the Exile. A second conclusion is, that the exigencies of the Evolutionary Theory necessitate a large change of opinion concerning the books of Scripture. The Evolutionary Theory makes great demands upon its advocates. It requires, for example, the denial of the Davidic authorship of the Psalms attributed by the original Hebrew text to David; it also requires belief in the unhistorical character of Joshua; it also requires the acceptance of the view that the ascription of Deuteronomy to Moses by Deuteronomy itself, is a literary expedient; it requires, in short, belief in the complicity of the holy men of old in a series of pious frauds in authorship extending from the days of Moses to those of Ezra. A theory should have the most certain proof which calls for such changes of view.

From a comparison of the Historical Books with the Levitical Legislation, let us now pass to a comparison of the Prophetical Books proper with the same Priestly Code. For the Prophets prior to Ezra know nothing, say the Evolutionary theorists, of the Priestly Code.

"The account of prophecy given by the prophets themselves involves," we are told, "a whole theory of religion." But "the theory," we are also told, "moves in an altogether different plane from the Levitical ordinances, and in no sense can it be viewed as a spiritual commentary on them."[1] Further, those who maintain the traditional theory as to the date of the Levitical legislation are determined to do so, the same writer says, "at any cost," seeing that "the prophets before Ezekiel have no concern with the law of ritual." In short, so far from the Prophets continuing the work of the Law, as has been commonly held, the Evolutionary contention is that "the Law continues the work of the prophets." "Great part of the Law was not yet known to the prophets as God's word."[2]

The contention is startling. But is it true? Is it true that the Prophets did not know the Levitical legislation, did not know that part of the Law which has been called, by the Evolutionary theorists, the Priest's Code? Let a careful and inductive study of the writings of the prophets decide.

The problem is this,—to inquire whether the prophetical writers prior to the Exilian period show any acquaintance whatever with the Levitical legislation.

[1] *Old Testament in Jewish Church*, p. 285.   [2] *Ib.*, pp. 288-306.

The reply is not doubtful. Isaiah certainly knew the Levitical legislation and Deuteronomy; so did Jeremiah; so did Zephaniah, Haggai, and Micah; so did Amos and Hosea.

The works of the two last, of Amos and Hosea, shall be selected for close examination. They shall be selected because of their acknowledged early dates. By common consent both flourished before the time assigned by the Evolutionary theorists to Deuteronomy, to say nothing of the time of the so-called Priests' Code. Amos lived in the eighth century before Christ, according to his own statement in the days of Jeroboam the Second of Israel, the contemporary of Uzziah of Judah; in other words, Amos lived more than a century before Josiah, in whose reign Deuteronomy is supposed to have been written, and about two centuries before the Exile, when those parts of Exodus, Leviticus, and Numbers, which form the so-called Priestly Code, are supposed to have been written. Hosea belonged to the same age. Further, both Amos and Hosea concern themselves with the affairs of the Northern Kingdom, where confessedly adherence to the Levitical Law had ceased with the disruption at the death of Solomon. If these two prophets show any acquaintance whatever with the Levitical legislation as found in the Priests' Code, the positions of the Evolutionary theorists fall to the ground.

That Amos knew the Levitical legislation is certain. Amos addressed himself to the condition of religious affairs in Northern Israel. There, it is true, during the days of the Divided Empire, "Jehovah was worshipped in many sanctuaries, and in forms full of irregularity from the standpoint of the Pentateuch;" there, it is also true, "were images of Jehovah under the form of a calf or steer in Bethel and Dan, and probably elsewhere;" but there, it is not true, that "these sanctuaries and their worship were viewed" by the prophet Amos "as the fixed and normal provision for the maintenance of living relations between Israel and Jehovah."[1] Does not the prophet Amos, taking his firm stand upon the Divine origin of the Levitical legislation, persistently represent the ritual of Dan and Bethel and Gilgal as wilful sin which must meet in due time with woful and merited punishment? "Hear ye and testify against the House of Jacob, saith the Lord God, the God of Hosts," runs the Divine message to him, says Amos; "for in the days that I shall visit the transgression of Israel upon him, I will also visit the altars of Bethel,[2] and the horns of the altar shall be cut off and fall to the ground." And this message to Israel is otherwise expressed by Amos thus: "Bethel shall become vanity,"[3] and thus "the high-places of Isaac shall be desolate, and the sanctuaries of Israel shall be laid waste;"[4] and thus "I saw the Lord standing upon the altar, and he said, Smite the chapiters that the thresholds may shake; and break them in pieces on the head of all of them."[5] Does all this sound like Divine toleration of the altars of Bethel? Does it not imply as pronounced a Divine anger against these illegal altars in the days of Jeroboam the Second as in the days of Jeroboam the First? What recognition is there here of these northern sanctuaries as the legal " provision for the maintenance of living relations between Israel and Jehovah"? These northern sanctuaries are, in the view of Amos, glaring instances of

---

[1] *Old Testament in Jewish Church*, pp. 225, 226.
[2] Amos iii. 13, 14.   [3] *Ib.* v. 5.   [4] *Ib.* vii. 9.   [5] Amos ix. 1.

rebellion against the Lord, and are denounced accordingly.

The fact is that Amos makes even popular acquaintance with the Levitical legislation the ground of his appeals to the Ten Tribes. The prophet desires to convince the subjects of the Northern Kingdom that they sin against light because they sin against known law. The following passage is an excellent illustration of this method of appeal. "Come to Bethel, and transgress," the passage reads in the Revised Version; "to Gilgal, and multiply transgression; and bring your sacrifices every morning, and your tithes every three days: and offer a sacrifice of thanksgiving of that which is leavened, and proclaim freewill offerings and publish them; for this liketh you, O House of Israel, saith the Lord."[1] Yet more closely rendered, the passage would run thus: "Go to Bethel, sin at Gilgal, multiply sin; and bring your festal offerings every morning, your tithes every three days; and offer by fire a thank-offering with leaven, and proclaim the freewill offerings (you make), publish them abroad, for this are ye fond of doing, O ye children of Israel." Of course the passage is ironical. But the significant feature of the irony is—*it turns upon the contrast between the habitual worship of the Northern Kingdom and the provisions of the Levitical legislation, assumed to be commonly known.* To worship at Gilgal or Bethel is sin, to the prophet, because the worship contravenes the Levitical legislation: festal offerings are unwelcome, not in themselves, but because they are presented in a manner which is contrary to the Levitical legislation: tithes, in themselves good, are abuses when offered differently to the instructions of the

[1] Amos iv. 4 5.

Levitical legislation: thank-offerings and voluntary offerings, also in themselves good, are really wicked because offered, in the one case with leaven, and in the other case with publicity, both details of mode contrary to express commands of the Levitical legislation. Suppose the relative provisions of the Levitical legislation to be familiarly known, and the rebuke is as pertinent as striking: suppose those provisions to be neither born nor thought of, and the edge of the reproof is blunt. It is necessary to read between the lines of the denunciation to see its full force, and it is the Levitical legislation which alone enables us to read between the lines. A sound paraphrase would run somewhat as follows: "GO TO BETHEL, SIN AT GILGAL, MULTIPLY SIN," *you who have received the express Divine injunction to worship at that one altar alone where the Lord hath set His name.*[1] [In this instance the command, a knowledge of which is implied, is given in Deuteronomy, but the date ascribed by the Evolutionary theorists to Deuteronomy is posterior to Amos.] "BRING YOUR FESTAL OFFERINGS EVERY MORNING," *and slay for your own festive enjoyment at an idolatrous altar the beasts which should form the daily burnt-offering at the altar of Jehovah.*[2] [Here the injunction, a knowledge of which is implied, is part of the so-called Priests' Code.] "YOUR TITHES AFTER THREE DAYS." *Jehovah has bidden you give tithes every three years, but you, in the unhallowed profusion of your idolatrous reverence, and in your eagerness to sin, bring your tithes after three days.*[3] [Here again the latent command which gives point is Deuteronomic, but,

---

[1] Deut. xii. 26, 27.
[2] Exod. xxix. 38-43; Lev. vii. 1-4; Numb. xxviii. 2-8.
[3] Deut. xxvi. 12.

by hypothesis, posterior to Amos.] "AND OFFER BY FIRE A THANK-OFFERING WITH LEAVEN" *in deliberate transgression of the express commands, on the one hand, to put all leaven away from bloodless sacrifice,*[1] *and, on the other hand, to place altogether in the background leavened bread when a thank-offering was made.*[2] [The laws concerning leaven are peculiarly Levitical, being mentioned, it is true, in Deuteronomy,[3] but only in connection with the Passover.] *And those voluntary offerings which you need not give unless you like, but which when given receive their value very largely from their secrecy and free will, give them ostentatiously to your idols:* " PUBLISH THEM, PROCLAIM THEM, FOR THIS YOU LOVE TO DO, O HOUSE OF ISRAEL." [The mention of freewill offerings—Amos gives here the technical term for such—is only met with (in the Pentateuch) in Deuteronomy, in the chapters in Leviticus attributed by the Evolutionary theorists to Ezekiel, and in the Priests' Code.] In this passage, then, a careful exposition finds a whole string of references to the legal portions of the Books of the Law,—Deuteronomic references before Deuteronomy was written (if the Evolutionary theorists are correct in their dates), Ezekielic references before Ezekiel, Levitical references a couple of centuries before the Priests' Code was framed. That Deuteronomy and the Priests' Code existed in the time of Amos, whatever the Evolutionary theorists say, is thus evident.

A similar conclusion follows upon the examination of another crucial passage in Amos. "I hate," Amos represents Jehovah as saying, "I despise your feasts, and I will not smell in your solemn assemblies: yea, though ye offer me your burnt-offerings and your meal-

---

[1] Lev. ii. 11. [2] *Ib.* vii. 12. [3] Deut. xvi. 3, 4.

offerings, I will not accept them, neither will I regard the peace-offerings of your fatlings (or *possibly* fatted calves). . . . Did ye bring me bloody and bloodless sacrifices (the whole round of sacrifice, that is) in the wilderness forty years, O House of Israel? Now ye shall take up Siccuth, your king, and Chiun, your images, the star of your god which ye made for yourselves, and I will cause you to go into captivity beyond Damascus, saith Jehovah, the God of Hosts is his name."[1] Now if there are many difficulties in the interpretation of the local references in the latter part of this passage, these difficulties do not in any way interfere with the interpretation of the facts which concern us. Amos uses here a series of technicalities which belong to the legal system of the Pentateuch. That legal system was not written even in outline in the days of Amos, say the Evolutionary theorists, and yet Amos is acquainted with these unwritten laws. The Evolutionary theorists cannot, therefore, but be wrong in their contention. The whole terminology of this passage is Levitical. Let the facts of the case decide. The Hebrew word for "feast" cannot be regarded as decisive, seeing that it occurs in what are called the Jehovistic sections of the Pentateuch; but other words are decisive. The Hebrew term, translated "solemn assembly," a rare term, is only found, in the Books of the Law, in Deuteronomy, in the chapters of Leviticus ascribed to Ezekiel, and in a part of Numbers attributed to the Priests' Code.[2] Further, the Hebrew words for "burnt-offerings," "meal-offerings," "peace-offerings," "blood-sacrifices," "bloodless-sacrifices," are all legal terms (of which the

[1] Amos v. 21-27.
[2] Compare Lev. xxiii. 36; Numb. xxix. 35; Deut. xvi. 8.

term translated "meal-offering" and "bloodless-offering" is never found in Deuteronomy, is never found from the beginning of Exodus to the close of Numbers in Jehovistic sections, is only found twice in the parts of Leviticus ascribed by the Evolutionists to Ezekiel, and is found in the so-called Priests' Code more than ninety times). Further, does not the meaning of the passage bear out the idea of a previous knowledge by Amos of the Levitical system? For what does the passage convey? Is not its gist this—a declaration that the day of atonement was past? The round of sacrifice had been instituted in the mercy of God, and borne with for forty years in the Wilderness, despite the stubbornness of the people; there had been great long-suffering ever since; but the idolatry and disobedience of Israel had been so persistent that Divine punishment was at length, after centuries of forbearance, about to fall; the sinful nation were now about to go into captivity, carrying their favourite, but helpless gods with them. The religious life of the Wilderness, which Israel would not have, henceforth it should not have. Does not the whole point of the appeal turn upon the near withdrawal, because of the long misuse, of the privileges conferred upon Israel by the Levitical system? The Ten Tribes have deliberately preferred idolatry to the law of Jehovah; the idolatry, says Amos, shall receive its due meed of Divine displeasure, and the law of Jehovah shall no longer be a possible mode of worship. At least, such an interpretation of this difficult passage does no strain to text or context.

That Amos, therefore, had a tolerable acquaintance with the Levitical legislation seems evident after the preceding examination; and Hosea, it would appear, had a like knowledge. The task of Hosea, who also addressed himself to the Northern Kingdom, was, it is true, rather to denounce the actual idolatry of Israel than to emphasize the ideal cultus which Israel had neglected. "Israel is joined to idols, let him alone," was the burden of his message. Those who forsook Jehovah for idols, it was his mission to proclaim, should lose their idols at Jehovah's hand. "The children of Israel shall abide many days without king, and without prince, and without blood-sacrifice, and without pillar, and without ephod, and without teraphim,"[1] the agents and instruments of idolatry (not the agents and instruments of a lawful worship, as some expositors have very superficially declared). Nevertheless, even in the statement of the impending doom of idolatrous Israel, Hosea uses terms which are Levitical; for Hosea declares the Divine determination to "cause all" the "mirth" of Israel "to cease, her feasts, her new moons, and her sabbaths and her set times,"[2] where all the terms used are technicalities of the Levitical legislation, and where the term translated "*set* times" is the word so frequently employed for the Tabernacle, the "*set* tent."

Again, according to Hosea, the front of Israel's offending is that they "have transgressed the covenant of Jehovah and rebelled against his law."[3] What is this Law of Jehovah? The question grows yet more weighty when another passage of Hosea's is considered, where he writes: "Because Ephraim hath multiplied altars to sin," says Jehovah, "altars have been unto him to sin: I wrote for him *the ten thousand things of my law*, but they are counted as a strange thing: as for the blood-sacrifices of My offerings, they sacrifice flesh and eat

[1] Hosea iv. 17.   [2] *Ib.* ii. 1.   [3] *Ib.* viii. 1.

it, but Jehovah accepteth them not; now will he remember their iniquity and visit their sins; they shall return to Egypt."[1] Are we not in such words again, to use Reuss's phrase, *en pleine Léviticisme* ? For what law has Jehovah written of "ten thousand precepts" other than the complete Levitical law? Would it not be an impossible exaggeration to speak of the Ten Commandments and the precepts of the twenty-first to the twenty-third chapters of Exodus (which, according to the Evolutionary theorists, alone existed in Hosea's days), as the "ten thousand precepts" of the Law? Even if the word which is rightly translated "law" be translated "instruction," as the Evolutionary theorists have felt themselves constrained to demand, contrary to the whole traditional evidence of meaning and usage, where, upon this view, were "the ten thousand" precepts of Jehovah's "instruction" WRITTEN for Israel's guidance? Must not the reference be to the legal portions of the Pentateuch, including the Priests' Code? Further, did not Israel's "sin" in the multiplication of altars lie in the contravention of the Levitical commands as to the centralization of ritual? Further, with respect to the Divine objection that "as for thy blood-sacrifices of My offerings," the Children of Israel "sacrifice flesh and eat it," does not the force of the criticism lie here, that the common practice of idolaters was to slay all their sacrifices in the groves and eat them, whereas the practice enjoined by the Levitical Law was to slay and offer in worship of Jehovah, and only exceptionally to eat, the burnt-offerings being wholly given to God, the sin and trespass offerings being wholly given to God and His priests, and the exceptional festal offerings being them-

[1] Hosea viii. 11-14.

selves also first given to God and then partially consumed by the offerers? Further, is there no emphasis placed upon the return to Egypt? Is not the stress of the reference this; that Israel having come forth from Egypt with the Divine help that they might receive the sacrificial religion given at Sinai, Israel shall be sent back, by Divine arrangement, to a parallel Egyptian bondage, because Israel has exchanged that Sinaitic worship for the altars of Bethel? Surely, if the prior existence of the Levitical Law be not conceded, the entire passage is robbed of its significance.

Or let another passage of Hosea's be examined. "Ephraim shall return," Hosea says, "to Egypt, and they shall eat unclean food in Assyria: they shall not pour out wine to Jehovah, neither shall their blood-sacrifices be pleasing to Him; (their blood-sacrifices) shall be unto them as the bread of mourners; all that eat thereof shall be polluted; for their bread shall be for themselves; it shall not come into the House of Jehovah. What will ye do in the day of the set time, and in the day of the feast of Jehovah?"[1] Here again we have Levitical terminology throughout. This is evident on the most superficial reading. For instance, where apart from the so-called Priests' Code in Leviticus, and apart from Deuteronomy, will any explanation be found of the common legal terms, "unclean," "unclean food"? A reference to the related page of a Hebrew Concordance would show once for all that the Evolutionary theorists cannot be correct here. It is true that the term is met with in Ezekiel, but surely no Evolutionist even will think that Hosea wrote subsequently to Ezekiel. Again, what explanation which is not due to the so-called

[1] Hosea ix. 3-5.

Priests' Code, can be given of the curious expression that the sacrifices of Israel are as "the food," the "polluted" food of mourners, food that should not "come into the House of Jehovah"? Is not the only tenable meaning of the words this, that the offerings of Israel shall be unto Jehovah as the offerings of those who mourn the dead, and who are, by their proximity to death, unclean, and as such cut off from religious privileges? The Priests' Code enables us to give a meaning to the singular phraseology as forcible as clear. According to the Levitical legislation the bread of the mourner, and the mourner himself, and his whole environment were polluted, and therefore interdicted from approach to God or use in Divine worship; "whosoever toucheth the dead body of any man that is dead, and purgeth not from sin, defileth the dwelling-place of Jehovah, and that soul shall be cut off from Israel; his uncleanness is yet upon him;"[1] "the soul that eateth of the flesh . . . that pertains unto Jehovah, having his uncleanness upon him, even that soul shall be cut off from his people."[2] This is the usage from which Hosea derives his figure of speech. The punishment of Israel shall be, that "in the day of set time and in the day of the feast of Jehovah" when Jehovah would usually be approached in joyous offerings, then Israel shall be debarred from entrance into the courts of the Lord's House, the reason of this prohibition being that Israel is "unclean" in the eyes of Jehovah, unclean from association with sin and death. If this interpretation be correct, conclusive proof is given that Hosea was familiar with the so-called Priests' Code, that part of the Pentateuch ascribed by the Evolutionary theorists to a

[1] Numb. xix. 11-20. [2] Lev. vii. 20.

date a couple of centuries later than Hosea. There are also other Levitical references in Hosea, as to the Feast of Tabernacles,[1] and to the legal technicalities, "ransom" and "redeem."[2]

Surely the evidence from prophecy is conclusive. For, on the testimony of Amos and Hosea, it has been shown that the Levitical legislation, supposed by the Evolutionary theorists to have been outlined in the days of Josiah, and matured in those of the Babylonian Exile, was certainly known at an earlier date. Nor is it needful for our purpose to accumulate instances from other Old Testament writers, that the Prophetical parts of the Old Testament written prior to the Exile show familiar acquaintance with the legislation formulated in Exodus, Leviticus, and Numbers, although such instances are very numerous. From the evidence already given, it seems certain that characteristic details of that part of the Pentateuch called the Priests' Code were known in Israel and Judah long prior to the Exile.

The conclusion arrived at, therefore, after this critical examination of the Evolutionary Theory, is this—that, taken on its own ground, and judged according to its own methods, this theory falls to pieces. A series of crucial instances has shown that the Evolutionary Theory of the origin of the Pentateuch fails to account for the facts presented by the Old Testament.

Thus, after an inductive and patient inquiry into the facts, which alone should decide the questions of authorship and date at issue, we are entitled to affirm that the Journal Theory, in spite of attack, still holds its ground There is, as has been seen, strong positive evidence in

[1] Hosea xii. 9.   [2] *Ib.* xiii. 15.

its favour. At the same time the evidence advanced for the rival theory loses its cohesion on close investigation. Hence, we infer that the Pentateuch, as it itself affirms, and as the Jewish and Christian Churches have ever affirmed, was written during the lifetime of Moses.

And immediately the conclusion as to the probable Mosaic authorship has been reached, a host of minute touches, which cannot but proceed, it would appear, from a contemporary writer, come crowding upon the attention of the inquirer. Surely the details of the Tabernacle must have emanated from an eye-witness. Fiction would be stranger than fact if so circumstantial and detailed a structure was imagined and not described. That the Temple might be the basis of an imaginary Tabernacle is conceivable so long as generalities only are regarded, but that all the variety of adaptation actually narrated should have been pure imagination passes the bounds of what conception can frame. Should the general plan of the Tabernacle, with its divisions into Court, and Holy Place, and Holiest, not have verisimilitude, a sense of truthfulness grows as the minute character of the descriptions given are considered. Not only have we exact dimensions, but colours, shapes, materials, ornaments, articles of furniture, are exactly described. We have, so to speak, full working plans. We can reproduce the rods upon which the curtains of the Court hung, and the rings by which they were suspended. We can draw accurately the copper uprights with their silver-plated capitals and their copper sockets, their brass pegs and their taut ropes, even to the specific peculiarities of these uprights when adapted to stand at the corners. Four express and diverse coverings, to some extent incapable of being utilized elsewhere, and at other times, are explicitly named and described. Every piece of tapestry, every column, every species of ornament, every method of juncture, every variation of material, is most carefully recorded, after the manner of an eye-witness. There is not an utensil employed which is not delineated with sufficient accuracy for its reproduction. The names of the workmen employed are given. Most careful arrangements are made for transport. Every part of the sacred structure is expressly made to be movable: the tent could be readily taken to pieces and readily reconstructed; every utensil, from the ark to the laver, had rings and poles to facilitate its carriage. If all these details were imagined by a writer of the Exile, the realism of the most realistic of modern novels is outdone. The same line of observation might be illustrated from the details given of the priesthood and of the ritual enjoined for sacrifice. There is no hint anywhere of its being impossible for any member of the congregation to offer sacrifice at the door of the Tabernacle. The priests are always Aaron and his sons. It is Moses and Aaron to whom all the Divine commands are given. Breaches in observance, and their lamentable consequences, are ascribed to Nadab and Abihu by name. It is possible for Aaron and his sons to go rapidly without the camp. Certain sacrifices are ordered to be eaten by "all the males among the children of Aaron." The points of priestly ritual at the altar will not suit the altar of burnt-offering in its later form in Solomon's Temple. And so on, and so on. When realism has inspired another Zenophon to write such an Anabasis, with materials purely imaginative, it has worked a miracle.

Undoubtedly there is much that is attractive in

the Evolutionary Theory of the Pentateuch ; it so harmonizes with much of modern thought. Then, too, the genius of its advocates has given to the theory an added charm. So has its boldness. What, but the truth of their case, one naturally asks, could lead men and scholars, so to run counter to cherished convictions as to affirm—that Moses occupies a position inferior to Solon —that the references of Jesus to Moses and his words are extravagant—that the statements of Paul as to the origin and influence of the Law but display the credulity of their age—that the use of the names of Moses and Aaron as the recipients of a Divine revelation resolves itself into a not unparalleled literary trick—that the Law and the Mishna virtually belong to the same epoch —that the Divine operation in Israelitish history is simply an instance of the ordinary action of Providence misinterpreted—and that the salient features of Old Testament history illustrate nothing more than a natural evolution, unless it be that they also illustrate the myth-making propensities of man. Such being some of the affirmations which the Evolutionary theorist is compelled to make, it seems difficult to understand that he should make them except from the most assured and well-grounded belief that they are truth. Let it also be frankly allowed that the Evolutionary theorists have taught us much. They have enabled all students of the Old Testament to see that the prophets played a larger and more prominent part than has commonly been suspected in the religious life of Israel, indeed, that the influence of the prophets was as great as their heroism and singleness of purpose. They have opened the way to a more realistic presentation of Jewish history, its intellectual conflicts, its carnal victories, the ceaseless battle between the good and the bad, the religious and the formalistic, the liberal and the conservative, and the ultimate success of the right, and the true, and the free. These theorists have brought to light many an archæological detail; they have solved many an exegetical enigma. They have laid all students of Scripture under deep obligation, by their patient, and long-continued, and minute investigation. Last, and not least, they have been instrumental in recalling attention to the Old Testament, which it was becoming a fashion to treat as unimportant. Honour, therefore, to whom honour is due. But they have conferred benefit by their incidental labours, not by their main theory. They have appealed to the "higher criticism," and the probability is that the futility of their great hypothesis will be demonstrated on their own ground. The Mosaic authorship of the Pentateuch has much besides tradition to stand on. Indeed, let the claims of the Journal Theory of authorship and of the Evolutionary Theory be carefully weighed, and it is highly probable that the preponderance of evidence will be found on the side of the Journal Theory.

LECTURE VI.

THE DIVINE ORIGIN OF THE LAW.

LECTURE VI.

THE DIVINE ORIGIN OF THE LAW.

THE goal of our inductive inquiry into the Books of the Law lies before us. Hitherto our investigations, inevitable if long, have been preliminary. They have but prepared the way for examining whether or not the Pentateuch may be regarded as a revelation from God, and if it may be so regarded, in what sense and by what right. Not that the contents of this Lecture have not their own probative force, even if the Lecture stood alone. The Divine side of the Pentateuch very largely speaks for itself. Nevertheless there is a manifest advantage in following the course laid down. That the Five Books of the Law are, in a very real sense, a revelation from God, is a conclusion more certainly attainable after the preceding discussion.

For convenience, let the previous lines of our inquiry be rapidly retraced. The question presented at the outset for examination was—the Divine Origin of the Law. We set ourselves to inquire, by inductive process, whether the first Five Books of the Old Testament were the product of human art, or of Divine revelation, or of both. But on the threshold of this important, this decisive, study, we were met by the problem, whether the Book of Genesis and the four subsequent books narrated fact or fiction, whether, as we should say to-day, they formed a history of religion or a religious story. That these Books of the Law are really history, fact and not fiction, a fourfold line of induction has led us to infer. First, the collateral testimony of ethnic tradition has shown the historicity of the earlier, and, as many have thought, the more imaginative chapters of Genesis. Secondly, the collateral and highly significant testimony of science has emphasized the historical truth of the same earlier chapters. Thirdly, strong grounds have been seen for believing that Genesis was of high antiquity, having been penned not later than the days of Moses by an author who had access to, and utilized wisely, reliable sources of history. And, fourthly, excellent grounds have also been seen for believing that, although all his writings were very probably slightly re-touched by later hands, Moses himself was the responsible composer, not simply of Genesis, but of the five books commonly associated with his name. More briefly—compressing these four reasons into two—the historicity of the Law, and therefore its veracity appears, first from the truth of its contents, and, second, from its large contemporaneousness with the events described.

Of course, corroborations of so antique a record are only to be expected here and there; nevertheless we have seen that, wherever there are points of contact between the accounts of the Pentateuch and profane history or physical science, the truth of these accounts is confirmed in a very remarkable manner. These ancient books have shown themselves eminently reliable in matters of common knowledge. Modern research has afforded an altogether unexceptionable testimony to the minute and detailed truth of these early sacred books.

If the Books of the Law are credible *as* HISTORY, are they also credible *as a* HISTORY OF REVELATION? This is the crucial question which now confronts us. By revelation is meant the supernatural communication of truth, in other words, *knowledge of Divine and human things divinely imparted.*

On the mere statement of the question some, from speculative bias, will refuse to advance further. Revelation, as so defined, supernatural revelation, is impossible, they will say. Revelation, in the sense of a flash of natural insight, or in the sense of the initiation of the tyro into truth by the expert, or revelation in any sense which does not postulate supernatural interposition, of this they will concede both the possibility and the need. But supernatural revelation, revelation which is miraculous, revelation which presupposes the intervention of Deity in mundane affairs, they will hold themselves excused *a priori* from inquiring into.

Even *a priori* it would surely be legitimate to reply that the Theist—he who is not a Theist must be approached in a different manner to that adopted in these Lectures—must believe that revelation is, first, within the power of God to bestow, and, secondly, within the faculty of man to receive. Upon the former point there can be little doubt: God, being God, can surely reveal Himself if He will. Nor can there be much doubt upon the latter point. Surely man, being man, and being able to receive truth from his fellow-men, can also receive truth from the Creator of men, who, knowing what is in man, can adapt this Divine teaching to human faculties of reception. Further, as a citizen of two worlds, of the material world and the spiritual, man possesses, by his very organization, the needful faculties for receiving impressions from both worlds.[1]

Such a reply might be made *a priori*. But from the standpoint assumed, it is unnecessary to examine philosophical objections either against miracles in general, or against that specific form of miracle which is called revelation. The Inductive Method does not admit axiomatic statements as to possibility or impossibility. This is an inductive inquiry. It is characteristic of the inductive method that speculation may supply provisional hypotheses, but nothing more. Now so long as the impossibility of revelation is regarded as a working hypothesis to be still further tested, reason is found rather for continuing than ceasing inquiry. Our proper task is to ask, not whether revelation is abstractly possible, but whether revelation has actually occurred. For us the question is a question of fact, not of speculation. If evidence is forthcoming of the fact of revelation, speculative difficulties will have to shift for themselves as best they can. To the King of Siam, as the story goes, ice was an impossibility, for ice was an incredibility; he could argue learnedly upon the folly of believing in the solidification of water; but show the king ice, or give him reliable testimony of the existence of ice, and his speculative difficulties rapidly adjusted or despatched themselves. Similarly, not a bad method of dealing with speculative difficulties concerning the reality of a supernatural revelation, is to produce such revelation, to produce truth which it is manifestly beyond the faculties of man as such to attain. If it can

[1] Compare Macaire, *Introduction à la Théologie Orthodoxe, traduit par un Russe*, Paris, 1857, pp. 53-63.

be shown that revelations have actually been given, practical men will leave speculation as to the possibility or impossibility of revelation to afford gymnastic exercise for philosophers and debating clubs. One instance of supernatural revelation has been seen in the narrative of Creation, as has been shown at length in the Third Lecture.

That God has verily revealed Himself to man again and again, and in increasing measure, is the express testimony of the Books of the Law. Those books abound with phrases like these: "Jehovah said unto Abraham," "Jehovah said unto Moses," "And Jehovah said unto Aaron," "And Jehovah called unto Moses, and said unto him," "And Jehovah said unto Moses and unto Aaron," "And Jehovah said unto Moses and unto Eleazar, the son of Aaron the priest." In these books God is said to reveal Himself in history, and in law, and in life, and is also said to accredit His revelations by miracle. The cardinal question, therefore, is, whether these assertions are true. Can these putative revelations be explained by natural causes? Is it supererogatory to appeal to a Divine interposition to explain these special providences in history? Are these apparently supernatural miracles really but a high power of the naturally wonderful? These masses of laws, individual, social, political, religious, expressly attributed to a Divine origin, do they intelligibly emanate from an origin that is human? These seeming predictions, are they nothing but the forecasts of genius or the intuitions of superior human knowledge? These doctrines concerning God and man and their relations, put forward as Divinely given, are they after all the manufacture of diplomatic, or possibly philosophic, priests, palming off their own creations for their own ends as the thoughts of God? Such are some of the questions which must inevitably arise in the face of the evident claims of the Law, and which must be resolved in the light of the facts of the case.

In this Lecture, then, *an inductive inquiry is to be instituted into the* NATURAL OR SUPERNATURAL ORIGIN OF THE LAW, and the question of questions is to be asked, *whether, judging from our knowledge of the limits of human knowledge, it was within the capacity of man as such to write these five books, popularly, at least, ascribed to Moses.*

Have we, then, any evidence in the Pentateuch that its contents are wholly or partly beyond the capacity of man to compose? The following considerations may guide our judgment.

Notice, in the FIRST *place, that the legal injunctions of the Pentateuch are distinctly made in the interests of religion.* For the present, be it strictly observed, attention is drawn, not to the entire Books of the Law, but to the Law in the narrower sense of the legal system contained in Exodus, Leviticus, Numbers, and Deuteronomy.

This religious aim of the Old Testament Law is a feature as unique as striking. Believing with Burke that "religion is the basis of civil society," lawgivers have often utilized the religious tendencies of man for public ends, citing in their codes the religious rewards of good citizenship, and the religious punishments, tremendous as lasting, of citizenship that was bad. But in the Jewish Law another fact appears. Instead of religion being made subservient to the ends of law, law is made subservient to the ends of religion. The distinction between the sacred and the secular is deliberately abolished by making the secular sacred. Right relations are established between man and man by establishing right relations between man and God. Jehovah, as the supreme ruler and judge of Israel, is the maker and executor of Israel's laws. For instance, it is upon the Divine landlordship that the laws of land ultimately rest; it is upon the Divine claims upon human fealty that the laws concerning offences against the person are based; upon the kingship of Jehovah the laws of taxation as well as of ritual repose. The rights of the individual, whether prince or peasant, sprang, in this code, from his relationship to Deity. Liberty, equality, fraternity, were at once secured, and guarded, by the covenant between the Jew and Jehovah. "I am Jehovah thy God," was the pledge of privilege, the test of obedience, and the sting of penalty. Crime and sin were identical. The modern distinction between the morally and the legally permissible was unknown. Nor was it possible under such a law to say that the king or the priest could do no wrong, for king and priest were to be judged, not by their exalted relation to the people they ruled, but by their humble relation to the Divine King, whose vicegerents they were. Being sin against God as well as against man, adultery, for example, was visited as severely as murder. In fact, all offences are estimated in this Law rather as transgressions against God than as wrongs to man.

"I am Jehovah, thy God," this is the one governing principle which underlay all the equity of the Law. "I am Jehovah, thy God," THEREFORE "thou shalt love

Jehovah thy God with all thy heart, and with all thy might, and with all thy strength." " I am Jehovah, thy God," THEREFORE "thou shalt love thy neighbour as thyself." Throughout the Law, the ultimate sanction to which appeal is made is, not utility, nor the rights of the individual, nor the rights of the community, but the obedience due to the Divine King of the Jewish nation.

In this theocratic form of government, so different from the social experiments of government by the one or the few or the many, there is certainly a suggestive theory of society. Does it not also bear the stamp of the Divine? Does not the explanation of its origin given by the Law appear intelligible? Is such a view of rule, as happy as uncommon, adapted as it was both to correct the most subtle idiosyncrasy and to evoke the most splendid energy, eliciting, as it was fitted to do, the best in the one or the few or the many who rule, whilst neutralizing the worst, is such a theory of government to be attributed to human genius? Must not such an inspiration concerning the Divine relations of men be Divine? One cannot but inquire as to the primary source of this theocratic idea, and when this Divine government is expressly attributed to a Divine revelation, the assertion is certainly very intelligible. Are we not dealing with truth when we read, " In the third month, when the children of Israel were gone forth out of the land of Egypt, the same day came they into the wilderness of Sinai. . . . And there Israel camped before the mount. And Moses went up unto God, and Jehovah called unto him out of the mountain, saying, Thus shalt thou say to the house of Jacob, and tell the children of Israel ; Ye have seen what I did unto the Egyptians, and how I bare you on eagle's wings, and brought you unto Myself. Now, therefore, if ye will obey My voice indeed, and keep My covenant, then ye shall be a peculiar treasure unto Me above all people ; for all the earth is mine ; and ye shall be unto Me a kingdom of priests and a holy nation ? "[1]

Then, SECONDLY, *notice, both in general and in detail, the didactic, the theological significance of the legal injunctions of the Pentateuch.*

For assuredly much of this Jewish code was rather ideal and educational than repressive. This is noteworthy. Injunctions were expressly framed therein, for the guidance of the best and not the worst of the nation. These laws had the making of saints in view, quite as much as the deterrence of criminals. All acknowledge that it is the function of law to be a terror to evil-doers, but it was upon the minutely conscientious that this Levitical Law pressed most heavily. This characteristic is not common in legal codes. Usually the least number of laws compatible with social morality and the general welfare are placed upon statute books ; but in this Mosaic legislation very numerous laws appear, the sole end of which is the production of a very high state of personal and national righteousness. This law did deter ; it did punish ; it did take account of wrong-doing ; but its pre-eminent purpose was to teach—to teach ethics, to teach religion. Its didactic value was supreme, deepening the consciousness of sin, educating in holiness, instructing the immoral to be moral, moving the moral to be saintly. Besides, many of the injunctions commanded therein could not be as widely kept as known, the end of their promulgation being answered

[1] Exod. xix. 1-6.

apparently by their being known. In short, the great end of the Law, using the word in the narrower sense as equivalent to the legal system of the Pentateuch, was to present a standard of goodness so exalted as to be holiness. This educational value, so striking as well as unusual, makes this Law a high-water mark to which the tide of life only very occasionally rises.

This ideal, this didactic, this theological, this doctrinal value of the legal injunctions of the Pentateuch is, in fact, the rock upon which so much of modern criticism splits. It is shortsightedness, or worse, to ignore this intention to instruct. The great question is not, as some have thought, how the Tabernacle and Sacrifices and Festivals and Priesthood came to be, whether by gradual evolution or by sudden appointment,—this is but a subordinate question; the real question is, how these sacred places, and rites, and persons, and seasons, came to be full of a profound religious meaning. For example, in treating of the curious festal seasons of Judaism, its Passover, and Pentecost, and Great Day of Atonement and Merry Feast of Tabernacles, it is a very superficial explanation which thinks all said, when they are declared to be an outcome, in the course of time, of ancient agricultural festivals; the one thing needful to be shown is how these agricultural festivals, if such they were, came to be so transformed that they had their own splendid eloquence and influence for the religious life; what it is really necessary to explain is how Passover and Pentecost and Day of Atonement and Feast of Tabernacles became to the religiously-minded the Feast of Justification, the Feast of Consecration, the Feast of Absolution, and the Feast of the Joy of the Reconciled (to use modern terms for ancient facts), "made year by year continually." Again, let who will examine recondite archæological questions as to the relations of priests and Levites; such inquiries will have an archæological interest: but the vital question concerning the priesthood is how it came to be the channel of great religious privileges; the pressing question concerning the priesthood 'is its mediatorial functions. Is there not indeed, about this preceptive character of the Law, that which suggests most strongly the truth of its claim to supernatural origin?

This didactic element may be dwelt upon with advantage.

It cannot be denied, and should not be ignored, that this Law assumes to be the authoritative text-book for its age, for the preacher, the teacher, and the moralist as well as the judge. And very fittingly. Tested by the grand purpose of all true religion—the adaptability to evoke, cultivate, and satisfy the spiritual cravings of mankind—the Sinaitic legislation has no superior but Christianity. Truths of deep religious import it was fitted to convey effectually to fishermen, herdsmen, and shepherds. Awe was inspired thereby without despair, and trust without presumption. A beneficent religious ideal was notably realized. By means of the splendid and varied cultus which the Law enjoined, under tremendous sanctions, those perplexing contrasts of the spiritual mind, the bewildering contrasts of time and eternity, death and immortality, Divine anger and reconciliation, human lust and aspiration, sin and Divine salvation, the unacceptable sacrifice of the sinful, and the acceptable offerings of the saved, were taught so as to enter readily into common thought, and to tinge perceptibly common experience. This law of many ceremonies was, in fact, the basis of a theology as well as of a cultus. Indeed, if the great things for man to *know* are the existence of the supernatural world, the sinful state of man, his incapacity of self-restoration, the possibility of forgiveness by God, and of the renewed life through the Spirit,—if the great things for man to *do* are to fear, to repent, to revere, to forsake evil, to cleave to good, to live in purity and charity, and to die in hope, —then must this Levitical Law be regarded as astonishingly, as miraculously complete in the knowledge and the faculty it was capable of imparting. This Law pourtrayed a religion of a high type. If at first sight the multitudinous rites enjoined seemed, disastrously for its influence and claims, to blend a debasing materialism with an exalted conception of Deity, nearer vision shows the carnal to have a latent significance, wine and oil, blood and flesh, flour and incense, unleavened bread and firstfruits, running water and the ashes of a slaughtered heifer, being but the body of a soul of fine religious import, convincing of sin, and assuring of forgiveness, objectifying self-surrender, and conveying a holy joy of fellowship, now justifying an individual, and now sanctifying a nation. Doubtless, to the cursory modern inquirer, the constant round of sacrifices, daily, weekly, monthly, festal, appears simply appalling; that priests should be butchers, and an altar shambles, is foreign to all our ideas of religion; how seemingly subversive of all refinement! Yet survey more closely, and it is as if a thrilling landscape has suddenly burst, by steady vision, from rolling mist and dense darkness. God is seen, and man, in bright light and blessed relationship.

So much appears on a superficial examination even. But let this didactic aspect of the Law be viewed a little more closely. Let four points, for instance, be estimated.

First, let the teaching of the Law concerning the Supreme Being be observed.

That teaching is as remarkable for what it does not say as for what it says. There is no pictorializing, there is no idolizing of Deity. Neither is there any philosophic pretence of defining the Infinite and Absolute. The Mosaic Law is as free from the temerity of philosophic speculation as from the vice of idolatrous portraiture. That God cannot be depicted by "any graven image," or by "the likeness of any form that is in heaven above, or that is in the earth beneath, or that is in the waters under the earth," is an axiom everywhere. At the same time the name Jehovah, synchronous with the Law, lifts the Supreme Being into a Transcendent sphere, where human speculation, limited to the sphere of the mutable, cannot follow. Nevertheless, according to the Law, Deity, who may not be imaged, does personally reveal Himself, and that in two ways, by His self-description and by His deeds, both of which methods, notable as well for their silence as their utterance, repay attention.

For consider the "Great Name," to use the term of the Law, under which the Divine Being describes Himself at the Burning Bush, Jehovah (as we must still say in English, lest we sacrifice rich association to pedantry) that unique name, that eloquent name, that silent name, has it ever been approached in the literature of the world for fulness, for majesty, for simplicity? And consider further. Over against the pregnant words said to have been spoken by God to Moses in the Desert of Midian stand the equally pregnant words subsequently spoken to Moses in the Wilderness of Sinai, as, with bowed head and bared feet, Moses stood, with the tables of stone in his hand, whilst "Jehovah descended in the cloud," and "stood with him there," and "proclaimed the name of Jehovah." Let the magnificent words be weighed; they are as wonderful in thought as in expression: "And Jehovah passed by before him, and proclaimed, Jehovah, Jehovah, a God full of compassion and gracious, slow to anger, and plenteous in mercy and truth, keeping mercy for a thousand generations, forgiving iniquity, transgression, and sin, and that will by no means clear the guilty, visiting the iniquity of the fathers upon the children, and upon the children's children, upon the third and upon the fourth generation." Are not the words—so tender, yet so severe—divine, as they claim to be? When parallel words, as faithful as true, are produced from any writer who has not breathed an atmosphere where they are known, it will be time enough to defend their supernatural origin. What ethnic faith is able to match this miraculous utterance, asserting so fully, and so concisely that God is, that God is one, that God transcends time and space, that God is merciful, that God is gracious, that God is long-suffering, that God is true, that God is just, that God is good, that God is holy, that God is holy, just, and good, despite of, nay, because of, His unsparing visitation of wrong-doing with penalty!

And add to this revelation by names and attributes the constant self-revelation of God by His acts. According to the Books of the Law, the Divine Character, incapable of exact and adequate representation to man, is manifested, notwithstanding, by a continuous series of Divine deeds. Again and again, national prosperity or national misfortune are made to be declarative of the Eternal Mind. What are Sinai and the Red Sea,

Marah and Rephidim, the sedition of Miriam and the rebellion of Korah, but so many revelations of the nature of Deity? In short, the pathway through the wilderness, with its pillar of cloud by day and of fire by night, was meant to be a significant series of Divine Self-revelations, a striking course of religious object lessons. That Jehovah was good in will (holy and righteous), and good in thought (wise and true), and good in feeling (just and merciful), the incidents of the long march from Egypt to Canaan body forth more excellently than words.

Now that all this self-revelation of God, in names and in acts, is mere human thinking and imagining, who that possesses at once seriousness of mind, knowledge of human nature, and acquaintance with other religious systems, will be able to believe?

Secondly, let the teaching of the Law concerning the unfitness of man to approach the Most High be also considered.

How clearly human sinfulness is taught in the Law! How much of the enjoined ceremonial is inexplicable, except upon this postulate! Everywhere it is taught that man has no RIGHT *of approach* to God. This fact, indeed, which underlies symbol after symbol, and injunction upon injunction, is not a little remarkable. For, be it remembered, the religious cultus announced at Sinai was expressly addressed, not to man as man, but to man as Israelite, to a people, that is to say, who had been admitted into the closest intimacy with Deity. In the beautiful words of Exodus, Jehovah had " made a covenant " with these children of Israel. Their tribes had heard Divine words, which said, "Now, therefore, if ye will keep My covenant, then ye shall be a peculiar treasure unto Me among all people ; for all the earth is

Mine; and ye shall be unto Me a kingdom of priests and a holy nation." Nevertheless, despite this elect relation, again and again, by reiterated injunctions, by the greatest variety of symbols, by all the studied associations of days specially sacred in the calendar, and of days memorable for those common events of birth and marriage and death, of home-coming or of change of abode, the sinfulness of this kingdom of priests and of this holy nation, the sinfulness of this covenant people, of their ministers, and their laity, of their altars and their houses, was unmistakably taught. The Israelites were placed upon terms of Divine friendship, only as they recognized, at many times and in many ways, that the attitude of God towards them was one of the purest mercy. In the very act of admission into the Holy Presence, attention was always carefully bestowed upon reminding these recipients of favour of their desert of a very different welcome. This inculcation of sinfulness was expressly associated with all phases of life, and with all occasions of worship, and with all grades of ministrants, with birth and marriage and death, as has been just said,—with the beginning of the year, and with its course and close,—with all the sentiments of the religious life, with prayer and with thankfulness, with unconscious error and with deliberate reconsecration,—with all sorts and conditions of men, with priests as well as with Levites, with prophet and judge and king as well as with the common citizen. The detail of ceremonial designed to impress upon the mind this state of unholiness, this unfitness to approach the Majesty on high, is very large, and need not be touched upon here at any length. A few prominent instances only shall be given. Every priest needed special purification for office. Every holy spot—be it even the Holiest beneath the wings of the cherubim and under the brooding mist of the Shekinah—required purification too. Sabbath and New Moon, Passover and Pentecost, and Feast of Tabernacles, as well as the annual Great Day of Atonement, had their specific ritual to remind the nation and the individual of sin. The sacrifices of consecration and of religious rejoicing, as well as the sacrifices for sin and trespass, had their ceremonial emphasizing the sinfulness of the worshipper. In fact, let any one observe how prominent a place the need of "atonement," to use the legal phrase, the need of the "covering of sin," occupies in the Sinaitic ritual, and he will straightway perceive how the unworthiness of man to approach Deity was emphasized in this ancient religion. To arouse, to deepen, to express, this sense of human sinfulness, half the so-called ceremonial law was devoted.

Whence originated this wonderful insight, as true as deep, into the nature of man? Can man, who resents this view of things mostly, have originated it? Are these profound, and profoundly unwelcome, views of the natural and of the spiritual man, of purely human origin?

Thirdly, let the teaching of the Law concerning the forgiveness of sins be also weighed. For nothing characterizes, nothing differentiates, more the Levitical Law than its tenets concerning the fact and the method of *atonement*, to use the technicality which originated with the Law, and without a comprehension of which the Law is unintelligible.

And, primarily, as to the fact of "atonement." What was this "atonement," which so frequently recurs in the Law? To speak exactly, what did this Law itself mean by this common technicality therein—"atonement"? Etymologically considered atonement was "covering," and usage shows that by "covering" was meant "the covering of transgression." To atone was to spread a covering over sin so that it ceased to arouse the Divine wrath. If we probe this ancient Hebrew figure, to atone "was to throw, so to speak, a veil over sin, so dazzling that the veil and not the sin was visible. The figure which the New Testament uses when it speaks of the 'new robe,' the Old Testament uses when it speaks of atonement. When an atonement was made under the Law, it was as though the Divine eye, which had been kindled at the sight of foulness and sin, was quieted by the garment thrown around it; or, to use a figure much too modern, yet equally appropriate, it was as if the sinner, who had been exposed to the lightning of the Divine wrath, had been suddenly wrapped round and insulated."[1] Perhaps, however, it is sufficient for the immediate purpose to remember, that the invariable effect ascribed in the Law to this "atonement" is restoration to the covenant relation which had been imperilled by transgression, is, in brief, the forgiveness of sins.

Then, in the next place, as to the method of atonement. Atonement, this reconciliation with Jehovah, this forgiveness of sins, was wrought by "blood." The blood of bullocks, and sheep, and goats "covered" sin. And this method of atonement was expressly explained in the Law, in a pregnant message, professedly sent by Jehovah, through Moses, to Aaron, and to his sons, and to the Israelites generally. The more important part of this message ran as follows: "And

[1] *Scriptural Doctrine of Sacrifice*, pp. 482-486.

whatsoever man there be of the house of Israel, or of the strangers that sojourn among them, that eateth any manner of blood, I will set my face against that soul that eateth blood, and will cut him off from among his people." For why? "For the life of the flesh is in the blood, and I (Jehovah) have given it (the blood) to you upon the altar to be an atonement for your lives; for the blood atones by the life." The passage is remarkable. Its express statement is that the blood of animals, slain in sacrifice, has been appointed by the Deity as a means of covering sin, because the blood is the life of the animal sacrificed. Four truths, in fact, emerge: viz., first, that the sacrifices of the Law covered sin; secondly, that this covering only pertained to animal sacrifices; thirdly, that covering so attached to animal sacrifices because of the effusion of blood which was part of the ceremonial of their presentation; and, fourthly, that blood was thus efficacious, by the Divine will, because the blood represented the life of the animal poured forth. Such is the legal view of atonement. This view is characteristic of the Law. It is peculiar to the Law. Other religions know of the presentation of animals in sacrifice, and even the presentation of human offerings, sometimes even the presentation of the fruit of the body for the sin of the soul, but this heathen presentation, however costly, simply represents the idea of cost, it does not proceed upon a definite idea of a substituted life. Blood *as blood* covers sin in the Law: blood *as cost* is supposed to cover sin in heathendom. Obedience to a Divine command is the merit of Old Testament sacrifices of life; obedience to a human instinct is the supposed merit of the heathen sacrifices of life. In the Hebrew faith it is God who gives dignity to the sacrifice presented in atonement; in heathen faiths it is the intrinsic value of the sacrifice itself which is supposed to be of worth. The blood offered is as the blood of Passover in the Law; in other religions it is as the blood of personal sacrifice. To put the difference sharply: in heathendom atonement is supposed to be more or less according as the offering is more or less; in the Hebrew code it *is* not the actual, but the ideal value of the blood shed which works forgiveness. Compare the sentiments which prompt immolation at the great Indian festival of Jagganath with the sentiments which would be evoked by the great Day of Atonement, and the difference receives striking illustration. The Law knew the idea of cost, and utilized it largely in worship, but, with minute consistency, did not admit the idea of cost into its idea of atonement. Thus whereas burnt-offerings might consist of many victims, the sin-offering, which was pre-eminently the offering of atonement, might never consist of more animals than one, and that the same comparatively costless sacrifice for rich as well as poor.

Now whence came this Old Testament idea of atonement? The question is vital. Is it enough to say, that " the life of which the blood was regarded as the substance had for the ancient Semites something mysterious and divine about it; they felt a certain religious scruple about destroying it, . . . the pouring out of blood was ventured upon only in such a way as to give it back to Deity; what was primarily aimed at was a mere restoration of His own to Deity"?[1] Is not this idea as to restoring to God His own a pure imagination? Is there any evidence whatever for

---

[1] Wellhausen, *Prolegomena to the History of Israel*, translated, p. 63.

saying that the Semites as such (of whom it is the fashion to say we know a good deal more than we do), knew ought of the Levitical idea of atonement? Or is there any evidence whatever for saying that the effusion of animal blood was regarded as restoring to God the life which was His own? Besides, this explanation is altogether beside the mark. What requires to be accounted for is, how the blood of animals came to be regarded as a means of atonement, as a means of the forgiveness of sin, as a means of restoration to Divine favour. As a matter of fact, there is no evidence that blood was regarded from early times as peculiarly sacred. The sanctity of blood began with the giving of the injunctions concerning the Passover. The sanctity of blood, the interpretation of blood as life, the association of blood and life with atonement, are contemporaneous with the giving of the Law to Moses. The fact is, that, whoever will fairly confront what the Law says concerning the covering of sin by the blood of beasts, and will divest his mind of prepossessions, will find the readiest explanation of this singular rite in the express words of the Law: "I (JEHOVAH) have given it (blood) to you to be an atonement for your souls." Surely, both the legal idea of atonement, and its method, are wholly mysterious viewed alone, and only intelligible as interpreted by Christianity, are, in short, Divine revelations approved by Divine revelation. But we must return to this point presently. At the moment it is enough to accentuate the method of atonement enjoined, and its manifest truth as evidenced by the results worked, both objective method and subjective results emphasizing the probable Divine origin of the Mosaic soteriology.

And, fourthly, let the teaching of the Law concerning the entire religious life of the covenant people be also carefully estimated.

The fact is that the complicated and protracted ritual of the Law, at first sight so materialistic as well as so onerous, was, after all, a splendid provision for the deepest religious needs of man; and it would even appear that this Law has also about it a splendid unity as well as a marked completeness. There was a massiveness and rotundity about this Levitical worship and law which grows upon one the more closely it is studied. In that sacrificial constitution were pourtrayed for any man who believed in God, and in the possibility of His revealing Himself, all the essentials of true religion. As the pious Jew regarded, though it were but in thought, the sacred structure of the Tabernacle or Temple, the eye whispered to the soul that God Most High dwelt in the midst of his nation, and might be approached in worship. As his attention was engrossed by the gorgeous vestments and busy ministrations of priests and Levites, he would recognize a divinely appointed organization, by whose mediation and intercession Divine worship might be beneficially and innocuously conducted. In the performance of the rites of purification, the truth was palpable, that those hereditary taints and personal faults which might intelligibly hinder approach to God if the spiritual sense was alert, might be neutralized. At the same time, the divinely arranged series of animal and bloodless gifts would deliver the messages with which they were divinely laden, the welcome and inspiring messages of the forgiveness of sins and a possibility of uninterrupted, or only momentarily interrupted, fellowship with God. In the sin-offering he recognized the divinely arranged instrument for obtaining forgiveness for sins of weakness and ignorance; in the trespass-offering, a fitting retribution for frauds against God or man: the burnt-offering was an aid to consecration, the peace-offering a channel of communion with God. In short, the Levitical injunctions brought into prominence those consolatory and instructive truths of the Divine nearness and approachableness, of human sin in its stupendous effects upon the physical nature and the conscience, together with the possibility of atonement, of forgiveness and of restoration to Divine favour. The Jew who could devoutly say, "I believe in Jehovah, maker of heaven and earth," could, by virtue of the Law, add to his creed the further articles, "I believe in the Shechinah, in the Tabernacle, and in the priesthood, in the communion of saints, the forgiveness of sins, and the life of reconciliation"—no inconsiderable spiritual equipment. Must not He who made the lock of the human heart have made this key also which so fits its many wards?[1]

The question must be fairly faced, Whence came all this remarkable insight into the religious needs of man, all this remarkable satisfaction of those needs? A religion is often best judged by its noblest products, and under this religious system of the Law the beautiful blossom of spiritual desire bore, in men like David, Isaiah, and Daniel, the rich fruits of holy content and aspiration. Nor can the spiritual character of such men be accounted for apart from the Law; the Law is the postulate everywhere in their spiritual character; they

[1] Compare *The Scriptural Doctrine of Sacrifice*, pp. 108, 109.

breathe its air, they have fed upon its fulness. Upon such a religious system, indeed, the Hundred and Nineteenth Psalm is not too lofty a panegyric, the Lamentation of Jeremiah is not too bitter an elegy. Complicated this system was, but exquisitely impressive; gorgeous, but appropriate; bloody, but merciful. Further, whilst its general purport was patent to the simplest, express Divine explanations having been given of its more prominent features, there was, as is evident upon close consideration of its provisions, food for the lifelong meditation of the wisest and greatest. This Law evoked the religious sense and appeased it; and, better still, in appeasing, stimulated, importing at once an ever-widening content and an ever-enlarging aspiration. This Law both gave truth and made experience. On the one hand, it imparted truth. It could convince of the love and holiness of God, of the heinousness and ruin of transgression, of the forgiveness of sins, of the satisfaction of the cravings after a Divine life; above all, it could convince of the possibility of an entire life of reconciliation and fellowship with God. On the other hand, this Law gave birth to experience. It could transform knowledge into personal conviction, effecting in man a sense of sin, an assurance of reconciliation, a growth in goodness, and each in increasing measure. Further, it was no small element in the value of this Law that, as we shall see presently, it prepared the way for a more spiritual and reasonable religion of the future.

Thus, the Law, discloses itself as, at once, a profound recognition of the religious needs of men, and a splendid response to those needs. Everywhere therein are emphasized man's need of redemption from sin, the

Divine willingness to save, and the reality of redemption. Everywhere therein the self-surrender of man to God is declared to be acceptable to Jehovah, so long as the Divine method of atonement by sacrificial blood is recognized. The practical value of this religious system was immense—how measureless let such a Psalm as the hundred and nineteenth testify, with its hundred and seventy-six verses in praise of this Law of Jehovah, which is described as a fitting guide of youth, an object of great delight, a mine of wonders,—as the rule of the free and the song of the exile,—as sweeter than honey and better than riches,—as life, light, and health,—as pleasant to meditate on in this world, and as pleasant to hope for in fuller measure in the world to come.

Once more the question is irresistible, Whence came this Law? Is it in harmony with human experience to say that the natural genius of any one man, or of any number of men, even with the element of time thrown in, these men elaborating their purely human faith throughout centuries, could have evolved this exceptional knowledge, not only of the ways of man, but of the ways of God, knowledge which approved itself in strong spiritual conviction? Surely knowledge of God must originate with God: surely knowledge of man in his Divine relations must also originate with God. Further, the astonishing collection of civil and religious precepts called the Law, is expressly stated to be of supernatural origin; the God of Israel is expressly said to have constructed as well as communicated this elaborate code for the entire government of life. Can this Law which so conspicuously advocates religious as well as civil morality, be itself an egregious instance of literary dishonesty? Did the writers of the Law deliberately lie when they ascribed to Divine authorship what they knew to be of purely human composition? Could, or would, priests have framed such a law in the ecclesiastical interest, as some have maintained? Could, or would, priests, or even prophets, of their own motion simply, have elaborated such a law in the religious intetest, as others have supposed? Could the Jewish people have produced such a law if they would, or would they if they could, as Henry Rogers would have said? If the full assimilation of such a law is beyond the faculty of man, is its origination purely human? If, as an apostle afterwards said, this law was "a yoke which neither they nor their fathers could bear," was it in human nature that this law their fathers could frame? Is not the more intelligible explanation of the origin of the Law given in the words " Jehovah spake"?

So much appears on the examination of the Law itself; but, THIRDLY, in further support of the supernatural origin of the Law, *notice the kind of evolutionary process this Legal Code illustrates.*

Here two points call for consideration, namely, the relation between the Law and the religion which preceded it, and the relation between the Law and the religion which followed it. In other words, it is necessary to inquire, whether the Law is a natural or supernatural successor of the religion of Jacob and Joseph, and also to inquire whether the Law is a natural or supernatural forerunner of the religion of Jesus. Have we, or have we not, in the several grades of Biblical religion, instances of a purely natural development, or instances of a development which discloses at intervals a supernatural intervention?

Is then the Law, upon comparison of its specific features with those of the religion of the Patriarchs, a natural growth from what preceded it, or is the Law a conspicuous instance of Divine interposition? Is the Law a stage in a naturalistic evolution, or is it a stage in a developing purpose of revelation? The answer is not difficult if we compare the pre-Sinaitic religion of the Israelites with the Sinaitic. The Law can neither be explained by a purely human enlargement of the faith of the Patriarchs, nor by a purely human compounding of the faith of the Patriarchs with the only other religious system which might be in question, the religion of Egypt. The evidence is clear. As surely as the Law designates itself a revelation, the facts available declare it to be a revelation.

Thus, judging by the evidence available, it would appear that the earlier and later faiths of the sons of Abraham differed in authority, in complexity, in centralization, in fulness of doctrine, and in practical value. The Sinaitic laws are more explicitly attributed to Divine origin than the details of the pre-Mosaic faith; and, throughout, the Sinaitic laws are stated to be a product of the mind not of Moses, but of Jehovah. So, too, it is evident that the Sinaitic worship was an advance upon its lineal predecessor in complexity; for hereditary priests have taken the place of the father of the family or tribe, all the varied ceremonial of the Court, the Holy Place, and the Holiest has superseded the very elementary worship of earlier times. Then, in the Levitical laws, the localization of worship is most manifest. Further, there is a clearness and a fulness about the doctrinal implications of the Law conspicuously absent from the earlier forms of worship. And, of course, a more developed and authoritative theology being always followed by large effects in practical life, all these differences culminated in large diversity of practice. Now, manifestly, of these five points of difference, the crucial point for our problem, as to the natural or supernatural origin of the Law, is the enlarged doctrinal significance. Greater complexity might be of human origination; so might centralization; the practical value of the religion would follow upon its doctrinal value; so would its authority. Is there, then, evidence in the doctrinal teaching of the Law, as contrasted with that of the earlier patriarchal faith, that the Law was of Divine origin?

Assuredly. The evidence is large. The evidence is clear. The evidence grows upon one the more it is considered. The Patriarchal Age prepared the way for the religion of Sinai, but these two phases of the Old Testament Faith are marked by such subtle links of connection, the agreements and the differences are so unexpected, that natural growth is no sufficient cause why the earlier faith became the later. That designing priests, as one school of evolutionists have said, or that earnest prophets, as another school have thought, might desire to palm off their individual contrivances, whether ambitious or fanatical, as the daily practice of great men and of a revered antiquity, would be nothing wonderful; the wonder would be that such men should have palmed off such practices. Things which the shallowest could see to be favourable to their designs are omitted; things that no amount of ingenuity can show to be otherwise than prejudicial are inserted. Intellectual might is affirmed in one breath to deny it in the next. The desire is, we are told, to constitute the Temple the one legitimate place of service; to this end these priests, or prophets, represent the patriarchs as worshipping when and where they would. These inventors of a faith wished to surround the Altar of Burnt-offering with the halo of an exceptional Divine presence; to this end they describe Abraham and Isaac and Jacob as erecting altars at their own will with signal success. These leaders of a new age aimed at usurping the sole priestly dignity; they depict therefore every father of a family, in the old revered times, as the priest of his household, every prince as the priest of his tribe. Their prominent purpose was, it is said, to hold in subjection by a varied and magnificent and imperative ritual; that purpose, however, they do not pretend to have been familiar to their greatest ancestors, who knew but one kind of sacrifice available at any time and for the expression of any religious emotion. In fact, on the theory of a purely natural evolution, it is a problem indeed to account for the fact that the religion of Jacob merges into the religion of Joshua. On the theory that the sacred narratives themselves speak truly of a Divine revelation to Moses, the problem immediately vanishes.

Let one fact, out of very many, be carefully weighed? That one fact is the stress laid in the Law upon *atonement*. The patriarchal worship knew nothing of atonement. There is not a single reference in Genesis, direct or indirect, whether by express statement, by ritual, or by any mention of an express manipulation of the blood of the sacrificial victims presented, to the Levitical idea of atonement. Yet this idea underlies the entire subsequent life and thought of the Old Testament. Whence came the idea? After our previous exposition, is not its Divine origin the most probable explanation of its entrance into human thought and experience? And let the Patriarchal doctrines of God, of man, of sin, of salvation, and of the Church be compared with the Mosaic doctrines of the same subjects, and it will appear that we have more than natural growth: we have supernatural addition, we have new revelation. The origin of the Law is only explicable upon Divine imparting. No purely natural process could transform the faith of the Patriarchs into the faith of Moses.

Nor can the Law be explained as a natural growth from the earlier Patriarchal faith, *as modified by a residence in Egypt*. Mosaism is not an eclectic compound of the faith of the children of Abraham and that of the subjects of the Pharaohs. The influence of Egypt upon the religion of Moses used, it is true, to be a favourite theme of discourse with many, but the theme has now been definitely abandoned. It is sufficient proof to quote the words of one of the most prominent of the Evolutionary theorists upon the origin of the religion of Israel. Says Dr. Kuenen, after describing this explanation of Sinai by the Nile as "a hypothesis now antiquated,"—"Amongst students of Israelite religion, there is not, as far as I know, a single one who derives Yahwism [the religion of Israel] from Egypt. The documents which form the basis of their studies favour the idea that Yahwism was roused from its slumbers by the Egyptian religion, and was made conscious of its own characteristics by its conflict with it, rather than that it sprang out of a faith from which it is seen to be radically different." And Dr. Kuenen goes on to quote approvingly the opinion of one of the greatest Egyptologists of the day, Le Page Renouf, who has categorically written: "It may be confidently asserted that neither Hebrews nor Greeks borrowed any of their ideas from Egypt;" adding, "I have looked through a number of works professing to discover Egyptian influences in Hebrew institutions, but have not even found anything worth controverting."[1] If Renan[2] desires to revive this now exploded theory of Egyptian influence once again, it will be time enough to consider his views, when he has settled his account with Kuenen and Renouf and those who think with them. The Laws of Sinai are confessedly no product of the Residence in Egypt; but such a confession does not make the natural origin of "Jahwism" any the more credible.

When, therefore, the question is asked, upon a comparison of the Patriarchal and Mosaic faiths, whence came the latter, whether by natural growth or supernatural revelation, the answer may surely be made by those who have studied the facts of the case by a rigid process of induction, that the Law was, as it claims to be, the gift of Jehovah to Moses, and forms part of that developing plan of revelation recorded in the Bible.

And this comparative argument for successive Divine interpositions in revelation, gathers irresistible force when the Sinaitic dispensation is compared with the Christian. If there are those who still, after the preceding discussion, see in the Law nothing incompatible with a skilful and ingenious adaptation, nothing more than an imaginary code written with a bias, it will scarcely be maintained by any one that these clever priests or earnest prophets of the captivity, whose inspiration be it remembered is, by hypothesis, but a human inspiration,

---

[1] Kuenen, *National Religions and Universal Religions*, Hibbert Lecture for 1882, pp. 58-61.
[2] *Histoire du Peuple d'Israel.*

not only harmonized the past with their aims, but *adroitly forecast the future.* Yet a miraculous continuity undoubtedly exists between the Law and the Gospel. From the Law alone the Gospel could not be inferred: from the Gospel alone the Law could not be inferred: but, on comparison of the Law with the Gospel, a continuity, which demonstrates a far-reaching Divine design, undoubtedly discloses itself. As the immature picture of the artist has its subtle links of connection with his maturest work, this foretelling that and that dignifying this with apotheosis, so the teaching of Christ and His apostles bestows the crown of immortality upon Mosaism. Nor are the witnesses to continuity difficult to array. They consist of all those elements of law and ritual, the likenesses amidst unlikenesses so indicative of a common author, which must have remained totally inexplicable had not Christianity appeared.

Let the general facts of the case be borne in mind. Very much of the meaning of the Law lay bare to the intelligence of the spiritually minded Jew; he knew that this elaborate religious constitution was symbolic; he also knew that so much of the significance of the symbols employed was disclosed as conveyed certain truths of the highest importance in eliciting and developing a truly spiritual life; he even recognized in these symbols a series of sacraments, which by the mercy of God became, as a matter of experience, the channels of many a religious blessing; but there still remained many things unsolved; there still remained many perplexing and eluding principles and details, displaying a very visible relationship he would confess, but very like the medley of a cipher the key of which he did not hold. Wherever he looked there was discernible, for example, a most appalling insufficiency in these rites. To recapitulate the prominent rites alone: the Tabernacle was called the dwelling-place of Jehovah, it was in bare fact a structure of wood and skin ornamented; the priesthood were to be regarded as the peculiarly holy servants of Deity, as a matter of fact too frequently their righteousness was imputed and their service official; or, thinking of the purifications and sacrifices, what power had water to palliate the curse, what efficiency lay in animal blood to atone sin? Such reflections must have presented amazing difficulties to the thoughtful, unless the hope grew strong that all these things were "shadows of coming blessings,"—σκίαι τῶν μελλόντων ἀγαθῶν, as the author of the Epistle to the Hebrews expresses it. Only with the certainties of the New Testament do the difficulties of the Old vanish. Immediately the Jewish and the Christian faiths are compared, these ancient stumbling-blocks are the very things which prove most conclusively the fact of a common source. The priesthood has its *rationale* in the "Priest for ever"; the Tabernacle in the Incarnation; atonement by blood has its ground in Calvary; the non-dissected feast, in the great Paschal Lamb; the Passover in the feeding upon the crucified Jesus; the Feast of Ingathering in the dispensation of the Spirit; the Feast of Tabernacles in the rejoicing of the saints through Christ. Christ is everywhere the missing key. The Divine foreknowledge supplies the unifying idea which underlies type and antitype.

In short, there is a *predictive* element about the Law which shows its leading features to have been divinely revealed. The Law is not explicable alone; the Gospel is not explicable alone: the Law has many features only adequately explained by the Gospel; the Gospel has many features only adequately explained by the Law: in other words, the Law is a prophecy of the Gospel, and the Gospel is a fulfilment of the Law. What follows? Even supposing the faculties of man capable of producing the Law, the pre-established harmony, so to speak, which exists between the Law and the Gospel, it is beyond the faculties of man as such to have invented. The Law cannot be an afterthought of Christianity; Christianity is no mere natural development of the Law; there are, however, points in both which only their similarity of origin can explain; whether the Law be revealed, or whether the Gospel be revealed, these common features are immediately seen to result from a Divine pre-arrangement. In so far as the Law is explained by the Gospel, —in so far, that is to say, as the Law has a typical, a prophetical, a predictive element, proof positive is given of the Divine origin of the Law.

"To those who rightly understand," said Augustine, "the Old Testament is a prophecy of the New." The thought is just. This thought an attempt is now being made to illustrate. For note this characteristic of prophecy—No prophecy is absolutely clear in itself; were it so, it might be alleged that the prophecy wrought its own fulfilment; but a prophecy only becomes perfectly lucid on comparison with its fulfilment. At least, these are the principles—partial unintelligibility when delivered, complete intelligibility on fulfilment—which underlay the prophecy of the Old Testament, the initial latency of which subsequently shows the more conclusively the Divine source from which the prophecy sprang.

If the induction appear abstract, it well repays attention. It may be stated as follows : The Old Testament has truth of its own to convey to the times in which it was written—it seems intelligible ; it has also much other truth, the importance of which only the times subsequent to its composition can disclose—it is really partly unintelligible ; but once those later times have come, the latent truth coming into the light of day—becomes wholly intelligible, and, as a consequence, it then becomes manifest to all who attend to the matter, that none but the Spirit of God can have originated the truth, once latent, but now disclosed.

An illustration may make the point clearer. That illustration shall be drawn from the preparation of the earth for man. All through the geological ages there has been a manifest adaptation between the flora and fauna of the globe and its atmosphere and climate. Detail is needless, seeing that this adaptation between geological life and its environment is one of the commonplaces of science. But all through the geological ages another process has been going on. There has been a sort of prophecy of a coming time written in the changing crust of the earth. Soil, for example, has been steadily forming, with what purpose ? Coal and lime and minerals of many kinds and forms have been building themselves up, shall we say, aimlessly ? A vast evolution has been progressing, to what end ? As yet, and prior to a later stage of the life-history of our planet, the prophecy, if such it be, is largely unintelligible. At length the epoch of man arrives, and all is clear. The problem is solved ; the prophecy has become intelligible. This soil of ages is for man to plough ; the lime of ages is for him to calcine; the coal of ages is for him to burn; the evolution of ages has had for its end to provide man, for instance, with the barley and oats and millet and wheat and maize and rice, which only appear with man, upon which he feeds, and without which he would die; the progress of humanity would have been impossible, we see, but for this long preparation for his advent. Manifestly man's advent upon the globe has been foreseen, and, at the same time, most thoughtfully prearranged for. What follows? Does not this,—that past ages are, so to speak, a prophecy of the coming of man, if unintelligible for a time, yet wholly intelligible, most lucidly intelligible, when the prophecy has passed into fulfilment? And does not this,—that the prophecy itself is written with a Divine finger? Similarly the Law is a prophecy of the Gospel; and, again, the Law as a prophecy is only fully intelligible upon the entrance of the Gospel; and yet again, both Law and Gospel, with their very subtle links of connection, have originated in the Divine Mind.

As a matter of fact, this prophetic, this typical, element was latent everywhere in the Law. At least, so comparison with Christianity clearly shows. Fulfilment and antitype have made the meaning of prophecy and type evident. In the Law, as we can see to-day, the seed, so to speak, of the Divine purpose in revelation had reached its leafage, and naturally possessed its own characteristic beauties and significance, not the least of which was the promise in this spring-tide of a glorious summer yet to come. Or, to use another figure, in the Law the Divine revelation had reached its youth, this youth again being full of its own riches and purpose, one important portion of which was its promise of a riper day to follow. The complete evidence in the Law for this promise, this prophecy, of a future flowering, of a future virile stage, would require a minute examination of the entire range of injunctions catalogued in the books of Moses; such a survey cannot, of course, be attempted here. A brief outline of the kind of evidence may, however, be presented.

The large evidence available must be examined as follows: First, the characteristic features of the Law, in general and in detail, must be carefully catalogued and classified. Secondly, the characteristic features of the Christianity of the New Testament must also be carefully catalogued and classified. Thirdly, a comparison must be instituted between the two sets of characteristics.

Upon such a comparison some highly important conclusions appear.

One conclusion is that both Law and Gospel teach very much the same religious truths. To select a few salient examples only. Both teach that the Deity desires to be approached in human worship. Both teach that, in such approach on the part of man, two conditions must be observed, the one condition being a recognition of the revealed method of atonement, and the other being a willinghood to draw nigh to the throne of the Heavenly Grace. Both teach that access to God is to be gained through the mediation of a priesthood. Both teach that near access to God is reserved for certain select souls. Both teach that God delights in that service of His worshippers which most conclusively illustrates their readiness to surrender themselves wholly to Him. In short, both teach—first, the Divine accessibility; secondly, by mediation; thirdly, upon atonement; fourthly, and upon voluntary self-surrender; fifthly, of a priesthood.

But this conclusion straightway leads to another. Law and Gospel teach these truths in a very different fashion. In the Law, the Divine accessibility is taught by a visible Tabernacle of material construction; in the Gospel, it is taught by the Incarnation of God in Christ. In the Law, mediation pertains to a hereditary and very fallible high-priest; in the Gospel, it pertains to the one sinless High-priest for ever. In the Law, atonement is by the blood of bulls, and of goats, and of lambs; in the Gospel, atonement is by the blood of the Incarnate Word of God. In the Law, priesthood pertains to an hereditary class, whose worship is official and ritualistic; in the Gospel, priesthood pertains to a regenerate class, whose worship is spontaneous and real. In the Law, surrender of the soul to God found expression in a ceaseless round of ceremonial acts; in the Gospel, it finds expression in a devout performance of all the manifold duties of life—personal, social, civil, and religious. In a word, whereas the Law taught by symbol, the Gospel teaches without figures.

Whereupon yet another conclusion discloses itself. The Law gives us *types*, and the Gospel *antitypes*, to use a technicality as concise as useful. By a type is meant the symbolical presentation of a truth; by an antitype is meant the presentation of the same truth as a matter of fact and not a matter of symbol.

And upon this yet another conclusion follows. It is beyond our human faculties to invent types, prior to the appearance of their antitypes. Types are prophetic symbols; at least, types are seen to be prophetic symbols, when once their antitypes appear. Symbols only become types when they have this element of prophecy, inadequately representing a truth by symbol which the future alone will adequately reveal. To take an instance. The Jew believed in atonement by the blood of beasts; Why? Certainly not from knowledge of the tragedy of Calvary. Why then? Is it easy to say? This much is evident: this method of atonement might arouse him to think out many a piece of inconsequent reasoning; it might suggest some possible solution of his intellectual difficulties in the far future; it might even tell a mystic and eluding tale to the imaginative and spiritually minded; but what express statements had the Jew upon the many perplexing details of this ritual of blood? That is to say, the Jew, who had any faith at all in the Divine origin of the Mosaic worship, might, as he presented his blood-sacrifice, rest, with priceless advantage, upon the words, "I have given it to you on the altar to make an atonement for your souls," he might put his trust in the Divine Wisdom, though that Wisdom spake for a while in parables; but what more did he, or could he, know? That blood was symbolic he might infer from the Divine command; that the symbol would be explained in the future he might also infer from the same reason; but of the exact ground of the symbol, of the *fundamentum relationis*, he could in his day know nothing clearly. When once, however, the symbol has passed into the actual exhibition of the truth symbolized, when prophecy has merged into fulfilment, when type has given place to antitype, when the Law has received its complement in the Gospel, then it is as clear as day why the symbol, the prophecy, the type was given. After the death of Christ, it is possible to find a Divine preparation for that fact, its significance, and its necessity, in the blood of the ancient sacrifices. So it is ever. Type is inexplicable indeed, is scarcely known as type until the antitype appears.

But if this is so, a further inference is inevitable. If types have no meaning apart from antitypes, and if types and antitypes are separated by centuries, then the very existence of types argues their supernatural origin. The course of reasoning is this: the Law, as judged by the Gospel, is full of types; types are predictive symbols,[1] but prediction is impossible unless the thing predicted is known; now knowledge of the thing predicted, in the long interval between Law and Gospel, was not within the reach of the faculties of man as such; such predictive knowledge is superhuman. The conclusion is that all the injunctions of the Law which are typical, are of Divine origin. The conclusion can only be avoided by denying that any relations whatever of type and antitype are to be found in Law and Gospel.

This typical character of so many of the injunctions of the Law has been too frequently ignored of late, especially by those we have called the Evolutionary theorists. These theorists have been too ready to assume the impossibility, or at least the improbability of a Divine revelation. Too frequently their objection to the Mosaic origin of the Law has arisen from initial objection to the supernatural. But the question as to whether there is any pre-established harmony between the Law and the Gospel, cannot be shirked by inductive inquirers. If there are any types whatever in the Law, the supernatural origin of those types is proved. Types—using the word as previously defined—cannot but be of Divine origin.

One series of instances, then, of genuine revelation, one series of examples of truth beyond the power of man

[1] Compare *The Scriptural Doctrine of Sacrifice*, pp. 392-405.

to impart, has been discovered. The Law, using the word in its narrower sense of the code given to Israel in the Wilderness, was a series of revelations.

FOURTHLY, *notice that the Law is only part of a long-continued series of revelations.* The Law did not stand alone; it was no isolated message from the heavens, which preserved both before and after a most rigid silence. That the Law was veritable revelation, Divine knowledge divinely imparted, we have seen; but the fact, the reality, of revelation once proven by the phenomena displayed by this Sinaitic Code, the veracity of the Pentateuch having been demonstrated in this particular, the truth of many other revelations in the same record is rendered highly probable. Now Genesis records many specific revelations, besides the narrative of Creation, immediately derived from a Divine source. There are revelations of God to Adam, and Noah, and Abraham, and Isaac, and Jacob, to mention only the more prominent instances. The narrative of these revelations is closely interwoven in a narrative which, wherever tested, has approved itself historical and thus reliable. If the narrative of common events has shown itself eminently veracious, there would be little reason to distrust the veracity of the narrative when it dealt with uncommon events, but for one consideration, the initial improbability of Divine interference in human affairs. The witness, who so testifies to natural things within his cognizance that his testimony is regarded as unimpeachable, might be trusted when he testifies to supernatural things within his experience, were not the fact of any Divine revelation altogether improbable. But the reality of Divine revelation has been demonstrated. The

Sinaitic Code, as well as the narrative of Creation, is Divine knowledge divinely imparted. Philosophical objections to the possibility of revelation are neutralized by the actual existence of indisputable revelations. What follows? Does not this? That the reality of revelation once shown, the testimony of Genesis, which has maintained its credit for truthfulness, wherever tested, compels us to see a long series of Divine interpositions in human affairs. Seeing that the Sinaitic Law is Divine in origin, as our investigation has shown, no initial objection to revelation can now warrant us in setting aside the actual statements of Genesis. Historical in common things, Genesis must now be regarded as historical in things uncommon and supernatural.

FIFTHLY, *notice that these Divine revelations* recorded in the Pentateuch, like all the revelations recorded in the Bible, *are represented as substantiated by miracles.*

The point has its importance. There is, it is true, in the record, no prodigality of miracles; nevertheless, according to the common Biblical law, there are marked demonstrations of miraculous power at certain crises in the religious development of man. The Bible has nothing to say of a continuous exhibition of miracle throughout the times it depicts; but it certainly does call attention to a massing of miracles at precise epochs of revelation. Miracles in the Law, as in the Bible generally, first, are sparingly distributed, and, second, make their appearance in order to accredit certain special instruments of Divine revelation to man. This restriction of miracles to epochs in revelation, when they were the credentials, so to speak, of ambassadors extraordinary from the King of kings, is seen in the days of the Patriarchs, in those of Moses, in those of Samuel, in those of Elijah, in those of Isaiah, and Jeremiah, and Daniel, and in the days of Jesus and His apostles.

These two considerations, viz., that Scripture miracles are rare, and that they are employed to accredit special Divine messengers, might possibly have been worthy the attention of Mr. Matthew Arnold. "Suppose," he has said, "I could change the pen with which I write this into a pen-wiper, I should not thus make what I write any the truer or more convincing."[1] The sentiment is a mere truism. But had Mr. Matthew Arnold claimed to have been a special Divine messenger the case would have been otherwise.

Quite consonantly, therefore, with the customary law of revelation, Moses is said to be endowed with miraculous power. As a chosen ambassador from God to man, Moses received the Divine credentials of miracle. Very fitly, surely. What can be credentials of the supernatural but the supernatural? The miracles accredit the revelation: the revelation demonstrates the Divine, and not the diabolic, origin of the miracle.

The Books of the Law being, then, records of Revelations, as well as of much else, being records, that is to say, of much Divine knowledge divinely imparted, *notice*, therefore, SIXTHLY, *that human knowledge of revelation implies inspiration.*

The discussion is not yet sufficiently advanced for the full treatment of this fertile distinction. Even here, however, before closing the consideration of the Divine origin of the Law, a few remarks may be fittingly

---

[1] *Literature and Dogma*, 4th edit., p. 128.

made, in anticipation of a more elaborate consideration later on.

Inspiration is a well understood term for the influence exerted upon man by the Holy Ghost. Further, the gifts of the Spirit being various, so the varieties of inspiration are various. Even, as associated with revelation, or the Divine impartation of truth to men, there are varieties of inspiration. Thus there is an *inspiration* which assists in the making *of character*, revelations being necessarily given by means of holy men, and holiness being a gift of the Spirit of Holiness. Then there is an *inspiration of intelligence*, man being incapable of receiving revelations except as he is divinely fitted for such reception, objective revelation demanding subjective inspiration. Then, too, there is an *inspiration of authorship*, the impulse to write the record of the Divine revelations being itself of Divine origin.

All this, it is hoped, will become clearer later on. But even now, it is suggested, after the series of facts already considered, that the following conclusions are warranted. In the first place, Divine revelations cannot be delivered to man by anybody. Secondly, the receptivity for revelation implies a long training by the Holy Spirit. Thirdly, all revelations further imply an immediate inspiration by means of which the faculties of man are expanded to receive what is divinely taught. And fourthly, if it is part of the Divine design that any revelation be committed to writing, written revelation implies another form of inspiration, prompting to the permanent embodiment in a faithful record. In short, revelation as such implies inspiration—an inspiration of character, an inspiration of understanding, and an inspiration of authorship.

LASTLY, *notice that*, there being, as has been seen, very good reasons for associating the authorship of the entire Books of the Law with Moses, and Moses being evidently inspired, in character, in receptivity, and in authorship—*there is a very real sense in which the entire Pentateuch may be called inspired, and therefore Divine in origin.* In this instance, at any rate, a holy man wrote as he was moved by the Holy Ghost and thus became an inspired organ of revelation. This conclusion is of the highest interest. It cannot be fully expanded here. Presently it will call for, and repay, the closest attention.

LECTURE VII.

THE DIVINE ORIGIN OF PROPHECY.

LECTURE VII.

THE DIVINE ORIGIN OF PROPHECY.

WHEN speaking of the Sacred Books of the Old Covenant, our Lord described them, evidently in terms familiar to His hearers, as "the Law and the Prophets,"[1] and once as "the Law and the Prophets and the Psalms."[2] A parallel phrase occurs in the Apocrypha, where mention is made of "the Law and the Prophets and the Rest of the Books."[3] It thus appears that where we say, briefly, "the Old Testament," the Jews were accustomed to speak, with more circumlocution, of "the Law and the Prophets," or of "the Law and the Prophets and the Psalms," or—the Psalms being but the first section of a series of writings—of "the Law and the Prophets and the Writings (or the Holy Writings)." Indeed, a similar series of designations is found in the modern Hebrew Bible, where even to-day, no single word appearing such as our word Bible or Testament, the title-page runs, "The Law and the Prophets and the Writings." This triple division of the Old Testament into Law and Prophets and Hagiographa is acknowledged by scholars to be the ancient arrangement.

[1] Matt. xi. 13, xxii. 40; Acts xiii. 15, &c.
[2] Luke xxiv. 44.
[3] Ecclus., Prologue.

Of course the Law, in this ancient mode of describing the contents of the Old Testament, consisted of the Five Book constituting the present Pentateuch. As for the Prophets, they were divided into two sections, the Earlier Prophets and the Later. The Earlier Prophets, let the reader of the English Bible observe, consisted of the Historical Books of our Old Testament—of Joshua, Judges, First and Second Samuel, and First and Second Kings. The Later Prophets consisted of the Prophetical Books proper of our Old Testament, three of which are ascribed to the so-called Greater Prophets (Isaiah, Jeremiah, and Ezekiel), and twelve to the so-called Minor Prophets, those prophets whose writings are extant in our Bibles from Daniel to Malachi, the Book of Daniel itself, however, belonging to the Holy Writings and not to the Prophets. The Writings, or Holy Writings—or Hagiographa, as they have come to be called—included the remaining books of our Old Testament, but arranged differently, the order running, Psalms, Proverbs, Job, the five Rolls (Canticles, Ruth, Lamentations, Ecclesiastes, Esther, kept in separate rolls, because they were publicly read in the synagogues on certain feast days by the later Jews), Daniel, Ezra, Nehemiah, and First and Second Chronicles.

Of these three divisions of the Old Testament the first has now been sufficiently considered. By a strictly inductive method, the veracity of the Five Books of the Law, their veracity both as history and revelation, has been shown to be highly probable. The Divine Origin of the Law, and therefore its inspiration, has approved itself the only hypothesis really explanatory of the facts.

From the Books of the Law we now pass to the

Books of the Prophets, using the word in the larger sense just explained, by the Books of the Prophets being meant the second great division of the Old Testament.

Respecting these Prophetical Books, two lines of inquiry must be prosecuted. Before it is possible to frame any solid conclusions upon the inspiration of these books, it is necessary to be assured both as to their historicity and as to their supernatural character. Possibly, however, after our previous inquiry into the inspiration of the Law, little needs be said upon the question of method. The method of search into the Inspiration of the Prophets is identical with that already employed for ascertaining the nature of the Inspiration of the Law.

Happily the general historical veracity of these Earlier and Later Prophets has not been challenged in the same manner as the historicity of the Law has been. If some have said, "Revelation is impossible, therefore I cannot accept the historical character of these prophets"; few, if any, have said, "The historical character of these prophetical books is unsustained, therefore I cannot believe that they contain revelation." We may pass therefore at once to the crucial question, whether these Earlier and Later Prophets are, in any degree, credible records of Divine Revelation, of Divine knowledge, that is, divinely imparted.

In this Lecture, then, FIRST, *the Divine Origin of Prophecy*, and, SECONDLY, *the Inspiration of the Books of the Prophets, as well as of the Prophets themselves, will be examined.*

That Prophecy and Law are the two prominent

features of the Religion of Israel, existing side by side, and exerting reciprocal influence, all are agreed.

Now what was Prophecy? What was its nature? What was its course? More definitely still, what, according to the Old Testament writers themselves, were the characteristics and history of Old Testament prophecy?

What the Old Testament has to say about the appearance of prophecy in the sphere of history is as follows:

For a time, it is said, the prophetical gift was possessed and exercised by isolated individuals at rare intervals. Abraham is called a prophet.[1] So is Moses.[2] Miriam was, we are told, a prophetess.[3] Moses anticipated that prophets would arise from time to time.[4] In the days of the Judges, Deborah is called a prophetess.[5] Again, in the same epoch, when the children of Israel were harassed by the Midianites, a prophet is said to have been sent to them, in response to their cry for Divine help.[6] So, too, in the extreme age of Eli, a man of God, a prophet apparently, foretold the violent death of Hophni and Phinehas:[7]

From the days of Samuel, however, the rare prophetic gift is represented as becoming continuous, or nearly so. At that time, it would seem, the prophets became organized into a distinct religious order, existing side by side with the priestly and the ruling orders.[8] Samuel, seeing the advantage of association, founded what came to be called "schools" of the prophets, these schools naturally giving power, status, and permanence to the

---

[1] Gen. xx. 7. [2] Deut. xviii. 15. [3] Exod. xv. 20.
[4] Deut. xiii. 1; xviii. 20. [5] Judg. iv. 4. [6] Ib. vi. 7-10
[7] 1 Sam. ii. 27-36. [8] Jer. xviii. 18; Ezek. vii. 26.

prophetical career. The original school was at Ramah.[1] Subsequently similar institutions are read of at Bethel and Jericho, and Gilgal, and at other places near the Jordan.[2] How long these "schools" survived we do not know. But we read of them expressly in the days of Samuel, in the days of Elijah, and in those of Elisha; indeed, a phrase in Amos,[3] when Amos describes himself as "no prophet, neither one of the sons of the prophets," would seem to imply the continued existence of these "schools," at least as late as the days of King Amaziah. The purpose of these schools was educational. They obeyed a sort of monastic rule, and exerted a sort of monastic influence. Into these "schools" were gathered suitable young men, known as "sons of the prophets," who were trained, under the guidance of their elders, for their specific work, sometimes numbering fifty, a hundred, and even four hundred.[4] The head of these schools was an "anointed" prophet,[5] who became at once leader and teacher, and who was technically called now Father,[6] and now Master.[7] Under the guidance of this head, these "sons" studied amongst other things, it would seem, how and what to teach orally, spoken addresses being given by prophets on new moons and sabbaths;[8] they also, it would appear, studied sacred music.[9] It was from these "schools" apparently that the more prominent prophets passed out to their public duties, although the instance of Amos, just quoted, shows that, occasionally, conspicuous prophetic gift was bestowed outside the "schools." Of course the existence of these "schools" demonstrates that there were many prophets

[1] 1 Sam. xix. 19, 20. [2] 2 Kings ii. 3, 5; iv. 38; vi. 1. [3] Amos vii. 14.
[4] 1 Kings xviii. 4; xxii. 6; 2 Kings ii. 16. [5] 1 Kings xix. 16.
[6] 1 Sam. x. 12. [7] 2 Kings ii. 3. [8] *Ib.* iv. 23; vi. 32.
[9] Exod. xv. 20; Judg. iv. 4, v. 1-30; 1 Sam. x. 5; 2 Kings iii. 15.

whose names have not descended to us, men who lighted the lamp of truth in a dark age, and who, having served their generation, passed away without record. To some prophets a more lasting fame was given. Their names have come down to us, immortalized in some cases by their deeds, like Samuel and Elijah, and in some cases by their writings, like Isaiah and Ezekiel. The practice of writing prophecies commenced with Hosea, whose ministry lasted nearly sixty years, from the days of Uzziah to those of Hezekiah. Contemporary with the earlier or later days of Hosea—to take the more probable dates when the several prophets flourished—were Amos and Joel and Jonah in the Northern Kingdom, and Isaiah and Micah and Nahum in the Southern Kingdom. A little later in order of time came Habakkuk, and Jeremiah, and Zephaniah, and Ezekiel, and Daniel, all more or less associated with the great epoch of the captivity of Judah. Then the prophetic message was taken up by the prophets of the Return, Haggai and Zechariah, the splendid era of open vision closing with Malachi, after whose death there was a lapse of several centuries before the prophetic mantle fell on John the Baptist, the great forerunner of the antitype of all prophets.

This rapid sketch of the course of prophecy in the Old Testament will suffice for the purpose in view. The evidence available shows us one long chain of prophets, if not from the days of Moses, at least from the days of Samuel until the close of the Old Testament canon.

The next question that arises is as to the nature of prophecy. What, according to the Old Testament, was the nature of this prophetic gift? What were the functions, therefore, of these religious leaders called prophets? Does prophecy of the Old Testament type occur only in the history of Judaism, or is it common to mankind? We are not concerned, be it observed, with popular conceptions or misconceptions of prophecy; but, as pursuing an inductive inquiry into the contents of the Old Testament, we are simply dealing with the data afforded by the Old Testament. What, then, according to the Old Testament, was the differentia of prophecy? Prophecy was, of course, religious utterance (which was occasionally committed to writing): the question is, utterance of what kind?

Happily there is little diversity of view as to the Old Testament conception of prophecy. Biblical interpreters, while differing widely as to the etymology of the Hebrew word translated prophet, are largely agreed upon its actual meaning. In fact, Biblical usage makes the significance clear. The *nabhi*, the prophet, was the medium, the spokesman, the interpreter, the ambassador, between God and man—the inspired messenger who, having heard words from God, transmits those words to man. The utterance of the prophet was an inspired, a revealed utterance.

A few instances of the employment of the word "prophet" will make this meaning quite evident. Here is one. When Moses pleaded his slow tongue as a reason for shrinking from the mission to Pharaoh, Jehovah encourages him by saying, "(Aaron) shall be thy prophet (*nabhi*) unto the people, and it shall come to pass that he shall be to thee A MOUTH, and thou shalt be to him AS GOD;"[1] by *nabhi* is meant, then, the mouth of God; Moses should be as the Divine source,

[1] Exod. iv. 10-17.

and Aaron as the human channel of revelation. Here is another instance: "I will raise them up," we read in Deuteronomy, "a prophet from among their brethren like unto thee, and will put MY WORDS in his MOUTH, and HE SHALL SPEAK ALL THAT I COMMAND HIM."[1] In the Psalms, again, where we read, "Touch not mine anointed ones (Abraham, Isaac, and Jacob), and do my prophets no harm,"[2] the patriarchs, it is evident, are called Jehovah's prophets, being the select media of Divine communications to men. Parallel instances abound. Throughout the Bible the prophet is the Divine messenger, who, having been told the mind of God, declares that mind to his people. This idea the other names given to prophets illustrate. It is as the messenger of heaven that the prophet is called now the "disciple"[3] of Jehovah (as eager to catch the faintest word of his Master that he may repeat it to others), and now Jehovah's "servant"[4] (the confidential steward, armed with plenary authority), and now the "seer"[5] (from his open vision of Deity), and now the "man of God"[6] (from his Divine relationship), and now the "man of the Spirit"[7] (as inspired by the Spirit). In short, the prophet, according to the Old Testament view, was a Barnabas, a υἱὸς παρακλήσεως, "a man endowed with the gifts of the Paraclete." Further, because the prophet was regarded, as Augustine expressed it, as an "enunciator verborum Dei hominibus," the Seventy Translators of the Hebrew text into Greek, rendered the word *nabhi* by προφήτης, the προφήτης being an interpreter, so to speak—one who speaks for another—one who makes intelligible words

---

[1] Deut. xviii. 18. [2] Psa. cv. 15. [3] Isa. l. 4. [4] Hosea iii. 7.
[5] 1 Sam. ix. 9. [6] *Ib.* ii. 27; ix. 6-8, 10. [7] Hosea ix. 7.

spoken in an unknown tongue. Further still, from this Greek word, by direct transference into our English speech, comes the word prophet. The prophet, that is to say—meaning by prophet what the Jews meant by *nabhi*—is, according to the Old Testament conception, one who utters to man the Word of God, *the human exponent of Divine revelation.*

The prophet, then—according to the Old Testament view of his function—interpreted to man revelations he personally received from God. Prophecy was not divination, but revelation. Soothsaying rested upon human presentiment; prophecy followed upon Divine inspiration. The prophet was conscious of being an organ of Divine communications. The words he spake he knew to be Divine words. His messages did not originate in natural facts, but in supernatural gifts. The prophet was a herald who announced the royal will of heaven. In a word, prophecy was revelation, Divine knowledge divinely imparted. At least, such is the conception everywhere current in the Old Testament.

The same view of prophecy, as revelation, follows upon an examination of the functions ascribed in the Old Testament to the prophet. It was as men who were inspired of God to declare revelations that the prophets were everywhere represented as exerting their wide and mighty influence. The prophets were the national annalists, but this they were as Divine historians, as the recipients of Divine guidance in the emphasizing of the Divine side of human history. The prophets, again, were the custodians of the national morals; but this, again, they were as inspired preachers of righteousness; for when they reproved or commended king or rulers, priests or laity, their Divine relationship was the ground of their praise or censure. The prophets were also exponents and upholders of the Law of Moses, decrying ritualistic observance, and demanding the obedience of the whole man, body, soul, and spirit; but they always relied, as a reason for earnest appeal and scathing denunciation, not on the revealed character of the Law, a revelation of the past, but on specific revelations in the present, granted to them personally. The prophetical order always claimed to be more than an order of lawyers interpreting an ancient code; they claimed, by virtue of their intimacy with Deity, to be an order of lawgivers, who made authoritative renderings of the code they advocated. So, too, the entire force of their proclamation concerning events about to happen to men and cities and nations, was consequent upon the fact of their Divine relationship. Further, it was as accredited channels of new revelation that the prophets declared the advent of a gracious future deliverer, who should palliate the curse of sin, and establish a kingdom of righteousness. Whether the prophets served as preachers or pastors, as moralists or judges, as poets or historians, as guides of the present or heralds of the future, the ground of their activity, however trivial or magnificent, however local or large, however fugitive or lasting, is ever ascribed, in the Old Testament, to the specific relation in which they stood to Jehovah. Jehovah inspired them both to understand and to utter His revealed will.

Prophecy, then, was *divine in origin*. The prophet spake the word of God. It was knowledge divinely imparted, whether of the past, the present, or the future, which the prophets communicated to their age, and through their age to all time. This is the invariable view in the Old Testament. There prophecy is unique; prophecy is miraculous; prophecy is supernatural; prophecy shows Divine interposition for the good of man.

Is this position warranted? This is the next question which must be asked in any inductive inquiry. Is it true as Peter said, that "no prophecy ever was brought by the will of man; but men spake from God being moved by the Holy Ghost"? IS PROPHECY DIVINE OR HUMAN IN ORIGINATION? What conclusion does a rigorous inductive examination of the related phenomena suggest?

Can Old Testament prophecy be explained on impersonal evolutionary principles; or is prophecy a fact which renders a merely natural evolution of things an inadequate theory of the universe? This is the important problem which must now be investigated in the light of the evidence available.

Is, then, the Old Testament conception of Prophecy as the human utterance of revelation warranted?

Now, in the *first* place, *notice that* what was seen in the case of the Law is equally seen in the instance of Prophecy. *The predominant interest of prophecy is religious.* Only secondarily was the aim of prophecy political, moral, or social; primarily, its aim was religious. The constant endeavour of the prophets was to put man in right relations with God, assured that right relations with man would necessarily follow. With every prophet the paramount, the supreme endeavour of his life was to bring the spirit of each of his hearers into the closest contact with the Spirit of God. Has not this religious import of prophecy some weight in determining its natural or supernatural origin? Is it so very human to accentuate strongly, nay, supremely, the Divine relations of man, "seeking first the kingdom of God and His righteousness," under the firmest possible conviction that all other good things will be added thereto? Surely there is something to be said for the supramundane source of so supramundane a life. Does man turn to God except when God turns to man? When the human soul trembles towards a fixed point in the heavens, may we not assume that God is the pole which attracts? It seems an invariable law that man is only full of God as God is full of man. Thus *the religious bent of prophecy seems to imply its supernatural source.*

The Divine origin of prophecy, it has just been said, is suggested by the crowning purpose of prophecy, of bringing man into close and conscious fellowship with God. However, it shall not be forgotten that this religious interest is not in itself sufficient proof, to some modern inquirers, of the supernatural character of prophecy. Some modern inquirers, with what consistency I do not stay to examine, accept the religious trend of prophecy, but deny its supernatural source. Thus a noteworthy recent book upon the Prophets of the Old Testament maintains strongly and strenuously this religious interest, "the high moral and religious character attained by the prophets," but sees no ground whatever for believing that "Israelitish prophecy was a supernatural phenomenon, derived from Divine inspiration."[1]

"Prophecy is," according to this view, "a phenomenon,

[1] Kuenen, *The Prophets and Prophecy in Israel, an Historical and Critical Inquiry*, translated from the Dutch by Adam Milroy, with an Introduction by J. Muir, London, 1877, Introduction pp. xxxvii, xxxix.

yea, one of the most important and remarkable phenomena in the history of religion, but just on that account a human phenomenon, proceeding from Israel, directed to Israel." From the religious bent of prophecy, which suggests, let us, therefore, pass to its predictive aspect, which demonstrates, its Divine origin.

Secondly, then, *observe that the Divine origin of prophecy is conclusively shown by its predictive character.*

Of course, as Old Testament students are now agreed, Old Testament prophecy is not entirely prediction. If, for many years, the value of the Old Testament in our modern life was all too seriously minimized by the wide acceptance of the view, to which Bishop Butler gave expression when he said that "prophecy is the history of events before they come to pass;" that limitation of view which is perilous to-day is of another nature. Prophecy is revelation, as we have seen—Divine knowledge divinely imparted; and if formerly mischief lay in so identifying prophecy with prediction as to ignore other forms of revelation which were equally prophecy, the danger now is of an opposite kind; the present error is in so excluding prediction from prophecy as to ignore that revelation may be of the future as well as of the present and past. Amongst other ends, prophecy frequently predicts, so it appears; certainly prophecy claims to predict as well as to preach. Prophecy pretends to a value beyond its significance at the moment. At the moment it may have comforted, warned, guided; but at the moment it was often largely unintelligible, because it was expressly predictive—at least so the evidence seems to declare. When the prophets preached, they frequently predicted. What follows? Does not this? That, whereas prediction before fulfilment may have a hortatory value (as when Isaiah spake to Ahab of the "Virgin who would bear," a prophecy which, although unintelligible, yet had its hortatory value for Ahab), prediction after fulfilment has a value that is evidential (as when Matthew regards the same prophecy as fulfilled in Jesus). To preach is human, but to predict is Divine. For preaching, for exhortation, the common faculties of man may suffice; prediction demands Divine co-operation with human faculties. Human faculties, as such, are confessedly incapable of repeatedly forecasting future events. Coincidence or chance might account for an isolated harmony of forecast and fact. But if it is true that Old Testament prophets are in the habit of predicting, their prophecies must partake more of Divine enlightenment than human gift.

Old Testament Prophecy must, then, be Divine in origin if it habitually predicts. Is this predictive element made out? The question is a question of fact. The problem is a historical problem. Whether or not Old Testament Prophecy blends a capacity for prediction with its capability of preaching, is peculiarly a matter of evidence, and therefore peculiarly a subject for inductive investigation. Dogma is here out of place, whether it be a dogmatic prepossession for or against prediction. The motto of the inductive inquirer is that of Horace, who was

"Nullius addictus jurare in verba magistri."

Our sole concern is with those conclusions which the facts critically weighed appear to warrant. Fulfilled or not fulfilled? this is the question for our inquiry. If fulfilment followed upon prophecy which undertook to predict, the prophecy must have been supernatural; on the other hand, as Dr. Kuenen has said with perfect justice, "unfulfilled predictions can never be derived from supernatural revelation."[1]

This, then, is the cardinal question to the careful consideration of which all energies must be now bent—DOES THE OLD TESTAMENT AFFORD SOLID GROUNDS FOR BELIEVING IN THE EXISTENCE OF PREDICTIVE PROPHECY? Dr. Kuenen and his school answer in the negative. Orthodox exegetes answer in the affirmative. To which side do the facts critically weighed compel the inductive inquirer to incline?

The facts of the Old Testament relative to prediction will be best studied under two heads, viz., *first, the predictive prophecies which are not Messianic*—that is to say, which have no reference to the future Prophet, Priest, and King who, born of Judah, was to be of universal import; and, *secondly, those predictions which are Messianic*, and do refer more or less directly to the coming Emmanuel.

First, then, *Does the Old Testament afford indubitable instances of non-Messianic predictions, of such predictions, that is to say, as must be supernatural in origin?* It is manifest that predictions which are supernatural in source must obey two conditions. On the one hand, *the prediction must be prediction*, that is to say, the prediction must actually precede its fulfilment; as Dr. Kuenen, who does not conceal his belief that every prediction in

[1] Kuenen, *The Prophets and Prophecy in Israel, an Historical and Critical Inquiry*, translated from the Dutch by Adam Milroy, London, 1877, p. 97.

the Old Testament was written *post eventum*,[1] yet rightly says, "it must be proved that the prediction actually preceded the event." [2] On the other hand, *the prediction must not itself produce the fulfilment*, as when the witches in *Macbeth* produced the murder of Duncan. The point was admirably expressed by Professor Briggs, when he wrote, "The peril to prediction is in efforts on the part of false prophets and impostors to realize it." But, as a matter of fact, to avoid this danger, Old Testament prophecies are largely unintelligible prior to their fulfilment. As the same capable writer goes on to say, "The clue is a secret clue, often so carefully hidden that centuries of study have not found it; prophecy is its own interpreter, and it is often designed by the infinite mind that its solution should remain unknown until the event itself occurred; like the predictive dreams of Pharaoh and Nebuchadnezzar, they need a Joseph or a Daniel to find the golden thread to guide through their labyrinthine mysteries." [3] These, then, it is clear, are the two necessary conditions of prediction indubitably supernatural—the prediction must be clear, and the fulfilment must be distinct. It is evident that if these conditions are anywhere observed in Old Testament prophecy, the superhuman origin of Old Testament prophecy is demonstrated. Predictions of such a kind are wholly beyond the powers of man, of

---

[1] *Prophets and Prophecy in Israel*, p. 388: "It is evident," he says, concerning prediction, "that the accounts embraced in our investigation date all, without exception, from the period when the prophetical predictions, with which they make us acquainted, had been fulfilled."

[2] *Ib.* p. 277.

[3] Briggs, *Messianic Prophecy, the Prediction of the Fulfilment of Redemption through the Messiah, a Critical Study of the Messianic Passages of the Old Testament in the Order of their Development*, Edinburgh, 1886, p. 49.

such human acts or states, for example, as we call forecast, anticipation, insight, foresight, augury (whichever word be preferred to express that pseudo-prediction which is possible to man). The problem is, bearing these two conditions in mind, to inquire whether the prophetical data of the Old Testament afford indubitable instances of supernatural prediction.

A good illustration of such Divine prophecying is seen in *Isaiah's Oracle of the Fall of Babylon*; or, as the prophet prefers to say, "Utterance concerning the Desert of the Sea."[1] In this connection a little careful attention bestowed upon this Isaianic prophecy will be richly repaid.

In the manner of a spectator who is actually witnessing the scenes he describes, Isaiah depicts a series of visions, with three of which only we need concern ourselves.

This is the first vision. "As storms in the south approach it cometh from the desert, from a terrible land. A hard vision is made known to me; the spoiler spoileth and the devastator devastates. Go up, Elam! surround, Media! To all their sighing will I put an end." So the prophecy of the future fall of Babylon opens. Isaiah sees the devastating advance of the Medo-Persian army against the fated city. The vision is "hard." Like a wind from the Arabian steppes the allied battalions are seen to move irresistibly onwards. The path of the march is strewn with the fiercest horrors of war. The tender-hearted onlooker sickens at what he sees. "Therefore my loins," he writes, "are filled with cramp; pangs have taken hold upon me as the pangs of a travailing woman; I am bent so that I cannot hear; I am dis-

[1] Isa. xxi.

mayed so that I cannot see. My heart beats fitfully; horror hath affrighted me; the twilight I love hath been turned for me into trembling." Thus, by describing not so much what he saw as the effect upon himself of what he saw, the prophet predicts that Babylon is to fall by a coalition between the Medes and the Persians, whose victorious progress shall be terrible. A century and more afterwards the prediction was fulfilled in the coalition against the Babylonian Empire of Darius the Mede and Cyrus the Persian.

The vision fades, and another vision follows. The scene has changed from the plains around Babylon to a banqueting hall within its walls. With a few rapid strokes Isaiah places before our view that wild night of idolatrous revelry, when, in bravado, Belshazzar gave a feast to a thousand of his lords, and when the finger of a hidden arm wrote, in letters of fire, its Mene, Tekel, Upharsin. Revelry he paints within, danger without. Hence the seemingly contradictory statements. "They cover the table, they set the watch, they eat, they drink; arise, ye princes! anoint the shield!" The lines may be filled in. With the prophet we can see the watch set without, the tables groaning within, the feast advancing, the vessels of the temple of Solomon resplendent; with the prophet we can hear the sudden cry that the hostile armies are within the city, the noisy rush to arms of the half-drunken princes. So accurate is the description that it might have been written after rather than before the event; or, to speak quite correctly, vague and unintelligible as the words read apart from any knowledge of the fulfilment, the clue once obtained, they are as pertinent as vivid. Isaiah foretells the famous episode in Daniel; Daniel fills out the famous prophecy of Isaiah.

Again the vision changes. The panic of the surprised revellers vanishes. Now the words of a guard upon the wall of Babylon are heard. "For thus saith the Lord unto me, Go set a spy, let him declare what he seeth." The spy announces the steady and persistent advance of the hostile army, battalions of horse, battalions of asses, battalions of camels, these last being adjuncts of the Persian army expressly mentioned by Herodotus. "And he saw a line of riders, an alliance of horsemen, a line of asses, a line of camels, and he listened intently, with much listening; and he cried, A Lion. Upon the watch-tower, my lord, I stand continually by day, and in my ward I keep my stand all the nights, and behold there cometh a line of riders, an alliance of horsemen." It is the Medo-Persian army, an alliance of horsemen, which the warder sees as it advances silently, stealthily, beneath the lion-banner of Cyrus, towards the breach in the wall. Still the watchman keeps his place. With dramatic force we are left to imagine the secret entrance through the river-bed, the hurried rush to arms, the shock of the collision, the hasty capitulation, the treachery of the princes, the slaughter of Belshazzar, the shout of victory, the applause at coronation. "And he lifted up his voice and said, Fallen, Fallen is Babylon, and all the graven images of her gods are broken unto the ground." By the will of Jehovah, and the instrumentality of Cyrus, the idols of the Queen of the Desert are shown wanting.

In this "utterance" a good example is seen of Old Testament prophecy. From the circumstances of the case the prophecy cannot have wrought its own fulfilment. Nor could the fulfilment have suggested the prophecy; for Isaiah, who wrote the series of visions, preceded Belshazzar by considerably more than a hundred years. It is true that a few commentators have expressly denied the Isaianic authorship, but inasmuch as their sole reason for such denial is an *a priori* disbelief in the possibility of prediction, their speculative opinion does not call for consideration in an inductive inquiry such as this. Indeed that we have here genuine and not simulated prediction, the characteristics of this utterance emphasize. It is not easy, indeed, to understand, the prophecy being such as it is, how such a description could have been given after the actual event of the fall of the great idolatrous city. Let the brevity, the vagueness, the generalization, the lack of detail be remembered, and at the same time let there be borne in mind, the singular reticence of the prophecy, and the great difficulties in comprehending the precise meaning of the words used, apparent to every reader of the original. If this prophecy be really the verbal photograph of a series of visions, the phraseology is intelligible. On the other hand, it is scarcely conceivable that any one who knew the exact historical details, as, for example, they were known to Daniel, could have expressed himself in such a manner. A comparison of the narrative of Daniel with this "utterance" of Isaiah's, ought to set the question of prediction, real or pretended, for ever at rest. Childhood can no more succeed manhood than this prophecy post-date the actual fall of Babylon. Style, atmosphere, contents, all substantiate the view that we have here visions written prior to their fulfilment : style, atmosphere, contents, all belie the theory that these visions were ideal representations written subsequently to the event described. But prediction must be supernatural in source.

VII.]   *Examination of Prophecy.*   365

Of such demonstrative instances of supernatural prediction the Old Testament is full. From Genesis to Malachi there are numerous instances of supernatural prediction, meaning by supernatural prediction, prediction which neither causes nor is caused by its fulfilment. A few instances—so important is the induction—shall be given, some of which relate to the History of Israel, and some to the History of Other Nations.

There are predictions concerning Israel of singular cogency.

For example, there is the *general prophecy that persistent national defection will infallibly be punished by siege, captivity, and dispersion.* This prophecy occurs in several forms, with more or less explicitness. In Leviticus it runs as follows—a few verses only are given from a long and significant passage:[1] "And if ye will not for all this hearken unto Me, but walk contrary to Me; then I will walk contrary to you in fury. . . . And I will make your cities a waste, and will bring your sanctuaries into desolation, and I will not smell the savour of your sweet odours. And I will bring the land into desolation. . . . And you will I scatter among the nations." The entire passage deserves to be read, depicting as it does, in remarkable language, the death of many in exile, the survival of a few, their repentance, and their subsequent return home. If, as our previous inquiry entitles us to affirm, Moses wrote this chapter, there is here a clear instance of prediction, and prediction of a supernatural order. However, should any Evolutionary theorist be inclined to insist that this chapter is a clear instance of prophecy after the event, this Book of Leviticus having been written after the

[1] Lev. xxvi. 27–45.

Exile had actually taken place, in that case he shall be confronted with a parallel prediction to be found in Deuteronomy, and written, as even the Evolutionary theorist allows, in the days of Josiah. In no less vivid and certainly in no less predictive words, Deuteronomy says—again selecting but a few verses out of many:[1] "The Lord shall bring thee, and thy king which thou shalt set over thee, unto a nation which thou hast not known, thou nor thy fathers; and there thou shalt serve other gods, wood and stone. . . . Thou shalt beget sons and daughters, but they shall not be thine; for they shall go into captivity. . . . The Lord shall bring a nation against thee from far, a nation whose tongue thou shalt not understand. . . . And he shall besiege thee in all thy gates, until the high and fenced walls come down." Is not this a manifest instance of supernatural prediction? Some, it is true, have found a difficulty in the mention of a king centuries before the establishment of monarchy in Israel, but this difficulty is as nothing in comparison with the difficulty of predicting this punishment by captivity. In this instance, too, neither can the prophecy have produced its fulfilment, nor can the fulfilment have suggested the prophecy.

As evident an instance of prediction is seen in the forecast of *the Captivity of Ephraim*. The subjugation and deportation of the Northern Kingdom by Assyria is one of the best attested facts in Jewish history, and took place in the reigns of Hoshea of Israel and Hezekiah of Judah. Now this captivity of the Ten Tribes was clearly foretold by Isaiah in the preceding reigns of Ahaz of Judah and Pekah of Israel. "And

[1] Deut. xxviii. 36–68.

the Lord spake again unto Ahaz, saying, . . . The Lord will bring upon thee, and upon thy people, and upon thy father's house, days that have not come, from the day that Ephraim departed from Judah ; even the king of Assyria. . . . The riches of Damascus and the spoil of Samaria shall be carried away before the king of Assyria." [1] Moreover, Isaiah predicts the time within which this dismay of Israel shall occur: " For the head of Syria is Damascus, and the head of Damascus is Rezin, and within three score and five years shall Ephraim be broken, and be no more a nation." [2] Is not the evidence complete ? Further, so troublesome does Dr. Kuenen find this actual statement of date, that he thinks it needful to say, without any satisfactory reason, that "the announcement" of time is "an addition by a later hand." [3] In this connection, again, it is desirable to observe that Hosea had uttered a similar prediction in a higher style of address, when, in a time certainly prior to the Assyrian captivity he had written : " Set the trumpet to thy mouth. As an eagle he cometh against the house of the Lord, because they have transgressed My covenant and trespassed against My law. They shall cry unto Me, My God, we Israel know Thee. . . . He hath cast off thy calf, O Samaria. . . . Israel is swallowed up. . . . For they are gone up to Assyria, a wild ass alone by himself;" [4] and in another place he had written, "Israel shall return to Egypt" (*i.e.*, to bondage as in the old days in Egypt) "and they shall eat unclean things in Assyria." [5] Here again the the canons of supernatural prediction are observed.

[1] Isa. vii., viii.   [2] *Ib.* vii. 7–9.
[3] *The Prophets and Prophecy in Israel*, p. 167.
[4] Hosea viii.   [5] *Ib.* ix. 3.

Another series of predictions, which, if made out must be supernatural, gathers around *the Captivity of Judah*. As all allow, this, the more famous Exile, did not take place till the beginning of the sixth century before Christ. Predictions, however, of this exile of Judah occur distinctly before that date, even a century before. Let, for example, the words of the Lord that came to Micah the Morasthite, in the days of Jotham, Ahaz, and Hezekiah, kings of Judah, be witness. "Therefore," says Micah, "Zion shall be ploughed as a field, and Jerusalem shall become heaps, and the mountain of the House as the high places of a forest";[1] a prophecy which Micah proceeds to make more definitive by saying that "Babylon"[2] will be the place of exile. Dr. Kuenen finds this reference to Babylon so perplexing that, first, he considers the reading doubtful, a common resource with perplexed commentators, and next, he thinks that, if the reading be correct, Micah mentions Babylon as an Assyrian city, whither Israel had gone into captivity.[3] But the point is, that, even if the explanation were in any degree permissible (which is doubtful in the extreme), ZION, and *not Israel*, is associated with Babylon. The same captivity of Judah is clearly announced by Micah's great contemporary, Isaiah, who "saw" visions in "the days of Uzziah, Jotham, Ahaz, and Hezekiah, kings of Judah."[4] As a specimen only of the predictions of Isaiah upon this captivity, let his well-known Parable of the Vineyard [5] be cited, "Therefore My people go into captivity without knowing; and their glory will be famished men and

---

[1] Micah iii. 12.   [2] *Ib.* iv. 10.
[3] *The Prophets and Prophecy in Israel*, p. 164.
[4] Isa. i. 1.   [5] *Ib.* v. 13, 14.

their multitude men parched with thirst; therefore the grave opens its jaws wide, and stretches open her mouth wide indeed, and the glory (of Jerusalem—the whole parable concerns Jerusalem) descends, and its tumult and noise, and those who rejoice within it." Or, if the captivity thus mentioned be regarded as nothing but the captivity of death—a very doubtful interpretation, let the entire passage concerning Ariel, the Hearth of God, as terrible in prediction as magnificent in language, be carefully read. As samples of this remarkable prophecy let the following verses be taken : " Woe to Ariel, Ariel, the city where David encamped! Add ye year to year; let the feasts come round; then will I distress Ariel, and there shall be mourning and lamentation ; yet she shall be unto me as Ariel : and I will camp against thee round about, and will lay siege against thee with a fort, and I will raise siege works against thee: and thou shalt be brought down."[1]   Again, as part of the evidence is this additional fact : in the Historical Books of the Old Testament, a prediction of the deportation of the Jews to Babylon is expressly attributed to Isaiah ;[2] which attribution, be it observed, is to Dr. Kuenen a fact so startling that he declares categorically Isaiah cannot be considered responsible for it—"it cannot be assigned to Isaiah "[3]—why, he does not say.

From Isaiah let us pass on to days nearer the great catastrophe. Naturally enough predictions of this coming disaster increase as the time of the Exile draws near ; they become very frequent indeed in the utterances of Jeremiah, growing in intensity, deepening in clearness, swelling in fulness, as the fate of Judah approaches,

---

[1] Isa. xxix. 1–3.   [2] 2 Kings xx. 14–17 ; compare Isa. xxxix. 1–8.
[3] *The Prophets and Prophecy in Israel*, pp. 170, 171.

"Lo I will bring," writes Jeremiah in the name of the Lord, almost in the words of Deuteronomy, "a nation upon you from far, O House of Israel; it is a mighty nation, it is an ancient nation, a nation whose language thou knowest not, neither understandest what they say. ... And they shall eat up thine harvest, and thy bread, which thy sons and thy daughters should eat. ... they shall beat down thy fenced cities, wherein thou trustest, with the sword."[1] In another place, Jeremiah describes how the fate of Ephraim shall overtake Judah. "And," says Jehovah, "I will cast you out of my sight, as I have cast out all your brethren, even the whole seed of Ephraim."[2] "Say thou unto the king," Jeremiah writes in another prediction, "and to the queen-mother, Humble yourselves, sit down; for your head-tires are come down, even your beautiful crown: the cities of the South are shut up, and there is none to open them: Judah is carried away captive, all of it; it is wholly carried away captive."[3] Yet again, to show how inflexible is the Divine purpose, Jeremiah adds, a little later on, the terrible passage, "Thus said the Lord unto me, Though Moses and Samuel stood before me, yet my mind could not be toward this people; cast them out of my sight, and let them go forth: and it shall come to pass, when they say unto thee, Whither shall we go forth? then thou shalt tell them, thus saith the Lord: Such as are for death, to death; and such as are for the sword, to the sword; and such as are for the famine, to the famine; such as are for captivity, to captivity."[4] Yet again, a little later, when Nebuchadnezzar has declared war, and Jeremiah is consulted as to the issue, "Then said

[1] Jer. v. 15-17.   [2] Ib. vii. 15.   [3] Ib. xiii. 18-20.   [4] Ib. xv. 1-4.

Jeremiah" unto these messengers, "Thus saith the Lord, the God of Israel, Behold, I will turn back the weapons of war that are in your hands, wherewith ye fight against the king of Babylon, and against the Chaldeans which besiege you without the walls, and I will gather them into the midst of this city. . . . And afterward, saith the Lord, I will deliver Zedekiah, king of Judah, and his servants, and the people, even such as are left in this city from the pestilence, from the sword, and from the famine, into the hand of Nebuchadnezzar, king of Babylon."[1] Yet a little later follow predictions, on the one hand, concerning Shallum, "For thus saith the Lord touching Shallum, the son of Josiah, king of Judah, which reigned instead of Josiah his father, which went forth out of this place, He shall not return thither any more; but in the place whither they have led him captive, there shall he die, and he shall see this land no more;"[2] and, on the other hand, concerning Jehoiakim "Therefore thus saith the Lord concerning Jehoiakim, the son of Josiah, king of Judah, they shall not lament for him, saying, Ah, my brother! or, Ah, sister! they shall not lament for him, saying, Ah, lord! or, Ah, his glory. He shall be buried with the burial of an ass, drawn and cast forth beyond the gates of Jerusalem."[3] In short, the prophecies of Jeremiah must be wholly dismembered, if their predictions of the captivity of Judah be not veracious, and therefore supernatural. It is true that Dr. Kuenen hints that these prophecies were collected together into one book *after* the events referred to. But surely a theory is weak indeed that is compelled to question the *bona fides* of Jeremiah! Who will believe that we have in this long series of prophecies,

[1] Jer. xxi. 1–10.   [2] *Ib.* xxii. 11.   [3] *Ib.* xxiii. 18.

with dates as precise as their statements are clear, simply a succession of "pious frauds" (if their motive could in that case be pious), claiming to be predictive, but proving themselves, when critically judged, descriptions, in the form of predictions, of events already past?

Another prediction, which was revelation, Divine knowledge divinely imparted, concerns *the Return of Judah from Exile.* Jeremiah expressly foretold the return from Babylon, an event which he certainly did not live to see. "Therefore, behold the days come, saith the Lord, that it shall no more be said, As the Lord liveth, that brought up the children of Israel out of the land of Egypt; but, As the Lord liveth, that brought up the children of Israel from the land of the north, and from all the countries whither he had driven them; and I will bring them again into their land that I gave unto their fathers."[1] Again, in another prophecy, having mentioned the name of Nebuchadnezzar, and "the astonishment and hissing and perpetual desolations" he will work, Jeremiah adds: "These nations shall serve the king of Babylon seventy years,"[2] a prediction which he subsequently expands in words like these: "Thus saith the Lord, Behold I will turn again the captivity of Jacob's tents, and have compassion on his dwelling-places; and the city shall be builded upon her own mound, and the temple shall be inhabited after the manner thereof; and out of them shall proceed thanksgiving and the voice of them that make merry: and I will multiply them and they shall not be few; I will also glorify them, and they shall not be small."[3] To which prediction Jeremiah adds yet another: "For thus saith the Lord, Like as I have brought all this great evil upon

---

[1] Jer. xvi. 14, 15. [2] *Ib.* xxv. 11. [3] *Ib.* xxx. 18–20.

this people, so will I bring them all the good I have promised them : and fields shall be bought in this land, whereof ye say, It is desolate, without man or beast, it is given into the hands of the Chaldeans : men shall buy fields for money, and subscribe the deeds, and seal them, and call witnesses, in the land of Benjamin, and in the places about Jerusalem, and in the cities of Judah, and in the cities of the hill country, and in the cities of the lowland, and in the cities of the South ; for I will cause their captivity to return, saith the Lord."[1] Have we not here supernatural prediction, neither influenced by nor influencing the fulfilment ?

And these supernatural predictions concerning the children of Israel may be fittingly closed—they cannot be here examined at length, such an examination would require a large volume—with the prediction as remarkable as manifest, concerning *the four great empires which would have relations with Judah* in the days subsequent to the deportation from Jerusalem. In the visions of the night Nebuchadnezzar, so Daniel describes, saw a great image.[2] Its head was gold ; its breast, silver ; its thighs, brass ; its legs, iron ; its feet, iron and clay mingled. Struck by a stone, the image crumbled away. This stone made without hands, became a great mountain, and filled the earth ; whereas the iron and the clay and the brass, the silver and the gold, became as the chaff of the summer threshing-floors. Such was the dream. Its interpretation, according to Daniel, was as follows. The dream represented symbolically the course of the great empires of the world, from the Babylonian Empire onwards, and at the same time the course of the divinely founded Kingdom of the God of Heaven, which, itself eternal,

[1] Jer. xxxii. 42-44. [2] Daniel ii.

should ultimately break in pieces the kingdoms of the world. The head of gold, said Daniel, was the Babylonian kingdom, this was to be succeeded by an inferior kingdom, of silver, so to speak; and this in turn by a kingdom of brass, destined to be the forerunner of a kingdom of iron; during the sway of this iron empire the everlasting kingdom of the God of heaven should be established. The course of history declares this prediction to be exactly true to fact. The Babylonian Empire merged into the Medo-Persian; the Medo-Persian became absorbed in the Græco-Macedonian; upon the ruins of the Græco-Macedonian dominion that of Rome was built. In other words, the kingdom of Nebuchadnezzar became, first, that of Darius and Cyrus, then that of Alexander, and then that of Augustus. So, too, it was in the days of this fourth empire that the kingdom of God in Christ was founded, and if this divine, but unobserved stone is to become a great mountain and fill the earth, the expression is by no means unintelligible in the light of history. The divine stone grows. *Regnum crucis gignit in regnum gloriæ.* Now even if the Book of Daniel were written in the days of Antiochus Epiphanes, as some have thought, mainly because of their antecedent disbelief in the possibility of supernatural prediction, surely there is supernatural prediction here, prediction prior, and not subsequent to, the events described.

Predictions also abound concerning the history of heathen peoples. The evidence is altogether too full to be treated here at length, but a few crucial instances of supernatural prediction shall be given.

One prediction concerning *Babylon*, as true as picturesque, has been examined. Let another be considered.

"The Burden of Babylon, which Isaiah the son of Amoz did see."[1] The following are the leading features of this "utterance" as given in the actual words of Isaiah. "The noise of a multitude in the mountains, like as of a great people! The noise of a tumult of the kingdoms of the nations gathered together! The Lord of Hosts mustereth the host for the battle." Armies, says Isaiah, are to come against Babylon. "They come," Isaiah continues, "from a far country. ... Howl ye; for the day of Jehovah is at hand; a destruction from Shaddai shall it come." The destructive armies will come from far. "Behold I will stir up the Medes against them. ... And Babylon, the glory of kingdoms, the beauty of the Chaldean's pride, shall be as when God overthrew Sodom and Gomorrah." Surely a remarkable precision of prediction. Isaiah depicts the downfall of mighty Babylon, and its subsequent desolation. To turn the edge of this evidence, it is true, some have said, largely on the ground of the accurate minuteness of the prediction, that this chapter, like the latter half of the same book, was, as a matter of fact, written in Babylon during the Exile. The evidence is slight indeed for so late a date. But supposing the later date to be conceded for the moment, have we not supernatural prediction in this chapter all the same? Let us read on. "It shall never be inhabited," says Isaiah of Babylon; "neither shall it be dwelt in from generation to generation, neither shall the Arab pitch tent there; neither shall shepherds make their flocks to lie down there; but wild beasts of the desert shall lie there; and their houses shall be full of doleful creatures, and ostriches shall dwell there, and he-goats shall dance there, and howling creatures shall

[1] Isa. xiii.

answer in the castles and jackals in the pleasant palaces." Is not this the picture of the site of Babylon drawn by all modern travellers? Is not this supernatural prediction? Was it so evident to any exile even in Babylon, that "the glory of kingdoms, the beauty of the Chaldean's pride," should speedily become a horrible desolation, echoing to the dismal shriek of the jackal?

And the evidence thus adduced of supernatural prediction is strengthened, when the more detailed prophecy of Jeremiah is taken into account, written as it was a century after Isaiah's, but still some years prior to the actual ruin of the great Mesopotamian city. "The word that the Lord spake concerning Babylon, concerning the land of the Chaldeans, by Jeremiah the prophet. Declare ye among the nations and publish, and set up a standard; publish and conceal not; say, Babylon is taken, Bel is put to shame, Merodach is broken down; her images are put to shame, her idols are broken down: for out of the north there cometh up a nation against her, which shall make her land desolate, and none shall dwell therein; they are fled, they are gone, both man and beast."[1] Then follow minuter details. "Flee out of the midst of Babylon, and go forth out of the land of the Chaldeans, and be as the he-goats before the flocks: for, lo, I will stir up and cause to come up against Babylon an assembly of great nations from the north country; and they shall set themselves in array against her; from thence she shall be taken; their arrows shall be as of a mighty man that maketh childless, and that returneth not in vain." Further, says Jeremiah, this disaster will be but the prelude of greater woes to follow. "Behold, she shall be the hindermost of the nations, a wilderness,

[1] Jer. l.

a dry land, and a desert: because of the wrath of the Lord it shall not be inhabited, but it shall be wholly desolate; every one that goeth by Babylon shall be astonished, and hiss at all her plagues. . . . How is the hammer of the whole earth cut asunder and broken! How is Babylon become a desolation among the nations!" Then, almost in the words of Isaiah, Jeremiah adds: "Therefore the wild beasts of the desert, with the howling creatures, shall dwell there, and the ostriches shall dwell therein; and it shall be no more inhabited for ever; neither shall it be dwelt in from generation to generation: as when God overthrew Sodom and Gomorrah and the neighbour cities thereof, saith the Lord; so shall no man dwell there, neither shall any son of man sojourn therein." Is not this revealed prophecy?

From Babylon let us pass to *Nineveh*, the twin empire of the Mesopotamian oasis. Assyria occupies a large place in the predictions of Jonah, Isaiah, Nahum, and Zephaniah. For our present purpose the prophecy of Nahum may suffice, itself wholly an utterance concerning Nineveh. The doom of this great city is proclaimed, writes Nahum, and the chariots and horses and ornaments so fresh in the remembrance of the Jews from Sennacherib's recent invasion, will soon pass into nothingness. With magnificent eloquence, indeed, Nahum describes the imminent destruction of the splendid city. "The Lord is good," he writes, "a stronghold in the day of trouble, and He knoweth them that put their trust in Him. But with an overrunning flood the Lord will make a full end of the place" of Nineveh, "and will pursue His enemies into darkness." And Nahum continues: "What do ye imagine against Jehovah? He will make a full end; affliction shall not rise up the second time. For though they be like tangled thorns, and be drenched as it were in their drink, they shall be devoured utterly as stubble fully dry. . . . Jehovah hath given commandment concerning thee that no more of thy name be sown." Of this utter destruction of Nineveh, Nahum speaks again and again. "He that dasheth in pieces is come up before thy face; keep the munition, watch the way, make thy loins strong, fortify thy power mightily: the shield of his mighty men is made red, the valiant men are in scarlet; the chariots flash with steel in the day of his preparation, and the spears are shaken terribly." And again, Nineveh "is empty and void and waste." And again, "And it shall come to pass that all they that look upon thee shall flee from thee, and say, Nineveh is laid waste." The very method of destruction is also foretold. "Behold thy people in the midst of thee are women; the gates of thy land are set wide open unto thine enemies; the fire hath devoured thy bars; draw thee water for the siege; strengthen thy fortresses; go into the clay, and tread the mortar, lay hold of the brick-mould; then shall the fire devour thee; the sword shall cut thee off, it shall devour thee like the cankerworm." "There is no assuaging of thy hurt," the prophecy ends, "thy wound is grievous: all that hear the bruits of thee clap the hands over thee." In such brilliant language Nahum foretold the utter destruction of Nineveh by fire and siege. What says the archæologist? Has he the same opinion? "It is evident," says Layard, "from the ruins that Khorsabad and Nimroud" (parts of Nineveh) "were sacked and set on fire."[1] As for the utter desolation of the once splendid city, she was no sooner taken by the allied

---

[1] Compare *Nineveh and Babylon*, London, 1853.

Medes and Persians than she vanished from history. Even garrulous Herodotus,[1] who visited the spot within two centuries of the destruction of the city, has no more to say of her than this : " The Tigris was the river upon which Nineveh formerly stood." Zephaniah's words have been fulfilled to the letter : Jehovah " will make Nineveh a desolation, and dry like the wilderness : and herds shall lie down in the midst of her, all beasts of every kind; both the pelican and the porcupine shall lodge in the chapiters thereof ; their voice shall sing in the windows ; drought shall be in the thresholds ; for he hath laid bare the cedar work : this is the joyous city that dwelt carelessly, and said in her heart, I am, and there is none else beside me : how is she become a desolation, a place for beasts to lie down."[2] Is not this also supernatural prediction ?

Concerning *Tyre* again there are two notable predictions. One, by Isaiah,[3] foretells that Tyre would be humbled by Assyria, that it would be "forgotten for seventy years according to the days of one king," and that subsequently it would recover for a while, "playing the harlot with all the kingdoms of the world upon the face of the earth." This prediction exactly accords with the punishment which was inflicted upon Tyre by Nebuchadnezzar, the dynasty of Nebuchadnezzar lasting seventy years from the days of the siege, just as this prediction is also correct in saying that the great merchant city would afterwards recover for a while its former glory. Isaiah's words are unmistakable. " The utterance concerning Tyre : Howl, ye ships of Tarshish, for it is laid waste, so that there is no house, no entering in. . . . Is this your joyous city, whose antiquity is of

[1] Bk. i. § 193.   [2] Zeph. ii. 13-15.   [3] Isa. xxiii.

ancient days? Who hath purposed this against Tyre, that giveth crowns, whose merchants are princes, whose traffickers are the honourable of the earth? The Lord of Hosts hath purposed it to profane the pride of all glory, to bring into contempt all the honourable of the earth." Afterwards the Divine purpose of humiliating Tyre is further described. "Behold the land of the Chaldeans; this people was not; the Assyrian hath founded it for them that dwelt in the wilderness; they set up the towers thereof, they raised up the palaces thereof; he made Tyre a ruin." And the prediction extends to details of time as well as of destroyer. "And it shall come to pass in that day, that Tyre shall be forgotten seventy years, according to the days of one king. . . . And it shall come to pass after the end of seventy years that the Lord will visit Tyre, and she shall return to her hire, and shall play the harlot with all the kingdoms of the world upon the face of the earth." A prediction sufficiently remarkable! A second prediction concerns the ultimate destruction of Tyre, and was uttered by Ezekiel,[1] in order to abase the proud looks of this Mistress of the Seas when Jerusalem was brought low by the invader. These are the words of Ezekiel: "The word of Jehovah came unto me, saying, Son of man, because that Tyre hath said against Jerusalem, Aha, she is broken that was the gate of peoples. . . . Therefore thus saith the Lord God: Behold I am against thee, O Tyre, and will cause many nations to come up against thee, as the sea causeth the waves to come up. And they shall destroy the walls of Tyre, and break down her towers: I will also scrape her soil from her, and make her a bare rock. She shall be a

---

[1] Ezek. xxvi.

place for the spreading of nets in the midst of the sea; for I have spoken it, saith the Lord God: and she shall become a spoil to the nations." Some centuries passed before the fulfilment; but the mouth of Jehovah had spoken. At length nation after nation did come against this city of merchant princes. Alexander the Great threw himself against her walls; so did the Saracen armies, in the seventh century of our era, under the Caliph Omar, when the true decadence of Tyre commenced; five centuries later, after the capture of Ptolemais by the Mahometans, the Christian colony of Tyre left the ancient site; and to-day a few inhabitants, Turks and Christians, live on the deserted spot by fishing. Again and again Tyre has "become a spoil to the nations." Tyre is a "place for the spreading of nets." Is not this supernatural prediction?

The predictions concerning *Edom* tell the same tale of Divine knowledge divinely imparted. For what says Isaiah? "Behold (My sword) shall come down upon Edom, and upon the people of My ban, to judgment. . . . The Lord hath a sacrifice in Bozrah, and a great slaughter in the land of Edom. . . . From generation to generation it shall lie waste; none shall pass through it for ever and ever. But the pelican and the porcupine shall possess it; and the bittern and the raven shall dwell therein; and He shall stretch over it the line of confusion, and the stones of emptiness. . . . And thorns shall come up in her palaces, nettles and thistles in the fortresses thereof. . . . And the wild beasts of the desert shall meet with the howling creatures, and the he-goat shall cry to his fellow; yea, the night monster shall settle there, and shall find her a place of rest. There shall the arrowsnake make her nest, and lay, and hatch, and gather under her shadow; yea, there shall the kites be gathered, every one with his mate."[1] And what says Ezekiel? "Thus saith the Lord God: Because that Edom hath dealt against the house of Judah by taking vengeance, and hath greatly offended, and revenged himself upon them; therefore thus saith the Lord, I will stretch out Mine hand upon Edom, and will cut off man and beast from it: and I will make it desolate from Teman; even unto Dedan shall they fall by the sword."[2] And what says Amos? "Thus saith the Lord: For three transgressions of Edom, yea, for four, I will not turn away the punishment thereof; because he did pursue his brother with the sword, and corrupted his compassions, and his anger did tear perpetually, and he kept his wrath for ever: I will send a fire upon Teman, and it shall devour the palaces of Bozrah."[3] And what is the testimony of modern travellers? The ruins of Petra, the capital of ancient Edom, have been one of the remarkable re-discoveries of this century, having been found by Burckhardt in 1812, when he penetrated thither disguised as a Mussulman pilgrim. In a country of utter desolation stand these monumental, if deserted, rock-temples and tombs, eloquent of Divine vengeance. In these Idumæan palaces the serpent crawls. The place is a prey to anarchy and brigandage; and the traveller who ventures thither must do so with a strong escort. "This region, prosperous for so long, offers only the sad picture of desolation and abandonment."[4] Well may Isaiah add to his remarkable prediction, "Seek ye out of the book of Jehovah, and read." In Bozrah, the

[1] Isa. xxxiv.   [2] Ezek. xxv. 12-14.   [3] Amos ii. 11, 12.
[4] Guèrin, *La Terre Sainte*, Paris, 1884, vol. ii. p. 314.

"strong" city, as the name implies, seemingly as lasting as the rocks from which its temple and palaces were hewn, the handwriting of God may be easily read.

Other instructive instances of supernatural prediction concern Philistia,[1] and Ammon,[2] and Moab,[3] and Elam,[4] but passing these by, after simply mentioning them, let one additional example suffice for the induction upon which we are engaged. *Egypt* was frequently the subject of prediction. Indeed a minute study of the prophetical references to Egypt would richly repay the inquirer. Here two of these allusions only shall be adduced. One occurs in Isaiah,[5] and many years before any such event had taken place, speaks to the existence of a strong Jewish element in Egypt. "And the land of Judah shall become a terror unto Egypt; every one that maketh mention thereof, to him shall they turn in fear, because of the purpose of the Lord of hosts, which He purposeth against it. In that day there shall be five cities in the land of Egypt that speak the language of Canaan, and swear to the Lord of Hosts; one shall be called the city of destruction" (or "of the sun," as some read). "In that day shall there be an altar to the Lord in the midst of the land of Egypt, and a pillar at the border thereof to the Lord." Surely there is here a remarkable historical fact forecast. After the Babylonian Exile many Jews, as is well known, settled in Egypt, and especially in the newly founded city of Alexandria, opening synagogues, maintaining worship, and, at length, to satisfy their religious needs, undertaking the translation of the Hebrew Old Testa-

---

[1] Zeph. ii. 4-7; Ezek. xxv. 15-17.
[2] Jer. xlix. 1-6; Amos i. 13-15; Zeph. ii. 8-11.
[3] Isa. xv.; Jer. xlviii.; Ezek. xxv. 8-11; Amos ii. 1-3; Zeph. ii. 8-11.
[4] Jer. xlix. 34-39. [5] Isa. xix.

ment into Greek. The presence, the importance, the influence of the Jewish element in later Egyptian history are indubitable, and should be regarded in connection with this prophecy of Isaiah's. The other prediction which shall be cited occurs in Ezekiel, who wrote, "In the tenth year, in the tenth month, in the twelfth day of the month, the word of the Lord came unto me, saying, Son of man, set thy face against Pharaoh, king of Egypt, and prophesy against him, and against all Egypt; speak and say, Thus saith the Lord God, Behold I am against thee, Pharaoh, king of Egypt, the great dragon that lieth in the midst of his rivers, which hath said, My river is mine own, and I have made it for myself. . . . Therefore thus saith the Lord God: Behold I will bring a sword upon thee, and will cut off from thee man and beast. . . . Therefore, behold I am against thee, and against thy rivers, and I will make the land of Egypt an utter waste and desolation, from Migdol to Syene and even unto the border of Ethiopia: no foot of man shall pass through it, neither shall it be inhabited fifty years."[1] But, as Ezekiel goes on to point out, the treatment of Egypt shall not be as the treatment of Babylon and Assyria, and the variation is noteworthy. "For thus saith the Lord God: At the end of forty years will I gather the Egyptians from the peoples whither they were scattered: and I will bring again the captivity of Egypt, and will cause them to return into the land of Pathros, into the land of their birth; and they shall be there a base kingdom. It shall be the basest of the kingdoms; neither shall it any more lift up above the nations; and I will diminish them, that they shall no more rule over the nations."

[1] Ezek. xxix.

Could there be a better description of that fair, but down-trodden land of the Nile, which has successively tempted the rapacity of Persians and Macedonians, of Greeks and Romans, of Arabs and Turks? "It shall be the basest of kingdoms; neither shall it any more lift up above the nations." Verily, as Ezekiel said at another time: "The pride of her power hath come down."[1] Is not this supernatural prediction?

A superficial and rapid survey only has thus been taken of the very fruitful and wide field of Old Testament prophecy concerning Israel and the several nations which came more or less in contact with Israel. In process the conviction has become pronounced as to the supernatural origin of these predictions. What the prophets themselves declared concerning the actual source of their utterances, an inductive examination has fully borne out. A study of the facts has corroborated the veracity of these prophetical writers. And, as a matter of fact, the corroboration would become stronger as our examination of the evidence became more full. Has not the Divine origin of much prophecy become clear?

Possibly, however, delaying upon this branch of evidence a little longer, it may not be unadvisable to present a little of the evidence for the Divine origin of prophecy in another manner. Let the predictions of some single prophet be examined, Jeremiah, for example. Jeremiah is selected for two reasons. On the one hand, his more prominent predictions have been carefully catalogued by one of the most cultured and liberal scholars of this century, the saintly Tholuck of Halle. On the other hand, this catalogue of Tholuck's has been criticized, formally and at length, by the most

[1] Ezek. xxx. 6.

thoroughgoing and able advocate of the purely natural origin of Old Testament prophecy, the scholarly Kuenen of Leyden, a name tolerably familiar by this time to readers of these Lectures. Able advocacy on both sides singularly aids an inductive decision. The very form Dr. Kuenen's criticisms have been compelled to take has its own great suggestiveness for the inductive inquirer.

First,[1] as Dr. Tholuck has pointed out, Jeremiah, at the commencement of his prophetic career, threatened his people with the appearance of an "enemy from the north."[2] This northern enemy, as the issue showed, was the Chaldeans. Here, then, is an instance of supernatural prediction. The prophecy did not bring the Chaldeans, and the Chaldeans did not cause the prophecy. Now what has Dr. Kuenen to say? He thinks it improbable that we possess the prophecies of Jeremiah in the form in which they were originally written. Originally Jeremiah might, he thinks, have meant some other people by the people from the north, although, for pious reasons, when he committed his prophecies to writing, he "so formulated" his "warnings" that they could be applied to the actual position of his countrymen, confronted by the hosts of Nebuchadnezzar. In short, Dr. Kuenen thinks that Jeremiah altered the record from a benevolent purpose, the end apparently being thought to sanctify the means. Let Dr. Kuenen's exact words be quoted:—

"Now it is certainly *possible*," he says, "in the abstract, that Jeremiah could . . . reproduce literally what he had said in preceding years; but it is, at the same time, *exceedingly improbable*

---

[1] The order adopted is ours.
[2] Jer. i. 14; iv. 6, 7; v. 15-17; vi. 1, 22.

that he was in a condition to do so. And, besides, such a verbal reproduction would have been *superfluous*, nay, utterly *at variance with the object* which he had in view. He wished, by the public reading of his prophecies in the temple, to bring the Judeans to repentance; but then the exhortations and warnings must be so formulated that they would admit of being applied to the position in which his countrymen were at the time. The book-roll written by Baruch might indeed reproduce faithfully the main contents of the earlier addresses, but not the references to place and time which they embraced; Jeremiah might, nay must, omit these. Regarded from this point of view, the predictions concerning the 'enemy out of the north' lose the miraculous character which Tholuck seems to regard as constituting their chief value."[1]

The inductive inquirer who has made himself familiar with Jeremiah will pause before accepting such a view.

Secondly, Jeremiah mentions in his early addresses, says Dr. Tholuck, a judgment which the Egyptian should execute in the apostate kingdom of Judah.[2] This prophecy was fulfilled about twenty years later, when Pharaoh Necho defeated and slew Josiah in the valley of Megiddo and subjugated his kingdom. What has Dr. Kuenen to say to neutralize this instance of manifestly supernatural prediction? Again he calls the veracity of Jeremiah in question. "That single utterance," says Dr. Kuenen, "concerning Egypt, on which Tholuck lays stress, assumes another aspect, as soon as we consider that it was committed to writing in the fourth year after the battle of Megiddo."[3] In fact, Dr. Kuenen seems to believe concerning prophecy what Hume averred concerning miracle—that it is less likely that prophecy should be true than that testimony should be false. Dr. Kuenen impugns the honesty of Jeremiah. Should not Dr. Kuenen be requested to

---

[1] *Prophets and Prophecy in Israel*, pp. 303, 304.
[2] Jer. ii. 14-17.   [3] *Prophets and Prophecy*, p. 304.

reconsider Paley's great defence of the supernatural? Is there not "satisfactory evidence" that Jeremiah, professing to be an original witness of supernatural prediction, "passed his life in labour, danger, and suffering, voluntarily undergone in attestation" of the accounts which he delivered, and solely in consequence of his belief of such prediction? *Is* it less likely that prophecy should be true than that such testimony as Jeremiah's should be false?

Thirdly—continuing the instances of Dr. Tholuck—"in the fourth year of Jehoiakim Necho was defeated at Carchemish by Nebuchadnezzar; shortly before and after that important event, which was very soon followed by the subjection of Judah to the Chaldeans, Jeremiah announced, in the most unambiguous terms, the desolation of Jerusalem, of the Temple, and of all Judea."[1] "Therefore, behold, the days come, saith the Lord, that it shall no more be called Topheth, nor the Valley of the Son of Hinnom, but the Valley of Slaughter; for they shall bury in Topheth, because there shall be no place else. And the carcases of this people shall be meat for the fowls of the heaven, and for the beasts of the earth; and none shall fray them away. Then will I cause to cease from the cities of Judah, and from the streets of Jerusalem, the voice of mirth, and the voice of gladness, the voice of the bridegroom, and the voice of the bride; for the land shall become a waste."[2] Concerning this prediction Dr. Kuenen says nothing expressly.

Fourthly, Tholuck instances the prediction as to the duration of the Exile. "Therefore thus saith the Lord of hosts: Because ye have not heard My words, behold,

---

[1] *Prophets and Prophecy*, p. 300.   [2] Jer. vii. 32-34.

I will send and take all the families of the north, saith the Lord, and I will send unto Nebuchadnezzar the king of Babylon, My servant, and will bring them against this land. . . . And this whole land shall be a desolation, and an astonishment, and these nations shall serve the king of Babylon seventy years."[1] "For thus saith the Lord, after seventy years be accomplished for Babylon, I will visit you, and perform My good word toward you, in causing you to return to this place."[2] Again, what has Dr. Kuenen[3] to say to this remarkable forecast, so well attested by the issue? He raises three objections. The first objection is that, if Jeremiah meant an exact time by the "seventy years" of his earlier prediction, he would not have given the same time eleven years later: an objection which would be fatal if there was any ground for saying that Jeremiah dated the seventy years from the year of his prophecy; but for this there is no evidence whatever; in each prediction, earlier and later, Jeremiah foretells the duration of captivity in Babylon—"shall serve the king of Babylon seventy years"; the seventy years are to be dated, not from either of the diverse years when the prophecy concerning them was uttered, but from the actual commencement of the captivity, an event posterior to both prophecies. The second objection taken by Dr. Kuenen is that the text of the second prediction is doubtful, as to which objection it is fair to remark that the text is only considered doubtful by those to whom its contents are unwelcome. The third objection taken is that if Jeremiah did predict the duration of the captivity as seventy years, he predicted wrongly, seeing that the

---

[1] Jer. xxv. 9–11.   [2] *Ib.* xxix. 10.
[3] *Prophets and Prophecy*, pp. 309–315.

exile was not exactly seventy years; concerning which objection all that it is necessary to say is, that the case of literal fulfilment has been conceded by all inquirers, except those who have an *a priori* and philosophical objection to supernatural prophecy. To these objections Dr. Kuenen adds another: "By its moral influence," he says, "Jeremiah's prophecy of Israel's restoration, effected, or at least powerfully promoted, that restoration itself." But the point which calls for explanation is this, not that the captivity lasted seventy years, but that Jeremiah knew that it would last seventy years— not that Jeremiah's prediction had some small influence in closing the captivity, but that Jeremiah knew when, by his influence, that captivity would close. Surely Dr. Kuenen's objections fall to the ground as far as the testimony of the facts themselves goes.

Fifthly—continuing Dr. Tholuck's instances of prediction in Jeremiah—comes the prediction concerning Jehoiakim. Baruch had written, from dictation, the prophecies uttered by Jeremiah, and the roll of writing had been brought under the notice of Jehoiakim, read in his hearing by command, and then angrily burnt by the king. Subsequently by Divine order the prophecies were re-written, and this second roll was presented to the king, with a most solemn warning: "Therefore thus saith the Lord concerning Jehoiakim king of Judah: He shall have none to sit upon the throne of David; and his dead body shall be cast out in the day to the heat, and in the night to the frost."[1] Seven years afterwards, as Dr. Tholuck reminds us, Jehoiakim "fell into the hands of the Chaldeans, and died a miserable death." Is not this manifestly supernatural

[1] Jer. xxxvi. 27–32.

prediction? Dr. Kuenen's reply is, that there is no evidence as to this falling into the hands of the Chaldeans. "This is nowhere related, and was not once predicted by Jeremiah; he had, in fact, only announced that Jehoiakim should have no honourable burial, or, as it is elsewhere expressed, that 'he should be buried with the burial of an ass, dragged forth, and cast far without the gates of Jerusalem.'"[1] So far the reply to Dr. Tholuck seems warranted. But we are concerned with Jeremiah rather than Tholuck. Dr. Kuenen says concerning this ignominious death of Jehoiakim "that this actually happened may be assumed as probable." But if there was this ignominious casting forth of the dead body of the king of Judah, is not this supernatural prediction?

Sixthly, Jehoiakim was succeeded by his son Jehoiachin, who was assisted in the government by his mother. To them the prophet brings this word of Jehovah: "Say thou to the king and to the queen-mother, Humble yourselves, sit down; for your head-tires are come down, even your beautiful crown; the cities of the South are shut up, and there is none to open them; Judah is carried away captive, all of it; it is wholly carried away captive. Lift up your eyes, and behold them that come from the north; where is the flock that was given thee, thy beautiful flock? What wilt thou say, when he shall visit thee?"[2] Now, as Dr. Tholuck reminds us, after a reign of three months the young prince and his mother were transported to Babylon. Is not this again manifest prediction? No, says Dr. Kuenen, the prophecy "does not require to be explained on supernatural principles." "The prophet could easily foresee that (Jehoiakim's)

[1] *Prophets and Prophecy*, pp. 305, 306.   [2] Jer. xiii. 18–21.

consort and his son would suffer the fate which would have been assigned to (Jehoiakim) if death had not intervened."¹ But why so? Was captivity the only, or probable, alternative? Might not the two have been slaughtered, to save all further trouble to the Chaldeans?

Yet, again, seventhly, Tholuck instances the singular meeting between Jeremiah and Hananiah the Gibeonite. Upon Hananiah's denial of the approaching victory of Nebuchadnezzar, Jeremiah was divinely commanded to visit Hananiah, and say: "Hear now, Hananiah; the Lord hath not sent thee; but thou makest this people to trust in a lie. Therefore thus saith the Lord, Behold, I will send thee away from off the face of the earth: this year thou shalt die, because thou hast spoken rebellion against the Lord." And the narrative adds: "So Hananiah the prophet died the same year in the seventh month."² What says Dr. Kuenen to this? "No one will certainly ascribe decisive weight to this narrative." Why? "Many a threatening of the wrath of Deity, such as we find there, has been ratified by the issue in as striking a manner, either because it produced a deep impression upon the imagination of him whom it concerned, or by accident, as it is called." Further, Dr. Kuenen goes on to say, "We do not know whether the death of Hananiah in that year was in fact foretold in terms so unambiguous."³ In this instance again Dr. Kuenen rather prefers to think the testimony of Jeremiah false than think supernatural prediction true.

Tholuck instances, eighthly, Jeremiah's prediction of the Fall of Babylon,⁴ already noticed. Here, again, the

---
¹ *Prophets and Prophecy*, p. 306.   ² Jer. xxviii. 15-17.
³ *Prophets and Prophecy*, pp. 304, 305.   ⁴ Jer. l., li.

prophecy is so remarkable, and is so demonstrably supernatural, that Dr. Kuenen sees no way out of it except by denying that Jeremiah wrote the prophecy at all. The prophecy must, he thinks, be ascribed to a younger prophet, who wrote after Babylon had fallen.[1] But is not this adapting facts to theory, rather than shaping theory upon facts?

Lastly, Tholuck calls attention to the exact fulfilment of Jeremiah's prediction concerning the manner and consequences of the defeat by Nebuchadnezzar of the troops of Zedekiah, when Jerusalem should be taken, the Temple burned, and the surviving population deported to Babylon. All this again Dr. Kuenen regards as certainly not supernatural prediction. It is simply, he thinks, an instance of the clearness of view of Jeremiah. "Jeremiah saw things as they really were, while the opposite party yielded to all kinds of illusion;" and, as Dr. Kuenen goes on to say, "we willingly give Jeremiah the credit which is due to him on that account; but it is impossible for us to see the proof of the Divine origin of his expectations in the fact that they are realized;" an opinion surely as individual as singular. Must not the inductive inquirer, when he sees a life like Jeremiah's, claiming at once to be inspired by God, and accredited by very numerous unmistakable fulfilments of the predictions made in the Divine name, hold a distinctly contrary opinion, and say, "that it is impossible for him to see anything else but the proof of the Divine origin of Jeremiah's expectations in the fact that they are constantly realized"?[2]

Surely, then, an inductive inquiry into the phenomena

[1] *Prophets and Prophecy*, pp. 308, 309.   [2] *Ib.* pp. 306-308.

presented by the Biblical Prophecies which are not Messianic shows the Divine origin of such prophecy. A similar origin, as will now be seen, is suggested by an inductive examination of the facts of Messianic Prophecy.

Upon the threshold, however, of this examination of facts as grave as fascinating, let a general principle be recalled, which has already engaged our attention once in the course of this inquiry, a general principle having reference indeed to all facts which concern any evolutionary process. The principle is this (it may be stated in a variety of ways), that enlargement of vision is often change of view; that what seems to be the main purpose of any fact, or series of facts, at one moment, may appear insignificant on a wider survey; that conclusions apparently warranted at one time may require to be amended upon a more inclusive look; that the reason of one phase of growth may not be the predominant ground of a later and more developed phase. A few simple instances may illustrate the principle. Thus the purpose of childhood studied in itself is one thing, whereas as regarded in relation to the whole life of man it is quite another. The end of a palm-tree may be at one moment to grow foliage and at another to grow fruit. Regard the Carboniferous Age in itself, and its *raison d'être* may seem to be its flora and fauna, the movement of its seas and the roar of its forests; but, regarded from the standpoint of the present geological epoch, its end may rather be thought to be the provision of coal-fields for man. Indeed, the whole wide range of growth might afford instances in point. Everything which has a life-history fulfils at least a double end; it has relations with its own time, and as part of a scheme of things, it has relation to the times to come.

This principle of a twofold relationship also holds in prophecy; and, for many reasons, it is desirable to bear the fact in mind. Every prophecy fulfils a twofold purpose; it has a purpose which is immediate, and a purpose which is prospective. What has been seen to obtain in types, which after all are but a variety of prophecy, obtains with prophecy most strictly regarded; it is at once a message to its own age, and a demonstration to the times which follow.

It is of the highest moment, at the present juncture of our inquiry, to remember that prophecy, Divine knowledge divinely imparted, may have a twofold significance in the intention of its Divine Imparter. *Before* fulfilment, a prophecy may *awaken expectancy: after* fulfilment, a prophecy may *afford proof*. For instance, before the actual event, the prophecy of the Fall of Babylon might serve to fan the dying confidence of the Jewish exiles; after the event, this same prophecy might demonstrate, not to Jews only, but to all peoples, the reality of revelation.

Further, like all prophecy, Messianic prophecy, or prophecy concerning the person and work of the coming redeemer, may also be viewed from two sides. Prior to fulfilment, the aim of Messianic prophecy was, it is manifest, to preserve among the Jewish nation, throughout its chequered history, a forward look to a coming day. After fulfilment, the effect of the same prophecy is, it is equally manifest, to disclose to all, who care to consider the evidence, a very remarkable series of Divine revelations, "spoken at sundry times and in divers manners." It is, of course, with this demonstrative value of Messianic prophecy that any inductive inquirer into the claims of the Old Testament is specially concerned. If, naturally, there is much interest in treating "the Messianic ideal of the Old Testament by itself and for itself," as has been so ably done by Professor Briggs, in his *Messianic Prophecy*,[1] still this is not the task before us now. For us there is a paramount interest in inquiring whether what are intelligibly called the Messianic Prophecies of the Old Testament and the several circumstances of the life and work of Jesus of Nazareth, are related to each other as prediction and fulfilment. For if they are, if what the Old Testament has to say about a coming Deliverer is unquestionably fulfilled in what the New Testament has to say about a Deliverer who has come, then another demonstration will have been given, and that of a very conclusive kind, of the reality of supernatural revelation.

Now ours is an inductive examination, and when we come to investigate the Old Testament records inductively—for the Messianic prophecies overflow the Prophetical Books as such, and it will not complicate our inquiry to regard the entire Old Testament at once in this Messianic respect—it is seen, as a matter of fact, that there is a very remarkable series of predictions, apparently belonging to a cycle of purpose all their own, and promising in no measured terms a remarkable future deliverance of an ever-widening and ever-deepening kind, a spiritual deliverance, a deliverance supernatural as well as extraordinary. If at first sight many of these prophecies appear to be local, temporary, and

---

[1] *Messianic Prophecy, the Prediction of the Fulfilment of Redemption through the Messiah; a Critical Study of the Messianic Passages of the Old Testament in the Order of their Development*, Edinburgh, 1866.

transient in their reference, further inquiry shows that should their realization be found in any common personage or ordinary event, then these prophecies appear singularly extravagant. Indeed, what Bishop Lowth says of the Second Psalm applies to most of these prophecies, "If on the first reading of the Psalm we consider the character of David in the literal sense, the composition appears sufficiently perspicuous, and abundantly illustrated by facts from the sacred history: through the whole, indeed, there is an unusual fervour of language, a brilliancy of metaphor; and sometimes the diction is uncommonly elevated, as if to intimate that something of a more sublime and important nature lay concealed within; if, in consequence of this indication, we turn our minds to contemplate the internal sense, and apply the same passages to an allegorical David, a meaning not only more sublime, but even more perspicuous rises to view."[1] So is it often in the Old Testament. Local fulfilment appears all too slight. The thoughts are carried on to a great coming Deliverance, although, as studied in the Old Testament alone, that future deliverance, whilst displaying some sort of order in development, shows also features not without apparent contradiction.

However, What are the facts of the case? For it is with facts we are concerned. The development of conception in the Old Testament, concerning the deliverance for which men should hope, ran somewhat as follows:—

The predictions are at first of a great coming deliverance. No sooner did sin enter into the world, upon subtle diabolical temptation, than a promise is made to

[1] *Lectures on the Sacred Poetry of the Hebrews*, vol. i. lecture xi.

Eve's offspring of successful conflict with Satan, in the memorable words to the serpent, "And I will put enmity between thee and the woman, and between thy seed and her seed; he shall bruise thy head, and thou shalt bruise his heel." [1] In this prophecy, be it observed, the future deliverance promised is associated with the seed of the woman. Many centuries pass away, and at length this First Evangel becomes a promise to Abraham of deliverance through Isaac, in whose "seed all the nations of the earth shall be blessed." [2] Two generations more, and the promise of blessing through Isaac becomes a promise of world-wide dominion to a prince who should come of Judah's loins; "the sceptre," said dying Jacob, "shall not depart from Judah, nor the ruler's staff from between his feet, until Shiloh come." [3] Thus the Patriarchal Age closes in such a way as to keep the eyes of the sons of Jacob intent upon a coming Deliverer, a son of Eve, a son of Abraham, a son, a prince of the house of Judah. All these are facts sufficiently curious:

Following on down the stream of time, the gaze is still forward, but the Messianic prediction of Moses' days assumes a different character. Moses foretells the advent of a prophet like himself. "And Jehovah said unto me, I will raise them up a prophet from among their brethren, like unto thee; and I will put My words in his mouth, and he shall speak unto them all that I shall command him. And it shall come to pass that whosoever will not hearken unto My words which he shall speak in My name, I will require it of him." [4] Thus the expectation of Israel is concentrated upon prophecy; and the future deliverance is associated

[1] Gen. iii. 15.   [2] Ib. xxii. 15–18.   [3] Ib. xlix. 10.   [4] Deut. xviii. 18, 19.

with a second Moses, a great prophet, whose words should be particularly Divine, and therefore peculiarly divisive, permanently winnowing because uniquely authoritative. If at first sight this looks like a promise of a prophetical order, further regard opens much difficulty in such an interpretation :

Four centuries pass, and a development of the older prince idea takes place. In recognition of the earnest desire of David to build a temple to Jehovah, the promise is divinely made to David, by means of Nathan, that the Davidic house shall know no end. "Moreover," said Nathan to David, "the Lord telleth thee that the Lord will make thee a house : when thy days be fulfilled, and thou shalt sleep with thy fathers, I will set up thy seed after thee, which shall proceed out of thy bowels, and I will establish his kingdom ; he shall build a house for My name, and I will establish the throne of his kingdom for ever, . . . and thine house and thy kingdom shall be made sure for ever before thee : thy throne shall be established for ever."[1] Here, again, if first thoughts seem to point to fulfilment in Solomon, second thoughts suggest difficulty, either in expression or in fact, in so speedy an execution of the promise. Still the forward glance is fostered :

This idea of the Kingly Messiah appears again and again in the Psalms. A few illustrative instances may suffice. In one Psalm David represents a Divine utterance made by Jehovah to the coming Messianic king, whom David recognizes as his lord, though his son.

"The Lord saith unto my lord, Sit thou at my right hand,
Until I make thine enemies thy footstool.

---
[1] 2 Sam. vii. 12-16.

> The Lord shall stretch forth the rod of thy strength out of Zion.
> Rule thou in the midst of thine enemies.
> Thy people are freewill offerings in the day of thy power :
> In holy attire, from the womb of the morning,
> Thy youth are to thee as dew.
> The Lord hath sworn, and will not repent,
> Thou art a priest for ever,
> After the manner of Melchizedek :
> The Lord at thy right hand
> Hath stricken through kings in the day of his wrath.
> He shall judge among the nations,
> The places are full of dead bodies ;
> He hath stricken through the head in a wide land.
> He shall drink of the brook in the way :
> Therefore shall he lift up the head."[1]

In which beautiful as well as remarkable utterance the future deliverance is associated with a descendant of David's, a great king, and therefore a royal priest. In the Second Psalm again the same idea appears of a great future deliverer, of royal blood, nay, of Divine relationship, the appointed king of Zion, Jehovah's anointed, who shall have the ends of the earth for his possession. A similar idea is expressed as forcibly as touchingly in the Seventy-second Psalm :

Further, this kingly character of the future redeemer several of the prophets develop, especially the prophets prior to Isaiah. They speak with eagerness of a noble scion of David's line, who should be at once a universal ruler and a universal blessing, approving himself for all time great David's greater son. Thus Hosea tells how, after a period of great trouble and humiliation, "the children of Israel will return, and seek the Lord their God, and David their king, and will come with fear unto the Lord and to His goodness in the latter days."[2]

[1] Psa. cx. [2] Hosea iii. 5.

And Amos writes, how, after the severe visitation of the Divine displeasure upon the chosen people, Jehovah declares that "in that day" He will "raise up the tabernacle of David which is fallen."[1] Micah, again, after a circumstantial prediction of woe, gives a circumstantial prediction of blessing. "But thou, Bethlehem-Ephratah, which art little to be among the families of Judah, out of thee shall one come forth unto me that is to be ruler in Israel; whose goings forth are from of old, from ancient days."[2]

Isaiah, again, who introduces quite other ideas of the future deliverer, has much to say about the Coming King and the Coming Kingdom. What David said vaguely, Isaiah states clearly. But Isaiah also introduces apparently contradictory conceptions. The coming deliverer, in his view, is to be a son of David, and of royal lineage, but, at the same time, is to be of Divine birth. Not only so, but although the kingdom was his birthright, this universal kingdom was also to be won by exceptional suffering. The Prince of Peace is, in his view, the Mighty God, and the Suffering Servant. To the features of the regal and Divine Messiah, Isaiah adds another of the Messiah who suffers vicariously for human sin.[3]

Such are the principal facts of a Messianic kind which meet the inductive inquirer. No attempt has been made to treat of them exhaustively. A few suggestive data have alone been collated. More was unnecessary. The facts are well known, and can be readily examined at length in specialistic treatises. All

---

[1] Amos ix. 11-13. [2] Micah v. 2.
[3] Compare *Scriptural Doctrine of Sacrifice*, pp. 210, 211.

that was needful was to point out the salient features of these Messianic prophecies. But, even thus slightly viewed, it is evident that, considered apart from all New Testament conceptions, the facts adduced present wholly unsolved problems. The problems suggested are many; the solutions are distant. Nevertheless, one conclusion soon shows itself as valid as inevitable. That conclusion is that, as has been previously said, a forward look was cultivated throughout the Old Testament times by this series of predictions, these predictions ceaselessly insisting that man never is, but is always to be blest, whilst, at the same time, hope in the future, if anywhere, is the only valid lesson of ideals which are constantly disappointed. Where in the seed of Eve, or the seed of Abraham, or the seed of Judah, or the seed of David is this coming Deliverer to be found? Does Moses satisfy the conditions of the promise, or Joshua, or Solomon, or Hezekiah? Nor are the difficulties personal only. There are difficulties of conception also. Side by side with this primary conception of a future deliverer, are the predictions that the deliverance is to be by a prophet, nay, by a priest, nay, by one of Divine birth. Yet again, together with the seemingly incompatible ideas of prophecy, kingship, priesthood, human birth, and Divine person, there comes in the further statement that the future deliverer will "pour out his soul unto death"—"be numbered with transgressors"—"bear the sin of many"—"prolong his days" only when he hath "made his soul a trespass-offering." Certainly the facts have their interest, but to the inductive inquirer into the Old Testament only, they cannot but be profoundly mysterious. Where is the key which can open this lock of many wards?

The perplexities of types vanish on the appearance of their antitypes. The problems of prophecies disappear on the advent of their fulfilments. Is there a great deliverer known to men, who can bring harmony out of apparent contradiction, and simplicity of view out of the bafflingly complex? To ask the question is a long way towards its answer.

As a matter of fact, which no serious inquirer can ignore, the unsolved problems of the Old Testament Messianic predictions receive a satisfactory solution in the New Testament Messiah. In Jesus of Nazareth there really appears a great deliverer, the greatest of prophets, the royal priest, the universal king, who, at once Son of David and Son of God, establishes an everlasting rule, not by right alone, but actually by vicarious suffering unto death. Jesus is the master-key which unlocks all the complicated wards of Old Testament prophecy. To use another figure, Jesus is the pure light in which all the colours of Old Testament prophecy may be found upon analysis. No inductive inquirer will overlook the striking fact. In Jesus the prophecies of the Old Testament concerning a coming deliverance — not without numerous difficulties and many apparent contradictions so long as they are viewed simply in themselves—find at once fulfilment, ratification, and explanation. On the advent of this Redeemer, the forecasts of redemption receive their necessary supplementing. In this instance, too, fulfilment has made forecast more intelligible.

But if this be so—if the Messianic prophecies of the Old Testament are fulfilled in Jesus—another conclusion also follows. These Messianic prophecies are demonstratively supernatural revelations, Divine knowledge divinely imparted. No other conclusion accords with the facts which have been cited. Prediction can only emanate from knowledge of the fulfilment; fulfilment can only emanate from knowledge of the prediction. Further, when the Messianic prophecies were uttered, the advent of Jesus was in the far future, and was unknown as such to the prophetic authors. And yet again, no mere human study of the Old Testament prophecies could have produced such fulfilment as is evident in the life and death of Jesus. The fulfilment cannot have suggested the prophecies, and the prophecies cannot have suggested the fulfilment. In other words, such prediction as this can only emanate from superhuman knowledge of the fulfilment; just as such fulfilment as this can only emanate from superhuman knowledge of the prediction. In short, the inductive inquirer, in face of the facts of Old Testament Messianic prophecy, is compelled to ask three questions—first, can the prophets themselves have originated such predictions?—second, could any mere man, upon the study of these predictions, have compassed their fulfilment, adducing credible evidence of his Divine as well as human birth, dying for men, convincing men that he had so died, establishing a world-wide kingdom, personating at once a great king, a great prophet, and a great priest?—third, do not such predictions and such fulfilment inevitably point to a Divine knowledge of both divinely imparted—in a word, to revelation? Was not Jesus able to fulfil the prophecies because He first planned them?

Thus far then, in this lecture, the Divine origin of Prophecy has been inductively considered, many grounds having disclosed themselves for believing that the Old Testament representation of prophecy as revelation is absolutely correct. Especially have the many and striking phenomena of prediction pointed to the supernatural origin of prophecy. Now, for a little while, the Divine relations of the Prophetical Books which chronicle this supernatural prophecy call to be considered.

The Divine origin of prophecy, then, as has been seen, follows from the demonstrable Divine relations of the prophets. From the Divine relations of the prophets also follow the Divine relations of the Books of the Prophets. As the Inspiration of Moses is the pledge of the Inspiration of the Books of Moses, so the Inspiration of the Prophets is the guarantee of the Inspiration of the Books of the Prophets. The point scarcely needs lengthy consideration.

Indeed, so far as the so-called *Prophetæ Posteriores* are concerned, there is little difficulty. That Isaiah, and Jeremiah, and Ezekiel, and the several minor prophets, as inspired men, wrote inspired books, is manifest. The prophet, as has been seen, was an organ of Divine revelation, and, as such, had been peculiarly fitted for his career by a life of Divine communion and by many specific hours when the Divine message became indubitable ; manifestly when such an inspired man committed to writing his communications from heaven, the literary product was an inspired product. Of this collection of prophetical writings Peter's sentiment is evidently just that " no prophecy ever was brought by the will of man, but men spake from God being moved by the Holy Ghost."

So much is clear concerning the *Prophetæ Posteriores*

—the Books of the Greater and the Minor Prophets. If there is revelation anywhere, Divine knowledge divinely imparted, it is in these books. If there is inspiration anywhere, Divine equipment, that is to say, for the transmission of revelation, it is also evidently in these books. These Later Prophets are very largely prediction, in other words, supernatural revelation concerning the future made available for mankind by supernatural inspiration.

But what shall be said of the *Prophetæ Priores* ? Are they also revelation? Are they also inspired ? Almost wholly history as these Earlier Prophets are, is this history to be regarded as in any sense supernatural ?

It would seem so. These Historical Books of the Old Testament, which form the so-called *Prophetæ Priores* are, it would appear, more than common annals. Rather are they a Divine interpretation of human history. They apparently embody an element of revelation. They are, it seems, the product of inspired men. Neither was anything in them, "ever brought by the will of man, but men wrote being moved by the Holy Ghost." These Earlier Prophets were written, there is reason for saying, by prophets,—by men, that is, who were at once chosen instruments of revelation and chosen vessels of inspiration. At least the inductive inquirer is confronted with considerable evidence of the prophetical authorship of these Historical Books, and of course, when satisfied as to the trend of the evidence, the inductive inquirer will not shrink from the implications of the evidence.

The evidence for the prophetical authorship of these books may be arranged under four heads :—

First : There is the evidence of the name. These books were called " Prophets " apparently as early as the days of Ezra. The only tangible explanation of the name is found in a belief on the part of Ezra, and the Jews of his day, that these books, these historical books, owe their existence to the prophets.

Secondly: These books, especially the books of Samuel and Kings, show a most intimate acquaintance with the sayings and doings of the prophets. Many prophetic conversations are minutely recorded, as are many strictly personal acts of the prophets. The numerous chapters upon the careers of Samuel and Elijah and Isaiah are good instances.

Thirdly: Certain portions of the history of Israel are expressly said to be due to certain prophets, whose names are mentioned. The evidence is noteworthy. Thus the history of David is attributed to three prophets, Samuel, Nathan, and Gad : " Now the acts of David the king, first and last, behold they are written in the words of Samuel the seer, and in the words of Nathan the prophet, and in the words of Gad the seer ; with all his reign and might, and the times that went over him, and over Israel, and over all the kingdoms of the countries." [1] Similarly the annals of Solomon's reign are ascribed to Nathan, Ahijah, and Iddo the prophets : " Now the rest of the acts of Solomon, first and last, are they not written in the words of Nathan the prophet, and in the prophecy of Ahijah the Shilonite, and in the vision of Iddo the seer, the vision against Jeroboam the seer of Nebat." [2] Similarly the story of the reign of Rehoboam is associated with Shemaiah and Iddo, the prophets : " Now the acts of Rehoboam, first and last, are they not written in the words of Shemaiah the prophet and Iddo the seer for a register." [3] The history

[1] 1 Chron. xxix. 29, 30.   [2] 2 Chron. ix. 29.   [3] *Ib.* xii. 15

of Abijah, again, is coupled with the name of Iddo: "And the rest of the acts of Abijah, and his ways, and his words, are written in the commentary (Midrash) of the prophet Iddo."[1] Further, Jehu the prophet is said to have written the annals of Jehoshaphat: "And the rest of the acts of Jehoshaphat, first and last, behold they are written in the words of Jehu the son of Hanani, which [the rest of the acts][2] was transmitted in the book of the kings of Israel."[3] Yet again, the narrative of Uzziah's reign is put down to Isaiah: "Now the rest of the acts of Uzziah, first and last, did Isaiah, the prophet, the son of Amoz, write";[4] just as the narrative of the reign of Hezekiah is also said to have been told by Isaiah: "Now the rest of the acts of Hezekiah, and his goodness, behold, they are written in the vision of Isaiah the prophet, the son of Amoz, in the book of the kings of Judah and Israel."[5] *At least* these various express references to prophetic authorship show that in the days of Ezra it was commonly believed that the several prophets mentioned by name were the writers of the national annals of their day; and *at least* these annals were the materials from which the Books of Samuel and Kings were composed.

But, fourthly: There is good reason for believing that the extant Books of Samuel and Kings are these very products themselves of the pens of Samuel, Nathan, Gad, Ahijah, Iddo, Shemaiah, Jehu, and Isaiah.

For mark the facts of the case. We have two parallel accounts of the kingdoms of Israel and Judah, the one

---

[1] 2 Chron. xiii. 22.
[2] Compare 2 Chron. xxvi. 22 and Bertheau, *Die Bücher der Chronik*, Leipsic, 1873, pp. xxix and 337.
[3] 2 Chron. xx. 34.   [4] *Ib.* xxvi. 22.   [5] *Ib.* xxxii. 32

manifestly written prior to the Captivity, and the other as manifestly written subsequently, the so-called Books of Kings and Chronicles. Into the diverse aims of these books, and into the minute questions of their date and authorship, we need not enter. But one peculiarity of the books calls for mention. Again and again, as we have already seen, Chronicles refers to a collateral series of documents as containing "the rest of the acts" of the kings, of whose history Chronicles consists. Now are there data for identifying this earlier series of documents? There surely are such data. For instance, Chronicles frequently refers (for supplementary matter not contained in itself) to the earlier authority—manifestly well known to the audience to which Chronicles appeals—as "*The Book of the Kings of Judah and Israel*": "And, behold, the acts of Asa, first and last, lo, they are written in the Book of the Kings of Judah and Israel";[1] or, again, "And the rest of the acts of Amaziah, first and last, behold they are written in the Book of the Kings of Judah and Israel";[2] or, again, "And the rest of the acts of Jotham, and all his wars, and his ways, lo, they are written in the Book of the Kings of Israel and Judah";[3] or, again, "And the rest of his acts, and all his ways, first and last, behold, they are written in the Book of the Kings of Judah and Israel";[4] or, again, "And the rest of the acts of Josiah, and his goodness according to what was written in the law of the Lord, and his acts, first and last, behold they are written in the Book of the Kings of Israel and Judah";[5] or, again, "And the rest of the acts of Jehoiakim, and his abominations which he did, and that

---

[1] 2 Chron. xvi. 11.   [2] *Ib.* xxv. 26.   [3] *Ib.* xxvii. 7.
[4] *Ib.* xxviii. 26.   [5] *Ib.* xxxv. 27.

which was found in him, behold they are written in the Book of the Kings of Israel and Judah."[1] Once a well-known collateral authority is referred to as the "Acts of the Kings of Israel." "And the rest of the acts of Manasseh, and his prayer unto his gods, and the words of the seers that spake to him in the name of the Lord God of Israel, lo, they are *in the Acts of the Kings of Israel.*"[2] However here, though the expression is peculiar, there is no valid reason for saying that "the Acts of the Kings of Israel" is a different book from "the Book of the Kings of Israel and Judah." Of course the "Book of the Kings of Israel and Judah" might contain the "Acts of the Kings of Israel." The Book of Chronicles—for both Chronicles and Kings now extant in two books were originally one book—refers then to a collateral authority which it names the Book of the Kings of Israel and Judah; just as—the fact need only be named—the Book of Kings again and again refers to supplementary histories, which it names the "Book of the Chronicles of the Kings of Judah" and the "Book of the Chronicles of the Kings of Israel." Is not the "Book of the Kings of Israel and Judah" to which Chronicles refers, the Book of the Kings of our present Bibles? The only objection which has been taken to such a view is, as Canon Rawlinson says, that it "is contradicted . . . by the fact that 'Kings' often does not contain the information for which the writer of Chronicles refers his readers to the work in question";[3] an objection fatal if true. But there is good ground for doubting its truth. "The Book of Kings contains,"

---

[1] 2 Chron. xxxvi. 8.   [2] *Ib.* xxxiii. 18.
[3] *The Holy Bible with an Explanatory and Critical Commentary by Bishops and other Clergy of the Anglican Church*, vol. iii., London, 1873, p. 160.

says Canon Rawlinson, "no account of the 'sons' of Joash, or of the 'burdens' uttered against him, which were written in the 'Commentary' of the Book of Kings." True, but the Commentary of the Book of Kings is not necessarily the Book of Kings; as the Canon has himself said, "the word used, *Midrash*, occurs but twice in the whole of the Old Testament, both times in Chronicles. It is common, however in Rabbinical Hebrew, *where it always has the meaning of something like an exposition or interpretation, not of a primary work.*" Surely ignorance as to what this commentary or *midrash* was, is no ground for identifying the "Commentary of the Book of Kings" with "the Book of Kings." "Nor does 'the Book of Kings,'" continues the Canon, "contain any record of the prayer of Manasseh, or the 'places' wherein he built high places and set up groves and graven images, which were recorded in the sayings of the seers." The Canon refers to a passage in Chronicles, which runs thus in the Revised Version : " Now the rest of the acts of Manasseh, and *his prayers unto his God*, and the words of the seers that spake to him in the name of the Lord, the God of Israel, behold, they are written among the acts of the Kings of Israel. His prayer also, *and how God was intreated of him*, and all his sins and his trespass, and the places wherein he built high places, and set up the Asherim and the graven images, before he humbled himself; behold, they are written in *the history of Hozai.*" But has not a series of mistranslations been made here which have misled both the Canon and the Revisers ? According to the Hebrew" his prayer *unto his God*" might equally be "his prayer *to his gods*" ; and "how *God was intreated of him*" might, much more literally, be "and *how incense was offered for him.*" Such renderings, too, harmonize most accurately, on the one hand, with the references to Manasseh's sins and trespass, and, on the other hand, with the accentuation of "the Lord the God of Israel" in whose name the *seers* expostulated with the king. Further, by the words translated "*the history of Hozai*" the Hebrew means no more than "*the words of the seers* (or *the prophets*)." Now, as a matter of fact, when we turn to the Book of Kings, just what *is* told us concerning Manasseh [1] is his doing after the abomination of the heathen,—his building of the high places,—his making an Asherah,—his setting up the graven image in the house of the Lord,—and the speaking of the Lord in expostulation by His servants the prophets. *There is therefore every reason for saying that the Books of the Kings of Israel and Judah referred to so frequently in Chronicles is just our Books of the Kings.*

But if so, then *our Book of Kings is expressly associated with the Order of Prophets.*

The evidence is as follows:—As has just been seen in reference to Manasseh, "the Acts of the Kings of Israel" (part apparently of the Book of Kings) is also called, it would seem, "the words of the seers"[2] (oddly translated "the history of Hozai)." Further, the words of the prophet Jehu, the son of Hanani, are expressly stated to form part of the Book of the Kings of Israel.[3] Yet again, the narratives of Uzziah's and Hezekiah's reigns in the Book of Kings are ascribed to Isaiah by name, as we have seen. These "words of Jehu," then, and these "words of Isaiah" are separate sections of the Book of Kings. And observe further, Chronicles refers again

[1] 2 Kings. xxi.   [2] 2 Chron. xxxiii. 18.   [3] *Ib*. xx. 34 (Hebrew).

and again, as we have seen, to *Kings* for supplementary matter; it does so concerning Asa, and Joash, and Amaziah, and Jotham, and Ahaz, and Josiah, and Jehoiakim. But for supplementary matter concerning Solomon Chronicles refers to *the words of Nathan and Ahijah and Iddo*, the prophets, and concerning Rehoboam to *the words of Shemaiah and Iddo*, and concerning Ahijah to *the words of Iddo*, and concerning Jehoshaphat to *the words of Jehu*, and so on. But the Books of Kings contain just these supplementary matters; in fact, precisely what is ascribed to the words of the prophets is found in the extant Book of Kings. The more detailed the examination the more evident is the fact. Now how came Chronicles to mention the "words of prophets" and omit the customary reference to the "Book of the Kings of Judah and Israel," unless the "words of the prophets" and the "Books of the Kings of Judah and of Israel" were one and the same? A most satisfactory explanation, in short, of the peculiar mode of reference of Chronicles to the supplementary historical source would surely be,—that, in the view of the Chronicler, the "Book of Kings" and the "words of the prophets" were identical. "The words" of Nathan and Ahijah and Iddo and Shemaiah were other sections of the Book of Kings. At any rate, the collateral authorities quoted by the Chronicler as the "Book of Kings" and the "words" of the several prophets named, exactly make up the Book of Kings as known to us. In fine, it is extremely probable that the Book of Kings, as we possess it, emanated from Nathan and Ahijah and Iddo and Shemaiah and Jehu and Isaiah—from the prophetical order, that is to say.

Further, if the two Books of Kings, known in ancient

time as the Book of Kings, emanated from these prophets, then the Books of Samuel are, by parity of reasoning, most probably the product of Samuel and Nathan and Gad; and Joshua and Judges are also the works of Samuel, as ancient tradition said. That Joshua and Judges most distinctly show prophetical handiwork, the contents of these books are evidence enough. The same great lessons concerning the relations of Israel and Jehovah which are the burden of prophetic speech and writing in Samuel and Kings are the great lessons of Joshua and Judges. Throughout these *Prophetæ Priores*, in fact, the same great religious lessons are taught, in all lights and with endless illustration, those lessons being two mainly—that *national misfortune* resulted from *national wrong-doing*, and that *national prosperity* followed upon *national obedience* to the Law of Jehovah.[1]

Several lines of evidence thus converge to deepen the impression that the entire Prophetical Books of the Old Testament, earlier as well as Later, Historical as well as Predictive, emanated from the order of prophets—are instinct, that is to say, with the inspiration of men exceptionally moved by God.

[1] Compare *Scriptural Doctrine of Sacrifice*, pp. 179-188.

LECTURE VIII.

THE DOCTRINE OF THE INSPIRATION OF THE OLD TESTAMENT.

LECTURE VIII.

THE DOCTRINE OF THE INSPIRATION OF THE OLD TESTAMENT.

TWO great sections of the Old Testament, the Law and the Prophets, have now been inductively considered, with what fulness the limits of our space would permit. The third section remains, the so-called Writings (or Graphia), Holy Writings (or Hagiographa). These Holy Writings consist, be it remembered, of certain Poetical Books (the Psalms, the Proverbs, the Book of Job, the Song of Songs, Lamentations, and Ecclesiastes), and of certain Historical Books (the Chronicles, and the Books of Ezra and Nehemiah, to which may be appended Ruth and Esther). Then, in addition to these poetical and historical books, these Holy Writings also contain—it has always been a great problem why—one prophetico-historical book, the Book of Daniel.

All these books deserve and will repay the most careful and minute investigation. Their consideration has, too, doubtless many discoveries in store for the inquirer who is at once scientific, thoroughgoing, and respectful, nay, for many generations of inquirers. For it would be idle to regard the past exegetical studies of these books, notably of the Psalms and Chronicles, as otherwise than preparatory. In fact, there is much need for lifelong devotion to such Biblical studies. Problems abound, concerning text, concerning interpretation, concerning authorship, concerning date, concerning purpose, and it can scarcely be said as yet that these branches of inquiry have been entered upon in a satisfactory spirit. "By particular persons attending to, comparing, and pursuing intimations scattered up and down," as Bishop Butler said of the Bible generally, there are, "in the continuance of learning and liberty," many things in these Holy Writings to be learnt, many difficulties to be removed, many enigmas to be solved. May the explorers be many, their methods competent, their tools fit, their attitude reverent as free, their perseverance prolonged as patient!

However, so far as the present inquiry is concerned, lengthy examination of these Holy Writings is not called for. One important principle, itself an induction from very extensive data, alone requires statement. This principle formulated, it will be seen that these Holy Writings supply no additional facts of importance in framing a doctrine of the Inspiration of the Old Testament. As far as the Book of Daniel is concerned, it is virtually one of the Prophetical Books; that is to say, it presents us with the same kind of data that they do; and as for the remainder of the Holy Writings, they all come beneath the principle of which we are speaking. The principle in question may be thus expressed. The Books of the Law, as has been seen, present us with a record of the progress of Divine revelation from Adam to Moses: the Books of the Prophets, again, present us with a record of Divine revelation from Moses to Malachi; whereas the Holy Writings *present us with a record*, not of revelation, but *of the assimilation of revelation*. It was a true perception which led the first compilers of the Old Testament Canon to put these Hagiographa in a category apart. Just because these books do not confront us with objective revelation they are invaluable. Their preciousness, their pricelessness, lies in their subjective qualities. These books mirror life in God. They rather reflect man as influenced by what he knows of Deity than God as moved by what He knows of man. They portray religion, not revelation; the Divine side of human life, not the human side of Divine life. Compare, for example, the Psalter with Isaiah. Both are poetry, and poetry of a very exalted kind; but the Psalter is lyric, Isaiah is didactic. Isaiah describes objective revelation; its key-note is everywhere, "Thus saith the Lord:" the Psalter depicts subjective experience; its constant undertone is "Thy law is a lamp unto my feet, and a light unto my path." Further, if Isaiah details experience, it is in order to emphasize revelation; if the Psalter dwells upon revelation, it is to accentuate experience. Even the Messianic references of the Psalter do not seem to be new revelation, but the reiteration, after assimilation, of revelations already received. Or contrast the Prophecies of Jeremiah with the Book of Lamentations. Both proceed from the same writer. Both deal with the same distressing epoch. Both utter the same wail of woe. But Jeremiah is revelation: Lamentations is experience. "The word which came unto Jeremiah from the Lord," is the subject matter of Jeremiah: "Is it nothing to you all ye that pass by? Behold and see if there be any sorrow like unto my sorrow," is the subject-matter of Lamentations. Or consider the historical books of the Hagiographa, idyllic Ruth, Oriental Esther, pragmatic Ezra. They are simply annals. They lack the didactic, the prophetic element. They recount history for its own sake, not for the sake of its Divine lessons. They rather show us man's interest in the ways of God than God's interest in the ways of man. In illustration, let the Books of Kings and of Chronicles be read side by side. In Chronicles we manifestly have the work of the historian; in Kings the work of the prophet. The same characteristic—of revelation assimilated—appears throughout the Hagiographa. These Holy Writings paint a picture of the holy life, both individual and national consequent upon a knowledge of the Divine revelation in Law and Prophets. Revelation is the theme of Law and Prophets; Holiness, resulting from revelation, is the theme of the Holy Writings.

After the express statement of such a principle—that the Holy Writings show us not so much revelation as revelation assimilated—it is possible to pass straightway to the consideration of the Inspiration of the Old Testament.

The main problem which has occupied our attention all through these lectures is, whether a Divine as well as human origin must be sought for the Old Testament. Of the human origin it has not been necessary to speak at length. What is written in human speech, and according to human laws of composition, must have emanated from human minds and hands. The human origin of the Old Testament has been taken for granted. But the question of questions which has engrossed us from first to last has been, whether human causes suffice to explain the existence of the Old Testament—in other words, whether a Divine cause must not be postulated for the production of this complex, this rare, this unique book, whether, in short, Divine co-operation with man is not the only adequate explanation of the existence of the Old Testament.

As our inquiry has progressed, supernatural causes for the data afforded by the Old Testament have had to be insisted on again and again. It has become more and more evident that without Divine assistance the Old Testament could never have been produced. When Moses and the prophets and the saints wrote the several books of the Old Testament, they did so as fellow-workers with Deity.

Thus, it was by Divine co-operation with man, as we have seen, that the Books of the Law were produced. The Books of the Law require the postulation of supernatural as well as natural causes. These books record revelations; they record many revelations; they record a series, an ordered series of revelations. From the narrative of Creation, supernatural in source, they pass on to the Divine self-disclosures to Adam, and Noah, and Abraham, and Isaac, and Jacob, which ultimately merge into the fuller revelations vouchsafed to Moses at the Burning Bush, in Egypt, and in the Wilderness. These Divine communications to man are interwoven, we have seen, with the very structure of the books of the Law, and demand the postulation of a Divine co-operation with man for the production of these books. No revelation, no Law; no God, no revelation: this is the attitude the inductive inquirer is compelled by the data of the Old Testament to assume.

A similar result has followed from our study of the Books of the Prophets. All prophecy, such as we have met with, demands a supernatural cause. Such prophecy can only accrue upon Divine co-operation with man. The prophets represented themselves as peculiarly the confidants, and, therefore, the messengers, of Deity; and our entire examination of their position has strengthened our conviction of the truthfulness of these speakers for God. No revelation, no Books of the Prophets ; no God, no revelation : this again is the attitude which the facts of the case compel the inductive inquirer to assume.

And a conclusion to some extent similar results from the brief epitome given of the mode of production of the Holy Writings. Not even they could have been produced without the Divine co-operation. For it is as manifest that there could be no assimilation of revelation without revelation, as it is manifest that there could be no revelation without Divine condescension. These Holy Writings are a record of a holy experience, either individual or social ; but this holy experience is necessarily based upon Divine knowledge divinely imparted, and thus calls for belief in a supernatural cause for its production. Nay more, as will become more evident presently, the very assimilation of revelation cannot take place without Divine co-operation. Again, therefore, the inductive inquirer arrives at the result: No revelation, no Holy Writings ; no God, no revelation.

From Divine co-operation, therefore, with man—summarizing all that has gone before—*the Old Testament has come.* Without Divine influence the Old Testament could not have been written. *But Divine co-operation with man, is just what is meant by Inspiration. Our previous inquiries may thus be compactly expressed by saying that this Sacred Book has been written by Inspiration of God.*

When we speak, therefore, of the Inspiration of the Old Testament, what we mean is that the Old Testament has been written by man with Divine aid. The conclusion is sufficiently important. It divides sharply between the Old Testament and many other books of high literary rank ; nay, it divides sharply between this and many other Sacred Books.

But can this Inspiration of the Old Testament be probed further, by the light of the facts educed by our previous investigation ? Divine co-operation with man is of many kinds. The Bible itself speaks of many kinds. Thus, there is an inspiration, a co-operation of God with man, which originates life :

> "The Spirit of God hath made me,
> And the breath of the Almighty giveth me life."[1]

There is an inspiration, a co-operation of God with man, which sustains life : " And the Lord said, My spirit shall not rule in man for ever ; in their going astray they are flesh."[2] There is an inspiration which imparts excellence to intellect, even infusing exceptional skill in artistic handicraft, as is said of Bezaleel ("And the Lord spake unto Moses, saying, See, I have called by name Bezaleel, the son of Uri, the son of Hur, of the tribe of Judah ; and I have filled him with the Spirit of God, in wisdom, and in understanding, and in knowledge, and in all manner of workmanship, to devise cunning works, to work in gold, and in silver, and in brass, and in cutting of stones for setting, and in carving of wood, to work in all manner of workmanship "[3]), and conferring exceptional prowess in leadership, as is said

---

[1] Job xxxiii. 4.   [2] Gen. vi. 3.   [3] Exod. xxxi. 1-5.

of Othniel, and Gideon, and Jephthah, and Samson.[1] There is an inspiration which endows with the gift of ethnic prophecy, as is expressly said of Balaam.[2] There is an inspiration which shows itself in the practical wisdom, the teaching aptitude, the visions, the miracles, the predictions of the Old Testament prophets. There is an inspiration which imparts the characteristic elements of the Christian consciousness—the sense of adoption into the Divine family ("The Spirit Himself beareth witness with our spirit that we are children of God"[3]), perception of the import of Jesus ("No man can say, Jesus is Lord, but by the Holy Spirit"[4]), grasp of supernatural truth ("And I will pray the Father, and He shall give you another Helper, the Spirit of Truth, whom the world cannot receive"[5]), availing prayer ("The Spirit also helpeth our infirmity; for we know not how to pray as we ought; but the Spirit Himself maketh intercession for us"[6]), and holiness of life ("through sanctification of the Spirit"[7]). There is an inspiration, further, which blends masses of individuals who possess the Christian consciousness into one great social organism, bestowing upon each member his special gift (with a view to the welfare of the whole), giving to each community its specific genius (also with a view to the welfare of the whole), imparting to each age its peculiar spirit (also with a view to the welfare of the whole).[8] In short, Inspiration, the co-operation of the Spirit of God with the spirit of man, assumes many forms, at one time vitalizing natural gifts and at another vitalizing gifts

---

[1] Judg. iii. 10; vi. 16; xi. 29; xiii. 25.
[2] Numb. xxiv. 2.
[3] Rom. viii. 15-17.
[4] 1 Cor. xii. 3.
[5] John xiv. 16, 17; xv. 26; xvi. 13.
[6] Rom. viii. 26.
[7] 2 Thess. ii. 13.
[8] 1 Cor. xii.; Ephes. iv. 4-16.

that are spiritual, now endowing individuals with new powers, and now raising communities to loftier ability. The life, the influence, the inspiration, the potency, whichever name be preferred for the co-operation of the Divine Spirit with the human spirit, has many functions. The genus has many species. Of these functions, amongst these species, is the inspiration which resulted in the production of the Old Testament. *Is it possible to define this Biblical inspiration more exactly ? can we find the differentia which may distinguish the Inspiration which resulted in the Old Testament from other varieties of Inspiration ?*

Our previous investigations lead us to infer that inspiration of various kinds was at work to produce the Old Testament; and it will best conduce to clearness of view if these several kinds of inspiration be considered in due order. *Thus,* FIRST, *there is the inspiration,* the co-operation of the Spirit of God with the spirit of man, *which resulted in the assimilation of revelation*—HAGIOGRAPHIC INSPIRATION as it may be called. SECONDLY, *there is the inspiration,* the co-operation of the Divine with the human spirit, *which resulted in the apprehension and communication of revelation*—PROPHETIC INSPIRATION as it may be called. THIRDLY, *there is the inspiration which prompts to commit to writing what was known of God and Divine things, and which guides during committal,* thus concerning itself both with the "*impulsus ad scribendum*" and with the "*assistentia in scribendo,*" as the older theologians would have said—TRANSCRIPTIVE INSPIRATION as it may be called. LASTLY, *there is the inspiration of the collectors rather than the authors*—CANONIC INSPIRATION. *Let each of these grades of inspiration be considered in order.*

FIRST, *then*, OF HAGIOGRAPHIC INSPIRATION, *or that Divine co-operation with man which issued in the assimilation of revelation.* If the line of thought be a little recondite, it is not a little important.

All knowledge implies two things—object and subject—something to know and some one to know. The subjective faculty of knowing is as necessary to knowledge as the objective fact to be known. It is but an instance of this universal truth to say that all knowledge of God also implies two things—object and subject; there must be a God to be known, and a human capacity to know God. There can be no human knowledge of God, without, on the one hand, the objective fact (God), and the subjective faculty (the religious sense). Even God cannot reveal Himself to man unless He has first endowed man with a perceptive faculty for the supernatural. Only spirit can apprehend spirit. If man be not made in the image of God, God must remain to him for ever unknown and unknowable. As has been as pertinently as bluntly said, "If man were not constitutionally religious"—endowed with a faculty, let us say, for knowing God—"the grossest ignorance could not have brought him to the consciousness of God; all the ignorance in the world could not have prevailed upon man to believe in God, had he not been organized to that effect; the animals are ignorant enough, and yet they have never arrived at a knowledge of God."[1] The sentiment is just. The anthropoid ape may imitate the attitude, but not the act of prayer.

This prior need of a faculty for knowing God before God can be known, will repay further examination.

[1] Frohschammer, *Das Christenthum und die Moderne Natur-Wissenschaft*, Vienna, 1868, p. 316.

Man has been so constituted that he may have knowledge of the Divine. This knowledge may, undoubtedly, vary considerably, from birth and from culture. Indeed some men seem to have a genius in spiritual things as some have genius, native faculty and native power of acquisition, in natural things. The same fact of man's capacity for religion may be expressed otherwise by saying that men have, though in very different degree, an *intuitive* knowledge of the supersensuous.

The validity of this term *intuitive* will probably require a few words. If there has been a large hesitation in confessing to the existence of this intuitive knowledge of the supensensuous, perhaps the real source of that hesitation was a lack of careful definition. By *intuitive* is not meant *innate*. Locke, acute, lucid, and conclusive as was his polemic against innate ideas, did not settle the question concerning intuition. The non-existence in man of innate ideas may be demonstrated, and, notwithstanding, the actuality of intuitions not be touched. That no knowledge as such is born in us or with us most are agreed. Long discussion has produced comparative unanimity upon the non-existence of innate ideas amongst psychologists of all schools. But although no knowledge is innate, given to us in our mental constitution, something is given to us: faculties of various kinds are given to us, and amongst these faculties, these abilities to know, these forms of thought, these moulds of ideas, are intuitive faculties. To have intuitions is part of the birthright of man, because he has intuitive faculties. Intuitions are the product of the intuitive faculties.

Intuition, as its etymology implies, is an analogous act to vision. The eye sees, it does not reason; it affords, as we say, intuitions, not arguments ; its knowledge is immediate, not indirect; it supplies percepts, not concepts; images, not ideas. If the eye be questioned as to the authority of its deliverances, it repeats them. Its ultimate appeal is to itself, not to any prior or subsequent conclusion. If the eye is an instrument for gaining much abstract knowledge, all such abstract knowledge follows from the action of the intellect upon the intuitions given by the eye. First comes that which is intuitive; afterwards that which is abstract. What is true of the eye applies to every sense. All our knowledge of the external world is primarily intuitive, the immediate declarations of our senses, which mirror, so to speak, what is presented to them. Further, what is true of the senses, is true of some other mental attributes of ours, which it is common to call senses too, inner senses, spiritual senses. Personal existence, for example, is an intuitive, not a reasoned truth. That I do see a tree is the only proof possible that I see a tree ; so, that I do exist is the only possible proof of my actual existence. No intuitive knowledge can advance in demonstration of its right to be any other than the woman's reason.

Intuitive knowledge being then immediate knowledge, perceptive knowledge, knowledge that is simply an image of some object presented to the outward or inward senses, the question arises whether, as man is endowed with eyesight to see, hearing to hear, and touch to feel (not to recapitulate all the senses), and as man has been gifted with intellectual organs which can discriminate and identify (not to recapitulate all his intellectual capacities), and as man has also been equipped for his destiny with a direct consciousness of self (not to recapitulate all the varieties of mental intuition), the question arises, whether man has not been made in addition with a faculty for apprehending the Divine. When the external world comes in contact with the senses, they image that external world; upon this all are agreed. Further, let the internal mental world present itself to our organs of introspection, and they again reflect that internal world; upon this also there is a general agreement. The additional question is, whether, when the spiritual world approaches the human spirit, that spirit has not also the capacity of mirroring, of consciously mirroring, that external world. To world-consciousness, as the Germans say, in its many phases, and self-consciousness in its many phases, does not man add God-consciousness in its many phases? Be it observed that the question is, not whether man can find God, but whether God can find man. The question is, whether, if the Spirit of God touch the spirit of man, man has any means of perceiving the supernatural contact. It is understood that the eye, except it be diseased, does not see unless there is something to see: it is also understood that the mind does not perceive self unless there is a self to be perceived; carrying on the great law, that in every act of perception there are given at once the person perceiving and the thing perceived, may it not also be understood that there is a spiritual, as well as a sensuous and rational intuition, an intuition in which are given in one indissoluble act both a spirit known and a spirit knowing? When God draws near to man, cannot man perceive the Divine proximity? Does not the soul of man vibrate consciously at the impact of Deity? Is our knowledge of God so bounded by the reasoning processes of the intellect, that we can only attain to thoughts of God not to God Himself? Or is man so constituted that, on the approach of the supersensuous world, the supersensuous may be felt to be near? As the brute knows his master, however feeble its faculty of expressing its knowledge, may not man know his Divine Father and Lord? All human knowledge is immediate or mediate, direct or indirect, intuitive or reasoned, seen or inferred, felt or argued, experimental or intellectual, apprehended or comprehended, perceived or conceived, beheld or demonstrated —to apply many names to the two great divisions of human knowledge; is there not an immediate, a direct, an intuitive, a seen, a felt, an experimental, an apprehended, a perceived, a beheld, knowledge of God? Is not the constitution of human nature such that, as it naturally grows up into a consciousness of self, and of the external world, being capable of reflecting objects presented both to mind and sense, it also naturally developes a consciousness of the Divine when the Divine draws near? When God approaches man, can man feel that God is at hand?

Surely the clear and precise statement of the question makes an affirmative reply easy. As Mulford has said in his suggestive *Republic of God*, " The being of God is the precedent and postulate of the thought of God;" and again, " From the beginning, and with the growth of the human consciousness, there is the consciousness of the being of God, and of a relation to God;" and again, " Man is conscious of the being of the eternal world, and lives and acts in this consciousness;" and again, "We cannot deduce the being of God from the existence of the world, nor the eternal from the temporal, nor the infinite from the finite, and yet the temporal has its ground in the eternal, and the finite in the infinite. . . . The knowledge of God comes through experience." Surely the reality of this intuitive knowledge of God is attested by individual experience. God finds us before we search for Him. We feel, before we reason, the fact of His Being. Surely, too, the reality of this intuitive knowledge is rendered certain by the *Argumentum a consensu gentium*. As said Epicurus in his work on the *Nature of the Gods*, "What nation is there, or what kind of men, who have not, previous to being taught, a certain impression of the gods?" As said Cicero in his *Tusculan Disputations*, "There is no nation so barbarous, no man so savage, as that some apprehension of the gods has not tinctured his mind." It is matter of fact that prayer is as universal as taste.

The fact of this intuitive knowledge of the supernatural has never been more consistently or more beautifully expressed than by Augustine in his many writings. "God is at the centre of the heart (*intimus cordi*)," he says in his *De Musica*. "Although removed from God by its affections," Augustine says in his *De Trinitate*, "the soul always feels the attraction of the Divine Being by a sort of occult memory (*per quamdam occultam memoriam*);" "We have a sort of notion of the Supreme Good by impression (*impressa notio ipsius boni*)." In his *Liber de Utilitate Credendi* he says, "All have a sort of internal consciousness of God (*interior nescio quid conscientia*)." This is always Augustine's view. Because God touches the soul, and because the soul thus becomes conscious of God, the soul, in his view, lives, knows, wills, and is restless. His phrases are singularly apt: the soul has a sort of "reminiscence" of God, a sort of "sense" of God, a sort of "consciousness" of

God. Was not Augustine right? To Descartes' axiom, "*Cogito, ergo sum,*" should we not add another, "*Deum sentio, ergo ego et Deus sumus*"? Cannot man as man say with Tauler, "I possess a power in my soul which is susceptible of God; I am as sure as I live that nothing is so near to me as God: God is nearer to me than I am to myself"? Cannot man as man say with John Wessel, "As no place is so dark as not to receive some degree of light from a sunbeam, so no rational soul is without some sort of indwelling knowledge of God"? "This is the crowning guilt of men," wrote Tertullian, surely in wisdom, "that they will not recognize One, of whom they cannot possibly be ignorant. Would you have the proof from the works of His hands, so numerous and so great, which both contain you and sustain you, which minister at once to your enjoyment and strike you with awe? Or *would you rather have it from the testimony of the soul itself?* Though under the oppressive bondage of the body, though led astray by depraving customs, though enervated by lusts and passions, though in slavery to false gods, yet, whenever the soul comes to itself, as out of a surfeit, or a sleep, or a sickness, and attains to something of its natural soundness, it speaks of God. . . . O noble testimony of the soul by nature Christian (*animæ naturaliter Christianæ*)."

There is, then, in man a spiritual sense, so to speak, whence intuitive knowledge of the supersensuous is received. But before applying this truth to the elucidation of the doctrine of Inspiration, let a few characteristics of this intuitive faculty, this spiritual sense, be stated. Possibly such enumeration may remove some of the difficulties necessarily attaching to the acceptance of such spiritual vision.

Observe, then, that this intuition of the Divine, like all intuition, belongs, as has been pointed out, to the realm of perception, sense, feeling, apprehension, not to the realm of conception, reasoning, intellect, comprehension. We have innate faculty of spiritual sight ; we have not innate spiritual knowledge. "As soon as man becomes conscious of himself as distinct from all other things and persons, he at the same time becomes conscious of a higher self; a power without which he feels that neither he nor anything else would have life or reality; this is the first sense of the Godhead, the *sensus numinis* as it has been called ; for it is a *sensus*, an immediate perception ; *not* the result of reasoning or of generalizing, but an intuition as irresistible as the impressions of our senses. In receiving it we are passive; at least as passive as in receiving from above the image of the sun, or any other sensible impression." [1] There is, therefore, something indeterminate about the intuitions afforded us by this spiritual sense. They are *im*pressions which have not attained to *ex*pression. It is the intellectual faculties which, bringing their discrimination, their analysis, their synthesis, to bear, can give to these or to any intuitions adequate embodiment in words. Who can define exactly the more voluminous impressions received by the eye and the ear, an undulating landscape or orchestral music? Who can define self? And who shall adequately describe that massive impression which the devout soul feels when God is present with his spirit in prayer? Only a long process of intellectual culture can fit us to communicate our intuitions to others. To say *that* I feel is easy ; to say *what* I feel is extremely difficult. Apprehension be-

[1] Max Müller, *Science of Language*, 2nd series, p. 145.

comes comprehension only after many a year of study and conflict. So it is with all intuitions. It is especially so with the intuitions of the spiritual sense. Further, it is with intuition of the Divine as it is with intuition of the natural. Receptivity varies with emotional state. Love clarifies our impressions; hatred confuses them. That men should sometimes interpret their spiritual intuitions very differently only follows the analogy of all intuitions.

Further, observe, that, like all our senses, external and internal, the spiritual sense may become blurred and dulled by misuse. Muscles which are not used become flaccid. Eyes, for which there is no need, become sightless. The parasitic sense which lives upon the labour of another sense, dwindles. So, too, he who ignores the sense of God, finds that sense less and less impressive: he who puts that sense into an improperly subordinate place stunts it. The prominent attributes of the human spirit are two, self-consciousness and self-determination. These attributes in a healthy state are subordinated to the God-consciousness. But let there be either an exaggerated self-consciousness (which is selfishness), or let there be a misdirected self-determination (which is sin), and in either case, the spiritual vision suffers. As said Theophilus, a bishop of Antioch in the second century of our era, in his *Ad Autolycum:* "If thou sayest, show me thy God, I answer, show me first thy man, and I will show thee my God. Show me first whether the eyes of thy soul see, and the ears of thy heart hear; for, as the eyes of the body perceive earthly things, light and darkness, white and black, beauty and deformity, so the ears of the heart and the eyes of the soul can perceive God. God is seen by those who can see Him when they open the eyes of their soul. All men have eyes, but the eyes of some are blinded, that they cannot see the light of the sun. But the sun does not cease to shine because they are blind; they should ascribe it to their blindness that they cannot see. Thus is it with thee, O man! The eyes of thy soul are darkened by sin, even by thy sinful actions. Like a bright mirror, man must have a pure soul. If there be any rust on the mirror, man cannot see the reflection of his countenance in it; likewise, if there be sin in man, he cannot see God. Therefore, first examine thyself whether thou be not an adulterer, fornicator, thief, robber, &c.; for thy crimes will prevent thee from perceiving God." A similar opinion was expressed by Gregory of Nazianzum, in his *Orations*, when he said, " Rise from thy low condition by thy conversation; by purity of heart unite thyself to the pure; would thou become a theologian, then keep the commandments of God, and walk according to His precepts, for the act is the first step to knowledge." *Beati mundo corde, quoniam ipsi Deum videbunt.* Who shall say how much of the darkened intuition of heathenism is due to pride and immorality, to selfishness and sin, continued through generations?

And yet further, observe that, like all the faculties which afford intuitions, the faculty which apprehends God may become finer and more skilled by suitable training. If Christian apprehension of God is superior to heathen knowledge of the all-pervading Spirit, the fact is no more anomalous than the more precise vision of the draughtsman, and the more delicate ear of the musician. Drill the touch of the dyer or the tongue of the tea-taster by constant practice, and hand and taste become daily surer and more sensitive. Cultivate introspection by introspection, and the philosophical capacity of self-analysis becomes daily more minute, accurate, and full. Similarly strengthen the consciousness of God by attention to the God-consciousness, and Divine intuitions will become ever clearer and more significant. Wise thought upon God will be of slow birth, and will be to some extent dependent upon intellectual power; it will also be largely dependent upon strong sense of God; and strong sense of God is dependent upon spiritual exercise. The real relation between thoughts and intuitions of the supersensuous is the relation which exists between all intuitions and thoughts. Intuitions are the materials of thought, and the more vivid the intuitions, the better the materials; thought is the structure, which must rely much for its solidity, however, upon the quality of the materials.

Further, from what has been said, it follows that the course of the journey from the relative blindness and ignorance of nature to clearer and more intense vision of God is evident. Clear vision of God depends on two things—upon God who is seen, the clearness of His self-revelation; and also upon the eye that sees, its clearness, its absence of distortion, its penetration. The Divine condition depends upon the Will of God. The human condition depends upon the will of man. Spiritual exercise will strengthen spiritual vision. The inner eye which has been weakened by misuse must be fortified by use. Two great lines of spiritual exercise especially must be deliberately entered upon. They are both modes of accentuating the spiritual nature by exercising it. Self must be subordinated, and the moral law must be observed. On the one hand, self-crucifixion, and, on the other hand, obedience, will purify the spiritual vision. Every moral law observed, every act of love to God or man, is a rung in the ladder which climbs to nearer view of the heavenlier world. As Abbé Gratry has said, as tersely as wisely, in his *Connaissance de Dieu*, "There is an initiation which embraces all; it is to die to oneself that we may live to God." An excellent illustration of the point is seen in the history of the Dispensations, the great Divine education of man: it is Law, obedience, which prepares for Gospel, and it is the Gospel, the Christian life where the supreme virtue is love whilst we still see in a mirror confusedly, which prepares us for the perfect state of vision face to face. As said Augustine, in his *Soliloquia*, "The look of the soul is (intuitive) reason; but every eye which looks does not see; right and true looking is virtue. Yes, true reason, right reason is virtue." This is one side of the vision of God; that vision becomes clearer and stronger as the vision itself, the organ of spiritual sight, is appropriately trained. The other side, as has been previously said, is consequent upon the object seen, and therefore, consequent upon the will of the Divine object of spiritual vision: a truth which may well recall another remarkable passage from Augustine: "I have loved Thee late, thou Beauty, so old and yet so new! I have loved Thee late! Thou wert in myself: I was outside myself. I was seeking Thee outside myself. Throwing myself into these beauties created by Thee, I was losing in them my proper beauty. Thou hast conquered my dulness; Thou hast shined; Thou hast lightened; and Thou hast triumphed over my blindness. Thou hast touched me; I have touched Thee; and my heart now knows no desire but the stability there is in Thee."

Three truths then have emerged.

First, man has a spiritual sense, an inner eye, which can give him intuitions of the supernatural world.

Second, these spiritual intuitions are, on the one hand, conditional upon the proximity and the nature of the supernatural objects presented to the spiritual sense.

Third, these spiritual intuitions are, on the other hand, conditional upon the character of the organ of vision, which may be improved by use, as it may be injured by misuse.

Applying these three truths to the question of Old Testament Inspiration, three further truths emerge:

First, the Books of the Old Testament were written, as their contents demonstrate, by men whose spiritual sense, whose apprehension of the religious, whose vision of the invisible, was most acute and full. This being so, and the spiritual sense as such *having no contents*.

Second, the products of this manifest spiritual sense, of this rare apprehension of the Divine side of things, must be largely due to the Divine object of vision. The Holy Spirit must have presented to the view of these Old Testament writers phases of the Eternal Mind. In other words, these Old Testament writers must have had revelations of God, as we know they had. But this imparting of revelation, this co-operation of the Spirit of God with the spirit of man, is one form of Inspiration.

Third, the products of this spiritual sense of the Old Testament writers must also be due to the quality and culture of their organ of spiritual vision. Seeing the Divine, they had desired to see the Divine. They surrendered themselves to become "holy men of God." They purified their spiritual vision by obedience, and prayer, and large love. But this culture of the spiritual sense was ever dependent upon the presence of God. Neither the spiritual eye nor the natural eye can be exercised by imaginary objects. It was by the Divine co-operation with the efforts of these men that they became holy and more holy. And this culture of the spiritual sense, this co-operation of the Holy Spirit with man, is another form of Inspiration.

Hagiographic Inspiration, therefore, *which underlies every book of the Old Testament has two forms; it is a co-operation of the Holy Spirit with the spirit of man in the maturing of spiritual character; and it is also a co-operation of the Holy Spirit with the spirit of man in the assimilating of revelation.*

From Hagiographic Inspiration, possessed by all the Old Testament writers, let us pass, SECONDLY, *to* PROPHETIC INSPIRATION, *possessed by many, enabling them to be the media of Divine revelation.* Having analysed, as far as the available data permit, the consciousness of the inspired man who lives, moves, and has his being in what has been revealed to him of God by the instrumentality of others, we are now to analyse, according to the available data, the consciousness of the inspired man who was divinely selected to be the organ of revelation.

Two great characteristics, the one negative, and the other positive, of the consciousness of the Old Testament prophet, have come before us in the preceding Lecture; and it is desirable to recall them.

On the one hand, the prophetic utterance was not the outcome of the natural faculties of the prophet. The prophetic word was not the product of personal reflection; it was not the outcome of past experience; it was not the flower of preliminary education. The speech of a man of good natural parts, however cultivated, was not of itself prophecy. Sometimes prophetic speech was eloquent; occasionally it was the highest oratory; mostly it was poetic; often it was poetry of the first rank; but neither eloquence, nor oratory, nor poetry, were of the essence of prophecy. Prophecy was more than the outcome of imagination, however lofty; it was more than the outcome of insight, however keen; it was more even than the natural outcome of the profoundest religious sense. Prophecy flowed from no natural or acquired talents as such. The prophets are agreed in saying that the gift they exercised was not to be attributed to natural parts. Indeed those who pretend to prophesy on the strength of natural gifts are declared by Ezekiel to be, *ipso facto*, false prophets: "And the word of the Lord came unto me saying, Son of man, prophesy against the prophets of Israel that *prophesy out of their own hearts*, and say thou unto them *that prophesy out of their own hearts*, Hear ye the word of the Lord, Woe unto the foolish prophets that *follow their own spirit, and have seen nothing*."[1] Jeremiah utters a similar sentiment when he says: "Thus saith the Lord of hosts, Hearken not unto the words of the prophets that prophesy unto you; they teach you vanity; they *speak a vision of their own hearts*."[2] On the one hand, then, prophecy is not the effect of natural parts, native or acquired.

On the other hand, the prophetic message was always declared to be the word of God expressly revealed to the speaker. What the prophet spake, he spake, he said, as the organ of Deity. The prophets always preface their messages by formulas like these:

[1] Ezek. xiii. 1–3.   [2] Jer. xxiii. 16.

"The word which came from the Lord;" "The word of the Lord which came;" "The word of the Lord came to me;" "Thus saith the Lord;" "Thus saith the Lord God;" "The Lord said unto me;" "Hear ye now what the Lord saith;" "The utterance of the word of the Lord." Upon this Divine origin of their words all the prophets insist. Says Isaiah: "The Lord God hath given me the tongue of them that are taught, that I should know how to speak a word in season to him that is weary; He wakeneth morning by morning; He wakeneth mine ear to hear as they that are taught. The Lord God hath opened mine ear."[1] Says Jeremiah: "Then said I, Lord God! behold I cannot speak, for I am a child. But the Lord said unto me, Say not, I am a child; for on whatsoever errand I shall send thee, thou shalt go, and whatsoever I shall command thee thou shalt speak. Then the Lord put forth His hand, and touched my mouth; and the Lord said unto me, Behold I have put My words in thy mouth."[2] Says Ezekiel: "I will open thy mouth, and thou shalt say unto them, Thus saith the Lord God."[3] The prophets spake— this is their constant testimony, and it has approved itself credible in our preceding investigation—not their own mind, but the mind of God.

Revelations, then, Divine knowledge divinely imparted, were made to the prophets. Is it possible to say how?

In the Old Testament there are four modes in which Divine communications are made to men—by *angels*, by *dreams*, by *trance*, and by *visions*. With the first mode, as when angels appeared to Abraham, we are not concerned. The three remaining modes, often confused,

[1] Isa. l. 4, 5. [2] Jer. i. 6–9. [3] Ezek. iii. 27.

require to be carefully distinguished. The dream was not the trance, and the trance was not the vision. Nor are vision and dream the same, although popular speech often leads to their identification.

The *dream* requires little consideration here. It was by this means that Divine communications were made to those who were not personally prepared to receive communications of a higher kind. The dreams of Pharaoh and the dreams of Nebuchadnezzar are good cases in point, in these instances requiring specific interpreters. But sometimes the dreamers of dreams were their own Josephs or Daniels, and a low type of prophetic activity is spoken of again and again as the dreaming of dreams. This inferiority of the dreamer one passage makes very clear. It is in connection with the rebellion of Miriam and Aaron against Moses. The ground of rebellion was a conviction that they were prophets equally with Moses. "Hath the Lord spoken only by Moses? Hath He not also spoken by us?" The Divine intervention settles the matter. Aaron and Miriam may be such inferior prophets as see dreams, but Moses is a prophet of a very different kind. "And the Lord spake suddenly unto Moses, and unto Aaron, and unto Miriam, Come out ye three to the tent of meeting. . . . And He said, Hear now My words: if there be a prophet among you, I, the Lord, will make Myself known unto him in an appearance by night,[1] I will speak with him in a dream. My servant Moses is not so: with him will I speak mouth to mouth, even manifestly, and not in riddles."[2] The dream was not

---

[1] Translated "vision" in the Authorized and Revised Versions, but this is misleading. The technical word "vision" should be reserved for the true prophetic vision, as in Isa. i. 1: "The Vision of Isaiah, which he saw."
[2] Numb. xii. 1–8.

the mode in which the Divine revelations were made to the Old Testament prophets.

The *trance* or *ecstasy* was of a different nature to the dream. The accompaniments of the trance show this clearly. Daniel was entranced, for instance, and in his case the accompaniments of this mental state are seen in distinct, if pronounced, form. Daniel falls into a deep sleep, he tells us: "And it came to pass, when I, even I, Daniel, had seen the vision, that I sought understanding; and, behold, there stood before me as the appearance of a man. . . . Now as he was speaking with me, I fell into a deep sleep with my face toward the ground; but he touched me, and set me where I had stood. And he said, Behold, I will make thee know." Further, after the Divine communication was ended, Daniel speaks of the great prostration under which he suffered: "And I, Daniel, fainted, and was sick certain days; then I rose up, and did the king's business: and I was astonished at the vision, but there was none to make it understood."[1] A somewhat parallel description is given by Balaam of the state of trance: "And (Balaam) took up his parable and said,

> Balaam the son of Beor saith:
> And the man whose eye is opened saith:
> He saith, who heareth the words of God,
> Who seeth the sight of the Almighty,
> Falling down, and having his eyes open."[2]

It was in a trance ("ecstasy fell upon him") that Peter received his commission concerning the Gentiles.[3] So, too, it was in a trance apparently that Paul was caught into the third heaven, and heard unutterable things,[4] not

---
[1] Dan. viii. 15–19, 27. [2] Numb. xxiv. 3, 4.
[3] Acts x. 10. [4] 2 Cor. xii. 1.

knowing whether he was in or out of the body. In this state of trance, then, the bodily senses were lulled as in profound sleep, whilst the inner eye, the spiritual sense, the faculty of spiritual intuition, was excited to the greatest alertness. Now undoubtedly this state of trance, or ecstasy, in which at once the body is quieted and the soul is aroused by Divine inspiration, plays a large part in the life of the Old Testament prophets. When, for example—so the facts of the case seem to imply—the communication to be made was wholly dissociated from the ordinary life and thought of the prophet, when the revelation, so to speak, had no point of attachment in the existing consciousness of the prophet, then recourse was had to the ecstatic state, the state in which one is carried out of oneself, the state in which, to use Paul's phrase, one knows not whether one is in or out of the body, the state of trance. Thus the revelations made to Daniel are wholly unintelligible to him; they form apparently no part of a series of revelations, the earlier phases of which he knew; they are out of continuity with his previous thoughts, and therefore they are made in trance. Similarly the vision of Isaiah, at his call to the prophetical office, when, in a dim haze, he saw the mysterious cloud-skirts of the Almighty, and heard the song of the seraphim, seems to have been given in trance; this revelation also was a breach in the continuity of consciousness. Similarly, again, the vision of Ezekiel, at *his* call to the prophetical career, when he saw the sapphire throne girt by its rainbow, from which went forth the monstrous figure, seemingly composed of four living forms, moving upon mystic wheels, sparkling as with gold, marching straight forward with a noise of wings, like the roar of waters, like the rush of a host, this vision, which had no continuity with the previous life of Ezekiel, seems to have been given in trance. The trance undoubtedly formed part of the prophetic experience. In such trance the bodily functions being palsied, so to speak, and the senses dead, the Inspiration of God quickened the spiritual sense into abnormal activity, so that the prophets verily saw the revelations presented to them.

But there was a yet higher state in which revelations were received by the prophets, the state of the prophetic *vision*. In this more exalted spiritual state, without trance, without coma, the inner eye, the spiritual sense, received such quickening that it directly apprehended the Divine revelation presented. In "vision" the prophet retained all his faculties in perfect balance, but as the keen gaze of thought may make the natural eye dead to the outer world, so, by the inspiration of the Spirit of God, the spirit of man was so accentuated as to be wholly engrossed with the revelation presented. The human spirit was vitalized to think the thoughts of God. It was, as had been said of Moses, as if the ear of the prophet, being more sensitive than the ear of ordinary men, could distinguish clearly, amidst the sounds of earth and above the hum of life, a deeper, a fuller, a more magnetic sound, the very voice of Deity as God spake to him "mouth to mouth." As, in those rare moments of loving fellowship, when sympathy makes words unnecessary, and when unison of feeling, born of close relationship, makes one soul understand the other, as it were, by instinct; so, but much more adequately, the heart of the prophet being in entire sympathy with God and His revelations, and the Divine influence streaming forth upon the prophet, without words the thought of God became the thought of man. Or, as in the rarer moments of prayer, when the sense of a great Presence grows upon us, doubts are solved by Divine help, and our pathway becomes clear because of Divine guidance; so, as the inspiration of the Almighty fell upon the prophet, his own thoughts were deliberately put aside for Divine thoughts, and his own ways for the Divine ways. This prophetic state—which, to judge from the large number of prophecies which seem to have been spoken to the prophets, as it were by a familiar Divine friend and guide, was the commoner as well as the more exalted mode of revelation—was spiritual intuition at its highest power, *vision*. As *vision*, the prophets themselves always describe this mode of revelation. Their words are peculiarly noteworthy. This is how they expressed themselves: "The *vision* of Isaiah, which he *saw*;" "The *words* of Amos, which he *saw*;" "The *vision* of Obadiah;" "The *utterance* which Habakkuk the prophet did *see*." Without the intervention of trance, with the intelligence fully alert, the prophets frequently *saw*, so to speak, the revelations of God. When God desired to reveal aught of Himself, the intuitive faculty of the prophet was so inspired by the Holy Spirit, that the prophet *saw* with God, became consentient with Deity. It was not that, in these hours of revelation, the prophets were altogether passive; they were more than lyres upon which God could play; they were more than pipes through which God might speak; these figures of speech of the older theologians are wholly inadequate to represent the prophetic mode of revelation: they were more than phonographs (if the term may be allowed) in which the words of God were mechanically preserved for subsequent reproduction; they were men, made in the image of Deity, restored by Divine inspiration to the image of Deity, who, with intelligence and insight clarified by holiness, heard once more the "voice of God walking in the garden towards the time of the breeze." They were silent, but from reverence, not stupor; they were passive, but from choice, not lassitude; they were receptive, not involuntarily, but from strong desire; they saw, not by clairvoyance, but by the inspiration of God. There was no break in the consciousness of the prophet; he did not live a sort of dual life, now in the body, and now out of the body; but, whilst living his life, just as he may have had memorable hours of intercourse with man or woman when he had learnt much whilst he had been much moved; so the prophet had hours, signal hours, of intercourse with God when he had learnt much whilst he had been divinely inspired. In these hours, by means of a co-operation of the Holy Spirit with his spirit, the prophet saw things he could never have seen of himself, and heard words which no acumen of his would have enabled him to hear. Miraculously exalted in spirit, his spirit became the medium for apprehending and communicating thoughts and plans and purposes of the Supreme Spirit. *Vision*, then, prophetic vision, was a sort of internal intuition wrought by inspiration. The subject, being inspired, perceived as object the revelation of God. Upon this brief outline of the more exalted and the more common prophetic state—words thrown out, as Matthew Arnold would have said, at a difficult theme—the whole of the Books of the Prophets are comments.

Prophetic Inspiration, then, which implies the previous

*reception of Hagiographic Inspiration, had two forms—
the ecstatic form, and the conscious form ; in the ecstatic
form which was the rarer, as well as the less exalted, the
ordinary faculties were rendered unconscious, and the
spiritual sense was divinely quickened to receive revelations ; in the conscious form, there was no break in the
conscious life, but here, too, whilst the ordinary mental
functions continued, the spiritual sense was divinely
quickened to receive revelations.*

Thus far, then, the Divine co-operation with the spirit of man which enabled the several writers of the Old Testament to be recipients and promulgators of the revelations from above, has been dealt with. But these several human media of revelation might have remained satisfied with declaring to their own age what they knew, and might not have thought of or desired the immortality of letters. Isaiah, for instance, like Elijah, might have spoken and not written his messages from heaven. It might have been enough for Solomon to instruct his own times in wisdom. Moses, without permanently embodying his revelations in writing, might have committed the Law to faithful men who would have been able in turn to teach others. Therefore, THIRDLY, *there was a* TRANSCRIPTIVE INSPIRATION, *which worked upon the authors of the several books of the Old Testament, that is, there was a co-operation of the Spirit of God with man, prompting the literary preservation of their contributions in the sphere of religion, and at the same time superintending that committal so that its record should be at once faithful and adequate.*

Two points arise here: first, the inspired act of

VIII.]   *Transcriptive Inspiration.*   449

committal to writing; second, the superintendence which imparted adequacy and faithfulness.

Sometimes, as we have seen, the committal to writing was in obedience to an express command. Thus Moses was instructed to write the circumstances of the discomfiture of Amalek "in the book" as "a memorial," an injunction which, given on other occasions also, he interpreted to mean that he should write a history of the memorable dealings of God with men, and especially with the Jewish nation, a history which only closed with his relinquishment of leadership: "And it came to pass, when Moses had made an end of writing the words of this Law in a book, until they were finished, that Moses commanded the Levites, which bare the ark of the covenant of the Lord, saying, Take this book of the Law, and put it by the side of the ark of the covenant of the Lord your God, that it may be there for a witness against thee."[1] Jeremiah was also expressly commanded to write his prophecies: "And it came to pass in the fourth year of Jehoiakim the son of Josiah, king of Judah, that this word came to Jeremiah from the Lord, saying, Take thee a roll of a book, and write therein the words that I have spoken unto thee against Israel, and against Judah, and against all the nations, from the day I spake unto thee, from the days of Josiah, even unto this day;"[2] a commandment which Jeremiah fulfilled by dictation to Baruch, as Baruch himself said, "He (Jeremiah) pronounced all these words unto me with his mouth, and I wrote them with ink in the book."[3] Further, when the roll of prophecies was destroyed in the anger of Jehoiakim, a Divine order was issued a second time to write all

[1] Deut. xxxi. 24–26.   [2] Jer. xxxvi. 1, 2.   [3] *Ib.* xxxvi. 18.

the prophecies of Jeremiah in a book. "Then the word of the Lord came to Jeremiah, after that the king had burned the roll, and the words which Baruch wrote at the mouth of Jeremiah, saying, Take thou again another roll, and write in it all the former words that were in the first roll. . . . Then took Jeremiah another roll, and gave it to Baruch the scribe, the son of Neriah ; who wrote therein from the mouth of Jeremiah all the words of the book which Jehoiakim king of Judah had burned in the fire : *and there were added besides unto them many like words."* [1]

To how many others of the writers of the Old Testament a similar express command was given to pen their thoughts and prophecies, it is impossible to say. Nor is it necessary to say. The issue shows that, as the several prophets wrote, in personal ignorance of the fact, successive parts of a developing scheme of revelation, "the spirits of the prophets being subject to the prophets" and yet at the same time being "borne along" by the Holy Ghost; so they and the other writers of the Old Testament, while apparently obeying their own impulses and fulfilling their own ends, were nevertheless divinely constrained to write. Not seldom, secondary agents, whose purview is definite but limited, find themselves instruments in the hand of Him whose plan is universal and eternal. He who utilized the free volition of a Nebuchadnezzar and a Cyrus, to say nothing of a Moses and an Elijah, to do His bidding, undoubtedly moved the several Old Testament writers, in perfect freedom yet with sure effect, to put into writing the things they had seen or felt or heard. That the Inspiration of the Almighty was not con-

[1] Jer. xxxvi. 27-32.

sciously felt as such would not show that the several writers were not inspired; for the co-operation of the Holy Spirit with us is so often unconscious, being subsequently evident by the results produced. How often, like Jacob, do we exclaim, as we start awake, "Surely the Lord is in this place, and I knew it not"! It is not necessary to the reality of *Transcriptive Inspiration* that its subjects should have been conscious thereof. Indeed the supernatural impulse to write would be the more conclusively shown by their ignorance.

The important fact for our inquiry is that the reality of this Transcriptive Inspiration is shown by its results. The unity of the Old Testament which it secured is sufficient proof.

The unity of the Old Testament is a common theme of religious writers, and it is as warranted as common. The authors of these several books were men of very different ages, extending over more than a thousand years; they were also men of very different ranks— prophets, and priests, and kings—rustics and courtiers— soldiers and civilians—some working in privacy and some in the blaze of public life. Now these writers themselves could not possibly know, as we know, their place and purpose in history. "To 'them' it was revealed, that not unto themselves, but unto us, they ministered the things, which now have been announced." With diligence they wrought at their own square of the great pattern of the Divine purpose, weaving their own threads, and balancing their own colours, not knowing the effect, nor even the law, of the whole. With faithfulness they served their day and generation, ignorant of the specific niche they were to fill in the great structure the Master-builder was erecting. But it is evident to us that these many and diverse writers form a unity; and that they were instruments in unfolding a revelation which was ever growing, despite its "many parts" and its "many modes" as the author to the Epistle to the Hebrews says, into one great whole and one beneficent method. There is a plan about this Old Testament, a plan which becomes more evident with more study, which we to-day can scarcely fail to understand, a plan to show the merciful ways of God to sinful man in a manner which is best suited to human needs, a plan, nevertheless, not evident to the several writers themselves. They were but agents in a vast work which was unintelligible to them. In short, the plan is Divine. Design is apparent everywhere—the Messianic prophecies are sufficient evidence—and the design is such that it points to a Divine Designer. Without Transcriptive Inspiration, without the co-operation of the Holy Spirit in suggesting directly or indirectly the committal of the several Old Testament books to writing, the plan of God to give to man a record of the Divine dealings, addressed not to a class but to man as man, could not have been carried out. The conclusion is an inference from the Divine Plan, and the Divine Plan is an induction from the whole facts of the case.

Further, the aim of the Divine revelations, namely, to reveal to men the Divine Self and the Divine purposes of grace, would have been impracticable, if the record of these revelations had been distorted. As then a form of Divine Inspiration was given to enable men to receive and assimilate the several revelations made; so, unless the Divine purpose was to be thwarted by its instruments, unless the Divine message was to fail because of its bearers, there must also be a Divine Inspiration which rendered the records of revelation received or assimilated adequate to their purpose. However clear the revelation, it would be valueless if its record was turbid. The Divine nature and aims would not be disclosed if they were wrongly delivered. He who inspired, therefore, that He might reveal, must add to Hagiographic and Prophetic Inspiration—Inspiration that was Transcriptive. So much, again, the nature of the case leads us to infer.

But, further, our previous inquiry has shown us, as a matter of fact, that the record is reliable. As a matter of fact, human ignorance and limitation do not so predominate in this record of revelation as to render the record untrustworthy. All our study of the Law has shown faithfulness in transcription; all our study of the Prophets, again, has shown faithfulness in transcription; the very existence of the Holy Writings demonstrates, by the reality of the experience they record, the veracity of the revelations upon which the experience is based. Indeed, tests of many kinds have shown that it is not open to any to reject the revelations of the Old Testament on the ground that the revelations may have become irrecognizable by the mode of their transcription. But this unperverted transmission of revelation is a supernatural effect, and points to a Transcriptive Inspiration.

Lastly, to the several forms of Inspiration already considered must be added CANONIC INSPIRATION, *that co-operation of the Holy Spirit with the spirit of man which resulted in the collection of the several books of the Old Testament into one canon.*

How this collection into one sacred book was brought about extant facts do not allow us to determine. We know that Moses set an example of an authoritative canon in his Five Books of the Law. There is good reason also for saying that the Schools of the Prophets, following the Mosaic example, constituted themselves the guardians of the several prophetical writings, which they preserved to form a steadily increasing whole, until the open vision of prophecy ceased. But who first made the collection of Law and Prophets and Holy Writings we know not, although the tradition has much in its favour which attributed to Ezra and his contemporaries this labour of combination. Nor is the knowledge of the actual framers of the Old Testament canon very important. To know who were the Divine instruments in this invaluable work is comparatively unimportant. What it is important to know is that these agents in construction were really unconsciously guided by a Divine architect. The reality of Canonic Inspiration is shown by the same line of argument as the reality of Transcriptive Inspiration. It follow from the manifest unity of the Old Testament, a unity which grows ever more sure with every attack. It is easy to object to the Books of Esther, or Solomon's Song, or Ecclesiastes, having a place in the canon, but such objection soon shows that it has proceeded from narrowness of view, a narrowness parallel to that which prompted Luther to call the Epistle of James, "a right strawy epistle." The Bible is a book for man as man. It is neither a treatise of theology, nor a manual of science; a handbook of law, nor a collection of sermons. Sermons are for an age: a law code would soon need lawyers for its interpretation; theology is for the theologian; science is for the scientist. But the Bible is not the book of an age or of a class. It appeals to all, and like the greatest of whom the Bible speaks, the common people hear it gladly. As has been well said : " The testimony of Church history and of general Christian experience to the profitableness and divinity of the disputed books is of greater weight than the personal impressions of the few who criticize it." [1]

IN FINE, *the Old Testament is, on the one hand, a record of revelation ; and, on the other hand, an inspired record of revelation.*

Revelation is Divine knowledge divinely imparted, and these Old Testament Scriptures are a record of a course of revelation.

Inspiration is a co-operation of the Holy Ghost with the spirit of man, guaranteeing the reliableness of the record. As a matter of fact this inspiration, a noteworthy part of the Providential Government of the universe with a view to its salvation, shows several grades. Inspiration is a general term applicable to any co-operation of the Holy Spirit with the spirit of man, and the Inspiration of the writers and collectors of the Bible shows four forms of that co-operation. First, there is Hagiographic Inspiration, enabling the assimilation of revelation. Next, there is Prophetic Inspiration, enabling the prophet to perceive and express without distortion the revelations presented to him. Next, there is Transcriptive Inspiration, which moves the writers to write. And lastly, there is Canonic Inspiration, that co-operation of the Holy Ghost which prompted the formation of the Canon.

[1] Strong, *Systematic Theology, a Compendium and Commonplace Book designed for the use of Theological Students*, Rochester, U. S. A., 1886.

This being so, of course the authority of these Old Testament records depends, on the one hand, on the co-operation which has enabled fallible and weak men to become the media of revelation; and, on the other hand, on the nature of the revelations vouchsafed. Inspiration guarantees the substantial truth of the record. As a record the record is infallible so far as it is true; it is substantially true, because it is inspired. Revelation guarantees the truth of the facts recorded. So far as the facts recorded are a guide in matters of faith and practice, they must be an infallible guide.

With one explanatory word, this investigation may end. If it has been said that the record is substantially true, the ground for this statement is that this substantial truth has been borne out in the course of this inductive inquiry. That the record is absolutely devoid of mistakes we do not know; the record is a human record of the Divine; but that the record is substantially true, is veracious, trustworthy, and historical, our whole inquiry has shown. It has also shown the need of the greatest caution before errors are attributed to the Old Testament. A great many pseudo-facts are abroad concerning the Old Testament, which call for the most painstaking and patient verification or disproof before they are repeated. As said the Psalmist: "The sum of Thy word is truth."

THE END.

APPENDICES.

APPENDICES.

APPENDIX I.

Tabular View of Typical Analyses of Genesis.

Typical instances of the Four Phases of Pentateuch Criticism are here represented.

The First Phase (see pages 159-161) is represented by its first and greatest advocate, Eichhorn, whose views are extracted from his *Einleitung in das Alte Testament*, 4th edition, 1823.

The Second Phase (see pages 161-164) is represented by Tuch, *Commentar über die Genesis*, 1838.

The Third Phase (see pages 164-166) is represented by Schrader, who still cleaves to this form of analysis, which he has most ably expressed and advocated. His views were stated in the eighth edition of De Wette's *Einleitung in das Alte Testament*, Berlin, 1869, which Schrader edited.

The Fourth Phase (see pages 167-169) has been given from Wellhausen, *Die Komposition des Hexateuchs*, published in the 21st volume of the *Jahrbücher für Deutsche Theologie*, 1876, and since reprinted in his *Skizzen und Vorarbeiten*, part ii. Berlin, 1885.

NOTE.—*Roman numerals stand for chapters; Arabic numerals for verses;* a *after a verse signifies its first half, and* b *its second half.* Chapters are only represented in different type when the entire chapter is attributed to Jehovist or Younger Elohist.

460 APPENDIX I.

EICHHORN.	TUCH.
[Roman type signifies Elohist, a writer prior to Moses; **clarendon** signifies Jehovist, Moses; *italic* signifies interpolations from other ancient sources.]	[Roman type signifies Elohist, who wrote in time of Saul; **clarendon** signifies Jehovist, who wrote in time of Solomon.]
I. II. 1-3, *4-25*. *III.* **IV.** V. 1-28, **29**, 30-32. VI. 1-2, **3**, 4, **5-8**, 9-22.	I. II. 1-3, **4-25**. **III.** **IV.** V. 1-29a, **29**b, 30-32. VI. **1-8**, 9-22.
VII. **1-10**, 11-16 (except last three words), **16** (last three words), **17**, 18, **19** (?), 20-22, **23**, 24. VIII. 1-19, **20-22**.	VII. **1-10**, 11-16a, **16**b, 17-24, VIII. 1-19, **20-22**.
IX. 1-17, **18-27**, 28, 29. **X.**	IX. 1-17, **18-27**, 28, 29. X. (wrought up by later hand).
XI. **1-9**, 10-32. **XII.**	XI. **1-9**, 10-32. XII. **1-4**, 5, 6, **7**, 8a, **8b-20**.
XIII.	XIII. **1-17**, 18.
XIV.	XIV.
XV. **XVI.**	**XV.** **XVI.**

APPENDIX I.

SCHRADER.	WELLHAUSEN.
[Roman type signifies the Annalistic Narrator (Elohist) who wrote in time of David; *italic* signifies the Theocratic Narrator (Younger Elohist) who wrote soon after the death of Solomon; clarendon signifies the Prophetic Narrator (Jehovist) who wrote in early days of Uzziah.]	[Roman type signifies Elohist, who wrote after the Exile; clarendon signifies Jehovistic document (a compound of Jehovist and Younger or Second Elohist of other writers) written after the Division of the Kingdom.]
I.	I.
II. 1-4a, **4b-25**.	II. 1-4a, **4b-25**.
III.	**III.**
IV. **1-22**, *23, 24* (?), **25, 26**.	**IV.**
V. 1-28, **29**, 30-32.	V. 1-28, **29**, 30-32.
VI. *1-3* (1 being revised by Prophetic Narrator) **4-8**, 9-22.	VI. **1-8**, 9-22.
VII. **1-5**, 6-9, **10**, 11, **12**, 13-16, **17**, 18-22, **23**, 24.	VII. **1-10**, 11-24 (except 12, 16b (last clause), 17, 22-23, which are Jehovistic).
VIII. 1, 2a, **2b**, 3a, 3b-5, **6-12**, 13a, **13b**, 14-19, **20-22**.	VIII. 1, 2a, **2b**, 3-5, **6-12**, 13-19, **20-22**.
IX. 1-17, **18-27**, 28, 29.	IX. 1-17, **18-27**, 28, 29.
X. *1-7*, **8-12**, *13-18a*, **18b**, *19*, *20*, **21**, *22-24*, **25**, *26-32*.	X. 1-7, **8-19**, 20, **21**, 22, 23, **24-30**, 31, 32.
XI. **1-9**, 10-32.	XI. **1-9**, 10-28, **29**, 30-32.
XII. **1-4a**, 4b, 5, *6a*, **6b**, **7**, *8* ("and Hai on the east"), 8 (the rest of the verse), *9*, **10-20**.	XII. **1-4a**, 4b, 5, **6-20**.
XIII. 1, *2*, *3*, **4**, *5*, 6, *7a*, **7b**, *8*, *9*, *10* (except "before the Lord destroyed Sodom and Gomorrah, as the garden of the Lord," which is Jehovistic), **11a**, 11b, 12 (except "and pitched his tent toward Sodom," added by Younger Elohist), **13-17**, *18*a, **18b**.	XIII. **1-5**, 6, **7-11a**, 11b, 12, **15-18**.
XIV. *1-24* ("Jehovah" in verse 22 added by Jehovist).	**XIV.**
XV.	**XV.**
XVI. 1a, **1b**, **2**, 3, **4-14**, 15, 1-6.	XVI. **1**, **2**, 3, **4-14**, 15, 16.

APPENDIX I.

EICHHORN.	TUCH.
[*Roman type* signifies Elohist, a writer prior to Moses; **clarendon** signifies Jehovist, Moses; *italic* signifies interpolations from other ancient sources.]	[*Roman type* signifies Elohist, who wrote in time of Saul; **clarendon** signifies Jehovist, who wrote in time of Solomon.]
XVII.	XVII.
XVIII.	**XVIII.**
XIX. **1-28**, 29-38.	XIX. **1-28**, 29, **30-38**.
XX. 1-17, **18**.	XX. 1-17, **18**.
XXI. **1**, 2-32, **33, 34**.	XXI. **1**, 2-32, **33-34**.
XXII. 1-10, **11-19**, 20-24.	XXII. 1-13, **14-18**, 19-24.
XXIII.	XXIII.
XXIV.	**XXIV.**
XXV. **1-6**, 7-11, **12-18**, 19, 20, 21-34.	XXV. 1-20, **21-23**, 24-34.
XXVI. **1-33**, 34, 35.	XXVI. **1-33**, 34, 35.
XXVII.	XXVII. **1-45**, 46.
XXVIII. 1-9, **10-22** (parts of 12, 17, 18-22, being Elohistic).	XXVIII. 1-12, **13-16**, 17-21a, **21b**, 22.
XXIX.	XXIX. (31-35 doubtful).
XXX. 1-13, **14-16**, 17-20a, **20b**, 21-24a, **24b-43**.	XXX. 1-13, **14-16**, 17-24a, **24b-43**.
XXXI. **1**, 2, **3**, 4-48, **49**, 50-54.	XXXI. **1-3**, 4-48, **49**, 50-54.
XXXII.	XXXII. 1-12, **13**, 14, **15-32** (?), 33.
XXXIII. (18-20, possibly an interpolation).	XXXIII.
XXXIV. (perhaps, however, an interpolation).	XXXIV.

APPENDIX I.

SCHRADER.	WELLHAUSEN.
[*Roman type* signifies the Annalistic Narrator (Elohist) who wrote in time of David; *italic* signifies the Theocratic Narrator (Younger Elohist) who wrote soon after the death of Solomon; **clarendon** signifies the Prophetic Narrator (Jehovist) who wrote in early days of Uzziah.]	[*Roman type* signifies Elohist, who wrote after the Exile; **clarendon** signifies Jehovistic document (a compound of Jehovist and Younger or Second Elohist of other writers) written after the Division of the Kingdom.]
XVII. (in verse 1 Elohim changed into Jehovah by Jehovist).	XVII.
XVIII.	**XVIII.**
XIX. (verse 29 is Elohist).	**XIX.** (verse 29 is Elohist).
XX. (verse 18 is Jehovist).	**XX.**
XXI. 1a, 1b-5, *6-32*, **33, 34.**	XXI. **1, 2a,** 2b-5, **6-34.**
XXII. *1-13* (in verse 11 Elohim changed into Jehovah by Jehovist), **14-18,** *19,* 20-24.	**XXII.**
XXIII.	XXIII.
XXIV.	**XXIV.**
XXV. **1-6,** 7-20, **21-26**a, 26b, **27-34.**	XXV. **1-6,** 7-11a, **11**b, 12-17, **18,** 19, 20, **21-26**a, 26b, **27-34.**
XXVI. *1-5,* 6, **7-31,** *32, 33*a, **33**b.	XXVI. **1-33,** 34, 35.
XXVII. **1-45,** 46.	XXVII. **1-45,** 46.
XXVIII. 1-9, **10,** *11, 12,* **13-16,** *17, 18,* **19,** *20-22.*	XXVIII. 1-9, **10-22.**
XXIX.	XXIX. **1-23,** 24 (?), **25-28,** 29 (?), **30-35.**
XXX. **1-5,** *6,* **7,** *8* (?), **9,** *10-13* (?), **14-16,** *17-20*a, **20**b, *21-24*a, **25**b, **26,** *27,* **28, 29,** *30* (revised by Jehovist), *31-43.*	**XXX.**
XXXI. *1, 2, 3, 4-17*a, 17b, 18, *19-47,* **48-50,** *51-54.*	**XXXI.** (except verse 18 from "and all his goods which he had gotten").
XXXII. *1-9,* **10-13,** *14-32,* **33** (?).	**XXXII.**
XXXIII. *1-17,* 18, 19, **20.**	XXXIII.
XXXIV.	**XXXIV.**

EICHHORN.	TUCH.
[Roman *type* signifies Elohist, a writer prior to Moses; **clarendon** signifies Jehovist, Moses; *italic* signifies interpolations from other ancient sources.]	[Roman *type* signifies Elohist, who wrote in time of Saul; **clarendon** signifies Jehovist, who wrote in time of Solomon.]
XXXV.	XXXV.
XXXVI.	XXXVI.
XXXVII.	XXXVII. **1** (?), 2–36.
XXXVIII.	**XXXVIII.**
XXXIX.	XXXIX. 1–5, 6–20, **21–23**.
XL.	XL.
XLI.	XLI.
XLII.	XLII.
XLIII.	XLIII.
XLIV.	XLIV.
XLV.	XLV.
XLVI.	XLVI.
XLVII. 1–27, **28–31.**	XLVII.
XLVIII.	XLVIII.
XLIX. **1–28**, 29–33 (possibly 1–27 are interpolations).	XLIX.
L. **1–11**, 12, 13, **14**, 15–26.	L.

Schrader.	Wellhausen.
Roman type signifies the Annalistic Narrator (Elohist) who wrote in time of David; *italic* signifies the Theocratic Narrator (Younger Elohist) who wrote soon after the death of Solomon; **clarendon** signifies the Prophetic Narrator (Jehovist) who wrote in early days of Uzziah.]	[Roman type signifies Elohist, who wrote after the Exile; **clarendon** signifies Jehovistic document (a compound of Jehovist and Younger or Second Elohist of other writers) written after the Division of the Kingdom.]
XXXV. *1–5*, 6a, *6b–8*, 9a, *9*b, 10–15, *16–21*, **22**, 23–29.	XXXV. **1-8**, 9-15 ("again" in verse 9 added by Reviser), **16-22**a, 22b-29.
XXXVI. (verses 40–43 doubtful).	XXXVI. **1-5**, 6-8, **9-39**,40–43.
XXXVII. 1, 2a, *2b–22*, **23–27**, *28*a, **28**b, *29*, *30*, **31-35**, *36*.	XXXVII. **1,** 2 ("These are the generations of Jacob"), **2-36**.
XXXVIII.	**XXXVIII.**
XXXIX.	**XXXIX.**
XL. *1–3*a, 3b, *4*, *5*a, 5b, *6–23*.	XL.
XLI. *1–40*, **41**, *42–48*, **49**.	XLI.
XLII.	XLII.
XLIII.	XLIII.
XLIV. (mostly).	XLIV.
XLV. (revised by Jehovist).	XLV.
XLVI. *1–5*a, 5b–27 (verses 15 and 20 interpolated), **28-34**.	XLVI. **1-5**, 6, 7, 8-27 (less certain), **28-34**.
XLVII. **1-6**, 7–10, 11 ("in the best of the land," inserted by Jehovist), *12–26*, 27 ("in the country of Goshen," Jehovist), 28, **29-31**.	XLVII. **1-4**, 5–6a, **6**b, 7–11, 12–27a, 27b, 28.
XLVIII. **1**, **2**, 3–6, **7**, *8–22*.	XLVIII. **1, 2**, 3–6, 7 (?), **8-22**.
XLIX. 1a, 1b-**28**a, 28b-33.	XLIX. **1-27**, 28 (?), 29–33.
L. **1-11**, 12, 13, *14–26* (revised by Jehovist).	L. **1-11**, 12, 13, **14-26**.

APPENDIX II.

Tabular View of the Analysis of Exodus, Leviticus, and Numbers, according to Wellhausen.

WELLHAUSEN, as has been seen, finds three sources of these books, viz., the writing he calls the Priestly Code, that which he calls Jehovistic (the joint product of the Jehovist and second Elohist of older writers), and Deuteronomy.

Of course, the Deuteronomist occupies a place apart from the present analysis.

Concerning the two remaining sources, a few points should be held in mind.

As regards the Jehovistic document, the only legislation it is supposed to contain is Exod. xx.-xxiii.

As regards the Priestly Code, it wholly belongs, in this view, to a date subsequent to Ezekiel. A small part of its laws, Lev. xvii.-xxvi., is supposed to belong to the time between the flourishing of Ezekiel and the writing of the entire code; and it is therefore regarded as a little earlier in date than the whole. With this exception the Priestly Code belongs to the time after the Exile : it is Post-exilic. This Priestly Code is mainly a legal code, and contains, speaking generally, the great body of laws found in the latter part of Exodus (after chap. xxiv.), the whole of Leviticus, and the first ten chapters of Numbers. To these laws, however, some historical matter has been added. The laws have been illustrated, so to speak, by historical notices based upon the contents of the Jehovistic document very largely, but expressly accommodated to support the aims of this Priestly Code. But compare pages 167-169 and 252-254 of this book.

HERE THE PARTS SUPPOSED TO BELONG TO THE PRIESTLY CODE ARE ALONE GIVEN; the remainder, of course, belongs to the Jehovistic document.

1. *The numbers in brackets after each chapter show the number of verses in each chapter.*

APPENDIX. II.

2. *The letters* a *or* b *after a number stand for the first or second half of a verse.*

BOOK.	CHAPTER.	VERSES BELONGING TO THE PRIESTLY CODE.
Exodus	i. (22)	1–5, 7 (except "and multiplied, waxed mighty"), 13, 14 (except "in mortar and in brick and in all manner of service in the field; all their service").
	ii. (25)	23 (from "and the children of Israel sighed"), 24, 25.
	vi. (30)	2–30.
	vii. (25)	1–13, 19, 20*a*, 21*b* (latter half), 22, 23.
	viii. (32)	1–3, 11*b*–15.
	ix. (35)	8–12.
	xii. (51)	1–21, 28, 37*a*, 40, 41, 43–51.
	xiii. (22)	1, 2, 20.
	xiv. (31)	1, 2, 4 ("and they did so"), 8*b*, 9 (except "all the horses and chariots of Pharaoh, and his horsemen, and his army"), 10 (from "and they were sore afraid"), 15 (except "wherefore criest thou unto Me"), 28 (very doubtfully).
	xvi. (36)	1–3 [6–8 inserted by the Redactor], 9–13*a*, 16*b*–18*a*, 22–26, 31–35*a*.
	xvii. (16)	1 (to "in Rephidim").
	xix. (25)	1 ("the same day came they into the wilderness of Sinai"), 2*a*.
	xx. (26)	[11 inserted by Redactor.]
	xxiv. (18)	15 ("and a cloud covered the mount")–18 (to "gat him up into the mount").
	xxv. to xxxi.	All, except possibly the last verse of chap. xxxi.
	xxxiv. (35)	29–32, 33–35 (35 being doubtful).
	xxxv. to xl.	All.
Leviticus	All.	All.
Number	i. to x.	All, except verses 29–36 of chap. x.
	xiii. (33)	1–17*a*, 21, 25, 26 (except the last clause), 32 (to "eateth up the inhabitants thereof").

BOOKS.	CHAPTER.	VERSES BELONGING TO THE PRIESTLY CODE.
	xiv. (45)	1*a*, 2*a*, 5–7, 10, 26, 27, 28 (doubtful), 34–36.
	xv.	All.
	xvi. (50)	1 and 2 (partly), 8–11, 16–22, 35.
	xvii. to xix.	All.
	xx. (29)	1*a*, 2, 3*b*, 6, 12, 22–29.
	xxi. (35)	4*a*, 10, 11 (doubtful).
	xxv. (18)	6–18.
	xxvi. to xxxi.	All.
	xxxii. (42)	16–19, 24, 28–33.
	xxxiii. to xxxvi.	All.

BY THE SAME AUTHOR.

In one vol., 8vo, price 12s.

THE SCRIPTURAL DOCTRINE OF SACRIFICE;

INCLUDING INQUIRIES INTO

THE ORIGIN OF SACRIFICE; THE JEWISH RITUAL THE ATONEMENT; and THE LORD'S SUPPER.

SOME OPINIONS OF THE PRESS.

E Pluribus Perpauca.

"Mr. Cave is evidently a trained Biblical scholar, strong in his grasp of the progressive teaching of revelation."—*Academy.*

"This is one of those specialist English treatises in theology which appear in increasing numbers. Although there is a great deal in this book which does not commend itself to our judgment, we have nothing but praise for its clearness, its method, its thoroughness, and its tolerance. We most warmly commend Mr. Cave's book to the study of the clergy, who will find it full of suggestiveness and instruction."—*English Churchman.*

"We wish to draw particular attention to this new work on the important subject of Sacrifice. If we can induce our readers not only to glance through the book, but to read every line of it with thoughtful care, as we have done, we shall have earned their gratitude."—*Church Bells.*

"To any one who wishes to get a precise and comprehensive idea of the significance of the Jewish ritual, or a satisfactory standpoint from which to discover the real meaning of whole fields of New Testament phraseology, Mr. Cave's work is simply invaluable. The study of it will discipline the reader to accuracy of thought and definition, whilst the literary style is such as to invest the pages with a charm often conspicuously absent from the treatises of English and, still more, of German divines. We confidently anticipate for this noble treatise a cordial welcome even on the part of those who may not altogether sympathize with the author's somewhat conservative position in matters of Biblical criticism; and we unhesitatingly commend it as worthy of a place alongside the standard theological works that should fill the bookshelves of every minister."—*Glasgow Herald.*

"The extent of Mr. Cave's reading is altogether exceptional. He seems to have traversed the whole field of theological inquiry, and can refer with ease to the writings of the Fathers and Reformers, as well as to endless treatises of more recent days. Ewald, Dorner, Schleiermacher, Kalisch, Oehler, Baehr, Maurice, Fairbairn, Bushnell, Dale, and other representative writers have all been diligently studied, and the validity of their opinions tested. On this ground alone the volume will amply repay thoughtful perusal. The examination of the theories of Bushnell, Campbell, and Dale should be read by all students of their writings."—*Freeman.*

EDINBURGH: T. & T. CLARK.
LONDON: HAMILTON, ADAMS, & CO.
NEW YORK: SCRIBNER, WELFORD, & ARMSTRONG.

BY THE SAME AUTHOR.

In one vol., 8vo, price 12s.

AN INTRODUCTION TO THEOLOGY:

Its Principles,

Its Branches, Its Results, and Its Literature.

SOME OPINIONS OF THE PRESS.

E Pluribus Perpauca.

"I have just seen your excellent 'Introduction to Theology,' and feel prompted to thank you for this excellent help to students. I have been lecturing on this subject for forty years, and long wished for some such substitute for Hagenbach (too German to be translated or even reproduced), which I could recommend to my students."—PHILIP SCHAFF, D.D., LL.D.

"Cave's Encyclopædia pursues the practical aim of introducing beginners to the study of Theology, and fulfils this aim, so far as the reviewer is able to judge, in important fashion. The execution is luminous, clear, always keeps the main point in mind, and rests upon diligent knowledge of the subject. As regards the selection of literary aids, it must be acknowledged that the selection has been made with knowledge, caution, and skill."—Dr. LEMME in the *Theologische Literaturzeitung.*

"Years of diligent research must have preceded the production of a work like this. It surveys the whole field of Theology, and offers to the student the guidance of which he stands most in need, carefully mapping out the ground to be traversed, showing the approaches to its several divisions, and specifying their peculiar features, their relations, and inter-relations, putting us in possession of results which have been obtained, and indicating also the processes by which they have been reached. His long list of books recommended to students at the end of each section are a tribute to his erudition and good judgment. He knows precisely the books which are of most service, and expresses in a few terse sentences, and often in a few words, his estimate of them. We can only say that we have rarely read a book with more cordial approval."—*Baptist Magazine.*

"In reading this volume we have been over and over again delighted by the clearness of the distinctions drawn and the fulness of the information conveyed. Such a help in our student days would have been prized beyond all price. Especially to be commended is the admirable bibliography appended to each department. We cordially commend this volume as the best, indeed the *only*, sufficient handbook for students, and as one not likely to be superseded except by such enlarged editions as the progress of theological study may demand."—*British and Foreign Evangelical Review.*

"This work is not only a valuable contribution to theological literature, but an interesting indication of the progress of theological study in this country. The convenience of the book as an introduction is enhanced by the orderly and uniform method of treatment of each branch of theological science, under name, definition, and problem of the science in question, its utility, divisions, history of its study, and 'outline' or sketch of what would be a complete and separate treatment of the subject. At the close of each section an extensive and very carefully prepared bibliography is given—one of the best features of a work designed to be a practical handbook. The work may be confidently recommended to those to whom it is addressed—beginners in theology on the one hand, and those who have made it a professional study on the other. The specialist will find that it will aid him in rounding and compacting his ideas of theological science as a whole; and the beginner will be saved from being a smatterer, and will be stimulated to research by having the subject exposed in the fulness of its outlines and arranged in a practicable shape. Even the non-professional student will find many suggestions of great practical value, and learn that theology is capable of clear scientific treatment." —*Scottish News.*

EDINBURGH: T. & T. CLARK.
LONDON: HAMILTON, ADAMS, & CO.
NEW YORK: SCRIBNER, WELFORD, & ARMSTRONG.

In four vols., 8vo, price £2 2s.

A SYSTEM OF CHRISTIAN DOCTRINE.

BY

DR. I. A. DORNER (of Berlin).

TRANSLATED BY

REV. PROFESSOR ALFRED CAVE, B.A.,

AND

REV. PROFESSOR J. S. BANKS.

"We are pleased, however, to state that, in our judgment, this translation, considering the great difficulty of the original, has, as a whole, been successful. We thank Mr. Cave for his work, and wish the English edition a wide circulation among all who cannot read the original German."—Prof. C. A. BRIGGS, D.D., in the *Presbyterian Review.*

EDINBURGH: T. & T. CLARK.
LONDON: HAMILTON, ADAMS, & CO.
NEW YORK: SCRIBNER, WELFORD, & ARMSTRONG.

PUBLICATIONS OF THE CONGREGATIONAL UNION OF ENGLAND AND WALES,

MEMORIAL HALL, FARRINGDON STREET, E.C.

The Congregational Union Lectures.

Demy 8vo, 5s. net; Crown 8vo, 4s. net.

THE ATONEMENT.

(With a New Preface.)

By R. W. DALE, M.A., LL.D., Birmingham.

Demy 8vo, 5s. net; Third Edition, Crown 8vo, 3s. net.

PRIESTHOOD,

In the Light of the New Testament.

By the Late REV. E. MELLOR, D.D., Halifax.

Second Edition. Crown 8vo, cloth, 3s. net.

THE BASIS OF FAITH.

By REV. E. R. CONDER, M.A., D.D., Leeds.

Demy 8vo, cloth, 5s. net.

CHURCH SYSTEMS OF ENGLAND

In the Nineteenth Century.

By REV. J. GUINNESS ROGERS, B.A.

Cheap Edition. Two Vols. in One, 8vo, cloth, 3s. net.

JUBILEE LECTURES.

A Historical Series delivered on the occasion of the Jubilee of the Congregational Union of England and Wales.

With an Introductory Chapter by Principal A. M. FAIRBAIRN, D.D.

Contributors:

R. W. DALE, M.A., LL.D.	J. KENNEDY, D.D.	E. WHITE.
H. ALLON, D.D.	S. PEARSON, M.A.	J. GUINNESS ROGERS, B.A.
J. STOUGHTON, D.D.	J. BALDWIN BROWN, B.A.	H. RICHARD, M.P.
E. R. CONDER, D.D.	A. MACKENNAL, B.A., D.D.	

Or the above, in complete sets of 5 vols., 12s. net. (Special terms to Ministers.)

Orders and all Business Communications should be addressed to the Manager, Mr. HENRY THACKER, Memorial Hall, Farringdon Street, to whom also cheques and postal orders, crossed "City Bank, Ludgate Hill Branch," should be made payable.

Crown 8vo, cloth, 1s. 3d.

CONGREGATIONAL CHURCH POLITY.
By R. W. DALE, M.A., LL.D., of Birmingham.

Or, IN PARCELS FOR DISTRIBUTION, 10s. for 12 Books.

CONGREGATIONAL UNION TRACTS.

A Declaration of Faith, Church Order, and Discipline. Christian Baptism. Deacons: their Office, Duties, and Qualifications. The Relation of the Church to the State.

The remainders of these issues are offered at 1s. per 100 (assorted or otherwise).

JUBILEE SERIES. 1d. each, or 4s. per hundred (assorted or otherwise).
1. Confirmation. 2. Plain Words to the Perplexed about the Soul's Salvation. 3. The Obligations of Nonconformists as Citizens. 4. On Joining the Church.

TRACTS ON CHURCH PRINCIPLES.
By EUSTACE R. CONDER, M.A., D.D., of Leeds.

Price 1d. each, or 4s. per hundred (assorted or otherwise).

1. Authority and Liberty to Preach. 2. Schism. 3. Baptism. 4. The Lord's Supper. 5. The Church. 6. Church Membership.

"ON THE CHOICE OF A PASTOR."
FOR DISTRIBUTION IN CHURCHES SEEKING A PASTOR.

By JOHN KENNEDY, M.A., D.D.

Price 7d. per dozen, or 4s. per 100, post free.

Price 2s. ; or, in cloth, 3s.

THE CONGREGATIONAL YEAR BOOK.

Containing Statistics of the Denomination ; Information concerning over 150 Societies, Colleges, Institutions, and Trusts; Obituary Notices of Ministers Deceased; Views and Descriptions of New Churches ; Legal Information on matters affecting Nonconformists ; Lists of Congregational Ministers in Great Britain and the Colonies, with their Addresses ; the Proceedings of the Congregational Union of England and Wales (including the Chairman's May and Autumnal Addresses), and general information indispensable to Pastors, Deacons, and others. ADVERTISEMENTS should be sent to Messrs. ALEXANDER & SHEPHEARD, 21, FURNIVAL STREET, E.C.

CONGREGATIONAL CHURCH RECORDS.

A Series of Papers prepared by the Committee of the Congregational Union for recording Historical Facts relating to Churches, Minutes of Proceedings, &c. Folio, bound in green vellum.

1st size, containing 2 quires	net price	14s. 0d.
2nd ,, 4 ,, ...	,,	20 0
3rd ,, 6 ,, ...	,,	26 0

The Contents and Proportions of the smallest-sized book are as follows :—

Title Page, &c.	6 pages	Roll of Church Members	...	32 pages
Historical Account	12 ,,	Marriages		12 ,,
Church Minutes	96 ,,	Baptisms		24 ,,
Collections	12 ,,	Burials		12 ,,

The second size contains twice these quantities; and the third three times.

BICENTENARY OF 1688.

"The Revolution of 1688 in its Bearings on Protestant Nonconformity."
By Rev. J. STOUGHTON, D.D.

This work has been prepared for the use of Classes carried on in connection with the scheme for "*Examinations in Religious Knowledge.*" Paper wrapper at 6d. per copy, or may be had in parcels for distribution—twelve copies, 4s. ; twenty-five copies, 7s. 9d. Postage or carriage extra. Copies in cloth may also be had at 8d. each.

Orders and all Business Communications should be addressed to the Manager, Mr. HENRY THACKER, Memorial Hall, Farringdon Street, to whom also cheques and postal orders, crossed "City Bank, Ludgate Hill Branch," should be made payable.

Congregational Church Hymnal.

LIST OF EDITIONS.
(NOW ON SALE.)

(IN ORDERING, PLEASE QUOTE NUMBER AND PRICE.)

Words Only.

No.							s.	d.
1.	CROWN 8vo, PICA (Pulpit Edition), Hymns only, *Cloth*					...	3	6
2.	,,	,,	,,	,,	Paste Grain	...	5	0
3.	,,	,,	,,	,,	Best Morocco	..	8	0
4.	,,	,,	,,	Hymns, Chants and Anthem. *Cloth*			4	6
5.	,,	,,	,,	,,	,,	Paste Grain	6	0
6.	,,	,,	,,	,,	,,	Best Morocco	10	0
7.	,,	,,	,,	Chants and Anthems only, *Cloth*		...	1	4
8.	,,	,,	,,	,,	,,	Paste Grain	3	0
9.	,,	,,	,,	,,	,,	Best Morocco	6	0
10.	FCAP. 8vo, LONG PRIMER, Hymns only, *Cloth*					...	2	0
11.	,,	,,	,,	,,	Paste Grain		3	6
12.	,,	,,	,,	,,	Best Morocco		6	0
13.	,,	,,	Hymns, Chants and Anthems, *Cloth*				3	0
14.	,,	,,	,,	,,	Paste Grain		5	0
15.	,,	,,	,,	,,	Best Morocco		7	0
16.	,,	,,	Chants and Anthems only, *Cloth*			...	1	2
17.	,,	,,	,,	,,	Paste Grain...		2	6
18.	,,	,,	,,	,,	Best Morocco...		4	0
19.	LARGE FCAP. 8vo, Double Cols., Hymns only, *Cloth*...					...	1	6
20.	,,	,,	,,	,,	French Morocco		2	6
21.	,,	,,	,,	,,	Paste Grain...		3	0
22.	,,	,,	Hymns, Chants and Anthems, *Cloth*...				2	0
23.	,,	,,	,,	,,	French Morocco		3	6
24.	,,	,,	,,	,,	Paste Grain		4	0
25.	,,	,,	Chants and Anthems only, *Cloth*			...	0	8
26.	,,	,,	,,	,,	French Morocco		1	4
27.	,,	,,	,,	,,	Paste Grain ...		1	6
28.	MEDIUM 16mo RUBY, Hymns only, *Cloth*				...	...	0	10
29.	,,	,,	,,	Limp, cut flush ...		...	0	6
30.	,,	,,	Hymns, Chants and Anthems, *Cloth*...			...	1	0
31.	,,	,,	,,	,,	Limp, cut flush		0	8
32.	,,	,,	Chants and Anthems only, *Cloth*		...	...	0	6
33.	,,	,,	,,	,,	Limp, cut flush...		0	4

Editions with Music.

No.							s.	d.
34.	CROWN, 8vo, Hymns, *Cloth*	...	...	...	...	...	3	0
35.	,,	,,	Superior Paper and Binding, *Cloth* ...			...	4	0
36.	,,	,,	,,	,,	Paste Grain	...	6	0
37.	,,	,,	,,	,,	Best Morocco ...		7	6
38.	,,	,,	Hymns, Chants and Anthems, *Cloth*		...	...	5	0
39.	,,	,,	,,	,,	Paste Grain	...	7	6
40.	,,	,,	,,	,,	Best Morocco	...	10	0

A New Edition in Demy 8vo (Old Notation) is in the Press

Orders and all Business Communications should be addressed to the Manager, Mr. HENRY THACKER, Memorial Hall, Farringdon Street, to whom also cheques and postal orders, crossed "City Bank, Ludgate Hill Branch," should be made payable.

Congregational Church Hymnal.

Editions with Music.

No.						s.	d.
41.	Crown 8vo, Chants and Anthems only, *Cloth*				...	3	0
41A.	,,	,,	,,	Superior Paper and Binding, *Cloth*	...	4	0
42.	,,	,,	,,	,, Paste Grain	...	5	0
43.	,,	,,	,,	,, Best Morocco	...	7	0
43A.	,,	Chants only, *Cloth*...			...	1	4
43B.	,,	,,	,, Superior Paper, Paste Grain		...	3	0
44.	,,	Anthems only, *Cloth*			...	2	0
45.	,,	,,	Superior Paper, Paste Grain		...	4	0
46.	,,	Music for Hymns only, *Cloth*			...	3	0
47.	,,	,,	,,	,, Paste Grain	...	4	0
48.	,,	,,	,,	,, Best Morocco	...	6	0
49.	Large Royal 8vo (Organ Edition), Hymns, Chants and Anthems, *Cloth*				...	12	0
49A.	,,	Hymns only, *Cloth*			...	7	0
49B.	,,	,, Paste Grain...			...	10	0
49C.	,,	Chants and Hymns, *Cloth*			...	7	0
50.	,,	Hymns, Chants and Anthems, *Paste Grain*			...	15	0
50A.	,,	Chants and Anthems, *Paste Grain*			...	10	0
50B.	,,	Anthems only, *Cloth*			...	6	0
50C.	,,	,, Paste Grain			...	9	0
51.	Medium, 16mo, Chants and Anthems only, *Limp Cloth*				...	2	6
51A.	,,	Chants only, *Limp Cloth*			...	1	0
51B.	,,	,, Cloth Boards, Red Edges			...	1	4
52.	,,	Chants and Anthems only, *Cloth Boards, Red Edges*			...	3	0
52A.	,,	Anthems only, *Limp Cloth*			...	1	6
52B.	,,	,, Cloth Boards, Red Edges			...	1	9

Tonic Sol-Fa Editions.

No.						s.	d.
53.	Crown 8vo, Hymns and Tunes, *Cloth*...				...	3	0
54.	,,	,,	,, Paste Grain, Gilt Edges		...	4	6
55.	,,	Hymns, Chants and Anthems, *Cloth, White Edges*			...	5	0
56.	,,	,,	,, Cloth, Gold Lettered and Red Edges		...	6	0
57.	,,	,,	,, Paste Grain, Gilt Edges		...	7	6
58.	,,	Chants and Anthems only, *Cloth, White Edges*			...	3	0
59.	,,	,,	,, Paste Grain, Gilt Edges		...	5	0
60.	,,	Anthems only, *Cloth*			...	2	0
61.	,,	,, Paste Grain, Gilt Edges			...	4	0
62.	,,	Chants only, *Cloth Lettered*			...	1	4
63.	,,	,, Paste Grain, Gilt Edges...			...	3	0
64.	Medium, 16mo, Chants and Anthems only, *Limp Cloth*				...	2	6
65.	,,	,,	,, Cloth, Red Edges		...	3	0
66.	,,	Chants only, *Limp*			...	1	2
67.	,,	,, Cloth			...	1	6
68.	,,	Anthems only, *Limp*...			...	1	8
69.	,,	,, Cloth			...	2	0
70.	Crown 8vo, Music for Hymns only, *Cloth, Red Edges*				...	3	0
71.	,,	,,	,, Paste Grain, Gilt Edges		...	4	0

and will be ready shortly. For Specimen Type see next page.

Orders and all Business Communications should be addressed to the Manager, Mr. HENRY THACKER, Memorial Hall, Farringdon Street, to whom also cheques and postal orders, crossed "City Bank, Ludgate Hill Branch," should be made payable.

THE ETERNAL GOD.

28 *1st Tune.* Elijah.—7 7.7 7.7 7.

G. ELVEY, Mus. Doc.

28 *2nd Tune.* Mount Zion.—7 7.7 7.7 7.

ARTHUR SULLIVAN.

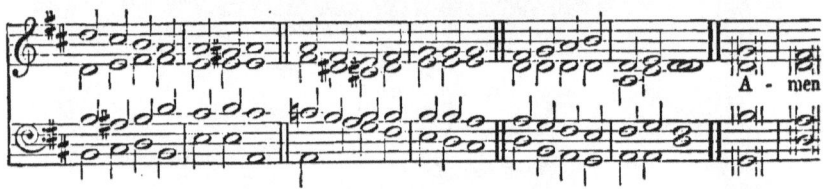

f O GIVE thanks to Him who made
    Morning light and evening shade;
Source and Giver of all good,
Nightly sleep and daily food;
Quickener of our wearied powers;
Guard of our unconscious hours.

f 2 O give thanks to nature's King,
    Who made every breathing thing:
His, our warm and sentient frame,
His, the mind's immortal flame.
O, how close the ties that bind
Spirits to the Eternal Mind!

f 3 O give thanks with heart and lip,
    For we are His workmanship,
And all creatures are His care:
Not a bird that cleaves the air
Falls unnoticed; but who can
Speak the Father's love to man?

f 4 O give thanks to Him who came
dim In a mortal, suffering frame—
    Temple of the Deity—
Came, for rebel man to die;
In the path Himself has trod,
f Leading back His saints to God. Ame

J. CONDER

DEMY 8vo EDITION SPECIMEN OF TYPE.

The Congregational Hymn-Book.
(INCLUDING THE SUPPLEMENT.)

No.			s.	d.
1.	48MO, without Supplement	} discontinued.		
2.	,, ,, ,,			
3.	ROYAL 32MO, Cloth, Lettered		1	4
4.	,, Purple Roan		2	0
5.	,, Levant Roan, Gilt Edges		2	6
6.	,, Calf, Marbled Edges		3	6
7.	,, ,, Gilt Edges		4	0
8.	24MO, Purple Roan		3	0
9.	,, Turkey Morocco, Gilt Edges		5	0
*10.	16MO, Double Cols., Special Edition, Cloth		1	0
10.	,, ,, Roan, Gilt Edges		1	8
11.	,, ,, Levant Roan, Gilt Edges		3	0
12.	,, ,, ,, ,, with Reference Bible		6	6
13.	,, ,, Turkey Morocco, Gilt Edges		4	6
14.	,, ,, ,, ,, with Reference Bible		9	6
15.	,, ,, ,, ,, extra ,,		11	0
16.	ROYAL 18MO, Cloth		3	0
17.	,, Purple Roan, Red Edges		4	6
18.	,, Calf, Marbled Edges	} discontinued.		
19.	,, ,, Gilt Edges			
20.	,, Turkey Morocco, Gilt Edges		7	0
21.	CROWN 8VO, Double Cols., Levant Roan, Gilt Edges		4	0
22.	,, ,, Turkey Morocco		5	6
23.	,, ,, ,, Gilt Edges, with Reference Bible		11	6
24.	,, ,, Turkey Morocco, extra ,,		13	0
25.	,, Pica Type, Special Edition, in Canvas		3	6
26.	,, ,, Purple Roan		6	6
27.	,, ,, Levant Roan, Gilt Edges		7	6
28.	,, ,, Calf, Gilt Edges		10	0
29.	,, ,, Morocco, Gilt Edges		11	0
30.	,, ,, Turkey Morocco, Extra, Gilt Edges		12	6
31.	,, Brevier Type, Double Cols., Roan		5	0
32.	,, ,, ,, Limp Morocco, Gilt Edges		6	6
33.	,, ,, Dble. Cols., Turkey Morocco, Gilt Edges, Extra		7	6

NOTICE.—In ordering from the above List it will be desirable to mention the PRICE as well as the NUMBER of the Edition required.

SUPPLEMENT ONLY.

	s.	d.		s.	d.
32MO, Cloth	0	4	18MO, Cloth	0	10
24MO, ,,	0	9	CROWN 8VO, Double Cols., Cloth	0	10
16MO, Double Cols., Cloth	0	6	8VO, Pica, Cloth	1	2

The Congregational Hymnal;
OR,
BOOK OF PRAISE FOR YOUNG PEOPLE.

	s.	d.		s.	d.
16MO, Pearl, Double Col., Paper Covers	0	2	DEMY 18MO, Bourgeois, Large Type, Stiff Cloth	0	6
,, ,, Cloth Limp	0	4			
ROYAL 32MO, Nonpariel, Cloth Limp	0	6	DEMY 18MO, Bourgeois, Large Type, Roan	1	0
,, ,, Roan	0	10			

The Abridged Congregational Hymn-Book.

For use in Lecture and Mission Rooms, in Prayer Meetings, and in the Family.
Paper Covers, 2d. ; Limp Covers, 3d. ; Large Type Edition, 18mo, cloth, 8d.

Orders and all Business Communications should be addressed to the Manager, Mr. HENRY THACKER, Memorial Hall, Farringdon Street, to whom also cheques and postal orders, crossed "City Bank, Ludgate Hill Branch," should be made payable.

Congregational Church Hymnal.

NOTICES OF THE PRESS.

"The selection is characterized by excellent taste throughout, and the revised harmonies to some of the older melodies are distinguished by good judgment, as might be expected, considering in whose charge this matter has been placed. It is one of the best collections of tunes for general use in evangelical congregations which has been compiled : far superior to the former works of the same kind, issued under the like authority. The old melodies are good ; the new ones, furnished by such composers as Barnby, Brown, Borthwick, Bunnett, Calkin, Frost, Elliott, Elvey, Foster, Hiles, Hopkins, Leslie, Macfarren, W. H. Monk, Prout, Stainer, and others, speak for themselves."—*The Musical Times.*

The work is a fine collection of hymn tunes, and in the printing it has been arranged that ymn and tune—sometimes a choice of a couple of tunes—shall appear at one opening. The old favourites are here—favourites which the Church, with all its varying creeds and phases of thought, will not willingly let die ; also a large number of copyright tunes obtained from various sources ; and a further number of tunes specially composed for the volume by the musical editor himself, and by Mr. Barnby, Mr. J. Booth, Mr. J. Bowcher, Dr. Bunnett, Dr. C. J. Frost, Mr. Minshall, Mr. E. Prout, Dr. Stainer, and others. The book is a specimen of clean and clear printing."—*Musical Opinion.*

"The book contains the richest treasures of our psalmody. . . . If we were to select one section of the book for special praise it would be the second, entitled 'The Lord Jesus Christ,' which is as beautiful as it is full. . . . As to the music, we have the judgment of an accomplished choirmaster. . . . We have his report before us, in a distinct judgment on each separate tune, and the general result is very satisfactory. . . . On his recommendation the book will be at once adopted by the church of which he is the able choirmaster."—*The Congregational Review.*

"This volume is a perfect treasure-house of noble and solemn music. . . . The closest scrutiny which is not jaundiced can find little or nothing that falls short of what an ideal hymnal should be. . . . Noble words are married to fit music. The 'Congregational Hymnal' is sure to make its way."—*Sheffield and Rotherham Independent.*

"The hymns have been selected with great judgment and discretion, and include some of the best compositions in the language. The tone of the hymns is distinctly catholic. . . . The selection of tunes will not disappoint those who desire to retain the old, nor those who wish occasionally to sing a new song."—*The Halifax and District Congregational Magazine.*

"It is unquestionably a rich mine of sacred song. . . . The fruits of it ought to be seen in days to come in the improvement of our congregational worship, and the enrichment of our spiritual life."—*The Manchester, Salford and District Congregational Magazine.*

"A first glance shows that it will prove one of the finest collections of church music that has been given to any church."—*Christian World.*

"The wisdom of the Congregational Union in intrusting the preparation of the new 'Hymnal' to one sole editor has been amply justified by the masterly manner in which Mr. Barrett has executed the difficult task committed to him. . . . The book has evidently been edited with a practical view to use in public worship, and with a success which merits cordial appreciation."—*Nonconformist* (Notice of Hymns).

"The editors have produced one of the best collections of psalmody—most suited to the churches—published hitherto. No nobler tribute could have been found in this Jubilee year than this presentation of a work which is characterized by so high a standard of excellence."—*Leeds Mercury.*

The following opinions have been expressed in letters to the Editor :—"I consider the 'Congregational Church Hymnal' worthy to take rank with the best existing Hymnals."—*J. Barnby.* "As far as I can judge from careful perusal, I should say, without hesitation, that it possesses all the musical qualifications necessary to make it of permanent value and interest."—*John Stainer.* "I consider the volume as a whole decidedly one of the best collections of psalmody that I have met with."—*Ebenezer Prout.* "I have found it to be, upon the whole, one of the very best, if not the very best, of modern hymnals recently published."—*A. Galloway, one of the Editors of the new Scottish Hymnal.*

www.ingramcontent.com/pod-product-compliance
Lightning Source LLC
Chambersburg PA
CBHW021423300426
44114CB00010B/614